NEW THEORIES OF
REVOLUTION

*A commentary on the views of Frantz Fanon,
Régis Debray and Herbert Marcuse*

JACK WODDIS

INTERNATIONAL PUBLISHERS *New York*

Burgess
HM
281
.W63
1972b

ISBN: (cloth) 0–7178–0350–3; (paperback) 0–7178–0366–X

Printed in the United States of America

CONTENTS

Chapter One

Revolution and the Role of Classes

I

Revolution and the Role of Classes

When the twentieth century has been completed and we come to sum it up there is little doubt that we shall describe it as a century of revolt and revolution. A century in which man initiated wave after wave of battle against the entrenched positions of the establishment. A century of revolt against poverty and war. Revolt against tyranny and fascism. Against colonialism and racialism. Revolt against the education system and against bureaucracy. Revolt against feudal landlords, royal princes, military brass and corrupt politicians. A revolt which has found expression, too, in attitudes towards culture, sex, marriage, the family.

But above all, a revolution against capitalism and imperialism. A giant step forward in the building of socialism and in laying the basis for a fully classless society. A change and expansion in the whole character of democracy, based on the power of the working people, allowing for the fullest participation of each nation and each individual in deciding their own future and carrying it out. Not the limited democracy of *saying* what they want without the power to effect it. Nor the limited democracy of having no power to formulate or take the major decisions but only the possibility of participating in carrying out the decisions previously made for them by those who, from their paternal perch, or desk, judge themselves best capable of deciding the fate and future of others.

It is inevitable that, living in the midst of such an historic upheaval, with the whole world beginning to heel over from capitalism to socialism, that the most politically conscious people, those who are touched by revolutionary fire and are ardent to contribute to political and social change, should make constantly new assessments of past revolutionary experience and attempt to extract from it the surest path to victory in the future.

"How to make a revolution?" is, in short, the big question that dominates the thoughts of so many of those who earnestly want to see revolutionary change. And to find an answer to this persistent query they examine this experience and that, weighing up successes and defeats, noting strong points and shortcomings.

Established theories are re-examined with meticulous care. Alongside Marx, Engels and Lenin there is a new-found interest in the views of Rosa Luxemburg, James Connolly, Georgi Dimitrov and Antonio Gramsci. Some find their inspiration in Cuba and Che. For others it is China and Mao that are the source of all wisdom. Fewer have apparently read Ho Chi Minh or Vo Nguyen Giap.

New theoreticians arise, not necessarily men who have themselves played a key role in "making a revolution" but men who have sought to find solutions to today's big problems of revolt and revolution. Men such as Debray, Fanon, Marcuse and others.

Everything is scrutinised and submitted for judgment. The role of spontaneity and the function of a political vanguard. Mass struggle and military coups. Parliamentary activity and guerrilla warfare. The strike weapon, factory occupation, workers' control. Peaceful transition and armed uprising. The role of different classes, of the workers, peasants, national bourgeoisie, and *lumpenproletariat*. The specific function of students and intellectuals. The seizure of universities and the establishment of "red bases". Changes in the structure of capitalism and in the strategy and tactics of imperialism. Changes in the composition of the working class. The influence of the scientific and technological revolution.

Some, in their justifiable desire to be done swiftly with the old world of capitalism and cant, seek the shortest and most direct routes to the new society. Others limit their aims to destroying the old with no clear vision as to what to put in its place—and some even admit (not without a hint of boastfulness) that they have no idea what their new society will be like. Still others take refuge in counselling caution as an alibi for their lack of leadership and as justification for their refusal to make decisive challenge to the old order. A new form of *attentisme*, in fact.

In the midst of this great welter of prognoses and counter-prognoses, of the demolition of old gods and the erection of new ones, revolutionaries who must always take account of the new, must unhesitatingly discard what is no longer of value, no matter how hallowed it may be. They must re-examine, with the utmost scrutiny and ruthlessness, all past experiences, all past theories and all current practice and concepts in order to be able correctly to fulfil the role of all true revolutionaries, that of helping to change the world.

In doing this they must avoid all dogma. Not only the dogma of clinging to old ideas and experiences which are no longer valid; but also the new dogma of laying down new paths and creating new models for all on the basis of the exceptional experience and never-to-be-paralleled road of particular countries; or on the basis of their own misreading of certain recent experiences.

The questions to be discussed in this book are not only of concern to revolutionaries, still less solely of interest to Marxists. They are questions which affect the lives of all mankind, and are being discussed by wide circles of people in the socialist countries, in the West, and in the Third World. They are questions which are the subject of numerous articles and books, of seminars, debates and conferences.

If Marxists have a special contribution to make in this historic debate, they do not have—and do not claim—a monopoly of wisdom. Marxism is only a little over one hundred years old. In most continents the knowledge and experience of Marxism is much younger. *The Communist Manifesto* was written in 1848. By the end of the nineteenth century Marxism had become an established trend in Europe. Yet it did not reach Latin America in any decisive form until after 1917, nor Asia until then—apart from Japan where capitalism and large-scale industry developed earlier, and where Sen Katayama and the young socialists were able to commence their activity even before the Russo-Japanese war had given rise to the 1905 revolution in Russia.

As for Africa—apart from South Africa, where prior to 1917 Marxism was introduced by emigrés from Russia and Eastern Europe, and from Britain—decisive contact with Marxist ideas only began after the second world war, and that at a time of considerable divergence in the international communist movement, especially in connection with the views put forward by the Communist leadership in China.

We are, therefore, really only at the beginning of the process of using Marxism to guide our actions and to solve the problems of mankind. The experience of revolutions, especially in the twentieth century, is exceedingly rich, but by no means exhaustive—and each new revolution adds its own quota of new approaches, new methods, new ideas.

We are in a new epoch with one-third of the world building socialism and with scores of newly independent states facing immense and diverse problems of economic, social and political development. Imperialism is entering a new phase of its general crisis notwithstanding its continued strength and economic growth. New problems arise from the technological and scientific revolution, and from the ever-growing concentration of capital in the hands of giant monopolies which bestride the continents, ignore frontiers and governments, dispose of resources considerably greater than those of the entire national budgets of most Third World countries, and increasingly concentrate a correspondingly immense political power in their hands.

On a total world scale millions are involved now in political struggle. They are awakened as never before, and naturally bring with them their ideas as to what is wrong with the world and what needs to be done. Sometimes these are old ideas in new clothing—but often they are genuinely new ideas arising from the new conditions, and they need the most sympathetic and understanding examination, for otherwise man cannot advance under the most favourable conditions.

We are faced with so many new and acute problems that we cannot afford to adopt a rigid, dogmatic attitude towards new ideas as if everything had long ago been settled by Marx or Lenin. They, for certain, would have been horrified to find their names and their writings being used to uphold fossilised ideas and act as a brake on revolutionary action. Marx did not hesitate for one moment to stir up all the thinking about social change which had preceded his work. Lenin, in his turn, had no hesitation in bringing Marx up to date— as he did, for example, in his work on the growth of monopoly capitalism; nor did he regard it as revisionist to say outright that what Marx had written about the possibilities of peaceful revolution in Britain in the nineteenth century no longer applied in the midst of the bloody holocaust of the 1914–18 war.

But if we should not hesitate to discard, if necessary, old ideas which no longer apply, no less should we take care to avoid setting up new dogmas in place of the old—taking China as a new model for all, in place of the Soviet Union, or Cuba in place of China. On the contrary, we need to have a really open mind, to explore what is happening, to be receptive to all new phenomena and to new, more effective ways of advancing.

Marxists do not have all the ready-made answers. They have Marxism, which is a guide to action. It is this tool of Marxism which must be used creatively to examine what is happening in the world. Nothing less than the most concrete and rigorous examination of reality, of the different revolutions that have taken place or are in process, can help one to arrive at really valid conclusions.

Lenin was particularly emphatic on the necessity for Marxists to make their own independent contribution to revolutionary theory, and to base this on their application of the general principles of Marxism to particular countries and particular situations.

We do not regard Marx's theory as something completed and inviolable; on the contrary, we are convinced that it has only laid the foundation stone of the science which socialists *must* develop in all directions if they wish to keep pace with life. We think that an *independent* elaboration of Marx's theory is especially essential for Russian socialists; for this theory provides only general *guiding* principles, which, *in particular*, are applied in England differently than in France, in France differently than in Germany, and in Germany differently than in Russia.[1] (Emphasis by Lenin in original.)

The twentieth century has certainly been most rich in revolutions. And each has contributed its own share of experiences and lessons—negative and positive—on which later revolutionaries have been able to build. Each revolution, too, has had its own unique features which never arise a second time—not even in the same country let alone elsewhere.

The failure of the urban uprisings in Moscow and elsewhere in 1905 did not mean that barricade fighting was defunct; only that the Marxists had not yet won a majority of workers to their side, nor swung over decisive sections of the many million-strong peasantry to throw themselves into revolution against the tsar as distinct from revolt against their local landlord. And when the mighty roar of October, 1917, crumbled the walls of Russian capitalism it was seen that the achievement had been that of the majority of the workers in firm alliance with millions of peasants, marching behind the banners of the Bolsheviks. October, 1917, showed that even in a country that was overwhelmingly peasant it was possible for the revolutionaries to take power *first in the towns* and subsequently to spread to the countryside, in contrast to the later and very different experience of China where the relative weakness of the young Communist Party and its inability to hold to the towns after the counter-revolutionary massacre of 1927 compelled it to retreat to the countryside, to suffer a long, arduous, bitter protracted war, to *liberate the countryside first* and take the towns as the final climax after more than twenty years of armed struggle.

The Russian Communists were right to take power in the towns first and extend to the countryside afterwards. The Chinese

[1] V. I. Lenin: "Our Programme": *Collected Works*, Vol. 4, pp. 211–12.

Communists were right to retreat from the towns, to liberate the countryside first and win the towns last. Each of these revolutions faced its own particular problems, in time and space, in class structure, political forces at its disposal and arrayed against it.

There was no single model. Nor could there be, as Lenin had so often emphasised. This does not mean, however, that each revolution does not learn from another. It learns from successes and it learns from defeats.

Above all it learns that no two revolutions are alike, that each country, each internal situation and each international situation in which the internal change matures, is different; and that the task of revolutionaries is not only to understand laws of social change which have a general validity, but equally important (and certainly requiring greater effort and creative thought) to see what is new and different, to be able to search amid all the complexities of revolutionary change for what is distinctive and essential for winning decisive sections of the people, for moving them into action, and for choosing at each stage the forms of struggle in which the people are prepared to engage and which eventually prove most effective in breaking the power of the ruling class.

It was the great achievement of Marx, Engels and Lenin that they brought a scientific approach to the questions of revolution and socialism.

Following them, Communist Parties and their leading exponents in many countries have made important additions to Marxist theory and practice, making living contributions to Marxism in the course of their daily struggles for the advance of the revolution. Others, not in Communist Parties, but nevertheless basing themselves on the ideas of Marxism, have also made invaluable contributions to mankind's advance in many fields.

In recent years, in the field of revolutionary thought and political theory, a number of new names have attracted wide interest. Among these are Frantz Fanon, Régis Debray and Herbert Marcuse who, from a standpoint critical of the capitalist system, have elaborated their ideas on the revolutionary way forward. The questions they pose and the answers they attempt are of importance to all revolutionaries—and they need to be examined with patience and care. In doing so, our approach must strive to be scientific. Revolution is too serious a matter for one to ignore new concepts. For the same reason, we cannot afford to be guided by mere fashions of thought, to follow without question unsubstantiated slogans, or to accept uncritically loud and emphatic assertions of a somewhat general character but which, on examination and when subjected to the hard test of objective fact, are found to be seriously wanting.

We need to distinguish carefully between genuine contributions to the science of revolution, and, on the other hand, new myths and legends which gain a temporary favour with some circles because of their superficial attractiveness, the "revolutionary" flavour of their boldness or, more often, because of the fact that they contain an element of correctness applicable under certain specific conditions. Above all, we must discard any theories which life itself, the harsh experience of revolutionary struggle, disproves.

Marxists should be the last people to cling to past formulae or ideas if life itself proves them to be no longer valid. Marxism is a constantly developing science. It takes account of all new phenomena in society, endeavours to appraise them and extract from them what is significant for the further advance of the revolution.

At the same time, serious revolutionaries will reject any theories, no matter how new, no matter how revolutionary-sounding or attractive they may be at first acquaintance, if they are shown to be invalid, unhelpful and even dangerous to the cause of the revolution itself.

It was for this reason that Marx battled against Bakunin and the anarchists in the First International, just as strongly as he fought against the reformists. It was for the same reason that the early Bolsheviks fought against the ideas of the Narodniks (with their conceptions of revolutions being made by small groups of active heroes and through the form of individual acts of terrorism and desperation) just as strenuously as they opposed Martov and the Menshiviks. In the same way Lenin never allowed his unending struggle against the opportunist betrayal of the reformist leaders of the Second International to deter him from his equally uncompromising polemic against the ultra-lefts in the international working-class movement, exposed so brilliantly in his work, *"Left-wing" Communism, an Infantile Disorder*.

Marxists have always understood that while it is essential to expose and defeat the ideas and policies of the right-wing Labour leaders, who strive to persuade the working class to accept the capitalist system, it is no less important to combat and defeat ideas and policies which, apparently from the other flank, as it were, prove equally harmful to the revolution, even when put forward and supported by people with a sincere desire to assist the struggle against capitalism and imperialism.

What is the scope and character of the new theories of revolt and revolution which are understandably the basis of so much discussion today? What are the main ideas which we need to examine and to test in the light of fact and the practice of revolutionary struggle?

These are, of course, manifold; but it seems to me that right at the heart of all the new theories that embrace both the path to socialist revolution as well as that of national liberation, and thus encompass the countries of the Third World as well as those of the advanced capitalist countries, is the question of the *role of social classes in the revolution*. In dealing with this question as put forward in the writings of Fanon, Debray and Marcuse we shall require to examine the particular role played by workers, peasants, intellectuals, students, the "national" bourgeoisie, the petty-bourgeoisie and military circles, and the *lumpenproletariat*. We shall need to consider such concepts as the "main force", the "leading force", and the "decisive force". We shall also have to take into account the relations between the different classes and strata at each stage of the revolution. Our enquiry will cover the views of Fanon on classes in Africa, Debray and his views on classes in Latin America, and Marcuse and his characterisation of class forces in the capitalist world, especially Western Europe and the United States.

Connected with the role of classes in the revolution are the much-debated questions of forms of struggle—whether armed or "peaceful", whether in town or countryside. We shall also need to examine the relation of political activity to armed struggle; how valid is the theory of the "foco"; what instrument is needed for leading revolutionary change; can spontaneity and learning from experience replace the need for a revolutionary party based on Marxism-Leninism; the different forms of armed struggle itself; the theory and practice of "red bases" and "student communes".

It is this series of questions and their related problems which constitute the main substance of this book. In brief, they touch on fundamental questions of revolution—who can carry it out, who can lead it, how should it be carried out.

It is only natural, therefore, that we should briefly examine beforehand *what is a revolution*?

In the popular mind, in the capitalist press, and, unfortunately, in some left circles, revolution is regarded as a question of the most militant sounding slogans, the most extreme and extravagant ideas, and, above all, a question of violence and bloodshed, of barricades in the streets, battles with the police, armed warfare in the hills and jungles.

Sometimes, of course, a revolution requires street barricades, or armed warfare in town or countryside, or both—but these particular *forms* of struggle are not the essence of a revolution. A social and political revolution is a matter of change in the whole basis and structure of society—from feudalism to capitalism, from capitalism to socialism. It is a change in which decisive political and economic power passes from the hands of a declining ruling class which has outlived its day, into the hands of a new advancing class which is destined to take society forward to a new phase of development.

This was the essence, despite their complexities, of the English revolution of 1640, and of the French revolution of 1789, both of which marked the decline of feudalism and the assumption of power by the growing bourgeoisie, leading to a decisive growth of capitalism. This, too—a change of class power—is the essence of socialist revolution, as seen by the experience of all countries where the power of capitalism has been broken.

As Lenin put it:

The transfer of State power from one class to another *class* is the first, the principal, the basic sign of a *revolution*, both in the strictly scientific and in the practical political meaning of the term.

(*Letters on Tactics:* April, 1917)

For a socialist revolution this requires the transfer of State power from the hands of the capitalist class into the hands of the working class and its allies. State power means the armed forces, the police, security, judiciary, prisons, Government departments and ministries, economic institutions of the State, the mass media—all of which, under the capitalist system, are controlled by representatives of the capitalist class. The aim of socialist revolution is to ensure that these institutions are no longer in the hands of those loyal to capitalism, but that such organs of State should be firmly in the hands of the working class and its allies, in the hands of those who represent the majority of the people. And the workers and their allies need this State power in order to break the economic power of the big monopolies, of capitalism.

Such a fundamental and historical change requires a movement of millions of people. That is why Lenin insisted that a revolution is a transfer of power from one *class* to another, that it is not a conspiracy or a coup by a small group; nor is it just a single, dramatic and violent act—but a whole stage of struggles, taking different forms, and proceeding at different tempos, now advancing, now retreating, following a complex zigzag path, not according to any preconceived blue-print but constantly compelled to adjust itself in the very process of struggle, depending on the rapidly changing relation of forces that accompanies all periods of revolutionary change. It is in the course of such a process that the revolutionary organisations help to raise the whole level of political understanding of the people so that they clearly understand their role in history and are ready to struggle and suffer in order to make the great change. The socialist revolution is the exercise of force by the working people, the execution of their mass will for fundamental change, for a transfer of class power in order to build a new system of society, socialism.

The essence of this whole process is the use of what Marx termed the "collective power" of the masses, the establishment of their ability to compel by force if necessary. This requires the alliance of the working class with all other classes and strata of the people who are exploited by monopoly capitalism.

This brings us right to the core of Marxist teaching on the role of the working class in the socialist revolution.

In his article, *The Historical Destiny of the Teaching of Karl Marx* written in 1913, Lenin emphasised that:

> The main thing in the teaching of Marx is that it brings out the historic role of the proletariat as the builder of socialist society.[1]

In open challenge to this view, C. Wright Mills has declared:

> For Marx the proletariat was the history-making agency. Now any fool can see that it's not true.[2]

As we shall see, all three of the subjects of this study—Fanon, Debray and Marcuse—take up this question of the role of the proletariat, the first in relation to Africa, the second in relation to Latin America, and the last named in relation to the Western world. I shall endeavour, in subsequent chapters, to answer their contentions in some detail; but for the moment it is necessary to make some observations of a more general character.

These observations will be familiar to Marxists, and some may

[1] V. I. Lenin: *Marx, Engels, Marxism*, 1936 edition, p. 56.
[2] *Ramparts*, August, 1965.

even wonder why it is necessary, in a book of this character, to recall these ideas which have always been accepted by them. Regrettably, however, many of those who unthinkingly take up the new slogans and the new concepts often do so without having read or grasped certain basic ideas of Marxism. It is therefore necessary, at this point, to outline the main ideas of Marx and Engels concerning the decisive role of the working class in abolishing capitalism and constructing socialism.

In his Preface to the English edition of *The Communist Manifesto* in 1888, Engels noted that a stage had been reached at which the working class could not "attain its emancipation from the sway of the exploiting and ruling class—the bourgeoisie—without at the same time, and once and for all, emancipating society at large from all exploitation, oppression, class distinctions and class struggles".

The Communist Manifesto itself explains why the working class is the basic enemy of capitalism:

Of all the classes that stand face to face with the bourgeoisie today, the proletariat alone is a really revolutionary class. The other classes decay and finally disappear in the face of modern industry, the proletariat is its special and essential product.

In other words, the historic role of the working class does not arise from some special subjective quality of the working class but from its objective status in capitalist society.

As Marx pointed out in *The Holy Family* (1844), "The question is not what this or that proletarian, or even the whole proletariat at the moment *considers* as its aim. The question is what the proletariat is, and what, consequent on that being, it will be compelled to do".

That is to say, if some Tory-voting workers have their horizons limited by the ownership of a house or a car, or if some backward sections are taken in by Enoch Powell, this does not invalidate Marx's conception of the historic role of the working class, which is not dependent on its actual class consciousness or political activity at any given stage but on its special status in society.

Why is this?

Capitalist society is based on the private ownership of the means of production. It is based on private profit which is obtained by exploiting the working class. The source of this profit is the surplus value extracted from the wage-earning class.

The workers struggle to defend and improve their wages and

general conditions of life, while the employer strives to extract the utmost surplus value from the workers. Hence the daily battles over wages, hours of work, piece-rates, productivity, holidays with pay, tea-breaks, and so on—the outcome of each such battle determining the share taken by the workers and that taken by the employer. Hence, too, the organisation by the workers of their trade unions to assist these struggles; and hence the constant attempt by the employers, and the capitalist state, to weaken the trade unions, to limit their rights, and to corrupt and tame their leaders.

This irreconcilable antagonism between the working class and the capitalist class is the basis of class struggle. As capitalism develops, the economic and political strength of the biggest employers increases, and so does the power of the workers. On the one side there appear gigantic monopolies, created through expansion and merger, and assisted by the capitalist State. On the other, the army of workers, despite the important changes in its composition, increases constantly with the growth of capitalism.

The increased strength of the world's working class is indicated by its numerical growth from 30 million at the beginning of the twentieth century to 540 million in 1969. At the same time the expansion of its organisation is shown by its trade union membership—from 9 million members in 1910, to 50 million in 1920, 64 million in 1945, and 230 million in 1970.

All daily struggles by the workers for their immediate demands, whatever may be the limited horizon of those participating in such struggles, objectively are part of the struggle against capitalist exploitation. The only way in which the working class can end this exploitation is by taking over the means of production. This means that it is in the basic interests of the workers *as a class* to establish a form of ownership corresponding to social production. It is in this sense that Marx regarded the working class as revolutionary in distinction to all other classes.

The central contradiction of the capitalist system, as discovered and explained by Marx, is that between social production and private appropriation. This contradiction can only be ended by harmonising social production with social appropriation, which requires the social ownership of the means of production. The decisive class whose historic role is to make this fundamental change is the working class since, as we have noted, its own struggle to end the exploitation of itself brings it to the same historic necessity.

The technical changes in production introduced by capitalism resulted in a change from the individual producer to what Marx termed the "collective labourer". The consequence, writes Marx, is that "Not only have we here an increase in the productive power of the individual, by means of co-operation, but the creation of a new power, namely the collective power of the masses" (*Capital*, Vol. 1, p. 311).

Those who have experienced working in a large-scale enterprise, who have taken part in trade union activity, in strikes and other struggles, will have experienced this "collective power".

The worker owns no means of production. He sells his labour power in order to earn his living. He is connected with the most advanced form of production, factory production, which today is subject to sweeping changes arising from the scientific and technological revolution. In the course of his labour he works collectively with others and combines with them in defence of his interests. He acquires a sense of belonging to a class with common organisations, aims and aspirations. Left by itself this sense of belonging to a class remains limited to a trade union consciousness. The worker does not spontaneously acquire socialist understanding or an awareness of the historic mission of the working class to overthrow capitalism, solely through his own experience. He is subjected all the time to capitalist propaganda in a thousand and one ways, especially in these days of television and the monopoly daily press. Moreover, an upper crust of the working class is periodically bought over by capitalism and is able, for a time, to persuade considerable sections of workers to support its opportunist policies.

Under these conditions, the working class can continue to fight for a very long time for its immediate interests without acquiring any conscious aim of changing the system, of taking power and building socialism. A socialist understanding, a fundamental comprehension of what is wrong with society and how to change it, has to be injected into the economic struggles of the working class by the conscious effort of those who understand Marxism and are organised for this task. It is for this reason that the working class requires its own political party, a party based on the ideas of Marxism.

It is in the light of these preliminary remarks that we shall now examine some of the new theories of revolt and revolution.

Chapter Two

Fanon and Classes in Africa

2

Fanon and Classes in Africa

Frantz Fanon, who died tragically of leukaemia in 1961 at the early age of thirty-six, has already become something of a legend. Born in Martinique in 1925, he left the West Indies twenty years later and, after military service, studied medicine in France where he specialised in psychiatry. He left for Blida, in Algeria, in 1952, to continue working as a psychiatrist. He soon threw in his lot with the Algerian F.L.N. in the struggle for liberation and died in the United States on the eve of Algeria's victory, while awaiting treatment for his illness.

His writings have had considerable influence among educated Africans, and equally, if not more so, among European intellectuals. In Italy a Frantz Fanon Centre was established, seminars held on his work and a journal issued—*Bollettino di Note Informazioni e Documenti*. In France his writings have understandably had a wide currency, and their impact can clearly be discerned in the pages of *Présence Africaine*. In Britain, too, four volumes of his writings have been issued, and a circle formed at Oxford to study his work.

Fanon's short life, as shown particularly by his outstanding work, *The Wretched of the Earth*, was dominated by a fierce and burning hatred of colonial and racial oppression. No one can read a single page of Fanon without sensing the depth of his feelings. In vivid imagery, writing almost as if his nerve-ends were exposed, he attacks without mercy all those whom he regards as standing in the way of the liberation of the downtrodden millions of Africa. It is doubtful if any writer has ever been able to depict so vividly and with such passion the emotions of an oppressed people in the face of their hated oppressor. Every barbed word against the *colons* of Algeria is equally a shaft hurled at Vorster and Smith—and an indictment of the imperialist Governments which help to maintain them.

Yet, at times, one can equally detect a certain false note in his denunciation, a kind of over-grand exaggeration, and a conclusion which leads nowhere and which therefore is quite quickly contradicted by some equally grandiloquent judgment.

In this typical passage one can sense straight away the immense power of his style and, at the same time, note the questionable conclusion.

"The settlers' town is a strongly-built town, all made of stone and steel. It is a brightly-lit town; the streets are covered with asphalt, and the garbage-cans swallow all the leavings, unseen, unknown and hardly thought about. The settler's feet are never visible, except perhaps in the sea; but there you're never close enough to see them. His feet are protected by strong shoes although the streets of his town are clean and even, with no holes or stones. The settler's town is a well-fed town, an easy-going town; its belly is always full of good things. The settler's town is a town of white people, of foreigners.

"The town belonging to the colonised people, or at least the native town, the Negro village, the medina, the reservation, is a place of ill fame, peopled by men of evil repute. They are born there, it matters little where or how; they die there, it matters not where, nor how. It is a world without spaciousness; men live there on top of each other, and their huts are built one on top of the other. The native town is a hungry town, starved of bread, of meat, of shoes, of coal, of light. The native town is a crouching village, a town on its knees, a town wallowing in the mire."[1]

But Fanon knows only too well that the colonised people are not "on their knees". Some may be, especially the hangers-on of colonial society. Fanon, however, makes no distinction. Here, for the moment, he is content to hide the entire class-structured society of colonialism behind the non-class term "the colonised" and to attribute to it a single generalised characteristic.

With equal indifference to differing class attitudes he immediately plunges the reader into a contradictory, but equally generalised, assessment:

> The native is always on the alert. . . . He is overpowered but not tamed; he is treated as an inferior but he is not convinced of his inferiority. He is patiently waiting until the settler is off his guard to fly at him. The native's muscles are always tensed. You can't say that he is terrorised, or even apprehensive. He is in fact ready at a moment's notice to exchange the *role* of the quarry for that of the hunter.[2]

[1] Frantz Fanon: *The Damned*, Paris, 1963, p. 32. (Later published in Britain under the title, *The Wretched of the Earth*.)
[2] ibid., p. 42.

Fanon has many penetrating things to say about the relation between the colonialists and their victims. He writes splendidly and with wide knowledge on the question of national culture and its influence on the national democratic revolution. He exposes the baneful influence of colonialism on European society. He reveals the tragic results of sadism on both the torturer and his victim.

At times, however, the strength of his anti-colonial thinking is so great that it clouds his thinking and leads him into unscientific judgments.

He makes almost a mystique out of violence.

> Violence, alone, violence committed by the people, violence organised and educated by its leaders, makes it possible for the masses to understand social truths and gives the key to them.[1]

Fanon argues thus because he sees that the colonial system rests on violence. From the very beginning, writes Fanon, the relation between the African and the settler was based on a "great array of bayonets and cannon".[2]

In the face of such violence, he claims, the African people must resort to their own violence—that of "an armed and open struggle".[3] In fact, "the existence of an armed struggle shows that the people are decided to trust violent methods only".

That violence in the hands of the colonial powers was an essential part of the colonial system is undeniable. But to see only the violence is to take a very restricted and politically dangerous point of view. The violence wielded by the troops and the police was not violence for violence sake. It was violence for economic and political ends. The colonial system was a régime of foreign state power, of imperialist government, backed up by imperialist troops, police, laws, prisons and regulations, all designed to ensure absolute power by the big imperialist monopolies. It was a system based on particular methods and forms of economic exploitation—forced labour, poll tax, migrant labour, poverty wages, land seizures, bans on the cultivation of certain crops, legal barriers to skilled work, discriminatory wages, low prices to peasant cultivators. It was a system, moreover, based on an ideology directed to maintaining the colonial workers and peasants in passivity and defeatism, and relying on ignorance deliberately fostered. A system based on the support of internal, indigenous allies prepared to forego the honour of independence for the sake of their own privileges,

[1] ibid., p. 117.   [2] ibid., p. 30.   [3] ibid., p. 65.

pomp and profits. To see only the violence runs the danger of thinking that removal of imperialist violence is sufficient; thus the "non-violent" continuation of monopoly investment and exploitation is ignored.

Fanon's over-simplification of the colonial system and his failure to see it in all its complexities—military, political, economic and ideological—was, as we shall see, to lead him into dangerously over-simplified assessments of the role played by different classes in the African anti-colonial revolution and into mistaken opinions concerning the revolution's future path.

Nguyen Nghe, in his penetrating study of Fanon,[1] characterises Fanon's emphasis on violence as subjectivism arising from his position as an "intellectual individualist". This subjectivism, he argues, leads Fanon to neglect a fundamental revolutionary truth, namely that armed struggle, important as it may be when it becomes necessary, is only "a phase in the revolutionary movement which is, above all, and basically political. . . . When one neglects political, ideological work in order to concentrate purely on military art, one has to expect disappointments, especially when conditions of peace are re-established, even when victory has been won." This was written in 1963; and, in the light of what transpired in Algeria after victory, one cannot ignore Nguyen Nghe's warning.

Nghe cites the examples of Vietnam where it was known for veteran resistance fighters, after nine years with the guerillas, to return to their opium pipes; and of peasants, who fought with the guerrillas for years, only to return to their previous fear of ghosts because of a certain loss of confidence in the Party due to its mistakes in the way agrarian reform was carried out. It was only possible, he points out, to overcome such problems by political work, by courageous self-criticism, and by educating the people to understand what was involved in building socialism.

Nghe also makes the important point that imperialism does not conquer and dominate solely through the instrument of violence, but also by its politics—"and it will continue to win until it is opposed by a body of political thought superior to its own".

James Connolly also had to contend with the single-track advocates of "physical force".[2] Criticising the "latter-day high falutin 'hillside' man" who "exalts into a principle that which the revolutionists of

---

[1] Nguyen Nghe: "Fanon et les Problemes de l'Independence", *La Pensée*, No. 107, February, 1963, pp. 23–36.
[2] James Connolly: "Physical Force in Irish Politics", *Workers' Republic*, July 22, 1899.

other countries have looked upon as a weapon", Connolly emphasised that what was decisive was to first reach agreement "upon the end to be attained". That is to say, clear political objectives are paramount. "In other words, Socialists believe that the question of force is of very minor importance; the really important question is of the principles upon which is based the movement that may or may not need the use of force to realise its object."

Connolly was using the term "force" here in the sense indicated by his title, that is to say, *physical* force, or violence. And when, in Connolly's judgment, the time came in Easter 1916, for such force to be used he never flinched—and paid for his revolutionary courage and audacity with his life.

It is not out of place to cite Cabral on the role of armed struggle. Speaking to peasants at Maké he declared:

> The armed struggle is very important. But the most important is to have an understanding of the conditions of our people. Our people support armed struggle. We must give them the certainty that those who have arms in their hands are the sons of the people and that arms have no superiority over working tools. If one carries a rifle and the other a tool, the most important of the two is he who carries a tool. For one takes up arms to defeat the Portuguese, but if we want to chase out the Portuguese, it is to defend those who use tools.[1]

Although Fanon places so much emphasis on violence, he is not always clear on this question. "It is the intuition of the colonised masses that their liberation must, and can only, be achieved by force."[2] For Fanon the term "force" means *armed struggle*. And yet again, in that unscientific habit he has of frequently contradicting himself, he can write: "We know for sure today that in Algeria the test of force was inevitable; but other countries through political action and through the work of clarification undertaken by a party have led their people to the same results."[3]

So, on the one hand "liberation can only be achieved by force" (clearly meant in the sense of armed struggle), but in other countries liberation was won "through political action". This contradiction in Fanon's thought arises because he fails to distinguish what has been common in all the paths to liberation, namely *political struggle*. Struggle

[1] Quoted in *Lutte Armée en Afrique* by Gerard Chaliand, Paris, 1967. (Author's translation.)
[2] Frantz Fanon: *The Damned*, op. cit., p. 57.
[3] ibid., p. 154.

implies the use of force, that is to say the attempt by the colonised people to impose their will on the colonisers, and compel them to abandon their direct colonial rule. But struggle, force, need not involve *armed* struggle, or *armed* violence. A demonstration by thousands of people is the use of force. A strike is the use of force. The occupation of land is the use of force. So, in its own way, is the refusal to pay taxes, or to dip cattle. Every action by the people in their daily struggle against colonialism involved some display of force, a manifestation of the power and will of the colonised, and an attempt to use the display of this force in order to compel a retreat by the colonialists. In many cases in Africa, in fact in the majority of cases, the use of such forms of struggle and such use of force, was sufficient, in the context of the general crisis which imperialism faced after the second world war, to win national independence. In a number of other cases, some degree of armed struggle was necessary. In some instances a single military blow (as in Egypt in 1952, or Zanzibar in 1964) was sufficient to topple a government; later, under different conditions, such short military actions were to be successful in the Sudan, Libya and Somalia (1969). In some cases, more prolonged fighting characterised the process of the liberation struggle, even if the armed movements themselves and the forces they represented did not always achieve the military defeat of the colonial power (e.g. Morocco, Tunisia, Kenya, Cameroun). In Algeria a seven years' war was fought to compel the French to abandon their rule and to surrender power to the F.L.N. Today, armed struggle is taking place in Guinea-Bissau, Angola, Mozambique, Namibia, and preparations for such fighting are obviously being made in South Africa.

Thus, armed action was a feature of the anti-colonial struggle only in a *minority* of African colonies, and this fact alone contradicts Fanon's argument that "armed and open struggle" is the only way forward.

★　　　★　　　★　　　★

On the subject of race and colour, Fanon never allowed his justified hatred of white racialism to turn him towards black racialism. On the contrary, he was as deeply concerned with the corrupting and corrosive effect of white racialism on the whites themselves as he was with the terrible consequences of white racialism on the black people.

> The white man is sealed in his whiteness.
> The black man in his blackness.[1]

[1] Frantz Fanon: *Black Skin, White Masks* (Paris, 1952), London, 1968, p. 11.

Fanon's aim was "nothing short of the liberation of the man of colour from himself".[1] At the same time he strove "to show the white man that he is at once the perpetrator and the victim of a delusion".[2] Both black and white are warped and stunted by the system under which the black man is suppressed, exploited, discriminated against, scorned and despised—and yet feared—by the white man. There is no future for the black man in yearning to become like the white man. The only future for both is the complete destruction of racialism in all its forms.

In a plea against racial attitudes of either black or white, Fanon declared:

> I as a man of colour do not have the right to seek to know in what respect my race is superior or inferior to another race. . . . I as a man of colour do not have the right to seek ways of stamping down the pride of my former master. . . . There is no Negro mission; there is no white burden. . . . No, I do not have the right to go and cry out my hatred at the white man. I do not have the duty to murmur my gratitude to the white man. . . . I recognise that I have one right alone: That of demanding human behaviour from the other. . . . My life should not be devoted to drawing up the balance sheet of Negro values. There is no white world, there is no white ethic, any more than there is white intelligence. There are in every part of the world men who search.[3]

One cannot remain unaffected by Fanon's moving plea. His is a voice which, while it will give no satisfaction to the white racialists, will bring no comfort either to those who want to label Fanon as a black racialist. Cutting right across all thoughts of colour, Fanon asserts that everywhere, in all countries, whatever the colour of their skin, there are "men who search", men who struggle to create the brotherhood of man.

It is typical of Fanon's anti-racial stand that in the midst of the Algerian war he could write warmly and appreciatively of those Frenchmen in Algeria, including some of the *colons* (settlers), who assisted the Algerians in their struggle.[4] In the same way, and from the same principled motives, his support for a Moslem people did not prevent him quoting with approval the 1957 declaration of a group of

---

[1] ibid., p. 10.
[2] ibid., p. 225.
[3] ibid., pp. 228–9.
[4] Frantz Fanon: *Studies in a Dying Colonialism* (Paris, 1959), New York, 1965, pp. 157–78.

Algerian Jews attesting that "Jews have joined the ranks of the Algerians fighting for national independence. . . . Some have paid with their lives, others have bravely borne the foulest police brutalities, and many are behind the doors of prisons and the gates of concentration camps. We also know that in the common fight Moslems and Jews have discovered themselves to be racial brothers, and that they feel a deep and lasting attachment to the Algerian fatherland. . . ."[1]

Fanon was an anti-imperialist, an anti-colonialist, not a racialist, and he therefore never forgot, in his own words, that "there are in every part of the world men who search".

Fanon's fierce and sometimes extravagant attitude on many essential points has, unfortunately, resulted in his ideas being taken up and used in a distorted fashion by cold war warriors who ignore the main purpose of his work and fail to recognise (or wish to cast aside) the fact that he hated not only colonialism and racialism; he equally detested capitalism, both that of the imperialist oppressor and equally that of its miserable imitator in Africa, for whom Fanon had nothing but the most withering contempt.

Those who wish to isolate the Third World from their natural allies in the socialist countries and in the working-class and democratic movements in the imperialist metropolis itself have sought to use some of Fanon's most flamboyant and impassioned thoughts to this end. Confused at times, Fanon may have been. Unscientific and contradictory in his approach he often was. In no sense had he yet acquired a fully coherent conception of the modern world. But there is sufficient in his writing to challenge the attempts of those who would seek to use him for ends which he thoroughly despised. He declared without equivocation:

> For colonial peoples enslaved by Western nations, the Communist countries are the only ones that have on all occasions taken their defense. The colonialised countries need not concern themselves to find out whether this attitude is dictated by the interests of Communist strategy; they note first of all that this general behaviour is to their interest.[2]

At the same time, he saw, too, the importance of the colonial people themselves joining hands to strengthen their common anti-imperialist struggle.

[1] Frantz Fanon: *Studies in a Dying Colonialism*, p. 157.
[2] Frantz Fanon: *Towards the African Revolution* (Paris, 1964), New York, 1967, p. 94.

The independence of a new territory, the liberation of the new peoples are felt by the other oppressed countries as an invitation, an encouragement, and a promise. Every setback of colonial domination in America or in Asia strengthens the national will of the African peoples. It is in the national struggle against the oppressor that colonised peoples have discovered, concretely, the solidarity of the colonialist bloc and the necessary interdependence of the liberation movements.[1]

Neither did Fanon ignore the role of the working class in the capitalist centres, and the importance of colonial liberation to them.

... the dialectical strengthening that occurs between the movement of liberation of the colonised peoples and the emancipatory struggle of the exploited working classes of the imperialist countries is sometimes neglected, and indeed forgotten.

It is true that Fanon called on the people of Africa to turn their backs on Europe, but there is no mistaking that it is capitalist Europe which he condemned:

Colonialism and imperialism have not paid their score when they withdraw their flags and their police forces from our territories. For centuries the capitalists have behaved in the underdeveloped world like nothing more than war criminals. Deportations, massacres, forced labour, and slavery have been the main methods used by capitalism to increase its wealth, its gold and diamond reserves, and to establish its power. . . . For in a very concrete way Europe has stuffed herself inordinately with the gold and raw materials of the colonial countries: Latin America, China and Africa. From all these continents, under whose eyes Europe today raises up her tower of opulence, there has flowed out for centuries towards that same Europe diamonds and oil, silk and cotton, wood and exotic products. Europe is literally the creation of the Third World. The wealth which smothers her is that which was stolen from the underdeveloped countries.[2]

There is little here to justify the argument that Fanon's intention was to isolate Africa and the Third World from all else that is progressive in the rest of the world, although at times his unfortunate manner of writing does convey this impression, especially since he calls on the Third World to start "a new history of Man".[3] Yet even here, he immediately modifies this call by admitting the necessity to take into

---

[1] ibid., p. 145.   [2] *The Damned*, op. cit., pp. 79–81.   [3] ibid., p. 255.

account "the sometimes prodigious theses which Europe has put forward".

He asserted, without any equivocation: "The Cold War must be ended, for it leads nowhere."[1] He made a clear choice for socialism—"a régime which is completely orientated towards the people as a whole and based on the principle that man is the most precious of all possessions will allow us to go forward more quickly and more harmoniously, and thus make impossible that caricature of a society where all economic and political power is held in the hands of a few who regard the nation as a whole with scorn and contempt".[2]

He called for a great effort to "rehabilitate mankind, and make man victorious everywhere, once and for all", adding that this task "will be carried out with the indispensable help of the European peoples", who themselves must realise that in the past they have often "joined the ranks of our common masters where colonial questions were concerned. To achieve this, the European people must first decide to wake up and shake themselves, use their brains, and stop playing the stupid game of the Sleeping Beauty."[3]

No one who was anti-European and narrowly "Third Worldish" could have displayed such genuine concern for the real fate and future of Europe. Europe, argued Fanon, has been made a monster by colonialism and capitalism. Her most horrible crimes were committed "in the heart of man", leading him to "racial hatreds, slavery, exploitation and above all the bloodless genocide which consisted in the setting aside of fifteen thousand millions of men".[4]

So let us turn our backs on all this, proclaimed Fanon.

> For Europe, for ourselves and for humanity, comrades, we must turn over a new leaf, we must work out new concepts, and try to set afoot a new man.

Thus, in his typical fashion, Fanon, carried away by his own eloquence and passionate feeling for revolutionary change, throws the baby out with the bath-water. One moment he is asking for the "indispensable help of the European peoples"; the next he is conveying the impression that nothing is to be learnt from Europe, that "new concepts" must be worked out and a "new man" set afoot. But the basic concepts are already to hand, the concepts of that same socialism

---

[1] *The Damned*, op. cit., p. 83.   [2] ibid., p. 78.   [3] ibid., p. 83.
[4] ibid., p. 255. It is not clear why Fanon used this figure.

for which Fanon has already opted—concepts, moreover, that first arose in Europe itself, both in the theory and in practice.

But it is not only European socialist thought on which Fanon wants Africa to turn its back. He decries, too, Europe's industrial and technological developments since, for him, these bring only "a succession of negations of man, and an avalanche of murders".[1]

Commenting on this, Marton has rightly noted:

> It is not the machine, not automation which mutilates man. Industrial techniques free man from the blind forces of nature. They act as liberators if they are used in the service of man, but worsen his alienation if they are used to increase the profits of the capitalists.[2]

Nghe has made a similar critique of Fanon's views on Europe:[3]

> One cannot recommence history, as Fanon pretends. One is situated in the stream of history, or rather one needs to know where one is situated in the stream of history. However great may be the hatred which one can nurture against imperialism, the first necessity, for an Asian or an African, is to know that for three centuries it is Europe which has been in the forefront of history. Europe has thrown into the arena of history at least two developments which are still lacking in many Asian and African countries; two developments which run together, even if at certain times or in certain places, they are not necessarily linked: the renewal of the productive forces, and democracy.

To reject these contributions, warns Nghe, because they have their origins in Europe, runs the risk of playing into the hands of those who make use of traditional ideas and institutions in order to cover up their reactionary policies.

*   *   *   *

Central to Fanon's thinking are his views on the role of social classes in the African revolution. It was to his credit that he attempted to analyse class forces in Africa, for without this there can be no possibility of understanding the character and perspective of the struggle facing Africa today. It is doubly to his credit that he made this attempt at a time when it was fashionable among a number of African leaders to deny the very existence of social classes in Africa.

[1] ibid., p. 253.
[2] Imre Marton: "A Propos des Thèses de Fanon", *Action*, 8–9, 1965. (Revue Théorique et Politique du Parti Communiste Martiniquais.)
[3] Nguyen Nghe: op. cit., p. 34.

Fanon's weakness here, however, is that he relied too easily on superficial impressions gleaned from a few countries, and consequently tended to make sweeping generalisations which are not usually borne out by the facts. He provides no statistics at all to back up his analysis, nor does he usually provide details or specific examples to support his emphatic and colourful assertions.

This is not to deny the importance of much of what he wrote. Certainly, reading again in 1971 his book, *The Damned*, written nearly a decade earlier, one cannot but be struck again and again by his brilliant intuition on many points, and by his ability, even when indulging in his passionate exaggerations, to expose a facet of development which today has reached maturity and largely justified Fanon's foresight.

This is true, for example, of his withering judgment of most of the new capitalist rulers of the neo-colonialist states, and his warning that, through their inability to solve any of their country's problems and because of their parasitical clinging to imperialism, they would drag Africa along a Latin American path of instability and eventual military coups.

> In these poor, under-developed countries, where the rule is that the greatest wealth is surrounded by the greatest poverty, the army and the police constitute the pillars of the regime; an army and police force (another rule which must not be forgotten) which are advised by foreign experts.[1]

But the young African bourgeoisie, warns Fanon, is too intent on getting rich even to appreciate the danger to itself of this situation. "It is the army that becomes the arbiter."

Writing in the beginning of the 1960's, long before the era of African military coups had begun, Fanon wrote with impressive perception:

> The ranks of decked-out profiteers whose grasping hands scrape up the bank-notes from a poverty-stricken country will sooner or later be men of straw in the hands of the army, cleverly handled by foreign experts. In this way the former mother country practises indirect government, both by the bourgeoisie that it upholds and also by the national army led by its experts, an army that pins the people down, immobilising and terrorising them.[2]

1963, the year in which *The Damned* was originally published, opened with the military coup against President Olympio of Togo. By the

[1] *The Damned*, op. cit., p. 139.   [2] ibid., p. 140.

end of 1968 there had been no less than forty coups or attempted coups or government crises in Africa.[1] Admittedly their cause and character were not in all cases the same. Not all were purely military coups. Neither were they all a clear shift to the right. In some cases they represented merely a reshuffle within the ranks of the pensioners of imperialism. But amongst them there were certainly a number which answer well to the description of the process anticipated so intelligently by Fanon. And almost every other month seems to bring a further confirmation of his judgment on this point.

Similarly, his penetrating remarks on the virtual collapse of the big national parties on the morrow of independence unfortunately are true all too often.

During the period of the struggle for independence there was one (a party) right enough, a party led by the present leader. But since then this party has sadly disintegrated; nothing is left but the shell of a party, the name, the emblem and the motto. . . . Since the proclamation of independence the party no longer helps the people to set out its demands, to become more aware of its needs and better able to establish its power. Today, the party's mission is to deliver to the people the instructions which issue from the summit. There no longer exists the fruitful give-and-take from the bottom to the top and from the top to the bottom which creates and guarantees democracy in a party. Quite on the contrary, the party has made itself into a screen between the masses and the leaders. There is no longer any party life, for the branches which were set up during the colonial period are today completely demobilised. . . . After independence, the party sinks into an extraordinary lethargy. . . . The local party leaders are given administrative posts, the party becomes an administration, and the militants disappear into the crowd. . . . The party is becoming a means of private advancement. . . . Privileges multiply and corruption triumphs. . . . The party, a true instrument of power in the hands of the bourgeoisie, reinforces the machine, and ensures that the people are hemmed in and immobilised. It becomes more and more clearly anti-democratic, an implement of coercion.[2]

Once again one is compelled to admire Fanon's ability, so early in the life of independent Africa, to discern an important trend which was to become, all too tragically, a dominant characteristic of so many

[1] See Jack Woddis: "Military Coups in Africa", *Marxism Today*, December, 1968; Ruth First: *The Barrel of a Gun*, London, 1970.
[2] *The Damned*, op. cit., pp. 137–8.

new African states. Of many, but not all. And it is here that Fanon's powerful assertions begin to take on the character of a dogma which does not help us to understand fully the complexity of the situation that has overtaken so much of Africa. For what Fanon failed to foresee and to emphasise was the emergence of a group of African states in which the leaders and the parties were to strive (despite their own weaknesses and shortcomings, despite the heavy weight of imperialism which still was to press on their economy and politics alike, and despite the ambitions and careerism of so many in the top echelons of the party and the new state) to drag their people out of the orbit of imperialism, to lift them up out of their apathy, poverty and ignorance, and to commence the brave and heavy task of building a new Africa which would begin to correspond to the needs and aspirations of its people.

Thus Fanon's analysis fails to explain the important anti-imperialist stand and the domestic changes pursued after 1960 by the United Arab Republic, Algeria, Mali, Guinea, Ghana, Congo (Brazzaville), and Tanzania, and later by Sudan, Libya, Zambia and Uganda. Although reactionary coups subsequently took place in five of these countries—Algeria, Ghana, Mali, Uganda and the Sudan—the group of advanced states is numerically as large today as it was in 1960. Fanon, however, gives the impression that he sees no distinction between this group of states and such pitiful neo-colonialist dependencies as Ivory Coast, Lesotho, Malawi or Malagasy.

The weakness in Fanon's analysis on such points arises from his lack of scientific method, from his tendency to present a generalised and often brilliantly written picture which is apparently meant to apply to *all* African countries (since he nowhere refers to exceptions nor indicates the specific cases with which he is dealing), but which, in reality, applies in *all* its particulars to *no single African country at all*.

Nowhere is his failure to use scientific method so obvious as in his treatment of African social classes despite the fact that here, too, he has many penetrating things to say and certainly makes points that stimulate thought as often as they provoke annoyance and rejection.

Since other commentators have tried their hands at sorting out classes in Africa it would be as well if we began by defining terms. This is particularly important in view of the tendency of some writers on Africa to confuse peasants with agricultural wage workers, or to term highly paid specialist and technical workers as "middle class".

Lenin defined a social class in scientific terms which have a relevance to all societies and to all regions of the world:

Classes are large groups of people which differ from each other by the place they occupy in a historically definite system of social production, by their relation (in most cases fixed and formulated in laws) to the means of production, by their role in the social organisation of labour, and, consequently, by the dimensions and method of acquiring the share of social wealth that they obtain. Classes are groups of people one of which may appropriate the labour of another owing to the different places they occupy in the definite system of social economy.[1]

It is, Lenin wrote, how people stand in relation to the means of production which is the key to their class. It is this which "consequently" determines the "dimensions" of the social wealth they acquire and their "method" of acquiring it.

From this standpoint, Africa is indeed very complex. Even before the era of twentieth-century colonialism, most tropical African countries did not in general possess the same clear-cut class divisions as, for example, existed in Asia where systems of feudalism had developed over long periods. The European contact and the resultant slave trade wrought havoc in Africa. At a time when Europe was progressing from feudalism to capitalism and making enormous technological advances, Africa, by this same advancing Europe, was being dragged down and its society thrown into temporary stagnation. On the blood and bones of African slavery, European capitalism, and especially that of Britain and France, flourished. In Europe, new towns arose, inventions were made, factories were built, and Europe was enabled to lay the basis for her passage to modern industrial development. But at the end of the nineteenth century, Africa, already in a backward economic state, was to suffer yet a further heavy blow; before she could recover from her four hundred years of slavery, the imperialist whirlwind was upon her. Once more her normal development was frustrated, and new distortions imposed on her economy.

Consequently, Africa entered the present century with no developed capitalist class of its own, with only the barest beginnings of a working class, with pockets of large-scale feudal land-ownership (e.g. Northern Nigeria, Buganda, Ethiopia, Upper Volta, the northern regions of the "French" Cameroons), but with the majority of its people still carrying on subsistence agriculture on their communally-owned lands, and still practising local handicrafts and village industries. Only during

[1] V. I. Lenin: *Selected Works*, Vol. 9, pp. 432–3.

the past sixty years, and especially in the past two decades, has Africa begun to emerge from this pattern of development.

It is therefore understandable if the growth of new classes in African society—or of the basic classes of workers and capitalists—should sometimes be presented in an unsatisfactory way. These classes are still in a process of development, and are in no sense mature clearly defined classes such as we are used to in the industrialised societies of the West. Workers in Africa are usually part-time peasants, and peasants are part-time workers. The most common worker in Africa is the migrant, who periodically leaves his holding on the communal lands to take up wage labour in the mines or plantations, only to return after a year or two to his stake in the countryside. Differentiation amongst the peasants is taking place but is often not very far advanced; private ownership of the land is beginning to spread, but no decisive break-up of communal land ownership has yet taken place, and the main tracts of land are still owned by peasant communities. African capitalists are appearing, but they still comprise a relatively small group, and have not yet been able to wrest from the imperialist monopolies any substantial portions of the economy for themselves. When one takes into account, too, the ideological influence of the united fight for national independence that has engulfed all African countries without exception, it can more readily be understood why there is often a hesitancy by some African leaders to accept the significance of social classes when considering Africa's present phase of development. But the significance cannot be denied.

It is a special merit of Fanon that he was able to see that an understanding of the future of Africa required an analysis of the class forces. It is further to his credit that his motivation in seeking his way through the complexities of class formation and class action in Africa was to assist the liberation of Africa from imperialism, and to hasten the social revolution which alone can emancipate the millions of peasants to whom he expresses such attachment.

PEASANTS AS A REVOLUTIONARY CLASS

What then, are Fanon's views on classes in Africa?

First, there is his special emphasis on the role of the peasants, and this is linked with his insistence on the necessity of "violence".

The peasantry is systematically disregarded for the most part by the propaganda put out by the nationalist parties. And it is clear that in the colonial countries the peasants alone are revolutionary, for they have nothing to lose and everything to gain. The starving peasant, outside the class system, is the first among the exploited to discover that only violence pays.[1]

Quite apart from the specific question of the role of the African peasantry, which will be considered later, one notes straight away Fanon's unscientific approach. The peasant, we are told, is "outside the class system", yet, at the same time, "the first among the exploited" to see the need for violent action. But if the peasants are exploited they can only be exploited by another social class. Thus, they must be part of a class system, and have a clear relationship with another class— and that remains true whether that other class is that of foreign plantation or trading monopolies, or of white capitalist settlers, or of indigenous feudal landlords, or finally of indigenous capitalist farmers and traders. The whole point about imperialism and the twentieth-century colonial system is that it reaches out and brings within its orbit the whole of the oppressed people, disrupting their former way of life even while allowing subsistence farming and communal land ownership to continue in a stunted and distorted form.

But to continue with Fanon's analysis.

Not only does he assert that the "peasantry precisely constitutes the only spontaneously revolutionary force of the country"[2] but he maintains that in the course of the inevitable armed struggle "the peasants, who are all the time adding to their knowledge in the light of experience, will come to show themselves capable of directing the people's struggle".[3]

Thus, in Fanon's view, the African peasantry is the sole revolutionary class and not only provides the main forces of the struggle but also is capable of performing the function of the leadership of this struggle.

But this does not exhaust the principal points of Fanon's analysis of the peasantry. As Martin Staniland points out in a recent penetrating study of Fanon ("Frantz Fanon and the African Political Class": *African Affairs*, Vol. 68, No. 270, January, 1969, pp. 4–25), there is a good deal of confusion and contradiction in the way Fanon deals with this problem. Having stressed the spontaneously revolutionary character of the African peasantry (not its *potential* role, it will be noted), Fanon has to admit the essentially conservative attitude of the peasants, and the possibility, therefore, of the colonialists making use of them for reactionary ends.

[1] *The Damned*, op. cit., p. 48.   [2] ibid., p. 99.   [3] ibid., p. 114.

"We must remember", he admits, "that colonialism has often strengthened or established its domination by organising the petrifaction of the country districts. Ringed round by marabouts, witch doctors and customary chieftains, the majority of country-dwellers are still living in a feudal manner, and the full power of this medieval structure of society is maintained by the settlers' military and administrative officials."[1]

The role of the chiefs and feudal leaders, explains Fanon, is essentially conservative:

> The feudal leaders form a screen between the westernised nationalists and the bulk of the people. . . . These traditional authorities who have been upheld by the occupying power view with disfavour the attempts made by the élite to penetrate the country districts. They know very well that the ideas which are likely to be introduced by these influences coming from the towns call in question the very nature of unchanging, everlasting feudalism. Thus their enemy is not at all the occupying power with which they get along on the whole very well, but these people with modern ideas who mean to dislocate the aboriginal society, and who in doing so will take the bread out of their mouths.[2]

Fanon understands that previous bourgeois and working-class revolutions have shown that "the bulk of the peasants often constitute a brake on the revolution". It is not surprising, therefore, as he points out, that the colonialists are able to make use of the antagonism between town and countryside in the struggle against national independence. The colonialists "mobilise the people of the mountains and the up-country dwellers against the townsfolk".[3] Even after independence, "The colonial secret services which were not disbanded after independence keep up the discontentment and still manage to make serious difficulties for the young governments."[4]

The tribalism of the rural masses is also brought into play.

> Sometimes colonialism attempts to dislocate or create diversions around the upward thrust of nationalism. Instead of organising the sheiks and the chiefs against the "revolutionaries" in the towns, native committees organise the tribes and confraternities into parties. Confronted with the urban party which was beginning to "embody the national will" and to constitute a danger for the colonial regime, splinter groups are born, and tendencies and parties which have their origin in ethnical or regional differences spring up. It is the

---

[1] *The Damned*, op. cit., p. 89.   [2] ibid., p. 89.   [3] ibid., p. 91.   [4] ibid., p. 95.

entire tribe turning itself into a political party, closely advised by the colonialists.[1]

Having thus clearly exposed the basic conservatism of the peasantry —and this despite his parallel contradictory assertion that the peasantry is a *spontaneously revolutionary force*, and, in fact, the *sole* revolutionary force—Fanon then rallies to the defence of the chiefs whom he had previously denounced as "traditional collaborators",[2] as main supporters of feudalism and colonialism, and as major enemies of the national liberation movement. In describing the attitude of the nationalist parties—"The traditional chiefs are ignored, sometimes even persecuted. . . . The old men, surrounded by respect in all traditional societies and usually invested with unquestionable moral authority, are publicly held up to ridicule"[3]—Fanon cannot hide a certain sympathy for the chiefs. And this is linked with his conception of the role of traditional society as the only genuinely national expression in contrast to the modern, Western ideas coming from the towns. Thus, in a sense like Gandhi harking back to the idealised Indian village, Fanon, while himself a "modern, Westernised town dweller", plumps for the peasant who "stands for the disciplined element",[4] who remains "altruistic", submerges his own individuality "in favour of the community", and stands in contrast to the worker in whom Fanon finds "individualist behaviour". In explaining his preference for the peasant rather than the worker, Fanon attempts to find a basis for his contention that the former is more naturally revolutionary by arguing that the peasant "is excluded from the advantages of colonialism", in contrast to the worker who, we are led to believe, "manages to turn colonial exploitation to his account".[5]

Fanon attempts to cut through this mass of contradictions in his own analysis by decrying the role of the working class in the national revolution, by his clear hostility to the national democratic parties which helped lead the independence struggle, and in particular by his absolute disapproval of the role of all sections of the indigenous bourgeoisie.

In his picture militant individuals, driven out of the nationalist party, find their way to the countryside, there to be reinvigorated and to find the true basis of the revolution. These "revolutionary elements" from the towns "discover that the mass of the country people have never ceased to think of the problem of their liberation except in

[1] ibid., pp. 95–6. [2] ibid., p. 109. [3] ibid., p. 91. [4] ibid., p. 90.
[5] ibid., p. 91

terms of violence, in terms of taking back the land from the foreigners, in terms of national struggle, and of armed insurrection".[1] The militants rally these "mettlesome masses of people, who are rebels by instinct", provide them with political education and military training; weapons appear, "the armed struggle has begun". Before long, "On every hill a government in miniature is formed, and takes over power. Everywhere—in the valleys and in the forests, in the jungle and in the villages—we find a national authority."[2] Fanon fails to explain where this process has taken place. In no sense can it be regarded as an adequate description of the course of the revolution in Tropical Africa. It is not even a correct description of what happened in Algeria.

It is, of course, not easy to avoid mistakes when analysing such a complex problem as that of the African revolution, but it is not entirely without significance that when Fanon attempts to find an example to prove this theory of his about the course of the African struggle he falls into an appalling blunder, holding up Roberto Holden, the imperialist-backed tribalist, as a genuine national leader of guerrilla forces, when in fact this same Holden was responsible for the savage slaughter of hundreds of genuine Angolan patriots fighting under the banner of the Popular Movement for the Liberation of Angola (MPLA). Holden has since been denounced and thoroughly exposed by all the responsible revolutionary movements engaged in armed struggle in the Portuguese African colonies and in southern Africa.

FANON'S REJECTION OF THE WORKING CLASS

Fanon's treatment of the African working class is not so contradictory as is his assessment of the peasantry, although once again his unscientific method cannot prevent him from falling into typical contradictions. Thus, he commences by admitting that "the most politically conscious" elements are "the working classes in the towns, the skilled workers and the civil servants".[3] But although the working class is politically aware, it cannot be relied on, argues Fanon, to throw itself into the revolutionary struggle for above all else it is a privileged stratum.

> It cannot be too strongly stressed that in the colonised territories the proletariat is the nucleus of the colonised population which has been most pampered by the colonial régime. The embryonic proletariat of the towns is in a comparatively privileged position.

[1] *The Damned*, op. cit., p. 101.   [2] ibid., p. 105.   [3] ibid., p. 88.

In capitalist countries, the working class has nothing to lose; it is they who, in the long run, have everything to gain. In the colonial countries the working class has everything to lose; in reality it represents that fraction of the colonised nation which is necessary and irreplaceable if the colonial machine is to run smoothly; it includes tram conductors, taxi drivers, miners, dockers, interpreters, nurses and so on. It is these elements which constitute also the "bourgeois" fraction of the colonised people.[1]

So, to Marcuse's "bourgeoisified workers" of the capitalist countries we have added Fanon's "bourgeoisified workers" of Africa. There is a strange division of labour here. Fanon, it should be noted, regards the working class of the capitalist countries as a revolutionary force, with "nothing to lose", but takes a negative view of the revolutionary potential of the workers of Africa. Marcuse, in his turn, has at times been quite convinced that the working class in the capitalist world has lost its revolutionary potential, but that the masses in the Third World, from which at no time has he specifically excluded the working class, is one of the decisive revolutionary forces of our time. One thing Fanon and Marcuse have in common—in the particular field with which each of them deals, the relevant working class is written off as a non-revolutionary force.

Fanon, who has assessed the working class as the "bourgeois" fraction of the nation, is compelled to admit that the organisation of genuine trade unions, freed from imperialist control and influence, "is a fresh element of pressure in the hands of the populations of the towns upon colonialism. . . . The national unions are born out of the struggle for independence organised in the towns, and their programme is above all a political programme and a nationalist programme. Such a national union which comes into being during the decisive phase of the fight for independence is in fact the legal enlistment of conscious, dynamic nationalist elements. . . . During the colonial phase, the nationalist trade union organisations constitute an impressive striking power. In the towns, the trades unionists can bring to a standstill, or at any rate slow down at any given moment, the colonialist economy."[2]

But all this, believes Fanon, remains unknown to the mass of country-dwellers. The actions in the towns, he argues, are simply small islands of struggle within the fortress of colonialism. Conversely, he argues, when the peasants take up the armed struggle in the country-side the workers "go on living their lives in the towns as if they failed

[1] ibid., p. 88.   [2] ibid., pp. 97–8.

to realise that the essential movement for freedom has begun. The towns keep silent, and their continuing their daily humdrum life gives the peasant the bitter impression that a whole sector of the nation is content to sit on the sideline. Such proofs of indifference disgust the peasants, and strengthen their tendency to condemn the townsfolk as a whole."[1] Thus we are presented with a picture of an absolute gap between the workers and the peasants, each class immersed in its own struggles, cut off from and largely indifferent to the fate and effort of the other.

It will be necessary to put this idea of Fanon's to more close scrutiny, but at this stage one cannot avoid asking: To which country is he referring? In what African country has he discerned this phenomenon? Unfortunately, he once again has failed to provide any specific information.

After independence, continues Fanon, the workers and their unions become still more political. "The trades union leaders discover that they can no longer limit themselves to working class agitation".[2] They are compelled to become "more and more political", and to challenge the bourgeoisie for "governmental power". And so they take up the demand for an end to foreign bases on the national soil, they denounce harmful trade agreements and oppose the government's foreign policy. But, apart from this "they do not know where to go", for if they present their social demands "they would scandalise the rest of the nation", for the workers, repeats Fanon, "are in fact the most favoured section of the population, and represent the most comfortably off fraction of the people".

What is the conclusion which Fanon draws from this assessment? Back to the countryside. The militants "come to understand, with a sort of bewilderment that will henceforth never quite leave them, that political action in the towns will always be powerless to modify or overthrow the colonial régime".[3] And so they depart from "the useless political activity in the towns"[4] and flee to the countryside where they "rediscover politics, no longer as a way of lulling people to sleep nor as a means of mystification, but as the only method of intensifying the struggle".

And so the armed struggle begins in the countryside. The peasant masses are awakened. The struggle spreads from village to village, from tribe to tribe. In an attempt to head off the struggle the colonialists offer concessions. This succeeds as a temporary tactic. The peasant, too

[1] *The Damned*, op. cit., p. 114. [2] ibid., p. 98. [3] ibid., p. 101. [4] ibid., p. 108.

inexperienced and unsophisticated in politics, is momentarily diverted. But this is only a transitional setback. The struggle is taken up afresh. The liberation forces advance. But there can be no final victory without taking the towns. Fanon understands that "some day or another the rebellion must come to include the towns. . . . Although the country districts represent inexhaustible reserves of popular energy, and groups of armed men ensure that insecurity is rife there, colonialism does not doubt the strength of its system. It does not feel that it is endangered fundamentally. The rebel leaders therefore decide to bring the war into the enemy's camp, that is to say into his grandiose, peaceful cities."[1]

But Fanon has already dismissed the workers of the towns as being incapable of playing a revolutionary role. To whom then does he turn? On whom can he rely to act as the peasants' urban allies?

Here we come to another essential component of Fanon's conception.

> In fact the rebellion, which began in the country districts, will filter into the towns through that fraction of the peasant population which is blocked on the outer fringe of the urban centres, that fraction which has not yet succeeded in finding a bone to gnaw in the colonial system. The men whom the growing population of the country districts and colonial expropriation have brought to desert their family holdings circle tirelessly around the different towns, hoping that one day or another they will be allowed inside. It is within this mass of humanity, this people of the shanty towns, at the core of the *lumpenproletariat*, that the rebellion will find its urban spearhead. For the *lumpenproletariat*, that horde of starving men, uprooted from their tribe and from their clan, constitutes one of the most spontaneous and the most radically revolutionary forces of a colonised people.[2]

Fanon recognises that the *lumpenproletariat* is "the gangrene ever present at the heart of colonial domination", but, ignoring the dangers that this gangrene can bring, he expects it to be a decisive force for revolution.

> So the pimps, the hooligans, the unemployed and the petty criminals, urged on from behind, throw themselves into the struggle for liberation like stout working men. These classless idlers will by militant and decisive action discover the path that leads to nation-hood. . . . The prostitutes, too, and the maids who are paid two

[1] ibid., p. 102.　　　[2] ibid., p. 103.

pounds a month, all the hopeless dregs of humanity, all who turn in circles between suicide and madness will recover their balance, once more go forward, and march proudly in the great procession of the awakened nation.[1]

Yet, once again Fanon is compelled to modify his picture and admit that it has too often been the imperialists, not the revolutionaries, who have been able to utilise the *lumpenproletariat* against the national liberation struggle. The oppressor will make skilful use of "that ignorance and incomprehension which are the weakness of the *lumpenproletariat*. If this available reserve of human effort is not immediately organised by the forces of rebellion, it will find itself fighting as hired soldiers side-by-side with the colonial troops."[2]

And here Fanon cites the very relevant examples of the *harkis* and *messalists* used by the French against the Algerian liberation forces; the "road-openers" who preceded the Portuguese armed columns in Angola; the organised demonstrations of separatists in Kasai and Katanga in the Congo, the "spontaneous" participants in the mass meetings against Lumumba in Leopoldville.

This is not really surprising, for as Fanon notes, the *lumpenproletariat* is marked by "spiritual instability". It is a force of men "whose participation is constantly at the mercy of their being for too long accustomed to physiological wretchedness, humiliation and irresponsibility".[3]

THE INTELLIGENTSIA AND THE NATIONAL BOURGEOISIE

There remain two other sections of the people in the towns still to be considered. The intelligentsia, and the indigenous capitalists.

Fanon correctly draws attention to the two tendencies of the intellectuals in Africa. On the one hand there are those intellectuals who, in the course of struggle, emancipate themselves from the artificial values which they have soaked up from the colonial system, overcome their individualism, and, at one with the people, adopt the vocabulary of "brother, sister, friend"—although this process is one which Fanon considers possible only under the condition that there has been a "real struggle for freedom", in which "the blood of the people has flowed and where the length of the period of armed warfare has favoured the backward surge of intellectuals towards bases grounded in the people".[4]

---

[1] *The Damned*, op. cit., p. 104. [2] ibid., p. 109. [3] ibid., p. 110.
[4] ibid., pp. 37–8.

After independence, too, Fanon notes a progressive trend among a section of the intellectuals, a number of whom he finds "sincere", ready to accept "the necessity for a planned economy, the outlawing of profiteers and the strict prohibition of attempts at mystification. In addition, such men fight in a certain measure for the mass participation of the people in the ordering of public affairs".[1]

But again basing himself on the alleged cleansing and liberatory effects of armed struggle, Fanon points to a difference in those countries in which decolonisation has taken place under conditions which prevented those areas being "sufficiently shaken by the struggle for liberation".[2] In such cases, he argues, the "wily intellectuals", those "spoilt children of yesterday's colonialism and of today's national governments . . . organise the loot of whatever national resources exist. Without pity, they use today's national distress as a means of getting on through scheming and legal robbery, by import-export combines, limited liability companies, gambling on the stock exchange, or unfair promotion."

The timidity of the intellectuals and their lack of decisiveness is partly due, claims Fanon, to "the apparent strength of the bourgeoisie".[3] For this reason, after independence, in order to avoid the installation of corruption, economic decline and the introduction of a régime of tyranny, force and intimidation, the road to the bourgeoisie must be closed. This is "the only means towards progress".

For the indigenous bourgeoisie Fanon has nothing but contempt and hostility, for he finds it a force which is wholly negative as regards the struggle for national independence.

The danger, as he sees it, is that the reformist character of the struggle led by the national bourgeoisie will prevent the attainment of genuine national liberation, in the place of which there will only be "an empty shell, a crude and fragile travesty of what might have been".[4]

In explaining the role of the national bourgeoisie, Fanon finds an economic basis to its attitude.

The national middle-class which takes over power at the end of the colonial régime is an underdeveloped middle-class. It has practically no economic power, and in any case it is in no way commensurate with the bourgeoisie of the mother country which it hopes to replace. . . . The university and merchant classes which make up the most enlightened section of the new state are in fact characterised by

[1] ibid., p. 142.   [2] ibid., p. 39.   [3] ibid., p. 143.   [4] ibid., p. 121.

the smallness of their number and their being concentrated in the capital, and in the type of activities in which they are engaged; business, agriculture, and the liberal professions. Neither financiers nor industrial magnates are to be found within this national middle-class. The national bourgeoisie of under-developed countries is not engaged in production, nor in invention, nor building, nor labour; it is completely canalised into activities of the intermediary type. Its innermost vocation seems to be to keep in the running and to be part of the racket. The psychology of the national bourgeoisie is that of the businessman, not that of the captain of industry; and it is only too true that the greed of the settlers and the system of embargoes set up by colonialism has hardly left them any other choice.[1]

Again and again Fanon asserts that the national bourgeoisie in Africa is a kind of phantom bourgeoisie, a weak hanger-on of foreign capitalism, with no strength or intention of building its own capitalist economy since, in fact, "under the colonial system a middle-class which accumulates capital is an impossible phenomenon". And so, after independence, this weak capitalist class makes no serious effort to change the economy. It still concerns itself solely with producing raw materials, "and not a single industry is set up in the country".[2]

It would, of course, be comparatively simple to provide facts on the new industries set up in a number of African territories. The UAR and Ghana under Nkrumah, are two outstanding examples. But Fanon is not concerned with the facts, with reality, only with his own generalised assertions.

Having neither sufficient material nor intellectual resources, says Fanon, the national bourgeoisie insists that all the big foreign companies pass through its hands. "The national middle-class discovers its historic mission: that of intermediary".[3] Content with its role as "the Western bourgeoisie's business agent", the national middle-class is eminently suited to its function as imperialism's internal ally in the post-independence game of neo-colonialism.

In fulfilment of this role, it creates the single national party.

Powerless economically, unable to bring about the existence of coherent social relations, and standing on the principle of its domination as a class, the bourgeoisie chooses the solution that seems to it the easiest, that of the single party. It does not yet have the quiet

---

[1] *The Damned*, op. cit., p. 122.   [2] ibid., p. 123.   [3] ibid., p. 124.

conscience and the calm that economic power and the control of the state machine alone can give.[1]

Thus the single party system is established, "the modern form of the dictatorship of the bourgeoisie, unmasked, unpainted, unscrupulous, and cynical".[2] And at the head of this party stands the national leader, the man who had formerly embodied the aspirations of the people for independence but who now reveals his inner purposes: "to become the general president of that company of profiteers impatient for their returns which constitutes the national bourgeoisie".[3]

The Party becomes "a means of private advancement".[4] Privilege and corruption mount. "The party is objectively, sometimes subjectively, the accomplice of the merchant bourgeoisie." But this shadow of a bourgeoisie is unable to construct "an elaborate bourgeois society".[5] Here "no true bourgeoisie exists; there is only a sort of little greedy caste, avid and voracious, with the timid mind of a huckster, only too glad to accept the dividends that the former colonial power hands out to it".[6]

Elaborating his analysis of this national bourgeoisie, Fanon also draws attention to the way in which it endeavours to utilise its positions in government and State to compensate for its basic economic weakness, namely "that it lacks something essential to a bourgeoisie; money. . . . It is not its economic strength, nor the dynamism of its leaders, nor the breadth of its ideas that ensures its peculiar quality of bourgeoisie. Consequently, it remains at the beginning and for a long time afterwards a bourgeoisie of the civil service. It is the positions that it holds in the new national administration which will give it strength and serenity. If the government gives it enough time and opportunity, this bourgeoisie will manage to put away enough money to stiffen its domination. But it will reveal itself as incapable of giving birth to an authentic bourgeois society with all the economic and industrial consequences which this entails. . . . The basis of its strength is found in its aptitude for trade and small business enterprises, and in securing commissions. It is not its money that works, but its business acumen. It does not go in for investments and it cannot achieve that accumulation of capital necessary to the birth and blossoming of an authentic bourgeoisie."[7]

No one who looks dispassionately at the fate of the majority of independent African states in the past few years can afford to dismiss

---

[1] ibid., p. 133.   [2] ibid., p. 133.   [3] ibid., p. 134.   [4] ibid., p. 138.
[5] ibid., p. 140.   [6] ibid., p. 141.   [7] ibid., pp. 143-4.

Fanon's powerful indictment of the national bourgeoisie. The losses have been too great, the setbacks too heavy, for any serious revolutionary lightly to set aside the weight of his argument. Yet here again it will be found, on closer examination, that his picture is too generalised, and that it lacks that quality of precision and factual detail that can more correctly lead one to valid judgments. Nowhere does he allow for any differentiation amongst the bourgeoisie.

Having effectively demonstrated the utterly useless and dangerous role this African bourgeoisie plays, Fanon draws attention to the growing disenchantment of the masses who, gaining nothing from the achievement of national independence, become increasingly isolated from the Government, the national Party, and its leaders who, in their turn, have turned their backs on the masses.

> The former colonial power increases its demands, accumulates concessions and guarantees, and takes fewer and fewer pains to mask the hold it has over the national government. The people stagnate deplorably in unbearable poverty; slowly they awaken to the unutterable treason of their leaders. This awakening is all the more acute in that the bourgeoisie is incapable of learning its lesson. The distribution of wealth that it effects is not spread out between a great many sectors; it is not ranged among different levels, nor does it set up a hierarchy of half-tones. The new caste is an affront all the more disgusting in that the immense majority, nine-tenths of the population, continue to die of starvation. The scandalous enrichment, speedy and pitiless, of this caste is accompanied by a decisive awakening on the part of the people, and a growing awareness that promises stormy days to come.[1]

This in brief, is Fanon's analysis of the role of different classes in the African revolution. It has been necessary to expound his views at some length and to quote fairly extensively from his main work, *The Damned*, in order to provide an adequate framework for an essential critique of these propositions.

To sum up Fanon's theoretical views on classes in Africa:

> *The working class* is a privileged class, a "bourgeois" fraction, with everything to lose, and is therefore antipathetic to revolutionary struggle;
> *The peasants* are the sole revolutionary class, with nothing to lose and everything to gain, and therefore spontaneously ready to

---

[1] *The Damned*, op. cit., p. 135.

turn to violent action, to armed struggle which is essential for genuine liberation, and to lead this struggle;

The chiefs and feudal leaders are upheld by colonialism and are opposed to the national party, but they possess moral authority over the peasants with whose help they defend the traditional society, which is a source of the strength of the nation;

The lumpenproletariat is the force in the towns which will act as the main ally of the peasants, as the "urban spearhead" of the rebellion;

Some *intellectuals* will side with the masses, but many will participate in the looting of the national resources after independence and timidly back up the bourgeoisie;

The bourgeoisie is only a mockery of a capitalist class, unable to act as an independent class, and only capable of fulfilling the role of an intermediary of foreign capitalism, and of stuffing its pockets at the expense of the masses.

If the first reaction of Marxists is to be rather surprised by the unorthodox character of some of these views, they should not reject them out of hand simply because they are new, or because they conflict with previous beliefs. Fanon's views must be subjected to the test of scientific examination before one attempts even a partial and provisional judgment.

Fanon was a sincere man. He dedicated his last few years to the Algerian revolution, and his views were undoubtedly conditioned both by his upbringing in Martinique, where he had direct experience of colonialism and racialism, and by his experience in the Algerian struggle where he witnessed at first hand the barbarities of imperialist aggression against a people's just war for liberation.

The weakness of Fanon's position, as we have already noted, is that he tried to construct a generalised body of theory concerning the role of classes in the African revolution without a detailed and scientific study of African reality. His views on social classes contain many penetrating flashes of insight, but they tend to be intuitive, based on impressions and observations of limited scope or confined to very few countries, rather than founded on a scientific examination in depth and on a more comprehensive scale. He provides no figures for the numerical size of different classes, of the extent of land holdings, of standards of living, wages and other sources of income. Moreover, he makes general assertions as to the course of the African revolution before and after independence but with only a few specific examples and nowhere with any examination in detail of what has actually transpired.

An understandable exception here is Algeria, on which Fanon naturally provides some unique material, especially in *Studies in a Dying Colonialism* and in *Toward the African Revolution*. But even in the case of Algeria, informative as Fanon is, there is nothing in his analysis that could have prepared one for the complex path that Algeria has trod since independence. This in itself is not a very damning indictment, for no one was in a position in the early 1960's to indicate the tortuous road that the different independent states of Africa would have to follow. But the whole point about Fanon's method is that he is altogether too sweeping in his judgments, one way or the other. He believed that armed struggle by itself would provide the cleansing fire from which would emerge the new men and women, experienced, pure in thought and self-sacrificing in action, and adequately equipped to complete the task of liberation and carry through the African revolution against imperialism and national capitalism.

He clearly had the highest hopes of Algeria precisely because her people had been through seven years of the most rigorous liberation war. He under-estimated the task that lay ahead, and did not pay sufficient attention to the problem of creating a revolutionary political party, based on the working class, guided by scientific socialism, and therefore capable of helping the people find their way forward through the multitude of political, social and economic problems which they faced on the morrow of independence.

Since Fanon's assessment of Africa's new governments allows for no differentiation and nowhere seems to recognise any of these governments as progressive, one can only assume that he would have regarded Ben Bella as a representative of the national bourgeoisie, and his downfall simply as the defeat of the national bourgeoisie by the army which had become "the arbiter". In reality, although Ben Bella's overthrow has not resulted in the complete undoing of Algeria's revolution, it has certainly represented a shift to the right and a slowing down of the revolutionary process.

CAN THE PEASANTS LEAD THE REVOLUTION?

In order to test Fanon's views on classes in Africa and to reach valid conclusions it is necessary to examine, in some detail, what has actually been the role of classes in Africa during the past two decades. This involves some study of the formation, growth and conditions of the different classes, especially the workers and peasants; it also requires, without rigid pre-judgment, an examination of the liberation struggles in Africa and the part played in them by each of the main class forces, and especially the working class whose effort Fanon decries.

Fanon argues that the peasants are economically worse off than the workers, and that this somehow results automatically in the peasants being more revolutionary.

We shall deal later with the question of the standard of living of African wage workers and peasants, but it should be noted at this point that any attempt to make a comparison between the living standards of workers and peasants is very complex.

Certainly the highly paid skilled African copper worker in Zambia receives a much higher income than that of the average peasant in the same country; it is certain, too, that some categories of government employees and skilled workers in a number of African towns are better off than poor peasants. At the same time, there is a considerable stratum of African peasants which is not poor, such as the rich peasants in Ghana, Nigeria or the Ivory Coast, engaged in cocoa or coffee production; these peasants employ wage labour, especially in the harvest season, and certainly enjoy a higher standard of living than the workers they employ and exploit, and often, too, higher living standards than the majority of workers in the country.

But all this apart, even if the *average* worker's wage in Africa could be shown to provide him with a higher standard of living than that of the *average* peasant it still does not tell one much about the relative revolutionary qualities of each class. Poverty by itself does not produce militancy or revolutionary understanding. We need only consider the point by Lenin in connection with the 1905 revolution, during which it was demonstrated that the higher paid metal workers were more politically conscious, more revolutionary and more ready to fight on the barricades than were the low-paid textile workers who had to be brought into the struggle stage by stage, on the basis of first being helped to fight for their immediate economic demands:

> The metal workers were the best paid, the most class conscious and the best educated proletarians. The textile workers, who in 1905 were two and a half times more numerous than the metal workers, were the most backward and the worst paid mass of workers in Russia. . . .[1]

[1] V. I. Lenin: "Lecture on the 1905 Revolution", *Selected Works*, Vol. 3, pp. 5–7.

Similarly, the poor peasants in Czarist Russia, the landless and horseless peasants, were no doubt worse off than the engineering workers in the Putilov works in Petrograd, but there was no question but that the Putilov workers, solid supporters as they were of the Bolsheviks, were far and away the more revolutionary force.

It is not out of place here to cite Modibo Keita who explained the role of the Mali workers and peasants in the independence struggle in these words:

> Our foremost supporters were naturally the peasants and workers. You have just asked me how I assess the role of the working class: I think that the working class, under the colonial system, had the clearest understanding of its exploitation. We know that they were not the most exploited when they had work—we had a good deal of unemployment—but that is not the point; it is a question of political understanding.[1]

Amilcar Cabral, General Secretary of the African Party for the Independence of Guinea and Cape Verde, makes the same point:

> Many people say that it is the peasants who carry the burden of exploitation: this may be true, but so far as the struggle is concerned it must be realised that it is not the degree of suffering and hardship involved as such that matters; even extreme suffering in itself does not necessarily produce the *prise de conscience* required for the national liberation struggle. In Guinea the peasants are subjected to a kind of exploitation equivalent to slavery; but even if you try and explain to them that they are being exploited and robbed, it is difficult to convince them by means of an inexperienced explanation of a technico-economic kind that they are the most exploited people, whereas it is easier to convince the workers and the people employed in the towns who earn, say, 10 escudos a day for a job in which a European earns between 30 and 50 that they are being subjected to massive exploitation and injustice, because they can see.[2]

[1] An interview in *Révolution Africaine*, March 9, 1963.

[2] Amilcar Cabral: "Brief Analysis of the Social Structure in Guinea". Condensed text of paper read at a seminar held in the Frantz Fanon Centre in Treviglio, Milan, from May 1 to 3, 1964. See *Revolution in Guinea*, London, 1969, pp. 51–2.

Despite the perfectly clear views of Cabral and Modibo Keita on this point (see above, and also Modibo Keita's reference p. 119 to the workers and their unions as "the engine of the Revolution") it is possible to find "new left" commentators, influenced by Fanon's approach, falsely arguing that Modibo Keita and Cabral laid stress on "the primary role of the peasantry" and even on "the leading role of the peasantry". See Jitendra Mohan: "Varieties of African Socialism", *Socialist Register*, 1966, p. 266. Fanon's followers, in fact, are apt to be as unscientific and inaccurate as he was.

Ledda, too, points out the limited possibility of the peasants acting as a spontaneous and leading revolutionary force.

This peasant world, spread out over thousands of villages, with backward forms of production and agricultural technique, is the stronghold of tribal tradition. And, *for the moment*, it constitutes a mass of passive support for the power of the privileged groups, thanks in part to the influence of religious and feudal chieftains. This throws considerable doubt on Fanon's statement that in the African countries "only the peasants are revolutionary". We have no intention here of underrating the decisive revolutionary role that the peasants have in Black Africa—and not only by reason of their numbers: they represent 70-80 per cent of the population—or the fact that the struggle cannot develop rapidly and fully without them. This is not the problem. The question is whether they are capable of becoming an autonomous revolutionary force and playing a spearhead role in the struggle against neo-colonialism on their own. It would seem not. The present situation in rural areas is such that—if we exclude the agricultural wage-earners, who are by nature closer to the proletariat—only an *outside* force will be capable of carrying out the absolutely essential, but difficult job of mobilising and organising the peasant masses.[1]

Nghe also takes Fanon to task on this point:

The peasant, by himself, can never acquire a revolutionary consciousness: it is the militant from the towns who must patiently seek out the most gifted elements of the poor peasantry, educate them and organise them; and it is only after a long period of political work that one can mobilise the peasantry.[2]

Of course, it would be entirely wrong to underestimate the role of the peasantry in the democratic, anti-feudal and anti-imperialist revolution in Africa, Asia and Latin America. After all, the peasantry is the overwhelming majority of the population in these three continents, and a particular victim of feudal and imperialist exploitation. As Engels emphasised in *Peasant War in Germany*, the peasantry is an immense force in the anti-feudal revolution. At the same time, as

[1] Romano Ledda: "Social Classes and Political Struggle", *International Socialist Journal*, Vol. 4, No. 22, August, 1967, pp. 574-5.
Interestingly enough Antonio Gramsci noted the same shortcomings as regards the peasantry in Southern Italy in the 1920's. He found them "in perpetual ferment but, as a mass, incapable of providing a centralised expression for their aspirations and their needs".
[2] Nguyen Nghe: op. cit., p. 29.

Engels pointed out, the peasantry needs a class ally if it is to succeed in revolutionary struggle. This has certainly been proved so in history. The peasantry has been a powerful force against feudalism and imperialism but has never been able to achieve a major victory on its own. Success has only come either in alliance with and under the leadership of the bourgeoisie, as in the French revolution of 1789, or in alliance with and led by the working class, as in Russia in 1917. Only through such alliances were the peasants able to obtain the land and thus open up a different future for themselves. In the later struggles in Asia the same has held true. In China, Korea and Vietnam it was through the leadership of the working class that the peasants secured the land; in India, it has been the national bourgeoisie which, with the support of the workers and peasants, has introduced modifications in the feudal land system and opened the way to capitalism in the countryside; in Japan, it was the state of monopoly capital, supported by United States imperialism which, following Japan's defeat in 1945, broke the old feudal pattern of landownership and ushered in large-scale capitalist development in agriculture. In none of these very different cases did the peasantry initiate or lead the transformation of the agrarian system, still less provide leadership for wider political and economic aims for the country as a whole.

In Eastern Europe, too, and in Cuba, the land question was solved for the peasants as a result of social changes initiated by Marxist-led organisations, composed of workers and other class forces.

This does not mean that a form of peasant power cannot be established. The early experience of the people's Soviet republics of Khoresm and Bukhara is very instructive in this respect. The situation which developed in these two republics at the end of 1919 and 1920, under the impact of the October Revolution, resulted in a widespread struggle of the peasants against feudalism. The local Communist organisations were very weak at first, and, in any case, arising from the class structure of these backward societies, were mainly composed not of workers but of peasants and intellectuals. Although called "Communist", the Khoresm Communist Party has been characterised by Professor K. Mukhamedberdiyev as "an anti-feudal, anti-imperialist party".[1]

The revolutions in Khoresm and Bukhara, he explains, were revolutions of a new type "never before known to history". The overthrow of the feudal power did not result in the power of the

[1] K. Mukhamedberdiyev: "V. I. Lenin and the First People's Democratic States in the East", *Turkmenskaya Iskra*, April 9, 1970.

working class. Soviets were indeed established, but these were not proletarian in character, nor did they express socialist power. "They worked as revolutionary-democratic organs of power, mostly of a peasant character. . . . With the victory of the people's revolutions in Bukhara and Khoresm, *the peasantry became the dominating class* and exercised its power through the people's Soviets, constituting the state form of the revolutionary-democratic dictatorship of the working people." The new republics set up were, according to Prof. Mukhamed-berdiyev, "*peasant republics, people's in content and Soviet in form*". For this reason, since they were not socialist republics, they did not adhere to the Russian Federation, nor at first to the Soviet Union; and their Communist Parties were not included in the Russian Communist Party (Bolsheviks). This, of course, was only a transitional phase; by 1922 the Khoresm and Bukhara Communist Parties joined the Russian Communist Party; and by 1923-4 the two republics had become socialist and joined the Soviet Union.

The significance of this experience is that peasant power is possible under certain conditions; that it is a transitional phase; and that, with the support of a friendly socialist power and a friendly Communist Party, it is possible to make the transition to socialism. This experience, however, although it is rather unique in history, also demonstrates once again that the peasantry needs a class ally in order to complete the revolution and make the changeover to socialism. Left to themselves, the peasants of Khoresm and Bukhara would have been in danger of yielding once again to feudalism or turning to capitalism.

In assessing the role of the peasantry in anti-colonial revolutions one should not ignore that the peasantry is, in general, based on the petty ownership of the means of production. (One should note here that, to some extent, one must exclude large parts of tropical Africa from this characterisation, since the African peasantry is largely based on subsistence farming, has a system of communal land ownership, and, apart from the settler-dominated countries, is not generally faced with an acute shortage of land.)

The peasantry is really not one homogenous class. If one can imagine, for example, a tube of toothpaste open at both ends and being squeezed in the middle, one has to an extent a picture of what happens to the peasantry. From an army of smallholders a mass of poor and often landless peasants is squeezed out at the bottom, while a small stratum of rich peasants employing wage labour emerges at the top. In other words, the peasantry is in a stage of break-up into three distinct strata with largely different interests. In fact, the poor landless peasant often ends up as the wage labourer exploited by the rich peasant. Since the rich peasant is often a money-lender as well, he is able to exploit the poor peasant in this way, too.

Capitalist development, the growth of industry and urbanisation hastens the break-up of the peasantry. Many peasants migrate to the towns or take up wage-labour in the countryside. The number of peasants declines both relatively and absolutely.

Most peasants are illiterate, ignorant and a prey to religious dogma and superstition. They are dominated economically by the chiefs and feudal landlords who exercise considerable ideological influence over them.

It is significant, as the British military expert, William Gutteridge, has reminded us, that British imperialism generally chose peasants for its colonial armies rather than the workers or other urban dwellers (apart from those required for the upper ranks), because it found the peasants more inclined to be willing to perform the duties required of them, even when it meant acting against their own people.

". . . the ideal soldier was generally supposed to be an illiterate, uncontaminated by mission education, from a remote area", where his upbringing would have resulted in "political unconsciousness".[1]

Gutteridge explains that the preference of the imperial authorities was completely understandable, since the soldiers recruited from remote country districts "had little in common with the coastal peoples and were capable of impartial, even hostile, action when serious internal security problems arose".

Gutteridge has made the point that "The detachment of the warrior from the hinterland from the political involvement of the urban African was the compelling internal-security argument"[2] for the policy of choosing peasants for the colonial army rather than urban Africans. Thus, in the 1950's, at least 70 per cent of all other ranks in the colonial armies of Ghana and Nigeria came from the northern hinterland.

Speaking of African armed forces in general, Kwame Nkrumah has noted: "The rank and file of army and police are from the peasantry. A large number are illiterate. They have been taught to obey orders without question, and have become tools of bourgeois capitalist interests."[3]

[1] W. F. Gutteridge: *The Military in African Politics*, London, 1969, p. 9.
[2] W. F. Gutteridge: "The Military Legacy of the British Empire": *The Listener*, November 7, 1968, based on a radio talk.
[3] Kwame Nkrumah: *Class Struggle in Africa*, London, 1970, pp. 42–3.

The same policy of relying on peasant recruitment for the army was pursued by the French colonial authorities in Africa.

Waterbury[1] notes French colonialism's preference in Morocco for the "new rural élite" rather than its "urban equivalent", and adds in terms that recall British colonialism's preference for the desert inhabitants in the Middle East, the hill "tribes" in Burma, the up-country martial "tribes" in India, and the remote interior peoples in tropical Africa, that "it is certain that French military personnel and the *officiers des affairs indigènes* found the simple, pugnacious Berbers an appealing lot. Everything possible was done to seal the rural areas off from the 'corrupt' influence of the city Arabs and their 'religious fanaticism', a policy that was considered more and more judicious with the spread of nationalism from the urban centres." In practice, it should be noted, French hopes were not fulfilled. "Knowledge of the cities, and more particularly of the nationalist movement, filtered . . . into the rural world in general."[2] What the French overlooked (in common with Fanon who, from a different standpoint, as we have seen, believed that the rural populations and the city dwellers lived and struggled in complete isolation from one another) was not only the developing commercial relations between town and countryside but also the constant migration, to and fro.

It is interesting to note the behaviour of the Algerian peasants after the liberation war. As the Ottaways have observed:

> The peasants for their part, have not proven as revolutionary as they were during the war of independence. They have not agitated to obtain an agrarian reform or to force the government to give more attention to their problems.[3]

When appealed to by the government to provide voluntary labour for the post-war reconstruction of the Algerian countryside, the peasants, note the Ottaways, tended to pool their meagre resources to build mosques rather than schools or a public fountain. "The number of new mosques", they comment, "is just one indication that the peasants, after the interlude of the war, have returned to their old ways and values." The renewal of interest in the religious brotherhoods, which had become discredited as centres of reaction during the liberation war, is a further indication of the tendency of the peasants to return

[1] John Waterbury: *The Commander of the Faithful: The Moroccan Political Elite*, London, 1970, pp. 112–13.
[2] ibid., p. 114.
[3] David and Marina Ottaway: *Algeria: The Politics of a Socialist Revolution*, Berkeley and Los Angeles, 1970, p. 41.

to their old ways of conservatism unless constantly won and won again for progress by a consistent challenge of a revolutionary ideology and organisation. "In the absence of any leadership from the party or the government", conclude the Ottaways, "the peasants have fallen once again under the influence of the traditional authorities—*marabouts* (holy men), imams, and village chiefs and elders."

Fanon may have placed his faith in the spontaneous revolutionary attitude of the peasants and scorned the alleged conservatism of the urban workers; but the British and French imperialists were in no doubt as to where lay the greater danger to their system. They saw the threat as emanating from the urban centres and in the building of an alliance between workers and peasants.[1] It was this alliance, above all, that the imperialists strove to prevent. But Fanon contributes nothing to such an alliance. On the contrary, all his arguments have the effect of stoking up mistrust between workers and peasants, and of setting one against the other.

I do not mean that the peasantry, especially the middle peasant, and the poor, landless, agricultural proletariat, cannot and does not play a major role in the struggle for independence and against feudalism, as was seen in the armed struggle in China, in the liberation wars of Vietnam over the past twenty-five years, in the role of the peasants and sugar plantation workers in the Cuban revolution, of the peasants and plantation workers in the armed struggle in Guatemala, in the armed struggle of the peasants led by the Communists of Colombia, or today in Guinea-Bissau, Angola and Mozambique.

But the peasantry is not a clearly defined, organised class that can provide the ideology to lead the rest of the nation, although it is capable of absorbing Marxism, the philosophy of the working class, when this is brought to the peasantry by an organised Marxist force. It is only natural in countries with mainly a peasant population that the peasants should constitute one of the decisive forces of the revolution. It is, after all, a well known Marxist concept that the main axis of the bourgeois-democratic revolution is the agrarian revolution, that is, an anti-feudal revolution directed to destroying the feudal land system and its accompanying political and social superstructure. But here, too, in assessing the role of the peasantry it is dangerous to over-generalise. Each revolution has its own peculiarities which must be studied.

[1] In pre-war Japan, as Owen Lattimore has noted (*Solution in Asia*, London, 1945, p. 26), feudal attitudes in the army were maintained by "a deliberate screening out of students and urban workers in peace-time conscription, so as to keep the standing army heavily peasant-minded".

Moreover, it is important to distinguish between what is a *main* force, providing the numerically large masses for the struggle, and the *leading* force or principal revolutionary force which elaborates policy and provides the ideology and organisational experience and capacity. It is failure to make this distinction which is, perhaps, the most frequent cause of confusion on this question.

It is not without interest here to note how one of Vietnam's leaders, Truong Chinh, deals with this question:

> Who must lead the revolution in order to overthrow imperialism and feudalism? The four classes which constitute the people are the working class, the working peasants, the petty-bourgeoisie, the national bourgeoisie. They constitute the forces of the revolution.
> As for the driving force of the revolution, it is made up of the working class, the peasantry, and the petty-bourgeoisie.
> The leading role is played by the working class.
> The working peasants form the main army of the revolution.
> The petty-bourgeoisie and the national bourgeoisie are the allies of the working class, with this difference all the time—that the national bourgeoisie is a conditional ally.[1] (Author's translation.)

Truong Chinh's characterisation is, of course, based on the experience of the revolution in Vietnam, and, in the form provided, is not necessarily of help in understanding developments in Africa. Some may even doubt the value of setting out such a clear-cut scheme of the role played by different classes in the revolution. But for our argument here it is of value in helping to establish the difference between a *leading* class and that providing the main forces for the revolution.

When Fanon claims that the peasantry in Africa is the only revolutionary class, "capable of directing the people's struggle", and argues that the workers are pampered and corrupted, he is staking a claim for the peasantry as the leading revolutionary force, with only the *lumpenproletariat* of the towns as its firm ally. In arguing in this fashion, Fanon, in effect, is staking this claim not merely in relation to what happened during the stage of the struggle for national independence but for the post-independence period, too. Whatever his motive for doing this he provides ideological cover and justification for those who, with quite different motives in mind, wish to place the working class in a subordinate position after independence has been won.

It is significant that his views on the role of the African peasants

[1] Truong Chinh: see *Hoctap*, January, 1960: monthly review of the Vietnam Workers' Party; cited by Nguyen Nghe, op. cit.

are not shared by those who have led the liberation movements in Africa, and know, from their own bitter experience, what an immense task it is to win over the peasants for active participation in the anti-feudal and anti-colonial struggle. One thing which Fanon tends to ignore is that in Africa the majority of peasants under the colonial system, especially in tropical Africa, were and largely still are, subsistence peasants, not yet fully drawn into the money economy, except in so far as they migrate to take up wage labour in order to pay taxes and buy necessities, or when they participate in production for cash and so give rise to a stratum of capitalist farmers exploiting other Africans as wage labourers.

In large parts of Africa the peasants are widely scattered, live sometimes not even in villages,[1] tend to lead isolated, narrow lives, and can be organised for collective activity only with extreme difficulty. Majhemout Diop, a former leader of the Party of African Independence of Senegal, has pointed out that in Senegal "the peasants are mostly illiterate, unorganised and dispersed among 12,000 villages and rural townships.[2] Primitive forms of production and organisation and the superstructure corresponding to these forms lag far behind the requirements of the modern world, owing to which *the winning of the peasantry in* active struggle as the natural ally of the working class will obviously be a difficult task for some time to come."[3]

The same difficulties have been described by Cabral in Guinea-Bissau.

> Given the general context of our traditions, or rather the super-structure created by the economic conditions in Guinea, the Fula peasants have a strong tendency to follow their chiefs. Thorough and intensive work was therefore needed to mobilise them. . . . Here I should like to broach one key problem, which is of enormous importance for us, as we are a country of peasants, and that is the problem of whether or not the peasantry represents the main revolutionary force. I shall confine myself to my own country, Guinea, where it must be said at once that the peasantry is not a revolutionary force—which may seem strange, particularly as we have based the whole of our armed liberation struggle on the

[1] In Tanzania it became necessary after independence for the Government to launch a campaign for "villagisation" in order to group together the isolated individual peasants.

[2] This covers some two million people, giving an *average* of less than 200 per village or township. Clearly many of the villages must be inhabited by very few people.

[3] M. Diop: "Structure and Position of the Working Class in Senegal", included in *Africa—National and Social Revolution*, Collection of Papers read at the Cairo Seminar, Prague, 1967, p. 102.

peasantry. A distinction must be drawn between a physical force and a revolutionary force; physically, the peasantry is a great force in Guinea; it is almost the whole of the population, it controls the nation's wealth, it is the peasantry which produces; *but we know from experience what trouble we had convincing the peasantry to fight.*[1]

(Author's italics.)

Cabral describes, in some detail, how his Party first organised its cadres drawn from "people employed in commerce and other wage earners, and even some peasants" and trained them so that "they could acquire what you might call a working-class mentality". He explains that about one thousand cadres were trained in this way at the Party school in Conakry, and that it was these cadres who then went into the rural areas and "inculcated a certain mentality into the peasants". Explaining that the PAIGC[2] is not a Communist or Marxist-Leninist Party, Cabral asserts that nevertheless "the people now leading the peasants in the struggle in Guinea are *mostly from the urban milieux and connected with the urban wage-earning group*".[3] (Author's italics.)

This emphasises once again the point made earlier on the need to distinguish between what is numerically a main force and what is the revolutionary force which fulfils the role of leadership. Certainly, in tropical Africa, where the peasants are the overwhelming majority of the population, no deep-going revolutionary change can take place without their massive participation. And the experience of the past two and half decades illustrates only too clearly that in a variety of ways—by resistance to colonial land seizures, by tax boycotts, opposition to forced labour, support for national liberation movements and political parties, and solidarity with workers' strikes (as in Enugu, Nigeria, in 1949, and in the 1952 and 1955 strikes on the Copper Belt, in Zambia), the rural population in Africa has played an important part in the struggle against colonialism.

[1] Amilcar Cabral: op. cit., p. 50. Lenin, too, observed that the peasants were the "hardest to move".

[2] African Independence Party of Guinea and Cap-Verde.

[3] ibid., p. 55. It is interesting to note the developments that took place in the years following that remark of Cabral's in 1964. In a conversation with the author in October, 1971, Cabral mentioned that the peasants, as a result of the extension of the liberation war and the PAIGC's deliberate policy of promoting and training peasant cadres, were now playing a key part in the leadership of the struggle. On the Supreme Council of Struggle (the leading executive body of the PAIGC) peasants now supply 60 per cent of the 85 members, with workers about 15 per cent, and petty-bourgeoisie also 15 per cent. Thus the initial leadership of the workers and petty-bourgeoisie has been successful in winning over decisive sections of peasants, who are increasingly playing a role in the leadership. In fulfilling this role, the peasants have acquired political understanding and come to accept ideas which owe much to Marxism, i.e. the ideology of the working class.

In those African countries where armed struggles took place before independence was won—as in Algeria, Kenya and Cameroun, or later in Congo (Kinshasa)—the peasants played an active role in a very direct sense. The same is true today in Guinea-Bissau, Angola, Mozambique, Namibia and Zimbabwe. But even in these cases the peasants have been led by political movements created in the towns, and largely led by intellectuals, technicians, former trade union leaders, and workers; and these movements have been influenced to a considerable degree by Marxist ideas, that is by the philosophical outlook of the working class. The peasants have certainly participated but, just as certainly, they have not led. Similarly, in South Africa, there have been important struggles by the peasants, especially in recent years in Sekhukhuneland and Zeerust, and the peasants give considerable support to the national liberation struggle there in its new armed phase; but again, this is to a movement led by the African National Congress and the Communist Party, two organisations which draw important support from the working class and other urban strata.

THE EFFECT OF LABOUR MIGRATION ON THE PEASANTRY

In writing about the peasants Fanon seems to ignore many of the basic realities about peasant life in twentieth-century Africa. Whatever marginal improvements may have taken place since independence, there is no doubt that during the colonial period the prevalence of labour migration in tropical Africa had heavily crippled traditional agriculture, and left the villages considerably denuded of able-bodied men. I have gone into this question in some considerable detail in a previous study,[1] but it is necessary here to emphasise certain points which Fanon appears totally to ignore.

All the available statistics in the 1950's showed quite clearly that the colonial economies of the African territories were largely based on migrant labour.

A United Nations Survey in 1959 (*Economic Survey of Africa Since 1950*) estimated that "The vast majority of wage earners south of the Sahara are probably migrants."

Figures available at that time showed that the majority of the million mineworkers in Africa were migrant workers; nearly half the labour force in Southern Rhodesia was immigrant labour; a majority

[1] Jack Woddis: *Africa: The Roots of Revolt*, London, 1960 (especially Chapters 1 and 4).

of workers in Uganda were immigrants; a quarter of African mine-workers in Northern Rhodesia (now Zambia) came from outside the territory.

The traffic in the opposite direction was just as emphatic. Over half the able-bodied manpower of Basutoland (now Lesotho) was leaving the territory each year; 25 to 30 per cent of adult males were absent from home in Bechuanaland (now Botswana) and Swaziland; over 40 per cent of all adult males in Nyasaland (now Malawi) suitable for employment were employed outside the territory; well over fifty per cent of Mozambique's adult male population was away working for wages in European employment outside Mozambique.

But even these figures, striking as they may be, do not tell the whole story, for in addition to the immense volume of migration across frontiers, there was a similarly massive migration within each territory, from the countryside to towns and other centres of wage employment, usually for Europeans. Surveys showed that often 60, 70, 80 and even 100 per cent of adult males were at times absent from their villages.

For Northern Rhodesia, Lord Hailey estimated that "taking the territory as a whole at least one third to a half of the able-bodied men are normally away from the village".[1] Numerous reports at the time showed the devastating effect of this migrant labour system on African village life.

> I went into many villages in Northern Rhodesia hundreds of miles away from the Copper Belt where only old men and women were living. All the able-bodied men . . . were off to the mine. . . .[2]

> The villages of Nyasaland are threatened with the collapse of their entire economic structure by the absence of as high as seventy per cent of the adult males.[3]

Describing the effect of migrant labour in Southern Rhodesia Yudelman notes that "the population in the African areas is heavily weighted by women, children, and males over 35 years of age".[4]

A comprehensive survey carried out between 1947 and 1951 in the Keiskammahoek District, in a Reserve in the Ciskei area of the Union of South Africa, showed that "the majority of the people go

[1] Lord Hailey: *An African Survey Revised, 1956*, London, 1957, p. 1381.
[2] *Times Educational Supplement*, March 6, 1959, p. 388.
[3] John A. Noon: *Labour Problems in Africa*, Pennsylvania, 1944, p. 39.
[4] Montague Yudelman: *Africans on the Land*, Oxford, 1964, p. 132.

out to work for a period of a year or so at a time. . . . Some, however, emigrate to the cities, make their permanent homes there, and do not return to the Reserves."[1] By the late 1940's it noted that as a result of the migration of young men and, to some extent of young women, too, "the trend is leading towards a district population comprised mainly of aged and young".[2] Already, at the time of the survey, people of sixty-five and older, and children under fifteen, comprised more than half the population; it was calculated that these two categories of young and old "would constitute sixty per cent of the population in another generation".

This, then, was the pattern over vast areas of Africa under colonialism. Fanon's peasant "revolutionary" was in real life all too often a young child, an old man, or an overworked woman carrying on the heavy labour of traditional African agriculture, burdened with the upbringing of her children, fetching firewood, carrying water over long distances, making, repairing and maintaining her hut. And it was to these forces that Fanon looked for his "sole revolutionary force".

This pattern of economy, with the steady drift from the villages, has by no means been ended by the winning of independence. In fact, the trend has been accentuated. With the expectations that have arisen with the attainment of independence, thousands of young people have flocked to the towns in the hopes of securing employment, escaping the restricted life of the village, obtaining education, and getting on in life. This flood of young people to the towns, is, in fact, one of the major problems facing the new African states.

One should not, of course, exaggerate how far the process has gone. The overwhelming majority of African people still live in rural areas; and the extent to which migrant labour has denuded the villages of adult males is not so marked in West Africa as it is in the territories that have long been subjected to considerable white settlement, such as Angola, Mozambique, Malawi, Zambia, Southern Rhodesia, Lesotho, Swaziland, Botswana, and the Union of South Africa. Nevertheless, the consequences of the migrant labour system introduced by colonialism in Africa have been so considerable on the economy and life of the village that Fanon's complete neglect of this factor (or, perhaps, his unawareness of it), robs his attempted analysis of the role of class forces in Africa of much of its validity.

[1] D. Hobart Houghton and Edith M. Walton: *The Economy of a Reserve*, 1952, p. 4.
[2] ibid., p. 34.

CLASS DIFFERENTIATION AMONG THE AFRICAN PEASANTRY

In other respects, too, Fanon's views on the peasantry in Africa are unsatisfactory. Despite his reference to classes, he makes no scientific examination of the agrarian question in Africa. As Professor Potekhin has rightly pointed out: "One can hardly regard the African peasantry as some homogeneous mass of people, undifferentiated in class structure. There is no such peasantry in Africa today."[1]

Feudal land-ownership has been an important aspect of the African peasant problem which Fanon largely ignores. In Egypt, before the land reform, 72 per cent of the landowners held only 15 per cent of the land; the rest of the land was mainly in the hands of big landlords from whom the land-hungry peasants leased land, or on whose estates they worked as wage-labourers. In Morocco, the big landlords owned one quarter of all cultivable land. Large-scale feudal land-ownership is a marked feature of Ethiopia. Until the recent destruction of the Buganda Kingdom, feudal land-ownership predominated there. Feudal land-ownership is also a feature of Northern Nigeria, Western Nigeria, Barotseland (in Zambia), Upper Volta and the northern regions of Cameroun.

Under the colonial system the European occupying power helped to uphold these feudal patterns, relying on the feudal rulers and landlords to act as the main social pillar and ally of imperialism.

In most parts of Africa, however, this feudal system of land-ownership did not, and does not, exist. In the majority of African territories communal land-ownership has been preserved. Professor Potekhin has emphasised that "Communal land-ownership in itself does not determine the mode of production in agriculture, since this form of land-ownership exists in the primitive-communal system, in the slave-owning and feudal societies and even in the preliminary stages of capitalism".[2] Nevertheless, stating that the "main land tracts are still owned by peasant communities", he estimates that "the peasant economy of most African countries remains fundamentally a subsistence economy, and petty peasants, with a beggarly, semi-starvation mode of life prevail in the countryside".[3] And it is this subsistence economy, as we have seen, that is usually damaged so heavily by the migrant labour system.

[1] I. I. Potekhin: *African Problems*, Moscow, 1968, p. 59. [2] ibid., p. 57.
[3] ibid., pp. 59–60.

The subsistence farmer, working on his plot on the communal lands, usually has little surplus left over for sale. Moreover, since land-ownership is not yet general—the subsistence farmer being allowed to *use* a plot on the communal lands but not to own it—the emergence of capitalism on the land is slow. At the same time, the private ownership of land has grown in the past two decades, partly through the natural consequence of the introduction of growing cash crops, the pledging of land to meet debts, the donation of land as gifts, the leasing of land, and eventually the sale of land. Private ownership of land has also spread in East and Central Africa where it was deliberately encouraged by the British colonial authorities through the introduction of "model farmer" schemes, "yeoman farmers", "land consolidation" and the like. Part of the intention of British imperialism in introducing private ownership of land in Africa was to facilitate the emergence of an African "middle class" on the land, which would act as a conservative force in society, tending to support the *status quo*.

Thus, Mr. Lennox-Boyd, a former Conservative Secretary of State for the Colonies, argued that "A black African middle class in the country (is) of vital importance" for Central Africa, since it was "essential that this sort of social revolution should happen before people" found themselves "overwhelmed by political revolution".[1] Similarly, the Joint East African and Central Board placed its hopes on the emergence of "an African middle class".[2] Not without significance, a conference of West German diplomatists at Addis Ababa, in October, 1959, stressed that West Germany's policy towards Africa should take into account that "the social and economic structure must be stabilised by the building up of a middle class in the different African terri-tories".[3]

How far this process of creating a buffer class of African landholders has gone is difficult to ascertain with any degree of precision. Speaking of private land-ownership in general, Professor Potekhin indirectly reveals the problem by the element of inconsistency (for him, unusual) that creeps into his argument:

> Private ownership of land by peasants has become widespread in a number of countries. . . . It is impossible to define its extent; how-ever, we can safely assert that this type of land ownership has not yet spread to any considerable degree.

[1] A speech at Weymouth, May 1, 1959: cited in *East Africa and Rhodesia*, May 7, 1959, p. 1053.
[2] *East Africa and Rhodesia*, April 23, 1959, p. 991.
[3] *The Times*, November 17, 1959.

Whether it is "widespread" or "not yet spread to any considerable degree", one thing is certain—it is a *growing* trend; and under its impact communal land holdings, still predominant, are showing signs of break-up, even though this is still limited.

Chodak makes the same point:

> Generally speaking, the traditional forms of land ownership are still predominant. However, pure traditional economy is in decline, money squeezes into every nook and corner and permeates human relations.[1]

The growth of capitalism in the African countryside cannot be denied, and this in itself to a large extent cuts across the prognosis made by Fanon. In the last two decades class differentiation has begun to show itself quite clearly among the African peasantry, a small richer group hiving off at the top and a mass of impoverished peasants being created down below. A survey carried out in Basutoland (now Lesotho) in 1950 among 160,500 households on holdings under 80 acres showed almost 7 per cent landless, and a third living on holdings of less than 4 acres. Some 90,000 had 4 to 15 acres each, and at the top were 6,740 households with 15 to 80 acres. Above the 80 acre limit were a number of chiefs owning 100 to 200 acres; and at the top of the pyramid were the larger holdings of capitalist farmers.[2]

In Zambia, where the best land has been taken by the white settlers, differentiation among the African peasants has been taking place in recent years. A study by A. D. Jones[3] revealed that among the 600 African cultivators in 100 square miles of maize-producing territory, fifteen were classified as "commercial farmers". These 15 had more land, machinery, implements, labour force and income than the rest, and were clearly emerging as a separate stratum. Between them they owned four maize mills, one saw mill, six motor vehicles, three tractors, one wind pump, four stores, one bakery and one petrol pump. The remaining 585 cultivators owned only two maize mills between them, and none of the other items at all.

In Southern Rhodesia, where the white settler minority holds dictatorial power and heavily restricts the economic growth of the African majority, it is very difficult for an African capitalist stratum to

[1] Szymon Chodak: "Social Classes in Sub-Saharan Africa", *Africana Bulletin*, No. 4, 1966, Warsaw.

[2] *Special Study on Economic Conditions in Non-Self-Governing Territories*, United Nations, 1958, pp. 120–1.

[3] "Farmers Among the Plateau Tonga", seminar at Ibadan, July, 1964, on social classes and élites in Africa.

emerge on the land. The average income on the land there for African cultivators is only £14 a year over and above the immediate subsistence needs. Yet even under these difficult conditions there are signs of differentiation. A very small number of African farmers have been able to set up Development Groups, somewhat similar to co-operative societies, in order to pool their small savings and thus create an informal credit association to buy in bulk. By 1966 there were reported to be 1,100 farmers operating in these Development Groups, some of the farmers enjoying incomes of as much as £2,000 a year.

In Ghana, where Polly Hill produced her classic studies of the cocoa farmers, her analysis in 1954–5 of co-operative societies in ten different cocoa regions, revealed a considerable differentiation, with 34 farmers having a *net* annual income from cocoa of £500 each; 83 in the £200–£499 range; 98 in the £100–£199 range; and 542 earning less than £100, with 140 of this last group earning under £50.

Similar differentiation among the peasantry has been taking place in a number of other African territories since the second world war. An agricultural enquiry in Senegal in 1960–1961, where the main crop is ground-nuts, showed 127,800 holdings of less than 2 hectares each, totalling only 12 per cent of the cultivated land; another 40,700 holdings of more than 7 hectares each, totalled 43 per cent of the cultivated land. Right at the bottom of the scale were 63,500 holdings of less than a hectare each, covering 33,535 hectares on which worked 134,500 people. At the top were 2,800 holdings of more than 17 hectares each, covering 77,239 hectares.

More marked is the growth of a class of African planters in the Ivory Coast, especially in coffee and cocoa. Here, according to Raymond Barbé,[1] in the rich region of Bongouanou, 500 of the richest planters possess more than 12 hectares each of cocoa and coffee, and employ at least five wage workers each. They represent only about 7 per cent of the total number of planters, but produce about a quarter of the entire cocoa and coffee output of the region. For the whole of the Ivory Coast, he estimates about 8,000 to 10,000 planters, owning 10 to 12 hectares each, and employing at least five wage workers. "Some of them including Houphouet-Boigny, political leader and President of the Republic of the Ivory Coast, own more than 100 hectares." It is this stratum of planters, says Barbé, which is able to accumulate sufficient capital to branch out into commerce and transport, and thus

[1] Raymond Barbé: *Les Classes Sociales en Afrique Noire*, Paris, 1964.

establish an African bourgeoisie. This development has been very rapid over the past decade. The emergence of 10,000 better-off African planters in the Ivory Coast has been at the expense of hundreds of thousands of poor peasants, many of whom have ended up as wage workers on these plantations and who, Fanon notwithstanding, would find it strange to be regarded as having common "peasant" interests with the rich peasants who exploit them.

Even in a less developed region, such as Dahomey, where the main crop is palm nuts, a third of the proprietors, owning 60 per cent of the land under cultivation, are now employing wage labour. In Cameroun, by 1957, following on the lifting of the previous colonial restrictions on African production of coffee, there were 17,500 African coffee producers, owning 50–60,000 hectares of plantations, and making an average of 100,000 CFA francs each in that year—which is well up to the average in the richer Ivory Coast. In Mali, as Potekhin has noted, there are large cotton-growing farms employing wage labour for cotton-picking; and large privately-owned coffee and banana plantations in Guinea.[1]

A similar development of differentiation amongst the peasantry, consequent on the breakdown of the old communal land system, the drawing of the African countryside into the market economy, the change over from communal land-ownership to individual title and from subsistence farming to cash crop production, can be seen in Uganda, Kenya and Nigeria.

Thus seventy years of imperialist exploitation have brought about significant changes on the face of African agriculture. Understandably elementary forms of feudalism remain widespread and are expressed in the power of the chief to allocate land, to secure gifts, to demand labour, to control the "native" courts, and so on. Sometimes these powers are very marked, as in Northern Nigeria, for example. The main enemy of the African peasant, however, has been not so much the feudal landowner but rather the imperialist, who often robbed the peasant of his land (taken for white settlement, for mining, for urban development, for strategic purposes, for roads and railways, and sometimes simply to deny the land to the peasant in order to impoverish him and so force him off the land and into European wage employment), taxed him to the hilt, ruined his subsistence agriculture, culled his flocks, limited his participation in the production of certain cash crops, and so faced him with the economic necessity to abandon his

[1] Potekhin: op. cit., p. 86.

land and to enter the ranks of the working class, even if only as a temporary and migrant worker.

Even those who have prospered within the cash crop economy and have themselves become employers of African labour, have had to contend with the competition of the European farms and plantations and, even more, with the domination of the market by the big imperialist monopolies which strive to pay the African producer the lowest possible price for his cash crops and demand a constantly rising price for the machines and manufactured goods he requires.

The widespread agrarian crisis in Africa, which was a natural result of colonial rule, has been to some extent concealed by the migrant labour system. Communal land-ownership and subsistence agriculture remains, but it has suffered heavy blows from seventy years of colonialism, and is now under attack from the indigenous capitalist forces which are growing in the African countryside.

Because of his generalised and simplified assessment of the African peasantry, which he tends to view as a fixed, static category, unaffected by the important economic changes taking place, Fanon fails to note the emergence of different strata among the peasantry and instead presents us with an undifferentiated and really mythical "African peasant" in somewhat the same manner in which defenders of the Russian *kulaks* (rich peasants) used to prate about the non-class *moujik*.

AFRICAN CHIEFS

Logically enough, because he fails to understand the economic and social processes which are shaking up the old traditional agriculture, Fanon similarly fails to provide an adequate picture of the role of the African chiefs. It has already been noted that on this question Fanon, while admitting the reactionary role so frequently played by the chiefs, sees in them also the residual base of the only genuine traditions of the nation struggling against colonialism; and in this role he sees them in opposition to the national parties from the towns, which he regards as "modernised" and "Westernised", the terms quite clearly being used here by Fanon in a pejorative sense. Admittedly there are cases in which a chief, by standing with his people for the defence of the traditional lands of their forefathers against colonialist or white settler seizures, plays a role against imperialism, whether he is aware of this wider significance or not. A recent well-known example of this is the courageous and stubborn resistance of Chief Rekayi Tangwena, who, together with his people, has refused to quit their traditional lands from which the Smith régime ordered them to move by a special Government Proclamation of February 21, 1969.

In other cases chiefs have more directly thrown in their lot with the national movement itself, and in this way have played an important role in the general struggle for national liberation. The late Chief A. Luthuli, President-General of the African National Congress of South Africa, was an outstanding example of this kind. But he was not the only one to play such a role in South Africa. Hilda Bernstein has written that "Since 1948 no less than 133 Chiefs have been banished to different areas where they could not make a living."[1]

In Tanganyika and Malawi, too, during the struggle for independence the chiefs played a most positive role, and the same was the case in Zambia, many chiefs even giving direct material assistance to the copper miners during their big pre-independence strikes.

The dilemma of many of the chiefs in the post-1945 phase of the national liberation struggle in a number of African countries is well illustrated by the fate of Chief Nsokolo, whose conflict with British imperialism has been admirably dealt with by William Watson in his study of the Mambwe people in the former "Northern Rhodesia".[2] The position of the chief, explains Watson, is not simple. He plays, in fact, or tries to play, a dual role:

He is an agent of the British administration and the main instrument for the implementation of British policy; at the same time he is the representative of his people to the British, and the guardian and spokesman of what they (his people) consider to be their interests.[3]

When the inevitable conflict arises between these two sets of loyalties, the chief "is compelled either to find a compromise acceptable to both sides, or to identify himself with one of them". But this is precisely where the dilemma lies for the chief. "Complete identification with the British will deprive him of the respect of his people and thereby undermine his authority, and consequently his usefulness as an agent to the British; identification with his people against the British will endanger his tenure of office."

At the time of Watson's study the struggle in "Northern Rhodesia"

[1] Hilda Bernstein: *The World That Was Ours*, London, 1967, p. 176.
[2] William Watson: *Tribal Cohesion in a Money Economy*, Manchester, 1958.
[3] ibid., p. 187.

had become very sharp and the position of the chief more and more difficult. He was, rightly points out Watson, "at the point of contact between two systems which (were) becoming increasingly hostile". Chief Nsokolo's people were drawn into three major conflicts. Many had taken up wage labour, joined trade unions, taken part in demonstrations against the colour bar in urban centres, and also participated in strike action against the Central African Federation then being imposed by Britain; many joined the political movement, at that time the African National Congress; and the peasants defied the fishing and agricultural regulations of the British authorities, at the call of Chief Nsokolo, who identified himself with all his people's actions, including the protest strike against Federation.

"Industrial strikes and agricultural defiance", writes Watson,[1] "were the two final sanctions that Africans could employ against the Whites, and both were political actions. The people forced Nsokolo to take action as their representative." In consequence, the British authorities deposed him.

A very similar example is given by Rev. Charles Hooper in the case of Chief Abram Moiloa, in the Zeerust district of the Transvaal, in South Africa. Chief Abram's problem arose out of the refusal of the African women to submit to the Government's instruction that they take out passes. Arguing that the Government law was "not a tribal law", Chief Abram told the women: "The matter rests with you and the white authorities."

This attempt to avoid making a decision did not save the chief. The Government expected him to *enforce* their laws, not merely inform the women what the laws were, and leave it at that. Chief Abram was deposed. The chiefs in the lesser villages were thus faced with a similar dilemma. Like Chief Nsokolo, described by Watson as being "at the point of contact between two systems . . . becoming increasingly hostile", these chiefs in Zeerust were, wrote Rev. Hooper, "the meeting ground of inimical forces. They represented authority derived from two different sources, and the sources themselves were at variance."[2] Of this kind of conflict in which the chief "becomes a shuttlecock" (Hooper), resulting in the collapse of the system of chieftainship, Fanon has not a word to say.

Where chiefs represent more powerful feudal interests, as in Northern Nigeria or Uganda or Ghana, interests which are often extended

[1] William Watson: *Tribal Cohesion in a Money Economy*, p. 219.
[2] Charles Hooper: *Brief Authority*, London, 1960, p. 170.

into fields of capitalist enterprise; or where the chiefs are more directly mere puppet nominees of the colonial Government, the national liberation movements find it necessary to wage the most energetic struggle against them. In Guinea, the struggle for independence was linked with the fight against the chiefs who were repudiated by Diallo Sayfoulaye for having made themselves "the servile instruments of the state, against the permanent interests of the people. Most were designated illegitimately and hold their posts only because they made themselves spokesmen and defenders of the colonial authorities."[1] By limiting the power of the chiefs in Guinea during the period of the *loi-cadre*, Sékou Touré was able to ensure a majority vote against Guinea remaining part of the French Union. In Niger, where Djibo Bakary, one of Africa's outstanding progressive figures and leader of the Sawaba Party, had not yet taken parallel steps against the local chiefs, they were able to swing the votes of the peasants against independence, and thus Djibo Bakary and his Government fell, his Party was forced into illegality, and he himself into exile.

In Guinea-Bissau, Amilcar Cabral has found it necessary more than once to draw attention to the tendency of some traditional chiefs to play the role of "traitors to the nation". "The colonialists", says Cabral, "who had once counted on the treason of some traditional chiefs (who had promised the loyalty of the villages under their control) must actually admit their failure in that sense, and have arrested or dismissed some of these chiefs. Gradually abandoned by the population they had dragged along, the traditional chiefs, traitors to the nation, are today mistrusted by the colonialists and cannot hide their fear and their doubts in the face of the advances of our struggle."[2]

The late Eduardo Mondlane, too, has drawn attention to the problem presented by the chiefs and the obstacles which tribal chiefs have often placed in the way of the Mozambique revolution. He quotes a relevant example from the journal, *A Voz da Revolucao*, concerned with Chief Nhapale, one of those chiefs who, "afraid of losing their feudal privileges with the victory of the revolution and the installation of a popular government, allied themselves with the colonialists".[3] The people opposed Chief Nhapale and went to protest to him, declaring

---

[1] *La Liberté*, June 5, 1956. Cited by Ruth Schachter Morgenthau: *Political Parties in French-Speaking West Arica*, Oxford, 1964, p. 250.

[2] *The Struggle for Liberation in Guinea-Bissau and Cape Verde*. Extract from Report by Amilcar Cabral to the Executive Secretariat of the Tri-Continental-solidarity Organisation of the Peoples of Africa, Asia and Latin America, December, 1966.

[3] Eduardo Mondlane: *The Struggle for Mozambique*, London, 1969, p. 164.

that Frelimo[1] would bring him to justice. The Frelimo unit leader then addressed the gathering in front of the chief whom he denounced for burning two innocent people, two patriots, alive. "Do you want to keep such a chief?" he asked.

> The people answered NO, and, encouraged by the presence of the guerrillas, put the chief through a summary trial and condemned him to death . . . Nhapale was executed.

In "Nyasaland", notes Rotberg; the Governor "preferred by and large to regard members of the traditional hierarchy of authority—all of whom owed their appointments to the Governor—as the only authentic indigenous voices".[2] The Governor himself confessed that "the opinion he valued most was that expressed by tribal chiefs". The same preference was expressed in "Northern Rhodesia" in the early 1940's when provincial councils were set up as "a form of insurance against the growth of indigenous nationalism".[3] They included a majority of chiefs and other important rural personalities and "purposely over-represented country interests while devaluating the opinions of those who dwelled in towns".[4]

It can be noted that despite Fanon's clear commitment to the cause of national liberation his views here run largely parallel to the arguments of the colonialists who, like Fanon, claimed to find in the chiefs "authentic indigenous voices" which they contrasted unfavourably with "those who dwelled in towns".

Fanon's attempt to "have it both ways" with the chiefs, admitting on the one hand that they are "traditional collaborators" yet simultaneously acclaiming them as the defenders, with the peasants, of the true traditions of the nation as against the sophisticated nationalist politicos of the towns, simply won't do. Nowhere does he explain the problem and changing role of the chiefs in dialectical fashion, seeing the impact on them of the national liberation struggle which increasingly compels them to act as open traitors to the national cause or to abandon their imperial masters and throw in their lot with the liberation struggle. Nor does he note the difference in attitude of the powerful chiefs in the strongholds of feudalism in contrast to many of the weaker chiefs in the regions of subsistence agriculture and more

---

[1] Liberation Front of Mozambique.

[2] Robert I. Rotberg: *The Rise of Nationalism in Central Africa*, Cambridge, Mass., 1966, p. 122.

[3] ibid., p. 200.

[4] ibid., p. 201.

primitive communal farming, where, even in their economic status, the chiefs are much closer to the people.

THE LUMPENPROLETARIAT

Fanon's claim that the *lumpenproletariat* is a leading revolutionary force, cannot be seriously sustained, especially since he spells out what he means by his references to pimps, hooligans, petty criminals, prostitutes, "all the hopeless dregs of humanity". As David Caute has rightly written, "Fanon fails to distinguish between the hardcore, corrupted *lumpenproletariat*, and the migrant peasants who move to and fro between town and village, and who are more capable of the revolutionary activity he describes and desires."[1] Marx, on more than one occasion, drew attention to the danger which can come from the *lumpenproletariat*. In the *Communist Manifesto* it is described as the "dangerous class, the social scum, that passively rotting mass thrown off by the lowest classes of old society" which "may, here and there, be swept into the movement by a proletarian revolution; its conditions of life, however, prepare it far more for the part of a bribed tool of reactionary intrigue".

In *The Class Struggles in France, 1848–1850*, Marx, on the basis of the experiences of that period in France, extends his treatment of the *lumpenproletariat*, and explains the reactionary role which it played. The *lumpenproletariat* in the main towns, wrote Marx, was "a mass sharply differentiated from the industrial proletariat, a recruiting ground for thieves and criminals of all kinds, living on the crumbs of society, people without a definite trade, vagabonds, *gens sans feu and sans aveu*,[2] varying according to the degree of civilisation of the nation to which they belong, but never renouncing their *lazzaroni*[3] character". While recognising that some of the younger people in this category were capable of "the most heroic deeds and the most exalted sacrifices", Marx also warned that they were equally capable of "the basest banditry and the foulest corruption".[4] And this indeed was the role that such people, recruited into the Mobile Guard, came to play. Interestingly enough, Marx points out that the Paris proletariat regarded this reactionary force "as the *proletarian* guard in contra-

---

[1] David Caute: *Fanon*, London, 1969, p. 74.
[2] People without fire or faith.
[3] Idlers and beggars of Naples.
[4] Karl Marx: *The Class Struggles in France, 1848–1850, Selected Works*, Vol. 1 Moscow–London, 1950, p. 142.

distinction to the bourgeois National Guard. Its error was pardon-able."[1]

The consequences of this "pardonable error" were soon forth-coming. When the Paris proletariat rose in revolt against the bourgeois republic it found ranged against it "the aristocracy of finance, the industrial bourgeoisie, the middle class, the petty bourgeoisie, the army, the *lumpenproletariat* organised as the Mobile Guard, the intellectual lights, the clergy, and the rural population. . . . More than three thousand insurgents were butchered after the victory, and fifteen thousand were transported without trial."[2] As in 1848, so again in 1851, through his Society of December 10, Louis Bonaparte relied on the *lumpenproletariat* for his *coup d'état*.

Marx, it seems to me, made two essential points about the *lumpen-proletariat*. First, that its *main* tendency was to act as "the bribed tool of reactionary intrigue". Secondly, that here and there it could be "swept into the movement by a proletarian revolution", and that some of the younger members of this stratum were capable of heroism and sacrifice. Marx did not deny that some individuals, even of the *lumpenproletariat*, could play a positive role. But as a class, or rather sub-class, it could only be *swept* into movement by the proletariat at a time of revolution; it certainly could not initiate or lead a revolution. Nor could it be regarded as a main force of the revolution, let alone displace the proletariat as the leading force in the towns, as Fanon claims.

It is, of course, true that under conditions of colonialism and the mass poverty which imperialism has made endemic throughout the Third World, the question of the non-working-class elements in the big towns and villages presents in some ways a much bigger problem for revolutionaries in these countries than it does in the major industrial centres. But even so, as Aidit pointed out, its main tendency has been destructive and counter-revolutionary.

The loiterers and vagrants are one of the products of a semi-colonial and semi-feudal society in view of the fact that this society has given rise to unemployed in the villages and towns, and these unemployed then live a life of vagrancy without any idea of what to do, and (are) eventually dragged down into adopting the path of crime, becoming thieves, robbers, gangsters, beggars, prostitutes and (adopting) all other such abnormal ways of living or working. This

[1] Karl Marx: *The Class Struggles in France, 1848–1850*, p. 143.
[2] Karl Marx: *The Eighteenth Brumaire of Louis Bonaparte*, in *Selected Works*, Vol. 1, op. cit., p. 231.

group is wavering in character and some of them can be bought up by the reactionaries, while others can be brought into the revolution.[1]

But, Aidit emphasises, even when such people join the revolution they become "the ideological source of roaming destructive elements and of anarchism within the ranks of the revolution. They can easily be made to waver both with material bribes as well as with incitement to hatred and to the destruction of anything constructive. They can easily be told by the counter-revolutionaries to mouth revolutionary phrases so as to oppose and destroy the Party of the working class, the workers' movement and the revolutionary movement in general."

The same negative characteristics have been noted by Professor Epstein in relation to Latin America, where he finds "grounds for caution, if not pessimism, about the political potential of the urban 'non-working class'".[2] He admits the relative and absolute deprivation that these people suffer but points out that they "have often supported fundamentally conservative populist figures such as Odria in Peru and Rojas Pinilla in Colombia, or else have been integrated into clientelist patronage politics, as in Brazil".

In Morocco, Professor Waterbury found that the inhabitant of the *bidonvilles*[3] of Casablanca, often unemployed, "is not the political radical, the alienated proletarian that some would see in him".[4] In fact, notes Waterbury, "he may be politically docile, or, if not, he rejects authority in ways common to the rural world". Often he has "*never* been regularly employed". He finds himself, in most phases of his daily existence, "at the mercy of the state". Consequently, while he is capable of violence and protest, "his protest is brief, unguided, and formless. He is not a man with nothing to lose. The *bidonville* is more attractive to him than the blad"[5]—and this helps to explain his frequent displays of "political timidity".

If Fanon had evidence that the *lumpenproletariat* in Africa had played a different role, then he should have produced it. But his bold assertion is nowhere backed up by any specific details or example. In fact, as has been noted, his only examples are those in which the *lumpenproletariat* has been used on the side of colonialism—as in Algeria, the Congo and Angola.

[1] D. N. Aidit: *Problems of the Indonesian Revolution*, 1963, p. 56.
[2] David G. Epstein: "A Revolutionary Lumpenproletariat?", *Monthly Review*, December, 1969, p. 55.
[3] Shanty-towns.
[4] John Waterbury: op. cit., p. 202.
[5] Countryside.

It is interesting to note the different approach to this question made by Amilcar Cabral. Cabral distinguishes carefully between the real *déclassés*, the actual *lumpenproletariat*, and the young people from the villages who have come to the towns in search of work, and who are connected with the families of workers or the petty bourgeoisie.

Of the former group, "the permanent layabouts, the prostitutes and so on", experience shows, according to Cabral, that they have been "a great help to the Portuguese police in giving them information; this group has been outrightedly against our struggle".[1]

On the other hand, Cabral points out, the group of mainly young people recently arrived from the rural areas to the towns, and with contacts in both urban and rural areas, "gradually comes to make a comparison between the standard of living of their own families and that of the Portuguese; they begin to understand the sacrifices being borne by the Africans. They have proved extremely dynamic in the struggle. Many of these people joined the struggle right from the beginning and it is among this group that we found many of the cadres whom we have since trained."

In some cases individuals from the ranks of the *lumpenproletariat* may break with their environment and join the ranks of the national revolution, but there is no evidence whatsoever to claim, as Fanon does, that the *lumpenproletariat*, as a social stratum, "constitutes one of the most spontaneous and the most radically revolutionary forces of a colonised people". Fanon, obsessed with violence, too glibly equates revolution with destruction. In town riots the declassed and criminal elements are always ready to lend a hand, quick to let loose their blind anger against society in general, to burn, to loot, to destroy. But this cannot make them a "revolutionary force".[2] Revolution involves the replacement of the old society by a new higher form of society. Such a fundamental change requires an understanding of the class or classes against whom the revolution is directed, an appreciation of the class forces which make up the revolutionary alliance, and a comprehension of the shape of the new society which is to emerge.

Fanon has served a purpose, nevertheless, by his distorted emphasis on the *lumpenproletariat*. In so doing he has drawn attention to the need

---

[1] Amilcar Cabral: *Revolution in Guinea*, op. cit., pp. 49–51.

[2] It is interesting to note here Hobsbawm's comment on the pre-industrial city "mob" in Europe. "The 'mob's' readiness to riot has made the task of revolutionaries easy on the first days of revolutions, but has been offset by an almost total inability to understand that social agitation does not end when a riot has achieved its immediate objectives, and by its lack of discipline." (E. J. Hobsbawm: *Primitive Rebels*, Manchester, 1959, pp. 123–4.)

to examine more closely the various strata that make up the urban populations of Africa today. As already noted, Cabral has pointed out the special role of the new arrivals to the towns, a group for which, he says, "we have not yet found the exact term". It is, of course, a group which arises from the conditions of the break-up of the old society and from the prevalence in Africa of the migrant labour system already referred to.

There are no adequate statistics to show the extent of unemployment in the towns of Africa. But it is obvious even to the casual visitor that there must be many people with no regular job. A 1955 analysis of Dakar showed only 27 per cent of the African urban population with some kind of definite occupation; even of the able-bodied, the figure was still only 42 per cent.[1]

There is a further urban group which can and does play a major role in the struggle, and again it is one for which an exact term is not easy. This is the growing army of young school-leavers who are without jobs.

Sharp attention to this problem throughout the Third World has been drawn by Guy Hunter:

> In country after country children from 10 to 18 are pouring out of the schools into a world which can offer only to a tiny proportion of them any opportunity beyond the unchanged pattern of family and village subsistence farming. The International Labour Organisation has calculated the net increase in the labour force in developing countries as about 162 million in 1960–70, and 226 million in 1970–80 (against 50 million to 55 million respectively in the developed world). What proportion of these will have wage-paid employment? The estimate for Latin America is 9 per cent; in many countries it could well be lower. More than half of these new citizens will have been to school, and children under 16 make up 50 per cent of the total population in many developing countries. This immense problem of half-educated, half-employed young people is, after the demographic explosion which exacerbates it, perhaps the gravest which developing nations face.[2]

The families they come from are varied—sometimes working class, sometimes of the professional strata, sometimes traders and other petty-bourgeois sections, sometimes peasants. Thus these youngsters

[1] *Les Cahiers d'Outre-Mer*, 1961, No. 56, pp. 383–5. Cited by I. I. Potekhin, *African Problems*, op. cit.

[2] Guy Hunter: *Modernising Peasant Societies*, London, 1969, pp. 12–13. Mr. Hunter's warning has, to an extent, been borne out by the 1971 disturbances in Ceylon.

are of mixed social origin. Having never been employed they are not unemployed workers in the normal sense of the term; they have had no experience of wage labour. They are forced to live off their families and far-distant relations (the customary practice in Africa) or often by their wits. This growing army of partly educated, dissatisfied and frustrated young people is usually the solid core that participates in the big demonstrations, constitutes the Youth Wings of the national parties, and is responsive to radical slogans. It can also fall a prey to demagogy and be used for reactionary purposes as in Malawi.

Chodak has drawn attention to the fact that unemployment in Africa today is not entirely the same as it was under colonialism. "The new African unemployed worker has at least the rudiments of education, and is gaining more and more every day. . . . Today, reading and writing is no exceptional ability. Literacy, however, produces self-awareness and consciousness of one's own condition, more exigent needs, higher aspirations."[1] Chodak's assessment regarding the state of literacy in Africa today is, perhaps, too sweeping;[2] but it is certainly true of many of the new young generation of unemployed, and is undoubtedly a growing trend.

In general, this group is a potential base of discontent which can be won decisively for revolutionary change, but to which Fanon has given scant attention. In fact he regards it with obvious anxiety as a group most likely to succumb to "Western culture".[3] Despite Fanon, abstract anti-Westernism is not the hallmark of revolutionary understanding. Fanon himself was a product of Western culture. His anxieties for the youth of Africa are only another echo of his Gandhian distaste for the "modern world", his idealisation of the peasantry, of the village as against the town, of the lumpen "drop-out" as against the industrial worker.

IS THERE AN AFRICAN NATIONAL BOURGEOISIE?

Fanon, as we have seen, would appear to have written off entirely the possibility of any section of the African capitalist class contributing,

[1] Szymon Chodak: op. cit., p. 45.

[2] The Pearson Commission Report estimates that only 30 per cent of children entering primary school in developing countries finish their school period, and that 50 per cent only get as far as the second grade. (See *Partners in Development: Report of the Commission on International Development*, Chairman, Lester B. Pearson, New York, 1969, p. 67.) The report emphasises, too, that "it is in the volatile cities of the developing world that agricultural stagnation and industrial unemployment combine to produce their gravest consequences" (p. 60).

[3] Frantz Fanon: *The Damned*, op. cit., p. 156.

even partially and provisionally, to the further unfolding of the African revolution. The African capitalists, and those "wily intellectuals" who cling to them, are regarded by him as one reactionary mass, wholly dependent on foreign imperialism. There is, he argues, "no true bourgeoisie", only a group of greedy hucksters who eagerly pick up the tips which the former colonial power allows it.

Fanon is not entirely alone in this assessment of the African bourgeoisie. Ledda[1] outlines five main groups of the African bourgeoisie—compradores who function as middlemen for the large foreign trading firms; indigenous entrepreneurs; a bureaucratic bourgeoisie emerging from the nationalist élites, and including both new political leaderships and former state functionaries; local planters; and feudal landlords. In some cases, he points out, these groups merge and become, in fact, a single capitalist class. But such a class, he argues, cannot be regarded as a "national bourgeoisie" in the sense of "a social force capable of producing a high level of development of a country's productive forces on the basis of *its own* choices". The African bourgeoisie, he contends, is "tied, body and soul, to foreign capital" and its interests "cannot exist or be defended independently".

Facts about the African bourgeoisie are by no means plentiful, but they are sufficient to enable one to judge to what extent an African capitalist class is developing, what are its main characteristics, and what role it is playing in the present phase of the African revolution.

We have already noted the significant expansion of capitalism in the African countryside. But this is not the only sector of the economy in Africa in which one can note the emergence of an indigenous capitalist class. The origins of an African capitalist class are generally to be found in trade. Export and import trade, of course, was firmly in the hands of the big imperialist trading companies even prior to the twentieth-century colonial system. Internal trade, however, gave scope for the emergence of African traders, especially in West Africa where palm-fruit production and processing was already in the hands of Africans and where local trading was already widespread.

The imported goods given in exchange went into African hands and African markets. The produce-buying companies, gradually extending inland, found Africans to bring the produce in and Africans to distribute the European goods even to the smallest villages.[2]

[1] Romano Ledda: op. cit., pp. 565–6.
[2] Guy Hunter: *The New Societies in Tropical Africa*, London, 1962, pp. 129–30.

In East and Central Africa, the lack of an immediate crop for export, and poor transport facilities compared with West Africa, delayed the emergence of African traders connected with the European market. Much of the trade fell into the hands of the Asians, who later expanded into cotton ginning and sugar plantations. European settlement in East and Central Africa meant that Europeans, too, monopolised certain branches of trade.

In West Africa, however, African traders had more opportunity, and with the coming of the lorry at the beginning of the twentieth century, a veritable revolution began to take place in African trading. Now it became possible to carry larger loads over longer distances in a shorter space of time; the interior could be more easily opened up to the trader; the village store could be set up and constantly re-stocked.

During and after the second world war this process developed still more rapidly. In West Africa, says Guy Hunter:

> from the mass of petty traders and craftsmen, the market women and the wandering Hausamen, there began to appear . . . a group of more substantial Africans in a more modern way of business. These might be the big traders of Accra, Kumasi, Kano, Lagos, Port Harcourt, and Onitsha, trading both in produce and European goods; the building contractors, the owners of fleets of lorries. These were men concerned with bank and credit, wages and customs dues; in many ways they were seeking to become modern men of business. *This was the real start of a transition from the traditional market to the twentieth century sense of commerce.*[1] (Italics added.)

The majority of African traders, to this very day, are still petty traders and part-time traders. In any large African town one can see hundreds, in fact thousands, of small traders, some with a few goods spread on the bare ground, some with a stall, some with a small shop. Kumasi, in Ghana, has 8,000 traders. In the Onitsha covered market in Nigeria there are 3,000 shops. The great majority of African traders are very poor, making a few pennies a day, some more fortunate, making a few shillings. A large number of them are part-time traders, earning a little extra money from their surplus vegetables or from handicrafts. Among them are many women. D. McCall (see *Social Change in Africa*, edited by A. Southall, 1961) describes how in Koforidua, Ghana, he counted in the market "nearly 3,000 sellers on a market day. This did not include the numbers of women selling at the various crossroads

---

[1] Guy Hunter: *The New Societies in Tropical Africa*, p. 131.

and in the streets." He estimates that "not less than 70 per cent of the adult female population was engaged in selling".

Some traders sell locally, others act as wholesalers, buying from the foreign importers and, with the aid of their lorries, selling up-country. Some traders in West Africa are also cocoa farmers, who utilise part of their profits from cocoa to launch out into trading, and, conversely, ploughing back some of their trading profits to expand their cocoa production.

From amongst these thousands of African traders a considerable differentiation has taken place. Studies by Peter Garlick of African traders in Kumasi and Accra show that amongst the 150 traders who are the biggest men in Kumasi, a turnover of £5,000 to £20,000 a year is quite common, and a number reach £100,000 a year. Over 60 of these traders (at the time of the enquiry, 1959–60), were doing some direct importing from overseas, and most were employing up to three or four assistants (often relatives), and some were employing more. An analysis of 251 African traders in Ghana by Garlick shows six in the turnover class of £20,000–£25,000 a year, 19 between £25,000 and £50,000, 9 between £50,000 and £75,000, 4 between £75,000 and £100,000 and 6 in the £100,000 to £200,000 class. A further 55 were between £5,000 and £20,000. This means a total of 44 out of 251 who could be classified as rich traders, and a further 55 as middle-size.

In his study on *Road Transport in Nigeria* (1958), E. K. Hawkins points out that while foreign transport firms dominate in the freight trade, African firms dominate in passenger traffic and in the carriage of internal trade. The African capitalist, says Hawkins, "has asserted himself, notably in the field of road transport, but also in retail trade, building and contracting". He further notes that "a number of Africans have become prominent" in Nigeria in tyre retreading, woodworking, the supply of building materials and printing.

Similar developments have been noted in the Ivory Coast, in Senegal and Cameroun. J. L. Boutillier, in his study on the Bongouanou region of the Ivory Coast, shows how some of the richer peasants have in the past decade begun to invest their profits outside agriculture, buying cars and lorries, becoming transporters and traders, setting up village stores, and sometimes going in for money-lending as well.

A report on Senegal describes how the better-off cultivators are taking up trade, some of them having already given up cultivation in order to live entirely by trading. In Cameroun, the Bamilike are particularly active in trade; in some of the areas where they are heavily concentrated, a quarter of them are occupied in trading. Describing the activities of traders in the cocoa region of the Cameroun, Jacques Binet (*Budgets Familiaux des Planteurs de Cacao au Cameroun*), writes: "The traders represent the wealthy section of the population."

In general, one can say that an African industrial bourgeoisie does not yet exist. It is certainly the case that no large-scale industrial and factory production is in the hands of African owners. At the same time, a number of small-scale industries, owned by Africans, already exist in a number of territories, and in some cases are steadily growing. A study on the *Development of Small Industries in Eastern Nigeria*, prepared for the United States Agency for International Development, estimates that small industry in Eastern Nigeria provides employment for approximately triple the number of people engaged in large-scale manufacture. In fourteen towns surveyed in the Region, 10,728 firms were recorded, employing 28,721 workers—an average of 2·7 per enterprise. This average included the manager/owner and apprentices. Only 332, or 3 per cent of the 10,728 firms, employed ten or more people; 55 per cent employed between 6 and 9; and as many as 38 per cent were one-man businesses.

Some of the African capitalists in Nigeria have diversified their efforts, acting as directors of British trading firms, exporting rubber and timber in their own right, entering industry itself with timber mills or rubber processing plants, and eventually employing several hundred production workers, shipping clerks and so on. Some of these African capitalists, who commence as quite petty traders, evolve by stages into buying agencies in effect for the big foreign monopolies, subsequently emerging as direct exporters on their own account, accepting posts as directors of foreign monopolies, and then commencing their own manufactures. One can see, in this process, how interlinked with foreign monopolies are these African capitalists, yet, at the same time, the different points at which they enter into competition with these very firms, both in trade and in manufacture.

In the majority of cases, the older capitalist sections have been joined by a new bureaucratic bourgeoisie, a stratum of career politicians—lawyers, civil servants, and other petty-bourgeois sections (sometimes sons of landowners, traders, and richer farmers)—who utilise their new governmental and state positions to acquire wealth and economic position. As part of, but in some ways separate from, this bureaucratic bourgeoisie are the army and police officers, normally trained in Western military academies. Often, it is this new bureaucratic bourgeoisie which wields state power, sometimes in alliance with external imperialist forces. In his book, *Classes and Class Ideology in Senegal*,[1] Mahjemout Diop, former General Secretary of the African Independence Party, argues that it is this bureaucratic bourgeoisie, numbering over a thousand, which has usurped political power in Senegal and is acting as an agency of neo-colonialism. The trading bourgeoisie in Senegal, says M. Diop, is negligible, and its income puts it rather in the category of a petty-bourgeoisie. African manufacture, in 1961, owned only 15 out of 320 enterprises in the country. Thus it is the new bureaucratic bourgeoisie which is the main obstacle to Senegal's advance. "The bureaucratic bourgeoisie are the weeds on the fields of the nation," declares M. Diop. "If our people want to live and survive they must uproot them from our native soil."

In those new African states which are ruled solely by compromising sections of the African bourgeoisie, there is an open and obvious attempt to follow a capitalist path, to rely mainly on the growth of indigenous capitalist forces. Addressing the National Assembly of the Central African Republic on October 16, 1961, the President, David Dacko, declared himself in favour of "a Central African bourgeoisie. That's what we have decided, because we think that that's what the future of our country will be. And I say to this Central African élite which is daily growing before our eyes: don't be ashamed to be bourgeois, don't be ashamed to become wealthy. . . ."

Such conceptions are naturally encouraged by the imperialists who understand that these bourgeois forces can become a prop for continued imperialist exploitation. One important tactic of neo-colonialism which will influence the position of the African capitalist class is the drawing in of trading or bureaucratic capitalist sections into the apparatus and network of the big monopolies themselves. Thus the big imperialist trading companies, such as the UAC (United Africa Company), the SCOA (Société Commerciale de l'Ouest Africain), and CFAO (Compagnie Française de l'Afrique Occidentale), as well as Cie du Niger Français, the main subsidiary of the UAC in the former French territories in West Africa, Barclays Bank and other major companies, have deemed it necessary to "bring in" the African, in some cases offering him managerial posts, or even directorships, sometimes combining this with abandoning a large sector of trade, especially in raw materials and traditional consumer imports, to the African trader. The African traders are still, to a considerable extent, merely

[1] Mahjemout Diop: *Classes et Idéologies de Classe au Senegal*, 1963, pp. 51-61.

agents of the big European monopolies from whom the goods for sale are imported, and to whom, in the last resort, the raw materials produced in Africa are sold. But in general, the new situation has favoured a further expansion and enrichment of the African trader, especially the bigger ones who are already well-placed to take advantage of the new possibilities.

The imperialists, in adjusting themselves to the new situation, are not only concerned with economic questions. They also hope, as Barbé has stressed, that in return for making economic concessions to the African capitalists, the latter will "in return, assure them political support in the different countries".[1]

In Guinea the Government has kept a close rein on the African traders, rightly regarding them as a base for reaction and counter-revolution. The struggle there between the people and more forward-looking democrats on the one hand, and the trading bourgeoisie on the other, has been a major source of tension over the past few years. In 1962, Sékou Touré had to appeal for "revolutionary firmness" against the "trading bourgeoisie". The warning was clearly necessary for, in 1963, when the Government introduced a 10 per cent tax on all sales, a number of traders went on strike. Sékou Touré, in a message to the branches and committees of the Democratic Party of Guinea (PDG), demanded: "The traders must open their shops, or close them for good." The dangerous role of the trading bourgeoisie in Guinea has been noted on many occasions by Sékou Touré, who has characterised it as "the base of all subversive, deviationist and counter-revolutionary activities".

President Sékou Touré has made it abundantly clear that these capitalist elements in Guinea are not simply an economic obstacle to Guinea's advance. These elements, he has said, are "a primary form of the society of exploiting capitalism, which is a natural ally of imperialism and neo-colonialism". Thus the leaders of Guinea have recognised that to give licence to such a stratum would endanger national sovereignty, hamper economic progress, and prevent Guinea's advance.

In Ghana, in the period prior to the coup against Nkrumah, there was a considerable sharpening of the struggle between the most forward sections who wanted to press forward and open the way to socialism, and those trading and bureaucratic capitalist elements who wished to be the main beneficiaries of independence and to drag their country along a capitalist road. As early as 1961, the Ghana Government, in its

[1] Raymond Barbé: op. cit.

White Paper, *Statement by the Government on the Recent Conspiracy*, found it necessary to point a finger at the new potential bourgeoisie which, in alliance with imperialism, was sabotaging the development of the country:

> Colonialism was responsible for producing a small reactionary Ghanaian élite drawn from the professional classes and the agents and senior employees of the great Merchant houses and educated to look at every social problem from an essentially colonial standpoint. They hoped on independence to step into the shoes of the former colonial rulers, but they had no intention of altering the social system which they hoped to inherit.

This nascent bourgeoisie was to be found not only in the so-called "Opposition", but even within the Convention People's Party itself, and among the Ministers. In his famous "Dawn Broadcast", April 8, 1961, President Nkrumah castigated the new bourgeois elements in Ghana society, who were utilising their state positions to enrich themselves at the expense of national development and the people's interests.

Writing in *The Spark*, a Ghana weekly (November 27, 1964), Obotan Awuku pointed out that local traders in many cases are "helping to perpetuate colonialism since their interests coincide with the interests of the capitalists. It is the height of neo-colonialism." Developing his criticism of this section of the local bourgeoisie, Obotan Awuku writes:

> Some local entrepreneurs with greater flair for capitalist ventures tie up with foreign capitalists in unequal and disadvantageous partnerships in the establishment of productive ventures. By reason of experience, capital or other economic considerations, however, they turn out to be mere tools in the hands of capitalist adventurers. They operate businesses which by their labels appear to be indigenous but which are in reality entirely owned by foreigners. There have been several instances of this, even of ministers and men in high places having deals with foreign capitalist adventurers.

In his Easter message to the nation, April, 1965, President Nkrumah once again found it necessary to attack sharply those capitalist elements in Ghana which were lining their own pockets at the expense of the state and the national economy.

> Let us all resolve to wage a relentless war against all those engaged in the dirty game of extorting wealth from the workers and the masses. *We must smoke out these hoarders and profiteers from the holes of their illegal warehouses.*

President Nkrumah's correct intention to "smoke out the hoarders and profiteers" did not succeed. The developing bourgeois elements, who had been allowed to enrich themselves in the past decade, had no intention of seeing Ghana travel towards socialism. Reactionary forces in Ghanaian society, backed by foreign imperialism, and taking advantage of the failures of the Government, including its very failure to curb the nascent capitalist class whose greed and ostentation was arousing the disgust and anger of the whole people, reached out and struck down President Nkrumah's government and the CPP. The aim of the coup was not to eliminate corruption but to swing Ghana away from her progressive path, and turn her into an ally of neo-colonialism. And this was so notwithstanding the fact that corrupt bourgeois elements were to be found in the topmost ranks of the CPP itself.

From the above facts one can draw certain tentative conclusions as regards the role of African capitalists.

1. Even before the winning of national independence, a stratum of African capitalists—mainly engaged in trading, transport and farming—was beginning to emerge in most African states.

2. Though dependent on the big foreign monopolies (who were either purchasers of the peasant produce, or suppliers of the goods for sale by African traders), some sections of these African capitalists participated in the national movements. This helps to explain why it was possible for them, after independence, to emerge in a number of cases as the new rulers.

3. Since the winning of independence, *a national bourgeoisie interested in industrial development and the growth of the economy*, has begun to emerge in some instances. This section plays a progressive role, since it does not wish to see the national economy remain in the grip of imperialism. It has therefore thrown in its lot with the majority of the people who are struggling for economic independence and economic advance. The national bourgeoisie in Africa, that is to say that section of the bourgeoisie which is genuinely interested in national independence, national economic growth, the expansion of the internal market, and the creation of national industry, faces very great problems. Generally, it is economically weak, lacks capital, as well as managerial experience and knowledge as regards modern factory production, and has no body of skilled African workers and technicians ready at hand. For these reasons, it is in no position at this stage to initiate large-scale factory production itself—and understandably is often reluctant even to try. But, since it desires to see economic expansion and a growth in

national production, it understands the need for and supports the idea of the state itself taking the necessary steps to create new national industries. It is this forward-looking section of the bourgeoisie in Africa which, in alliance with the working class, the peasants, and revolutionary democrats, is resisting imperialism and struggling against the intrigues of the compromising sections of the bourgeoisie.

4. In the most progressive states, the economic and political power of the *trading bourgeoisie* is being weakened by State economic measures (the setting up of state trading agencies, fiscal and tax measures, etc.), and this is leading to a sharp struggle with these elements since what is basically involved is the whole question of breaking decisively with imperialism, and opening the way to socialism.

5. On the land, while there is in many cases a significant growth of co-operatives, there is also a *considerable differentiation taking place within the peasantry* practically in every state, with the emergence of a small but clearly defined capitalist stratum which exploits African wage labour.

6. The setting up of new States and new governments has meant the emergence of a stratum of *bureaucratic capitalists*, including army officers, which, when linked to imperialism, acts as its neo-colonialist agency. This stratum is sometimes in alliance with feudal forces, and usually with other sections of the African bourgeoisie, especially traders.

7. This total process is leading to the establishment not simply of sections of capitalists but of what can now be regarded in some African countries as *a definite capitalist class*, with common class interests expressed in its control of a political party, its domination over the state and government, and the growing cohesiveness of its economic and political power. In no case can one say that this process has reached an advanced stage, but it would be equally wrong not to note the tendency.

8. In all African states, both those which are under progressive leaderships and are cutting away from imperialism, and those which are under reactionary capitalist sections clinging to imperialism, *the internal class struggle is sharpening*. In reactionary states it takes the form of open class battles (strikes, demonstrations and even the overthrow of governments), ranging from simple economic demands over wages, prices, etc., to the challenging of the whole direction of government policy. In the advanced states, it takes the form of economic and political resistance by the reactionary capitalist sections to the steps of the government

and state which are aimed at the further unfolding of the national democratic revolution. In some cases, this resistance by the reactionary capitalist sections, acting in concert with imperialism, has been successful in overthrowing progressive governments, as in Ghana, Mali, and Uganda. Similar plots have been tried in Guinea and Congo (Brazzaville). The neo-colonialist counter-offensive which is now raging in Africa is based on an alliance between imperialism and indigenous capitalist elements in Africa who have a common interest in preventing African states from taking a path which would open the road to socialism.

It is against this examination of the African bourgeoisie as a whole that one needs to examine the particular question of the national bourgeoisie, especially since Fanon really makes no scientific differentiation between the national bourgeoisie and other sections of the African capitalists.

The question of the national bourgeoisie has dogged the international communist movement from its very beginnings. It was debated, in particular, at the Second Congress of the Communist International in 1920, when Lenin produced his well-known *Theses on the National and Colonial Question*, and at the Sixth Congress in 1928, which adopted a thesis entitled *The Revolutionary Movement in the Colonies and Semi-Colonies*.

When Ledda defines the national bourgeoisie as "*a social force capable of producing a high level of development of a country's productive forces*" it seems to me that he is, to an extent, confusing capacity with intentions, which arise from other objective factors. Certainly, among the groups he lists, some can be dismissed as outside the ranks of the national bourgeoisie, if one takes the term in its more normal sense as referring not to the whole indigenous bourgeoisie but to that section of it which is interested in controlling and expanding its own internal market (which necessitates an attack on, or at least a weakening of, feudalism, and competition and conflict with imperialism). Compradores and feudal landlords are not usually regarded as part of the national bourgeoisie. But can one so easily dismiss the African entrepreneurs, and even sections of the new bureaucratic bourgeoisie (which, to some extent, are to be distinguished from the older bureaucratic bourgeoisie reared by the colonial system)? And are not the petty-bourgeoisie, including sections of the peasantry, and sections of the élite, also linked to the aspirations of the national bourgeoisie?

Part of the problem arises from ignoring the present stage that Africa has reached, and misunderstanding the character of Africa's present revolution. Although the world as a whole is passing through a transition from capitalism to socialism, the African countries are at a very early stage of that process. They have, in the main, won their national independence, but the essential tasks of their democratic, anti-imperialist, anti-feudal, revolution remain to be fulfilled[1]—and some of these tasks, of course, may not be completed until the socialist stage is reached.

Fanon gives little help on this question. It is not clear whether he thinks that Africa's immediate task is the socialist revolution or whether he envisages a democratic transitional phase before the goal of socialism can seriously be set. Yet this is decisive, since the character of the existing revolutionary phase determines the forms of class alliance which are objectively possible and necessary, and the relations of the different classes within that alliance.

It is fashionable in some "New Left" circles these days to emphasise the dependent and compromising character of the indigenous bourgeoisie, and even of the national bourgeoisie. In fact, this is usually cited in respect of all Third World countries as proof that there is no longer any possibility of a national democratic phase of the revolution but that the immediate aim must be a workers' and peasants' government. It is, of course, true that the advance of socialism and its increasingly decisive influence on world processes to some extent circumscribes the national bourgeoisie and limits its possibilities of an independent capitalist growth since its fear of the growing strength of socialism will tend to push it back into the arms of imperialism. But it is equally true that the very existence of a socialist system provides new possibilities for the national bourgeoisie to secure help in building its independent economy and in lessening its dependence on imperialism, and in this very process to come into conflict with the imperialist powers.

These two possibilities now before the national bourgeoisie are only another expression of the dual character of this bourgeoisie—and this, it should be said, is the nub of the matter. It is not a question as to whether the national bourgeoisie is on the side of the revolution or the counter-revolution—for, in a sense, the answer is both. And this was a point already emphasised by Lenin in 1920. Talking of "a certain rapprochement between the bourgeoisie of the exploiting and colonial countries", he explained that as a result, while the bourgeoisie of the oppressed nation supports the national movement "it at the same time

[1] In some cases, of course, even earlier forms of society have to be replaced.

works hand in glove with the imperialist bourgeoisie, that is, joins forces with it against all revolutionary movements and classes".[1]

The whole point about the national bourgeoisie is that, like Janus, it faces two ways. As a bourgeoisie it is interested in exploiting its own workers and ensuring their submission to its domination. At the same time, its attempts to gain control over its home market and expand the national economy bring it into conflict with the big imperialist monopolies which naturally desire to maintain their dominant position in the market, and ensure that the economy of the given country evolves in accordance with their own profit-interests and not with the genuine development of that country itself.

Thus the national bourgeoisie finds itself in conflict both with its own workers and with the imperialists. Its very dependency on imperialism is a sign of its contradictions with imperialism. Its dependency is a form of its oppression at the hands of the big monopolies. However weak it may be, it would like to relax this grip. To do this it repeatedly makes use of the mass movement of workers and peasants, attempting to wield the movement like a big stick to win concessions for itself from the imperialists. But as soon as the workers and peasants begin to challenge the limits of the bourgeoisie's own aims, and start to press their own class demands, and even threaten to take over the direction of the struggle, the national bourgeoisie backs down in haste and will, at times, even turn to the imperialists for help in crushing the people's movement.

In China, the national bourgeoisie repeatedly sided with the revolution—and just as repeatedly abandoned it. Between 1924 to 1927 it was on the side of the revolution; from 1927 to 1931 important sections supported the counter-revolution. For a short period in 1931 it supported the national revolution—and then forsook it. From 1937 to 1945 it was once more on the side of the national revolution; and then in 1945, sections of it deserted once more. After the victory of the Chinese people in 1949, sections of the national bourgeoisie came back to the fold and played a positive role in building the new China.

No one would claim, for one moment, that the African bourgeoisie is analogous to that which existed in China. Even in Africa there is a considerable difference between the bourgeoisie that exists in Gambia —with less than half a million people—and that of Nigeria, with a population of some 50 million and far greater possibilities for the

[1] V. I. Lenin: "Report of the Commission on the National and Colonial Question". *Collected Works*, Vol. 31, p. 242.

growth of a relatively strong bourgeoisie. It is correct to draw attention, as Fanon and Ledda have done, to the exceptionally weak and dependent character of the African bourgeoisie, but this factor itself does not justify a complete write-off of the national bourgeoisie in Africa. No matter how weak, how vacillating, how dependent, it has points of conflict with imperialism which can be used to further the national struggle. It is a commonplace of Marxism that revolutionaries should never ignore allies, no matter how weak, how temporary, how unreliable and how downright treacherous they may be. In this respect, despite its obvious weakness, the African bourgeoisie is no exception.

As has been noted earlier, Fanon's view of the path of the African revolution allows no room for an explanation of the progressive changes introduced into Ghana during Nkrumah's presidency or in Uganda under Obote, in Zambia under Kaunda, in Tanzania under Nyerere, and similar developments in some other African countries. Neither does it really explain why the coups took place in Ghana and Uganda (nor why they succeeded, which is another question altogether). Obviously neither in Ghana nor in Uganda were the workers and peasants in power, nor was socialism being built. It is equally obvious that those in power in these two countries were not the old feudal and compradore classes through whom imperialism formerly ruled directly over the territories. Simply to say that they were governments of the petty-bourgeoisie or of sections of the élite is only half an explanation. Clearly pre-coup Ghana and pre-coup Uganda, each in its own way, and the former probably more decisively than the latter, were weakening the old pre-capitalist structure, modernising their countries, building new industry, creating a state sector of the economy, and loosening the grip of imperialism over certain sectors of the economy. In both cases, the government power represented the aspirations of the national bourgeoisie, even though it spoke often about building "Socialism".

The petty-bourgeoisie and educated élite in office is well-placed to evolve into a section of the bourgeoisie.[1] In taking important steps to build up the economy it is paving the way either for a transition to socialism—if the working people prove strong enough to take over power and carry through the changes still more fundamentally—or for the establishment of capitalism. The fact that the African entrepreneur

[1] See, for example, Joan Bellamy: "African Élites—a Study of Ghana", *Marxism Today*, February, 1967, pp. 37–43.

has generally speaking proved too weak (lacking in sufficient capital, technical and managerial skills, qualified and trained workers, etc.) to build large-scale industry has meant that this task devolves on the State; this does not rule out the further growth of indigenous capitalism. After the Meiji restoration in Japan, the State built up modern industries—and this paved the way for their being taken over later by the *zaibatsu* and so making possible the growth of Japanese monopoly capitalism. Africa is not Japan. But the existence of an important State sector of the economy and the creation of State industries by no means rules out the growth of private capitalism, nor the possibility that, at a certain stage, the private sector will take over part or even all of the State-built enterprises. The overthrow of Nkrumah in Ghana, for example, was followed precisely by a partial sell-up of many of the State-owned enterprises, mainly to foreign firms.

In examining the ideas of the New Left one is constantly struck by the thought that the essence of the controversies which their theories on revolutionary strategy and tactics pose for discussion have been repeatedly posed in the past, and just as repeatedly demolished. One should not be so dogmatic as to automatically rule out propositions simply because in the past, in entirely different circumstances, they had been found to be invalid and even dangerous to the advance of the revolution. But on the other hand, one should not totally ignore previous debate in the international revolutionary movement.

The differences expressed by Lenin and N. M. Roy over the *Theses on the National and Colonial Question* in 1920 were very much concerned with this question of the national bourgeoisie. Roy tended to see only its negative side, and wanted to pose the question of organising the workers and peasants as against that of assisting the bourgeois democratic revolution. In his *Memoirs*, Roy explains:

> I pointed out that the bourgeoisie, even in the most advanced colonial countries, like India, as a class, was not economically and culturally differentiated from the feudal social order: therefore the nationalist movement was ideologically reactionary in the sense that their triumph would not necessarily mean a bourgeois democratic revolution.[1]

In his own draft theses, which he prepared for the Communist International Congress, Roy went so far as to argue:

> ... in the colonies we have two contradictory forces; they cannot develop together. To support the colonial bourgeois democratic

[1] N. M. Roy: *Memoirs*, Bombay, 1964, p. 379.

movements would amount to helping the growth of the national spirit which will surely obstruct the awakening of class consciousness in the masses; whereas to encourage and support the revolutionary mass action through the medium of a communist party of the proletarians will bring the real revolutionary forces to action which will not only overthrow the foreign imperialism, but lead progressively to the development of Soviet power, thus preventing the rise of a native capitalism in place of the vanquished foreign capitalism, to further oppress and exploit the people.

On Lenin's advice, the whole of this section, Thesis No. 10, was deleted in the final version of Roy's theses.

On the basis of his view, Roy argued in the Commission against item 5 in Thesis No. 11 of Lenin's draft in which Lenin stressed the need to support the bourgeois democratic liberation movement. Roy, in fact, wanted this point deleted, and according to the Minutes argued that the Communist Party of India "must concern itself only with organising the broad masses to fight for their class interests".[1]

Lenin did not entirely reject Roy's view. He saw that there was a positive element in the latter's argument, namely that there was a dangerous negative side to the role of the national bourgeoisie which should not be ignored. For this reason Lenin made his own Theses more specific by amending his item 5, Thesis No. 11. The term "bourgeois democratic" movement was replaced by the term "national revolutionary" movement, Lenin explaining that this was done in order to make a distinction between the reformist and revolutionary trends. "The significance of this change", noted Lenin, "is that we, as communists, should and will support bourgeois liberation movements in the colonies only when they are genuinely revolutionary, and when their exponents do not hinder our work of educating and organising the peasantry and the broad mass of the exploited in a revolutionary spirit."

Roy's sectarian position, however, did not end there. Nor did his viewpoint disappear. There is more than a trace of it in the Thesis adopted in 1928 by the Sixth World Congress of the Communist International, on *The Revolutionary Movement in the Colonies and Semi-colonies*. Commenting on this thesis and its treatment of the role of the national bourgeoisie, Kuusinen commented "There was a tinge of sectarianism in that evaluation at the time the theses in question were

[1] See in particular G. Adhikari's interesting account: "Lenin on Roy's Supplementary Colonial Theses", *Marxist Miscellany*, No. 1, January, 1970 (New Delhi).

being formulated".[1] Kuusinen went on to point out that the consequence of underestimating the revolutionary potential of the national bourgeoisie resulted in a tendency to ignore the obvious fact that the liberation struggle was not just a movement for social liberation but for national liberation, too. Forgetting this fact could, and sometimes did, lead to the advanced revolutionary forces becoming isolated from other democratic forces of the nation and so weakening the revolution.

It would be dangerous to ignore these lessons. Lenin's arguments in 1920 still hold good today, notwithstanding the fact that the national bourgeoisie in Africa tends to be very weak. Prior to 1945 the national bourgeoisie in Vietnam was also extremely weak. In fact, Le Duan once noted that it was so weak that even if one had pooled together all the capital of the national bourgeoisie it would be insufficient to construct a single medium size modern factory. Even so, the Vietnam Workers' Party took the road of the national alliance of forces, including the national bourgeoisie; and it has been this concept that has enabled it to unite the overwhelming majority of the Vietnamese people and so withstand the powerful forces of US imperialism.

Any attempt to skip stages, to reject possible allies, even temporary and unstable ones, and to seek a more direct route based on the concept of a more limited alliance, formed primarily of workers and peasants, can prove disastrous. The lure of the short route, as the tragedy of Indonesia has shown, can lead to catastrophe—and so make the route longer in the end. By his attempt to write off completely the national bourgeoisie Fanon, and those who echo him, are feeding this dangerous trend.

No one should have illusions about the national bourgeoisie. It may be an *oppressed* bourgeoisie, but it is still a bourgeoisie. And as long as it plays a leading role in the African revolution it will prevent the transition to socialism. But if it is weak, so is the African working class which, in almost every African territory, has been unable so far to establish its own party, based on Marxism. This serves to underline the fact that Africa's road to socialism will not be easy or short. Enthusiasm for the socialist future should not be allowed to dim one's view of the stage one has reached, nor of the tremendous obstacles that have to be overcome. The economic, social and cultural backwardness of Africa is itself a powerful argument for the revolutionary forces to utilise every potential for change, and to make use of every possible contradiction between the national bourgeoisie and the imperialists.

[1] O. W. Kuusinen: *Selected Works*, Moscow, 1966, p. 509.

LIVING STANDARDS OF AFRICAN WORKERS

Decisive for Fanon's whole argument is his characterisation of the role of the African working class. One cannot avoid noting here that after the African capitalist class, for which Fanon has nothing but the most intense detestation and contempt which he also extends to the bureaucratic and intellectual hangers-on of the African capitalists, his greatest hostility is reserved for the African working class. He hardly has a single good word to say for it. On its martyrdom and sacrifices in the struggle for independence he remains absolutely silent. His dislike of the workers, his contempt for them, his fear of them, is thinly concealed. Since, as we shall see, his allegations against the African workers are nowhere borne out by the actual facts, one can only pose the question as to why Fanon is so angrily committed against them. It could be, of course, simply a question of lack of information. However, one cannot but feel and suspect that, despite his ignorance of the struggles and conditions of the African working class, it is not lack of information that has led him to his conclusions. It is rather, as Imré Marton[1] has wisely pointed out, a natural consequence of his basic petty-bourgeois attitude to the African revolution and its future. Fanon, in short, sees the working class as the rival of the petty-bourgeoisie of town and country on whom he relies to construct his new ideal Africa.

But let us first examine to what extent his views on the African working class are justified.

Fanon's attempt to set peasant against worker rests on the grounds of the latter's better material standards, which are alleged to turn him into a pampered, privileged and corrupt egoist who has a stake in the status quo and who therefore plays a conservative role in society. Fanon is not the only one to claim a conflict of interest between African workers and peasants. Leopold Senghor, President of Senegal, and, ironically enough, himself a typical example of the Westernised African leader whom Fanon has so sharply attacked for his attachment to imperialism, has been a particular advocate of this point of view. Arguing that the wages of workers are some twenty times the average income of the peasants, "who constitute more than 90 per cent of the population", Senghor has declared against wage increases, suggesting that "It could not serve the public interest to increase the

[1] Imré Marton: op. cit.

disproportion between the living standards of the classes now in process of formation."[1]

This argument entirely fails to take account of the peculiar class structure of Africa where, during the colonial period in which Fanon pretends the workers enjoyed a special luxury, the overwhelming majority of workers were casual, unskilled migrant labourers or seasonal workers in agriculture. For this absolute majority pay and conditions were abysmal. Elsewhere I have examined this in considerable detail.[2] Suffice it to mention that figures cited in my earlier work show that the minimum *daily* pay for such workers varied from between one shilling to under five shillings, depending on the country. Under colonial conditions the minimum tended to become the basic wage. In fact, the entire wage structure of African workers in the colonial epoch was built on the foundation of the basic minimum. Very often, too, the worker received even less than the miserable minimum. A further fact to bear in mind is that in many countries the basic minimum was calculated on what was known as a "Poverty Datum Line", a limit determined by what was assessed as being sufficient to maintain the absolute minimum standard of living for a single male worker, with no margin left for his wife or children.

The *Report of the Committee on African Wages* (commonly known as the Carpenter Report), which was issued by the colonial Government of Kenya in 1954, stated that "the minimum wage has become very much a *real* wage" which was acting "like a magnet to hold down wages". It added that it could find few witnesses prepared to say that the current minimum wage was "adequate to cover the cost of living of a single man living under urban conditions. Many, on the other hand, including witnesses with some claim to 'expert' knowledge, have had no hesitation in condemning it as being definitely inadequate."

The 1957 Minimum Wage Order for Nyasaland stated quite bluntly that the wage proposed in the Order "does not take into account a worker's family responsibilities". In the same way, the Plewman report on Salisbury, Southern Rhodesia (1958), pointed out that "it is always the single adult labourer who provides the foundation of the wages structure". A study on "Inter-racial Wage Structure in Africa", published in the International Labour Review, July, 1958, considered that the official aim of establishing a minimum wage sufficient to main-

---

[1] Report to the Constitutive Congress of the PFA, July 1, 1959.
[2] Jack Woddis: *Africa, The Roots of Revolt*, London, 1960 (especially Chapter 7, pp. 183 et sea.).

tain the "purchasing power of the lowest-paid workers at least equal to the cost of a minimum standard of living, at or above the subsistence level" has not always been achieved. It adds that the minimum rates had been fixed at a level sufficient to maintain the minimum standard of a single worker, and would not meet the cost of supporting a family.

The *Report of the Territorial Minimum Wages Board* for Tanganyika, 1962, prepared on the eve of Tanganyika gaining independence, revealed only too clearly how low the minimum wage had been, and the limited basis on which it had been calculated. "It is quite clear", it stated, "that at the existing lower wage levels, without additional supplementations, at least in urban centres, families with children cannot possibly escape malnutrition at whatever food scale is regarded as the necessary minimum." Referring to a memorandum submitted to the Board by the Kivukoni College, and dealing, among other things, with workers' indebtedness, the Report sums up: "In the cases explained none of the workers were receiving a sufficient income to support themselves with absolute necessities and a healthy diet, let alone support a family, and in practically every case investigated workers were supporting fully or partly other people in addition to their own wives and children. Their debts were incurred overwhelmingly to pay for necessities."

In the ILO's *African Labour Survey, 1958* (which covered the whole of Africa apart from North Africa), it is stated that the majority of wage earners work at "rates which do not cover even the barest necessities of life for a family". In its *Labour Survey of North Africa, 1960*, it stresses that "large sectors of the population, among which must be included the majority of wage earners, are living at levels which are very near to the minimum level of existence". It added that "Statistically at least, many seem condemned to exist in conditions which do not even attain that level."

In the Belgian Congo and in Ruanda-Urundi, the minimum wage regulations of 1954 and 1955 laid down that the minimum wage had to be calculated on the basis of a single man just starting his first job. Information submitted by the Portuguese Government to the Inter-African Labour Conference held in Lusaka in 1957 likewise stated that "the basis of the minimum wage does not include the worker's family responsibilities". In the French colonies, too, the minimum wage scales were based on a *minimum vital* calculated on the minimum subsistence needs of a single, childless, unskilled male. The ILO *African Labour Survey, 1958* pointed out: "In fact, the general minimum wages for all occupations . . . have not always quite corresponded to minimum subsistence wages but have tended rather to reach that level by stages."

That the minimum wage was based on the subsistence requirements of a single adult (usually unskilled) male was itself a limiting enough factor; but when one examines the basis on which these requirements were calculated, then the terribly low wage levels to which the African worker was bound by official calculation becomes still more evident.

In an appendix to the Carpenter Report on wages in Kenya, Dr. E. M. Case explains the dietary basis on which the minimum wage was drawn up:

> Foodstuffs, the constitutents of a diet, must discharge three primary and essential functions. Firstly, they must provide energy both for the maintenance of life on a basal level and for the performance of activities superimposed upon this; secondly, they must furnish material for growth, for perpetual replacement and repair of tissues, and for reproduction. Thirdly, they must contribute the substances that are implicated in the control and regulation of the innumerable bodily processes, physical and chemical, that constitute life.

The ideas contained in this paragraph recall those of Marx when he explained that a minimum wage amounted to "the cost of the existence and reproduction of the worker". Or, to put it in another way, the minimum wage represents the cost of keeping a worker alive, enabling him to maintain his physical and mental capacities and his ability to work, and permitting him to reproduce more of his own species, that is future workers, who will eventually replace him.

Under African conditions, however, with a plentiful supply of cheap, unskilled migrant labour, the minimum wage imposed under colonialism did not meet even these minimum requirements, for it did not allow for the reproduction of the worker, but provided solely for the continued existence of himself, and that only on the lowest possible level of subsistence. Thus, in colonial Africa, the minimum wage, even at the level fixed by the authorities, tended to be still lower than what a minimum wage, scientifically speaking, is supposed to represent.

Rhodesia provides perhaps the most clear-cut example of the methods used to calculate minimum wages for African workers. In essence, the approach made in Rhodesia and still being applied, underlay the method employed in all colonial Africa.

In the capital, Salisbury, Dr. D. Bettison elaborated a "Poverty Datum Line" for Africans living in the municipal area of the town and its surroundings. The purposes of this PDL, as it is called for short, was to calculate the very lowest basis on which a single adult male could *exist*—and nothing more. It was worked out on a weighting system which allowed for food, clothing, fuel and light, cleaning materials, transport to and from work, rent and taxation. According to Professor E. Batson (*The Poverty Line in Salisbury*), the Bettison PDL assumed that "as far as food, clothing, fuel, lighting, and cleaning materials are concerned . . . purchases are made in the cheapest market open to ordinary consumers."

In other words, as the *Report of the Urban Affairs Commission, 1958,* for Salisbury pointed out, the PDL "is simply a statistical calculation of what is required in the way of income to enable the basic and elementary needs of individuals to be met. It takes into account only the barest essentials of food, clothing, and shelter and includes no items which are not necessary for the maintenance of life, not even what are sometimes described as conventional necessities."

Professor Batson has commented that "such a standard is perhaps more remarkable for what it omits than for what it includes. It does not allow a penny for amusement, for sport, for medicine, for education, for saving, for hire purchase, for holidays, for odd bus rides, for newspapers, stationery, tobacco, sweets, hobbies, gifts, pocket money, or comforts or luxuries of any kind. It does not allow a penny for replacements of blankets, furniture or crockery. It is not a 'human' standard of living. It thus admirably fulfils its purpose of stating the barest minimum upon which subsistence and health can theoretically be achieved."

Thus, what was openly admitted to be a sub-human standard of living was regarded by the colonial authorities as "admirably" fulfilling its purpose. The purpose therefore stands revealed as nothing less than the deliberate pinning down of African wages to the very lowest level of subsistence—and not a penny more. Even this does not depict the worst, for the *Report of the Urban Affairs Commission* admitted that many workers received wages which did not reach even the PDL. Broadly speaking, the basis on which the wages of African workers were fixed throughout the colonial territories was rather similar to that prevailing in Southern Rhodesia. And it was wage levels such as these which, in Fanon's view, made the African proletariat the "most favoured", most "pampered" and "privileged", the "bourgeois stratum" of African colonial society. As ridiculous as the assertion may appear when set beside the real facts, it has to be admitted that too many students of African affairs, including some of the Left, have fallen for this unscientific guff

Official reports on colonial Africa in the 1950's, that is, on the eve of independence, underlined the appalling poverty of the African workers, and the incredible conditions they suffered. In Leopoldville (now Kinshasa), for example, "many children know hunger very early".[1] At the age of six an African child in colonial Leopoldville was reckoned to have learned to fast for twenty-four hours. "Hunger-training" was common among the families of poor workers. The proportion of undernourished children was estimated to be about half.

Under colonialism the African worker enjoyed practically no social security. This was especially so in the British colonies. There was no unemployment pay, no sick pay, no pension, no free education or hospitalisation.

"The average urban African", wrote Gussman, "is unhealthy, badly housed, uneducated, and he lacks any security in town even if he happens to have been born there."[2]

Describing housing in Mombasa, Kenya, in 1953, the *Report of the Municipal African Affairs Officer*, p. 21 (an unpublished report), stated that "in the course of a recent police investigation at night no fewer than sixty persons were found sleeping in one temporary single-storeyed house". In Dar-es-Salaam, in Tanganyika, it was calculated "that the average number of persons living in a room 16 feet by 20 feet is eight, and that in some rooms it is as much as twelve".[3]

The same report stated that "The wages of the majority of African workers are too low to enable them to obtain accommodation which is adequate by any standard. . . . The high cost of accommodation relative to wages is, in itself, a cause of overcrowding, because accommodation is shared in order to lighten the cost. This, together with the high cost of food in towns, makes family life impossible for the majority" (pp. 209-10).

The UNESCO report cited above shows that similar appalling conditions existed throughout colonial Africa. It sums up the conditions of urban Africans in these terms:

> . . . they are characterised by a high incidence of poverty, malnutrition and disease, and live in overcrowded conditions . . . (p. 211).

A United Kingdom report submitted to the Inter-African Labour Institute of the Commission for Technical Co-operation in Africa

[1] *Social Implication of Industrialisation and Urbanisation in Africa South of the Sahara*, prepared for UNESCO by the Africa Institute, 1956.
[2] B. Gussman: "Industrial Efficiency and the Urban African", *Africa*, April, 1953, xxiii, No. 2, p. 141.
[3] *East Africa Royal Commission Report, 1953-1955*, Cmd. 9475, 1955, p. 211.

South of the Sahara for the *Survey on the Human Factors of Productivity in Africa*, in 1956, stated: "All the information available suggests that the African worker's basic handicap is physical, *and arises from malnutrition*." Dr. Josué de Castro, describing Africa as "beyond question one of the darkest spots on the world's map of malnutrition and hunger", makes the significant point that it is the African wage workers (as distinct from "the traditional society organised in family groups, living by primitive agriculture, stock raising, hunting and fishing"), who "represent the lowest nutritional level of the continent *and perhaps, according to FAO experts, 'the lowest in the world'*."[1]

The war in Nigeria has brought home to millions of people outside Africa that there is such a disease as Kwashiorkor, or malignant malnutrition. The impression has been created that this disease has been caused by the war. In fact, it was already widespread in colonial Africa and was regarded by nutritional experts as a prime cause of African labour fatigue, since children who were fortunate to survive the disease carried its scars for the rest of their lives.[2]

But in their adult lives, too, African workers suffer from malnutrition due to their poverty. Dr. H. C. Trowell has drawn attention to the limited amount of food consumed by African workers in Kenya in the 1940's, many leaving home without food in the morning, doing without food midday, and only eating once in the day, late at night.

> Visits to the Railway location early in the day [he wrote], confirmed the statements made by many men that little food is usually taken before leaving home in the morning, and that in the middle of the day some labourers who receive only a low wage eat nothing. For long periods of the day some men are unable to satisfy hunger.[3]

Enquiries made at the houses of 153 African railwaymen in Kenya, in the Malongeni location, revealed that not even 25 per cent of the men had a full midday meal, and that many not only went without a midday meal but had only a cup of tea at 4.30 p.m. and waited until as late as 8.30 p.m. for their one daily proper meal.

J. Vincent, describing the plight of the Ivory Coast urban worker, wrote:

> In the last days of the month[4] he often takes an empty stomach to work. When his wage is spent, he eats very little and his output

---

[1] Josué de Castro: *Geography of Hunger*, London, 1952, p. 192.
[2] Jack Woddis: *Africa, The Roots of Revolt*, London, 1960, pp. 167–8.
[3] *African Labour Efficiency Survey*, ed. by C. H. Northcott, London, 1949, p. 87.
[4] African wages are normally paid monthly.

curve descends more steeply as the last pay-day recedes into the past.[1]

So much for Fanon's incredible claim that the African workers under colonialism were the "most pampered and privileged", and constituted a "bourgeois" fraction of the colonised people. It has been necessary to go into some considerable detail in order to counter this mischievous assertion.[2] All the available facts and statistics, which Fanon either ignored or of which he was not even aware (and if it was the latter, it was totally irresponsible for him to make such sweeping statements without even bothering to find out what were the real facts) completely refute Fanon's claim. Nearly all official and semi-official reports are compelled to admit that under colonial rule the African worker, far from being "pampered", had to put up with deplorable conditions. Low paid, ill-clad, ill-housed, ill-fed, under-nourished, diseased—this was too often the condition of the typical African worker.

Not only is Fanon's claim inaccurate in absolute terms, as we have seen, but it contains another fallacy, for he failed to take account either of the heavy expenses which fell to the lot of the urban worker (and still do) or of the family responsibilities arising both from the migrant labour system and from the traditional extended family relationship in Africa.

Submissions made by the Joint Action Council of the trade unions in Nigeria, prior to the 1964 general strike, calculated that a worker in Lagos had to pay £4 a month for rent, £1. 10s. for transport, and £1. 10s. for clothing—a total of £7 a month out of a wage of £9. 2s. leaving only 42s. for food for 30 days, let alone other items. No wonder the Morgan Commission found that "most workers are living under conditions of penury".[3]

Julius Nyerere, President of Tanzania, has rightly said: "We talk easily about 150 shillings a month as a wage, as if by raising the minimum to this level we have given a worker sufficient to keep himself and his family decently. Let us pause and think for a moment exactly what this means. Of his 150 shillings, a worker will probably have to

[1] *Brief Study of the African Worker's Output in the Ivory Coast*, École Nationale de la France d'Outre-Mer.

[2] See the author's *Africa, The Roots of Revolt*, London, 1960, and *Africa, The Lion Awakes*, London, 1961, for a fuller treatment of the wages, conditions and struggles of the African wage workers.

[3] *Report of the Commission on the Review of Wages, Salary and Conditions of Service of the Junior Employees of the Governments of the Federation and in Private Establishments, 1963–64*, Federal Ministry of Information, Lagos, 1964, para. 50.

pay about 40 shillings in order to rent one room in Kariakoo or Magomeni. He therefore has about 110 shillings a month from which to keep his family in food and clothes, to pay school fees, to buy water, heat and light, and all the other things essential to existence in an urban society. In other words, for all these things the worker has about 30 shillings a week—or less than many of us spend at a restaurant in one evening".[1]

In any case, Fanon's posing of the worker's wage against the income of the peasant fails to take account of the migrant character of much African labour, and of the close relationship that exists between the working class and the peasantry, with the worker's family often left behind in the countryside and partly dependent on the small savings from the worker's wage, since it is very difficult to exist solely on a peasant income. The poor peasant is usually driven out to be a wage worker by his very poverty as a peasant—and it is his hope that, as a wage worker, he will be able to earn sufficient to maintain not only himself in the urban area but also to provide something for his family left behind in the countryside. To limit the worker's wage to an absolute minimum, therefore, hurts the peasantry, which relies on a proportion of the worker's wage coming to the village.

This much is indicated in the ILO African Advisory Committee report on Methods and Principles of Wage Regulations (Tananarive, April, 1962): "To the extent that the same people are at different times of the year, or in different years, subsistence farmers and wage labourers, higher wages may benefit them or their families. . . ."

The same point is made by Yudelman who writes:

Cash incomes earned in traditional agriculture are low, but the combination of free land and the security provided through kin groups enable families to maintain themselves at low cost by producing subsistence crops. On the other hand, average returns to African labour in the wage sector are low in relation to the cost of maintaining a family at places of employment.[2]

He draws the conclusion that under these conditions the real income of a whole family remains low if all its members stay in the countryside and work their land—and it remains low if they all move into the wage sector. The only way to surmount this difficulty, even partially, is to divide the family between subsistence agriculture and wage employment.

---

[1] *Vigilance Africa:* November 4, 1964.   [2] Yudelman: op. cit., p. 131.

If the family splits and the male works for wages, while the other members of the family maintain themselves in rent-free housing by producing subsistence crops, total family incomes are higher than if the family remained together.[1]

These observations regarding the situation in Southern Rhodesia are generally true for most of Africa.

This is borne out by the findings provided by T. M. Yesufu in Nigeria:

> The very close family and village ties are shown . . . by the amount of money spent for the sustenance, education, or some other form of assistance to the workers' relations other than their immediate family of wives and children. At the Railway workshops, at the African Timber and Plywood sawmills, 80 per cent and 90 per cent of the workers, respectively, made regular remittance to their parents, brothers and sisters, or maintained within their households some of these or other relatives. The workers spent an average of 9 per cent (Railways) and 12 per cent (African Timber and Plywood) of their wages on such relations although the large number of the latter who lived with the workers often made it a very difficult matter to make a distinction.[2]

Interestingly enough, it is not only the radical Fanon who argues that the workers are the privileged class in Africa. The same argument has been repeated by a number of economists and commentators whose support for the establishment is obvious, and whose arguments have been put forward as a justification for holding back wage advances by the workers.[3]

A recent mimeographed study on wage problems in West Africa has indicated that in actual fact "the pattern in West Africa since independence has been one of governments' restraining changes in money-wages, and allowing real wages to fall, sometimes steeply and usually for long periods of time, in face of rising prices".[4] Rimmer also draws attention to the extent to which the African wage earner

[1] Yudelman: op. cit., p. 131.

[2] Dr. T. M. Yesufu: *An Introduction to Industrial Relations in Nigeria*, Oxford, 1962 pp. 120–1.

[3] See, for example, W. Arthur Lewis (*Reflections on Nigeria's Economic Growth*, Development Centre of the OECD, Paris, 1967, p. 42); Peter Kilby (*Industrialisation in an Open Economy: Nigeria, 1945–66*, London, 1969, p. 301); and Elliot J. Berg ("Major issues of wage policy in Africa", in *Industrial Relations and Economic Development*, ed. by A. M Ross, London, 1966, p. 189).

[4] Douglas Rimmer: *Wage Politics in West Africa*, Occasional Paper, No. 12, February 1970, Birmingham University, Faculty of Commerce and Social Science.

becomes the provider for all his poor or unemployed kinsmen, both in the form of long-term hospitality and in remittances of money and goods. Gutkind cites the case of a Lagos carpenter who complains "almost every month I have somebody come to me for help. I do not earn enough money to help all my relatives and friends, and what I do earn does not help me a great deal. The harder I work the more my friends demand money from me."[1]

A study of 188 permanent industrial workers in Dakar in 1965, carried out by Pfefferman, showed that no less than 1,802 persons were maintained at the expense of the 188 wage earners. Nearly a half of those so maintained were distant relatives rather than direct members of the family. The average number supported by each wage earner was 9·6, and there were some cases where the wage earner was maintaining more than twenty people on his single wage. Perhaps even more significant in Pfefferman's sample, the per capita income in the wage-earner's household came to only 2,075 CFA francs per month—*which was approximately the same as the then current average monthly per capita income in the groundnut area of rural Senegal*, according to the figures given by Claude Adam and cited by Pfefferman.

This may be an exceptional sample, but the general pattern revealed here is common throughout Africa. Rimmer remarks, with justification, "once the possibility is admitted of the ratio of dependents to income-earners being generally higher in wage-earning communities than in rural communities, the existence of a net differential in favour of wage-employment no longer necessarily implies a higher average standard of living in wage-earning communities".[2] As he wryly adds, the wage-earners are only aristocrats in the sense of being an "aristocracy of *noblesse oblige*, not of high living".

Bakary Djibo, in dealing with the question of relations between workers and peasants, has commented: "The raising of the minimum wage closely affects the peasants, firstly because peasant youth work during the slack season as wage labourers, and also because in the town workers continue to give material support to their parents in the countryside. Moreover, the workers' trade unions have no intention of obtaining gains which would worsen the conditions of the peasants."[3] Bakary Djibo makes the interesting point that following on the victory of the workers in the French colonies in Africa in securing the enactment

[1] P. C. W. Gutkind: "African responses to urban wage employment", *International Labour Review*, Vol. 97, 1968, pp. 151–2.
[2] Douglas Rimmer: op. cit., p. 57.
[3] *World Trade Union Movement*, No. 16, August, 1953, p. 25.

of the Labour Code in December, 1952, which gave better wages and conditions to the workers, the colonialists "undertook a campaign of lies designed to make people believe that the improvement of the workers' living conditions would necessarily increase the poverty of the agricultural workers".

In making his comparison between peasants and workers in Africa, Fanon forgets many things. The peasant grows his own food; the worker, especially in the town, has to pay for it at relatively very high prices. The peasant builds his own hut; the worker has to pay a relatively high rental.[1] The peasant working and living on his own plot of land has no fares; the worker often has quite high bus fares to and from work. All this is in addition to the family responsibilities we have already noted.

The United Nations Report on the World Social Situation in 1963, referring to the ILO report on "Employment and training problems connected with urbanisation in Africa", states that this latter report indicates that despite the fact that average earnings of wage labourers in towns are higher than those of rural workers, "the advantage is offset by the fact that the urban worker can only draw on the resources of the subsistence economy to a very slight extent while . . . he may be burdened in the town by the support of his family as well as by contributions to needy relations elsewhere."

The extent to which the peasants *rely* on the wages of African workers is well demonstrated by the figures provided by the United Nations and cited by Professor Potekhin: 95 per cent of the incomes of peasants in Northern Rhodesia were earnings from migrant workers, in Southern Rhodesia the figure was 78 per cent, in Kenya 73 per cent, in the Belgian Congo 55 per cent.[2]

A Salisbury report for 1961 states ". . . there can be little doubt that wage earnings now form a major part, if not the bulk, of the income of rural based families."[3]

In the light of these facts one cannot but see that Fanon's approach to this question is not only inaccurate and confused: it also carries with it implications that are positively harmful to the building of a close political alliance between the workers and the mass of peasants. Such an alliance is essential to the struggle for independence and, still more,

[1] "An important factor in reducing real incomes in the wage economy is the high cost of family housing" (Yudelman, op. cit., p. 266). Yudelman quotes a number of sources to back this statement.
[2] I. I. Potekhin, op. cit., p. 59. The figures are taken from *Enlargement of the Exchange Economy in Tropical Africa*, United Nations, 1954.
[3] *Report of the Mangwende Reserve Commission of Inquiry, 1961*, Salisbury, 1961, p. 30.

to complete the aim of national liberation and introduce fundamental social and economic changes that will really provide a better life both to workers and peasants.

No one would deny that, under the colonial system, there were sections of workers who enjoyed a more favourable standard than most. This was true of some strata of Government employees and of that minority of workers who were able to acquire qualifications as skilled workers. But only a limited number were so privileged. In the conditions of colonialism, the overwhelming majority of African workers remained unskilled, casual, migrant low-paid labourers who could in no sense be regarded as "pampered". Even where they were able to secure some improvement in their wages and conditions this was only by dint of the most intense strike struggles in which workers were sometimes shot, often arrested and sent to jail, usually in conflicts occasioned by demands for the merest increase of a few pence a day.[1]

There is one final point on this question of the worker's wages which Fanon ignores. We have already noted that keeping wages low can harm the income of the whole family since most of its members are so often left behind to work the land. But who would really benefit if wages of African workers are kept down? The main exploiters of African labour, despite the large sector of government employment, remain the foreign monopolies—especially the big mining and plantation companies; and it is they, not the peasants, who would be the main beneficiaries of any tendency to freeze African wages.

Dudley Jackson,[2] for example, in echoing Fanon's argument about the relatively high-paid worker and the low-paid peasant, has suggested that wage levels in Botswana should be brought down to a level in accordance with the standard of living of the majority of the population, that is "those in the rural areas". The real purpose of the proposal becomes clear when he argues that a severe cut in wages by the Government would then set a pattern of lower wages which could be followed by the mining companies which are poised for considerable development in Botswana. He avoids mentioning the increased benefits which this would mean for the mining companies. Nor is the proposal for lower wages, allegedly put forward to assist the economy of Botswana, accompanied by any suggestion of asking the mining companies to pay out in taxes at least part of the increased profits which the lower wages would produce.

[1] See Jack Woddis: *Africa, The Lion Awakes*, London, 1961 (especially pp. 85–115).
[2] Dudley Jackson: "Income Differentials and Unbalanced Planning—the Case of Botswana", *The Journal of Modern African Studies*, Vol. 8, No. 4, 1970.

A recent study by Weeks[1] points up a similar conclusion. Referring to the arguments of Kilby, W. A. Lewis, Elliot J. Berg and others who allege that "organised labour is already a highly privileged minority", Weeks asserts that "this judgment . . . has achieved the status of a prevailing orthodoxy" which has become the basis for a "growing assault on the role of trade unions in less developed countries, to the extent of providing a justification for undermining their organisational strength."

Weeks attacks in particular the attempt by such writers to utilise rural incomes as a criterion for urging wage restraint. Such a restraint, he points out, would naturally be to the benefit, theoretically speaking, of the non-wage earning sections—peasant cultivators, urban self-employed and employers. In practice, however, "peasant cultivators and the urban self-employed in general lack the political power to take what wage-earners are denied." That leaves the employers who, as Weeks logically points out, would be the only beneficiaries of restraining the wages of the workers.[2] Thus Fanon's argument about the "privileged" workers as compared with the peasants easily lends itself for use by those who really have no interest in helping the peasants but only in establishing a new "orthodoxy", which is then pressed into service in the interests of the employers.

Fanon, therefore, and those who consciously or otherwise are influenced by his ideas, are doing no service to the anti-imperialist struggle when they put forward theories about the "privileged" workers.

DID THE AFRICAN WORKERS PARTICIPATE IN THE NATIONAL STRUGGLE?

If Fanon was irresponsible in creating his myth about the bourgeoisi-fied African worker, he was no less irresponsible in attempting to invent the legend of the consequent innate conservatism and limited participation of the African workers in the struggle for national libera-tion. To Fanon the African peasant is the "sole revolutionary force",

[1] John F. Weeks: "The Problem of Wage Policy in Developing Countries with Special Reference to Africa", *The Economic Bulletin of Ghana*, Vol. 1, No. 1, 1971, pp. 31–44.
[2] British trade unionists will be familiar with this kind of argument since they have had to contend with it in British terms, having been told *ad nauseum* that they should forego wage increases in order to help the lower paid. Car workers at Fords or BMC know only too well that if they restrain their wage demands it will not be the lower paid dustmen or nurses who will benefit, but only the car manufacturers who have no intention of handing over the extra profit they thus earn to help dustmen or nurses or any other lower paid sections.

the worker "has everything to lose" from ending colonialism. The peasant is self-sacrificing; the worker is selfish.

Once again the facts refute Fanon. In country after country the workers acted as pace makers of the national liberation struggle. They staged major confrontations with imperialism, organised strike struggles most of which were fought with great tenacity and courage, sacrificed in prison and in front of the bullets of the imperialist troops, and helped to awaken the entire nation. General strikes became manifestations of national struggle and stirred millions into an awareness of the total system of colonial oppression and discrimination, of the necessity to fight against it, and of the possibility of defeating it. Their determined actions inspired the whole people and provided them with rich experiences. "They were the spark which set fire to the national liberation struggle."[1]

The African workers, whom Fanon accuses of selfishness, have been a class martyred by colonialism. Hundreds of them were killed, and thousands wounded and imprisoned over several decades of proletarian and national struggles.

In their conflicts with the colonial authorities the workers and their unions found it necessary to become involved in politics. This necessity grew out of their daily experiences. They could not but be aware that their low wages, poverty and limited rights sprang from the very soil of the colonial system under which they were compelled to live. Minimum wage laws, race discrimination, pass laws and restrictions on residing in urban areas, poll tax and forced labour, the shortage of educational facilities, the lack of industrialisation and mechanisation, the absence of sick pay, unemployment benefit and retirement pensions, the prevalence of bad housing and ill health, the reservation of the best land for European occupation, the hundred-and-one laws restricting the rights of Africans in their own country—all these conditions derived from the policies and actions of governments which represented the colonial power.

In their daily struggle against the effects of colonial rule the workers found themselves faced with the necessity to destroy the very roots of their oppression—and that involved the abolition of the colonial system. To maintain their domination over the African people the colonial authorities had established forms of government which

---

[1] Heinz Deutschland: *Trailblazers: Struggles and Organisations of African Workers Before 1945*, Berlin, 1970, p. 161. This study is a mine of information on the workers' struggles against colonialism in Africa.

denied the people political rights, used legal or extra-legal methods to suppress or curb the trade unions, and clamped down a system of arbitrary rule and exploitation which ate into every political, social, economic and cultural facet of the people's lives. The very lack of political rights only served to bring home to the African workers the relation of politics to their own miserable conditions of life and labour.

Every day this connection was driven home. The very absence of big African companies, of African-owned mines or other large enterprises —a natural consequence of the colonial system—turned the African workers in an anti-colonial direction. It was the European firms which paid them low wages and resisted the workers' claims for higher pay. It was the European government officials and their special "trade union advisers" who generally backed up the employers. All the laws which kept their wages low and limited their trade union activity, which made them pay poll taxes or carry passes, were laws enacted by the European colonial power. If, as a last resort, the workers went on strike to defend their union or to improve their standard of living, it was the European-owned newspapers which condemned them; the poor African papers which stood up in their defence constantly ran the danger of being closed down by the European authorities and their editors arrested for "libel" or "sedition". It was European officers who gave the orders to armed police or soldiers to fire on strikers or arrest union leaders. European judges passed sentence on those who came up for trial, and European chief warders controlled the prisons.

This experience of the African workers was underlined by Gasim Amin, an Executive Officer of the Sudan Railway Workers' Trade Union, writing in *El Sahara* (August, 14–17, 1953). Workers, he wrote, "must accept one indubitable fact, namely that when they endeavour to achieve some economic gains they are always brought in the Sudan into direct conflict with the political force in power. This happened in July, 1947, when the railway workers decided to walk in procession to the railway headquarters. Instead of being met by the General Manager, they were met by armed police. It also happenened on other occasions. It is therefore clear that if the workers want to achieve higher wages or a reduction of working hours, then they must direct their struggle first and foremost against the political force in power."

Thus the politics of anti-colonialism, of national liberation, sprang from the very soil of African working-class experience under the colonial system. Starvation wages, national humiliation, batons, bullets, prison— this was such a daily reality for the majority of workers that inevitably they came to realise that no fundamental change in their lives, no decisive social and economic advance was possible without political change, and that the essence of that political change had to be national freedom.

If Fanon was unaware of the factors which motivated the thinking and actions of the African workers and which led them to play such a key role in the struggle for national liberation the European authorities were certainly only too conscious of it and of the dangers this represented to the continuance of their rule. They realised that the African working class, if left to determine its own activities, would not limit itself to economic struggle and "non-political" trade unionism, for the essence of the situation was not whether the workers would choose to be political or not but whether they would submit passively to the political reality of the colonial system and take no part in the movement against it, or whether they would consciously embrace the politics of national independence and throw their organised and significant weight into the struggle to end colonialism.

There was, no doubt, a further, if unspoken, thought in the minds of the colonial authorities. The workers and their trade unions would add not only numerical and organisational strength and discipline to the anti-colonial movement; more important, perhaps, from a long-term point of view, they would bring a more radical element into the thinking and activity of the national movement. It was, after all, from the workers' organisations that the demand usually arose for nationalising foreign undertakings. Such a demand, for example, was voiced by Nigeria's tin miners at Jos, by the gold miners of Ghana, and by the copper miners on the Zambian Copper Belt. And despite Fanon's negative and almost uninterested attitude towards the nationalisation of imperialist enterprises in Africa, this is always one of the touchiest points for the foreign monopolies.

In drawing attention to the participation of the labour movement in the struggles for national independence in the different colonies, Dr. Yesufu has made the point that "This is natural enough because the workers are normally the best organised, the best educated, and the most articulate in the countries concerned, and the leadership of both the labour and nationalist movements have, therefore, tended to be closely identified."[1]

Elaborating this point he has written:

The workers constitute the bulk of the educated people in the country and are, therefore, the leaders of public opinion in the

[1] T. M. Yesufu: *An Introduction to Industrial Relations in Nigeria*, London, 1962, p. 137.

villages which they influence by constant visits, through family relations, and through the activities of the tribal organisations. In the towns where the workers are concentrated, it is they who attend the political rallies, shout the hallelujahs, and do the heckling. The wage-earners, therefore, constitute, so to speak, both the barometer and the thermometer of the country's political atmosphere. . . .[1]

Aware of the danger to colonialism stemming from the African wage workers, the authorities did everything they could to limit their struggles and organisation. For the first four decades of the twentieth century they strove to prevent the emergence of trade unions in Africa. When they had to retreat they attempted by propaganda and argument, by legal enactment, by the intervention of "trade union advisers" from Europe, and, when necessary, by direct restrictive and repressive action, to keep the African workers and their unions isolated from political and national movements.[2]

If the African workers were really so "pampered" and "privileged" as Fanon claims, and of so little account in the national liberation struggle, it would hardly have been necessary for the colonial authorities to have expended so much energy in holding the workers down and doing their level best to keep them away from the liberation movement. These efforts by the authorities, which Fanon ignores, caused serious difficulties to the workers and their unions, difficulties which harmed the national movements themselves, and which the unions have, in part, inherited to this very day in most independent African states. But at no time could the bans and pressures of the colonial governments be decisive, for life itself, the constant need and urge of the African workers to end colonialism and to carve out a new life for themselves, repeatedly broke through the barriers.

Moreover, their outstanding national leaders continually helped them to extend their horizons, to see beyond the frontiers of strict trade unionism to the needs of national independence which would give them new possibilities of bringing about economic and social change and advancing their class aims. Thus the relationship between the workers' trade union struggles and the wider fight for national liberation was constantly emphasised by Sékou Touré, Kwame Nkrumah, Albert Luthuli and others. That the more advanced workers understood their role was emphasised by Modibo Keita, former President of Mali,

---

[1] T. M. Yesufu: *An Introduction to Industrial Relations in Nigeria*, p. 148.
[2] For details see: Jack Woddis: *Africa: The Lion Awakes*, op. cit.

when addressing the first congress of the National Union of Workers of Mali, in July, 1963:

> The unions represent the engine of the Revolution in Mali; they are the most reliable guarantee of the socialist choice of the Party and the people.[1]

But it is not simply assertions by different African national leaders nor assessments of various Africanists which refute Fanon as regards the role played by the African working class in the national liberation struggle. It is the facts of those struggles themselves which are the most cogent argument.

Workers' strikes and attempts to set up unions can be noted in Africa quite early on in the twentieth century, and these generally pre-dated the creation of the modern national political organisations.[2] But it was in the post-1945 period that the organised workers of Africa demonstrated their greatest strength and revealed the significance of their role in the national liberation struggle. In territory after territory strike after strike unfolded. Many of them lasted several weeks; a number became general strikes; infrequently they led to sharp clashes with armed police and troops, to widespread arrests and shootings. In many cases the colonial authorities declared a State of Emergency and thus threw the whole territory into a state of political crisis and turmoil. Invariably the workers' actions posed political demands and merged with the wider struggles for national independence.

(a) West Africa

This was clearly so in West Africa. In Nigeria, for example, the actions of the workers, especially against the mineowners and against the powerful British trading firm, the United Africa Company, were undoubtedly a major factor in arousing national feeling. James S. Colman has pointed out[3] that, notwithstanding the relatively small percentage of wage labour in the total population of Nigeria, "the main weight of active nationalist support came from the 100,000-odd clerks, artisans and skilled labourers, especially in mining, transport, government employment and trade". He stresses that "it is not the number of wage labourers or salaried workers but their strategic position in the structure of the economy and administration" which

[1] Gilbert Julis: *L'Action des Masses Populaires au Mali*, Centre d'Études et de Récherches Marxistes, Paris, 1967, p. 22.
[2] For details see Jack Woddis: *Africa: The Lion Awakes*, op. cit.
[3] James S. Colman: *Nigeria: Background to Nationalism*, Los Angeles, 1958, p. 70.

explains their key role in the national movement. In the specific conditions of Nigeria, the actions of miners, railwaymen and United Africa employees were of particular importance in heightening the national feeling of the people as a whole and not merely that of the workers most directly involved in particular industrial actions.

The conflict with the United Africa Company (UAC) had a special significance, since other strata in addition to wage earners had for long been at odds with this giant trading monopoly which exploited peasant producers and ordinary consumers as well as the workers it employed, and had thus become a symbol of British colonial rule. Mr. Coleman writes that the 1945 general strike, in which the UAC employees played an important part, "served as a dramatic opening of a new nationalist era", and that it marked the beginning of a new radical and political feeling even in the feudal north "although few northerners had participated" in the strike.[1] Ananaba, a moderate trade union official of the ICFTU, has also noted the significance of the 1945 general strike, describing it as "one of the most important events in Nigerian labour history", and which, like the strikes of 1949 and 1964, shook "the foundations of the nation",[2] lasting 44 days in Lagos and 52 days in the provinces.

> With the exception of essential services like electricity and the hospitals, the strike hit practically all the technical and industrial establishments of the Government. Even office workers joined in the struggle. Railway and port services were paralysed; telegraph keys and telephones were dead. Never had the Nigerian workers demonstrated such impregnable solidarity. Never had they been more united in opposition to bad faith *and the injustices of colonial administration*.[3] (Author's italics.)

The 1949 general strike and nationwide protest, which followed the shooting of 21 defenceless miners and the wounding of a further 51, at the Enugu coalfields, had an even greater effect on the national movement. Richard L. Sklar has written: "Historians may conclude that the slaying of coal miners by police at Enugu first proved the subjective reality of a Nigerian nation. No previous event ever provoked a manifestation of national consciousness comparable to the indignation generated by this tragedy."[4]

Ananaba has described the Enugu slaying as "perhaps the most

[1] James S. Colman: *Nigeria: Background to Nationalism*, Los Angeles, 1958, p. 259.
[2] Wogu Ananaba: *The Trade Union Movement in Nigeria*, London, 1969, p. 44.
[3] ibid., p. 44.
[4] Richard L. Sklar: *Nigerian Political Parties*, New Jersey, 1963, pp. 76–7.

significant episode in Nigerian labour history".[1] Explaining its effect on the whole nation, he writes: "In terms of losses sustained, the emotion it excited and that grief it created in the public mind, no industrial dispute in Nigeria can be matched with it." The shooting took place on November 18, 1949. So great was the popular revulsion— "The country was outraged"[2]—that at a meeting of the National Emergency Committee of the National Council of Nigeria and the Cameroons on December 8, the slogan was proclaimed of "Self-government for Nigeria Now!"

Throughout the 1950's, too, the strike movement in Nigeria was a major factor in the national struggle, the strike of the 40,000 tin miners at Jos, in 1955, and several railway strikes being of particular importance.

In Ghana, the general strike of 1950 did more than arouse the national movement. It was, in fact, the biggest single action undertaken by any section of the Ghana people, and proved to be decisive in paving the way for the election victory of Kwame Nkrumah and the Convention People's Party in 1951, the achievement of internal self-government and so inevitably to the attainment of an independent Ghana in 1957. Describing the reaction of the workers to the strike call in 1950, Nkrumah wrote in his autobiography: "The response of the people was instantaneous. The political and social revolution of Ghana had started."[3] In a massive display of solidarity, the workers stayed out for ten days. Trains stood immobile. Offices were silent and deserted. The mines were empty. Building work came to a standstill. No ships left or put in to Takoradi harbour.

The Government's response to this surge of working-class unity was to declare a State of Emergency, impose a curfew, and arrest leaders both of the trade unions and of the CPP, including Nkrumah. In acting thus the Government showed that it understood the political significance of the strike. But its repressive acts only served to arouse national feeling and strengthen the desire for national independence. Ghana in 1950 was very different to 1940. It was no longer possible to repress one section of the people in isolation from the rest. Nor was it possible to push back a resurgent nation. And when the people went to the polls the following year the CPP won a resounding victory, and those elected with the biggest majorities were the union and CPP leaders who had been jailed in 1950.

---

[1] Ananaba: op. cit., p. 98.   [2] ibid., p. 109.
[3] Kwame Nkrumah: *Autobiography*, London, 1959, p. 97.

In Guinea, it was undoubtedly the activity of the workers and their trade unions, including their strike actions, which made possible the rapid growth of the political movement in the few years before the winning of independence in 1958. The sixty-six day strike of 1953 was of special significance. Called in protest against the authorities' slowness in implementing the Labour Code, it marked the beginning of a new phase in Guinea's independence struggle. "Previously inactive villagers within Guinea became involved" in this strike, wrote Ruth Schachter Morgenthau;[1] its impact "was profound". Noting that "after the strike the PDG (Democratic Party of Guinea) burst to popularity as an expression of revolutionary protest in the villages", Miss Morgenthau pointed out that "the strike had most important political consequences, since the trade unionists also led the PDG". She added:

> After the sixty-six day strike, they had territorial fame, a recognised leader in Sékou Touré[2] and the Party entered a new phase. . . . Within less than two years the PDG leaders displaced in elected office the leaders of the ethnic and regional associations; within four years they had destroyed also the *commandment indigenè*, particu- largly the *chefs de canton*.[3]

Miss Morgenthau has also pointed out how the modest trade union backgrounds of the Guinea national political leaders influenced their style of work:

> The trade union experience of many PDG leaders affected their ideas as well as their style of living, speaking, writing and acting. Since they held jobs low in the administrative hierarchy, they lived of necessity close to the people. Many had but irregular incomes; their housing was bad, few had cars, their clothes were simple. They relied on their colleagues or relations when in need, and made virtues of the labels pinned on them by their adversaries—"illiter- ates", "vagrants", and "badly dressed". . . . Their union background assured their familiarity with the techniques of mass action and protest, with boycotts, strikes and demonstrations. . . .

It will be noted how the picture of these leaders of the Guinea working people—relatively humble in their origins, modest in their way of life, deeply immersed in the struggles of the people—differs greatly from Fanon's picture of the "pampered" and "privileged" supporters of the colonial system.

[1] *Political Parties in French-Speaking West Africa*, Oxford, 1964, pp. 228–9.
[2] Note: he was simultaneously general secretary of the trade unions and of the Party thus symbolising the unity of the two wings of the movement.
[3] ibid., p. 230.

Admittedly, in most African territories in the final phase of direct colonial rule there were usually a group of trade union officials, mostly associated with the ICFTU, who were certainly "pampered" and "privileged"—but they were in no sense characteristic of the African working class as a whole.

Assessing the role of the Guinea trade union movement in 1956, Diallo Seydou was able to call on it to "integrate itself as the nationalist revolutionary and not the reformist force within the context of other progressive political forces. Its role at every instant is political."[1] In the decisive campaign in September, 1958, to register an overwhelming "No" to de Gaulle in the independence referendum, it was the trade unions, working alongside the PDG, that were largely instrumental in winning over the people.

In Mali, too, the workers and their unions, even though numerically small, played an important part in building up the political wing of the national movement. We have already noted the important assessment of their role made by Modibo Keita. In the same way Mamadou Fadiala Keita has termed the Mali working class "a fundamental base" of the political movement. Miss Morgenthau has described vividly how the workers of Mali (including Fanon's denigrated taxi-drivers) worked to help build the party, the *Union Soudanaise*:

> The Dakar-Niger employees carried messages and packages and publications. The postal employees used slack periods to cable party messages to "sure" militants. Most French officials touring the interior were driven by African chauffeurs, and these were among the first to be recruited into the unions.[2]

These chauffeurs were not only keen trade unionists but, according to Mamadou Keita, were the "best propaganda agents" for the party. It was the Mali wage earners, writes Miss Morgenthau, who "turned first" to the *Union Soudanaise*.

In similar fashion to the leaders of the PDG and the Guinea trade unions, the Mali national leaders strove to live modestly and in the closest contact with the masses whom they were organising for the national liberation struggle. Modibo Keita admirably caught this spirit of dedication in his report to the 1952 congress of the party. Recalling those "who have known prison and those who have died", he declared "we shall have marked the road to be followed, we shall

[1] *La Liberté*, the PDG newspaper, December 11, 1956.
[2] Morgenthau: op. cit., pp. 286-7.

have known the first pricks of the thorns, for we shall have been the first to break the path".[1]

In Niger, the workers and their unions were from the very start closely linked with the most advanced political sections of the national liberation movement. Niger's outstanding leader, Djibo Bakary, a main organiser of the trade unions and leader of the Sawaba (Freedom) Party, symbolised this connection. In the pre-independence struggle which Djibo led, the Niger unions, though understandably small, were the most disciplined and loyal supporters. "Virtually the only organised group that remained consistently loyal to Djibo was the CGT trade unions."[2]

Similarly, in Cameroun, the workers and their unions were closely identified with the spearhead of the national liberation struggle. Their strikes in the post-1945 period contributed to arousing national feeling and the fighting spirit of the people as a whole. "During the immediate post-war period", writes Le Vine, "the trade unions were the most politically active organisations in the French Cameroun."[3] And here, too, as in Guinea and Niger, the leader of the most advanced political party was a trade union leader. The former trade unionist, Ruben Um Nyobe (later to be killed by French colonialists during the guerrilla warfare which he led), became a founder and leader of the Union des Populations du Cameroun (UPC).

In Sierra Leone, where the first recorded strike took place as early as 1874,[4] and important railway strikes took place in 1919 and 1926, the workers' struggles contributed greatly to the national struggle, the general strike in 1955, in the capital, Freetown, playing a particularly important role.

This strike, which began on February 9, 1955, was in protest against the rise in the cost of living. The strike became general in Freetown; it lasted for five days and paralysed the city. Huge demonstrations of the strikers were joined by their families and by other strata of the population, and were turned into manifestations of popular discontent with the colonial system. In the face of this mass protest, the colonial authorities ordered their troops into the town. Shots were fired on the demonstrators and it is reported that many were killed and scores, if not

[1] *Afrique Noire*, October 16, 1952.

[2] Virginia Thompson: "Niger", in *National Unity and Regionalism in Eight African States*, edited by Gwendolen M. Carter, Cornell and Oxford, 1966, p. 164.

[3] Victor T. Le Vine: "Cameroun": *Political Parties and National Integration in Tropical Africa*, edited by James S. Coleman and Carl G. Rosberg, Jr., Berkeley and Los Angeles, and London, 1964, p. 137.

[4] In fact, Deutschland (op. cit.) notes one as early as 1793.

hundreds, wounded. It is significant that when news of the strike reached outside Freetown peasant protests began. Under the impetus of the workers' struggle, more than 100,000 peasants took part in rallies and demonstrations in the Western districts and before long open clashes with the authorities took place, a number of them lasting until early 1956. It was under the impact of these events that the leading political parties began to press for full independence.

In Gambia, too, it was the Gambia Workers' Union, formed in 1958, which became a major political instrument in the struggle for independence. The general strike which the union called on January 24, 1961, became a test of strength between the working people and the colonial government. Right from the start the government treated this industrial dispute over a wage claim as if it were an attempted revolt. Peaceful pickets were attacked and a mass meeting of workers broken up by the police, using batons and tear gas. One child was reported to have died from the effects of tear-gas, and a worker who had apparently not taken part in the meeting was reported to have died from injuries, following indiscriminate police raids on the workers' compounds. *The Times*, in a despatch sent three days after the commencement of the strike, stated that there had been 29 casualties. A number of workers, including the union general secretary, were arrested.

The events surrounding the strike, the police brutality and the trial of the union general secretary, aroused intense feeling far beyond the ranks of the port workers directly involved in the action. Thousands gathered outside the court-room, all the lawyers in the town rallied to the union's support, and civil servants struck in protest against the police brutality. This example from a small territory of only 300,000 people, with a working class of less than 12,000 at the time, illustrates once again the immense role which the workers' industrial actions and strike struggles played in arousing the people as a whole against the colonial system. The strikes may have had their origin in economic demands, but since they were a challenge to the low wage system imposed by colonialism and maintained by the colonial governments, they inevitably became a form of struggle against the whole system. This, too, is a fact, which Fanon ignores.

In Dahomey, an important role in the anti-colonial struggle was played by the workers and their trade unions, especially the railway-men's union which, between 1947 and 1948, carried on a strike for over five months uninterruptedly. After 1957, the Dahomey section of

UGTAN (General Union of Black African Workers) organised a substantial proportion of the country's workers and conducted its activities not on a limited programme of economic demands but on the basis of a political programme of anti-imperialism and anti-colonialism. For its uncompromising stand for national independence, the National Confederation of Labour of Dahomey (UNSTD–UGTAN) came under constant and intense attack from the French colonial authorities.

In Madagascar (Malagasy), it was above all the workers who, after the French Government's barbarous suppression of the people's independence movement in 1947 when 100,000 people were killed, first started to reorganise the movement. A congress of trade unions was held in November, 1949; a successful twenty-two day strike was waged at the Diego-Suarez ship-repair yards in December, 1950; and, in the same year, the Malagasy Solidarity Organisation (Fifanampiana Malagasy) was founded. By the mid-1950's political parties were being formed, and in August, 1956, the majority of trade unions on the island formed the Federation of Madagascar Trade Unions. In November, 1957, a 48 hour strike began, in which 15,000 workers participated. It rapidly spread to all main towns, and was supported by peasants, small traders and shopkeepers. The strikers did not limit their demands to calls for wage increases and an increase in family allowances, but also raised the fundamental demand for national independence. The political side of the national movement also grew in this period; and Madagascar gained its independence in June, 1960. It would be wrong to claim that the workers won Madagascar's independence—or even to argue that their contribution was necessarily the main factor; but it would be equally wrong to ignore their participation.

(b) East Africa

In East Africa, the actions of the workers over many years had repercussions far beyond their own ranks, and reinforced the general movement for national liberation. The strikes in Entebbe, Jinja, Kampala and other towns in Uganda in January, 1945, initially for higher wages, also voiced the demands of the people for wider representation in the Lukiko (the Assembly of the feudal kingdom of Buganda, the country's most developed province). The strikes were suppressed by armed force, and twenty Africans lost their lives, but they led to political gains by the people, and in November, 1945, the first three Africans were elected to the Uganda Legislative Council. Again, in 1949, strikes in

Uganda for higher wages were accompanied by demands for wider representation in the Legislative Council and in the Lukiko. In the 1950's, too, the strike wave continued as a component part of the national movement, at first for constitutional reform but eventually for full independence.

That the unions initiated the political and national movement is stressed by Roger Scott, who explains that from their beginning the unions in Uganda "served as a vehicle for political expression in the absence of any alternative".[1] It was only later that "the political functions . . . were taken over by overtly political organisations". It is significant, as Scott reminds us, that the British colonial authorities constantly strove to keep the unions away from politics and to sever the links between the workers and the national liberation struggle. Fanon may have had his reservations as to the role of the African working class in the national liberation struggle; but British imperialism was quite clear on this point and acted accordingly. In 1944 the Labour Department was already complaining that the activities of the Uganda Motor Drivers' Association "continue to be directed towards internal political affairs". The Commission of Enquiry set up after the January, 1945, general strike came to the conclusion that the motives behind the strike and the demonstrations were political rather than economic, and found Buganda "badly infected with the political virus". In 1952 a Trade Union Ordinance was adopted in order to bring the unions firmly under government control and to separate them from the political movement. In the ensuing years the colonial government, assisted by the International Confederation of Free Trade Unions, was able to have a considerable degree of success in keeping the unions away from the national movement, but the effort which it had made to bring this about was itself a refutation of Fanon's theory of the innate conservatism of the African working class, and its commitment to the colonial *status quo*.

In Tanzania, too, the workers played a key role in the conflict with imperialism, and confirmed R. B. Davison's observation that industrial communities in Africa, small as they may be, have acted as "flashpoints of social and political upheaval".[2] The dockers' strike in Dar-es-Salaam, when British troops and naval ratings fired on pickets in 1950, resulting in one worker being killed, and seven wounded, was followed

[1] Roger Scott: *The Development of Trade Unionism in Uganda*, Kampala, 1966, p. 9.
[2] *The Study of Industrial Relations in West Africa*, see Proceedings of the Annual Conference of the West African Institute of Social and Economic Research, Achimota, April, 1953.

oy heavy repression. By the end of the 1950's a new wave of strikes developed which did much to help forward the national movement. The eight day strike of Dar-es-Salaam dockers in 1958, the 55 day postal workers' strike of 1959–60, the strike of 10,000 railwaymen in 1960, the strike of miners at the Williamson diamond mine in December, 1960, all helped to pave the way to constitutional reform, to the election victory of the Tanganyika African National Union in August, 1960, and independence in 1961.

Of particular importance were the great strikes on the sisal plantations, especially between 1957 and 1960, which involved the loss of several hundred thousand working days. These were manifestations of bitter conflict with the colonial authorities, who did not hesitate to arrest strikers, attack them with tear-gas and batons, and even shoot on them, causing a number of casualties. Throughout all this period the workers and their unions maintained the closest relations with the political party, the Tanganyika Africa National Union. When one examines the strike statistics of Taganyika for the period 1955 to 1961 and notes the mounting wave of strikes coinciding with the steady rise of the national movement right up to the attainment of independence, one cannot but once again question most sharply Fanon's irresponsible denigration of the African working class.

In Kenya, which is so often regarded as the most striking example of a peasant revolt, it was the working class which pioneered the way, which shared the burden of exploitation and sacrifice in struggle right up to the "Mau Mau" Emergency, and which continued to play a key role during the Emergency itself.[1]

It is not without significance that the first major clash between the people of Kenya and the British authorities after the first world war was the upheaval of 1921–3 which was a fusion of working-class strike action with the wider demands of the peoples as a whole, linked with the political wing of the movement. In protest against unemployment, land evictions, wage cuts, increased poll tax, and forced labour, thousands of workers flocked into the newly formed Young Kikuyu Association. Mass demonstrations were held and a general strike was called—the first in Kenya and one of the earliest recorded in Africa's history. Thousands of workers struck. Their leaders were arrested. The government brought out troops, armoured cars and machine guns, and the troops opened fire. A massacre ensued,

[1] For full details on this aspect see Jack Woddis: *Africa: the Lion Awakes*, London, 1961 especially pp. 79–85, 117–22).

one estimate giving 150 killed apart from the hundreds wounded. Describing this struggle, Makhan Singh has justifiably commented:

> Thus on that historic day the tree of Uhuru was watered by the blood of our martyrs. They were martyrs of Kenya's national movement and trade union movement. The fight for Kenya's independence and for workers' rights began in great earnest with modern methods. And there took place the first General Strike of African workers in East African territories for political and economic demands.
>
> A new chapter in the history of Kenya had begun.[1]

Twenty years later, the period leading up to the Emergency was marked by major conflicts between the workers and the colonial government of Kenya. Employing a variety of different forms of repression, and through the introduction of new restrictive laws, the government struck heavy blows against the unions. General strikes took place in Mombasa in 1939, 1944 and 1947, on each occasion in the face of fierce repression.

Writing of this period in the 1940's, Waruhiu Itote ("General China") has stressed: "At that time the trade unions had the most militant leaders and were the most active groups working for independence in the city."[2] This is confirmed by Makhan Singh who constantly draws attention to the close working between the leaders of the trade unions and the national movement, and the extent to which trade union "officials and members were also active in the national organisation".[3]

How the government viewed the situation was indicated in the report of the African Affairs Department in Kenya, for the years 1946–7:

"There was a general strike in Mombasa in January and its repercussions assumed a political rather than a purely economic aspect."

The report goes on to quote the Municipal African Affairs Officer as follows:

> For the first time Africans began to hold mass meetings, numbering frequently as many as 5,000 people, in the open spaces in the locations. . . . At first these meetings were concerned chiefly with labour conditions of Africans in Nairobi, but they gradually became more and more political and concerned principally with conditions outside Nairobi.

[1] Makhan Singh: *History of Kenya's Trade Union Movement to 1952*, Nairobi, 1969, p. 16.
[2] Waruhiu Itote: *"Mau Mau" General*, Nairobi, 1967, pp. 38–9.
[3] Makhan Singh: op. cit., p. 132.

On May 1, 1949, the East African Trade Union Congress was set up in Kenya. Significantly, Jomo Kenyatta and other national leaders were present.

The settlers' paper, *Kenya Weekly News*, made no secret of its fears concerning the extent to which the workers and their trade unions were throwing their weight into the national struggle. Fanon or no, the settlers saw the workers as a threat to their colonial system. A long editorial on February 24, 1950, entitled "Trade Unions in Africa" warned against the unions being used "as a weapon of political agitation" and called on the government to exercise "restraint and sanctions" against those carrying on "subversive agitation".[1]

What the settlers were worried about became clear when the East Africa Trade Union Congress General Secretary, Makhan Singh, wrote on his May Day article, May 1, 1950: "This influence of the workers and trade unions in politics would go on increasing, because the problems facing the workers and the trade unions cannot be finally solved without the complete freedom of East Africa and ending of exploitation of man by man. . . ."[2]

On May 1 itself a representative meeting of trade union delegates meeting in Nairobi adopted a May Day pledge which contained these words:

> We pledge that our Unions and East African Trade Union Congress would do their utmost for the achievement of workers' demands, complete freedom and independence of East African territories.[3]

The settlers' demand for action against the trade unions was soon met. A wave of repression swept the country.

Armed with their new anti-trade union laws, the government banned meetings, raided trade union offices and on May 15, 1950, arrested Fred Kubai, the President, and Makhan Singh, the General Secretary. This was followed by a general strike in Nairobi, which spread to Nakuru, Mombasa, Kisuma, Kakamega, Kisii, Thika, Nyeri and other towns. It was the biggest industrial conflict seen in Kenya's history, and undoubtedly had an immense influence on the people as a whole. It lasted nine days in Nairobi and two or three days in most other towns, and involved 100,000 workers. Quite unprecedented force was used against the workers. One would have been justified in thinking that a liberation war had begun. The government em-

---

[1] Cited in Makhan Singh: op. cit., pp. 250-1.   [2] *Daily Chronicle*, May 1, 1950
[3] Cited in Makhan Singh: op. cit., p. 263.

ployed aircraft, armoured cars and trucks, and Bren-gun carriers. Hundreds were arrested. It can readily be imagined how this clash between the workers and the colonial authorities must have inspired the movement for national liberation which two years later was confronted with the government's Emergency measures. Makhan Singh has correctly called it "a great anti-imperialist demonstration".

Even during the Emergency, which largely took the form of an armed struggle in the rural areas, the workers continued to play an important role. The unions were under constant attack by the government. Many trade unionists were arrested and detained on allegations of being connected with the Mau Mau movement. Both in Nairobi and Mombasa, traditionally the strongholds of the Kenya labour movement, strikes and other forms of action were undertaken by the workers throughout the Emergency. That the workers of Nairobi, most of them Kikuyu, were regarded by the government as a constant thorn in its side and a dangerous ally of those fighting in the forests, was shown by the government's repeated attempts to "clean up" the town. The military were constantly in action. Under Operation Anvil, large-scale screenings, involving tens of thousands of workers, were carried out and thousands of workers detained behind barbed wire. The aim of this action was to prevent the urban workers providing material aid and young recruits to their brothers engaged in armed struggle.

The extent to which the workers were linked with the most radical wing of the Kenya national movement and with the Mau Mau itself, is shown by Donald Barnett in his valuable study of the Emergency.[1] Barnett brings out very well the way in which the movement, led by the illegal Kikuyu Central Association, and which prepared the ground for the later struggle, combined workers and peasants, trade unions and political movements; it was concerned with wages as well as land, colour-bar and political representation; it was ready to employ the weapon of general strike along with other forms of pressure such as boycotts (later, during the Mau Mau itself, a bus boycott in Nairobi, 1954, was to be one of the highlights of the urban struggle), and eventually armed action. As Barnett points out, "The migrant labour system, in terms of which the vast majority of urban workers were obliged to maintain dual residence in the city and reserve, lent itself nicely" to the process of extending the membership of the KCA both in town and countryside.

He also makes it clear that the organised leadership came largely

[1] Donald L. Barnett and Karari Njama: *Mau Mau from Within*, London, 1966.

from Nairobi, and that, following the arrests of the national leaders after October, 1952, when the State of Emergency was declared, "leadership passed into the hands of the now unlinked district and lower-level councils of Nairobi and the rural areas". Soon "links began to be fashioned between urban groups and those emerging within the forests of Mount Kenya and the Aberdares".

There would be no purpose in claiming for the working class of Kenya a bigger role than it in fact played in the struggle for national independence. But the quarrel that we are pursuing with Fanon is not on the degree of African working-class participation in the liberation struggle, but whether it really was or was not on the side of the national revolution. The events in Kenya, as in the rest of East Africa, again refute Fanon.

(c) Central Africa

In Central Africa, too, working-class discontent was a potent factor in the formation of the national liberation movement.

> The pressures of industrial life intensified the prejudice and discrimination to which the Nyasas and Rhodesians were subject during the years before World War II. Their experiences on the Copperbelt added significantly to the ferment of discontent that, perhaps more directly than elsewhere in the protectorates, ultimately sought to express itself aggressively. In time, workers with experience on the Copperbelt or in the mines of Southern Rhodesia or South Africa lent their services to the nationalist cause, but they participated equally in associational and religious forms of protest and, on important early occasions, in violent demonstrations against the white man's rule.[1]

The series of powerful strikes in Northern Rhodesia's Copperbelt, in 1935, 1940, 1952, 1955 and 1956, served to shake up national feeling throughout Central Africa both before and after the Federation. The strikes of 1935 and 1940 were met with the fiercest repression, police firing on the strikers on both of these occasions, causing six deaths and a further 22 casualties in the first, and 17 deaths and 69 casualties in the second.

The great strike of 1952 marked an important stage in the link up between the miners' actions and the wider struggle. In order to prevent

[1] Robert Rotberg: *The Rise of Nationalism in Central Africa*, Cambridge, Massachusetts, and London, 1966, p. 156.

the workers being starved into submission and to avoid food shortages being used to provoke the desperate workers into raiding the mining compound food stores, thus giving the police the excuse and opportunity to fire on the workers as in 1935, the union leaders arranged for rural areas to send in free food supplies. The chiefs, in contrast to previous occasions, helped; meat was dried, salted and stockpiled, thus providing the striking miners with their own food reserves. This was a major factor making it possible for the miners to stay out solid for three weeks and to obtain substantial wage concessions from the companies. In 1955, assisted with food supplies in the same way, the miners stayed out for 58 days. In 1956, a series of rolling strikes shook the Copperbelt, sixteen strikes being held between May and September that year, in defence of the union which was under attack by the companies and the government. Unable to break the strike, the government declared a State of Emergency. The union leaders were arrested and banished from the Copperbelt.

That the African miners involved in these major class battles did not limit their horizons to their own immediate economic demands can be seen from the complaints of the European mining companies as well as the attitude of the colonial authorities. It is significant that the Branigan Commission, which was set up "to inquire into the unrest in the Mining Industry in Northern Rhodesia" in 1956, condemned the African miners' union leaders on the grounds that they were not actuated "by a desire to protect and further the legitimate interests of the African employees but to achieve political or nationalistic advancement of all Africans generally in the Territory". The Report also quoted the copper companies as complaining that many of the union officials were also members or officials of the African National Congress (from which emerged the Zambia National Congress which subsequently became the United National Independence Party), and that officials of both organisations had made "political speeches" at each other's meetings.

Similarly, in Nyasaland (now Malawi), the strike of tea plantation workers was an important act in the crisis which hit the Central African Federation in its dying days. In Southern Rhodesia (Zimbabwe), there were a number of strike actions which played a key role in the political struggle against the Federation, against white domination and for national independence and majority rule. These included the strike at the Wankie coal mine (1954), and that on the Kariba dam (1959) which resulted in the declaration of a State of Emergency.

There were also a number of actions in Bulawayo, Harare and Que-Que, the steel centre.

Their relation to the general struggle against the rule of the white settlers has been indicated by Franklin. Writing specifically of the Wankie coal strike he points out that "though not directly connected with federation, (it) was to some extent related to the federation 'malaise' which saw through the flimsy veil of Partnership to the aim of white supremacy behind it".[1] Referring to later strikes, including the railway strike of 1956, Mr. Franklin points out: "In these incidents the deterioration of race relations and the rapid growth of African Nationalism due to the imposition of federation was plain."

When the Southern Rhodesian government arrested the leaders of the National Democratic Party (the forerunner of the Zimbabwe African People's Union—Zapu) in July, 1960, the workers responded by a powerful strike embracing over 100,000 workers in the eight townships around Bulawayo, and about the same number in the neighbourhood of Salisbury. Strikes and demonstrations continued for a week, in the course of which hundreds were arrested, and a number (at least nine) killed when police and troops opened fire. A year later, again in July, workers struck in protest against the government's referendum on the new constitutional proposals which were aimed at perpetuating white settler rule.

Significantly, in the "Belgian" Congo, too, it was the action of the unemployed African miners demonstrating against their plight on the streets of Leopoldville, and supported by tens of thousands of dockers, railwaymen and factory workers, that helped to spark off the national explosion at the beginning of 1959 which preceded the winning of independence a year later.

(d) North Africa

In North Africa, as well, the struggles of the working class constituted a key element in the national liberation movement. In the Sudan, the workers and their Trade Union Federation, from their very beginnings, understood the need to extend their struggles from the economic to the political sphere and to participate in the movement for national independence. A statement issued by the Executive Committee of the Sudan Workers' Trade Union Federation in 1951 declared: "We are opposed to any co-operation with imperialism. Our case with imperialism is one of enmity and therefore we do no

[1] Harry Franklin: *Unholy Wedlock*, London, 1963.

accept bargains and collaboration. . . . The Federation, which leads the workers in their daily struggle for their demands now sets before them the way in which they will lead the workers, together with other categories of the people, to get rid of imperialism. . . ." In fulfilment of these aims, the Federation supported the students' strikes early in 1951, helped the peasant protest movement, assisted the Gezeira tenants to organise themselves, and backed the Sudanese police in their strike for trade union recognition in May, 1951. The Federation took its politics seriously enough to organise special night classes for workers on political subjects. The December, 1951, Congress of the Federation openly espoused political aims, calling for full support for a united front of all anti-imperialist organisations, and for the workers to throw their weight into the struggle to achieve self-determination for the Sudan. There is no doubt that, quite apart from the Federation's energetic activity in pursuit of its economic demands, it was above all its determination to play its part in the wider struggle for national independence that made it and its leaders a constant target of the British authorities. The Federation's general secretary was imprisoned more than once, and the British trade union adviser repeatedly attempted to clip the power of the unions and to limit their political activity.

In Tunisia, the workers and trade unions played a very prominent part in the national struggle. Already, in 1951, in two great actions, involving strikes and street demonstrations, they had displayed their support for the people of Morocco (March, 1951), and of Egypt (November 2, 1951). A three day general strike was held from December 21 to 23, 1951, in protest against French colonial rule in Tunisia. Of outstanding significance was the three days' general strike which began on January 18, 1952, in protest against the Resident General's banning of the Neo-Destour Conference, and his arrest and deportation of the leaders of the Neo-Destour Party, the Communist Party, and the two trade union centres (the UGTT and the USTT). This strike was complete; everything came to a standstill, shops were closed, markets deserted, and no one went to work. On the big day of action called by the political leaders on February 1, 1952, again the workers and their unions responded overwhelmingly, not only by strike action but by their participation in the processions and huge demonstrations which took place in the main towns. When the union leader, Farhat Hached, was assassinated by French right-wing terrorists, mass strikes and demonstrations were held throughout Tunisia, on December 6, 1952. The extent of working-class and trade union involvement in the national struggle was also indicated when independence was at last won in 1956; no less than five members of the Government established in March, 1956, were members of the united UGTT.[1]

In Morocco, the large and well-organised working-class and trade union movement was at the centre of all the national actions which swept the country in the 1950's, especially in Casablanca and Rabat, the scenes of all the major demonstrations, marches, protest movements and other forms of activity against foreign rule. Describing the role of the workers Dr. Ashford has written of the 1952 period that "it was increasingly difficult to prevent popular demonstrations, especially in Casablanca where Moroccans had been joining unions and where the bond of workingmen's solidarity had been added to the desire for independence." [2] Symbolic of this period was the general strike of December 8, 1952, called in protest against the murder of the Tunisian trade union leader, Farhat Hached, and also in support of independence for Morocco. The strike was met by the French authorities with a wave of terror; hundreds were reported to have been killed between midnight of December 7 and the morning of December 9. These sacrifices by the Moroccan workers, like those of the workers in the other African territories mentioned above, challenge Fanon's claim that the African workers were completely selfish and concerned only with their own economic betterment. As Dr. Ashford's detailed account explains, the struggle of the workers of Morocco made them a key element in the national struggle. The trade union movement, he writes, derived considerable prestige from its sacrifices in the 1952 struggles and "managed to establish itself as a leader in the struggle for independence before" the return of the exiled King in 1955.[3] In dealing with the roles of the political party, the Istiqlal, and those of the resistance movement and the trade unions, Dr. Ashford asserts that "both the resistance and the trade unions could maintain with considerable justification that they had made sacrifices as great or perhaps even greater than the party over the preceding three years"[4] (i.e. 1954–6).

Explaining the role of the unions in Morocco, Dr. Ashford writes:

> Though it represented only a third of the membership of the Istiqlal, the Moroccan Federation of Labour enjoyed certain advantages in political activity. For the most part its members were concentrated in urban centres; this fact facilitated communications and

[1] The USTT had merged with the UGTT prior to Tunisia winning independence.
[2] Douglas E. Ashford: *Political Change in Morocco*, Princeton, 1961, p. 72.
[3] ibid., p. 75.
[4] ibid., p. 223.

supervision. The industrial and commercial occupations of most members introduced the workers to organised behaviour and provided experience that many Istiqlal members never had. By its working class composition the U.M.T.[1] possessed a ready-made appeal for post-independence solidarity. The obviously oppressive economic conditions and abuse to which Moroccan labourers had been subjected over the preceding thirty years were of immediate concern. . . . As a result, the U.M.T. has enjoyed a double life as nationalist spokesman and also as a working class spokesman. Where specific interests of the workers were involved, the union could halt all economic activity. Where national problems were at issue, the U.M.T. could speak with almost more legitimacy than the Istiqlal itself.[2]

Fanon has argued that the workers in Africa were "pampered" and "favoured". On the contrary, explains Dr. Ashford, the workers of Morocco under colonialism were "economically more vulnerable" than the political leaders, and were also "more vulnerable to police control and brutal suppression".[3] However Fanon may have viewed the role of the workers, the French authorities, notes Dr. Ashford, had no illusions about the workers' activity in Morocco. Their large demonstrations in Casablanca on May Day, 1951, "revealed their growing strength and may have caused French officials to step up plans to suppress all nationalist activity".

Even in Algeria, Fanon's adopted country, the role of the working class was quite other than that given in his assessment. The launching of the armed struggle in 1954 was undoubtedly a turning point in Algeria's struggle for national liberation, but before that decisive act, and during the seven years of the liberation war itself, the Algerian workers and trade unions fought energetically against the colonial authorities, made great sacrifices and gave up a number of martyrs to the national cause. The strike of 100,000 workers in 1947, which involved street fighting and the occupation of factories; the miners' strike of 1948, which in some pits went on for four months; the strike of tens of thousands of agricultural workers, also in 1948, in Oranie and Algerois; the repeated actions by the dockers; the wresting, by consistent struggle, of a social security system from the colonial authorities, in 1949; the six days' strike of tobacco workers in 1950; the strike of gas and electricity workers in March–April, 1951; the sixty days' miners' strike in September–November, 1951; the strikes in the

---

[1] L'Union Marocaine du Travail (Moroccan Union of Labour).   [2] op. cit., p. 270
[3] ibid., p. 272.

same year of dockers, tramwaymen, hospital workers, and agricultural workers—these are some of the significant working-class actions prior to 1954 which helped to strengthen the resolve of the Algerian people to take up the struggle for their national liberation.

The responsible attitude of the Algerian workers towards the interests of other strata of society, especially the peasants and agricultural population, runs counter to Fanon's picture of the "unselfish" peasant confronted with the "selfish worker". The important Fourth Algerian Trade Union Conference, held in Algiers in January, 1950, raised the whole problem of agrarian reform, demanding land for those who work it; and when the Algerian Agricultural Workers' Conference took place in November, 1951, this demand for land became a rallying call.

Commenting on the backing given by workers to the rural population, Braham Moussa, secretary at that time of the Co-ordination Committee of the Algerian Trade Unions, wrote:

> It is important to note that there is a growing understanding among the town workers of the necessity for helping their brothers in the rural areas as a result of which they are intensifying their solidarity with them. In this way the Algerian Agricultural Workers' Conference was financed to a considerable degree by the distributive and industrial trade unions in the towns as well as by the State employees' unions, each one adopting one or more delegates and pledging themselves to assist in their work of forming trade unions, as well as on organisational questions and in their fight for their demands. Solidarity also is shown by the effective help given by the town workers to their rural brothers who have been imprisoned, in monetary help and also by very important strike movements.[1]

The Algerian workers, at their Fourth Algerian Trade Union Conference, also went on record against colonialism, and called on all trade unions to participate in the struggle for national liberation. Neither did they limit themselves to declarations and appeals. By their actions, too, they demonstrated their devotion to the national cause. Thus there took place on April 27, 1952, the day of solidarity with the Tunisian and Moroccan people then engaged in struggle, an action organised by the Algerian trade unions together with the Algerian Front; the huge May First demonstration in 1952 in which nearly 100,000 workers participated, and which took the form of a show of strength between the workers and the colonial authorities; the strike

[1] "The Algerian Trade Union Movement Forges Ahead", by Braham Moussa: *World Trade Union Movement*, July 1-15, 1952.

of May 7 for the release of those arrested on May 1; and the mass participation of workers on the great day of national struggle against colonialism, May 23, 1952.

A further sign of the maturity of the Algerian workers and of their passionate commitment to the cause of anti-colonialism was the action of the Algerian dockers who, despite severe hardship and privation, consistently refused over many months to load ships with material for the "dirty war" which the French imperialists were then waging in Vietnam. What this meant in terms of sacrifice by the Algerian dockers is indicated by this extract from a report in 1957: "From the very beginning of the Vietnam war, the (Algerian) dockers refused to load war materials destined for Vietnam. But in 1949, they went very much further than this. They decided to refuse to handle *all* goods of every description whether rifles or boxes of matches, barrels of wine or corks, provided they were either being shipped to or coming from Vietnam. And, until the Geneva Agreements put an end to the war, nothing turned them from their decision, neither police threats, the withdrawal of their work cards, nor hunger. *They lost 4·6 thousand million francs in wages but remained obdurate.* Their wives and families equalled them in endurance and sacrifice. Other categories of workers and small traders supported them as much as they could, so as to back the struggle of the Vietnamese people. And this went on for five years."[1]

On May 9, 1953, in opposition to the attempt of the Administration to rig the local elections in Oran, the dockers and building workers led more than ten thousand people in mass demonstrations which continued throughout the day in front of the polling booths, despite police repression. During the whole of 1953 over 220 strikes took place in Algeria, involving more than 270,000 workers.

When the armed struggle began in 1954 it did not take the French authorities long to find it necessary to crack down on the workers and their organisations. The General Union of Algerian Workers (UGTA) was banned in 1956. Even prior to this, the declaration of a State of Emergency on April 4, 1955, was followed by widespread arrests of trade union leaders and active members, and their confinement in concentration camps. A number were brutally murdered, including Ladjabi Mohammed Tahar, Secretary of the Hospital Workers' Union of Constantine, Boudour Ali of the Algerian Union of Railwaymen, Bouzour of the Municipal Workers' Union, and miners' delegates from Sidi Maarouf.

[1] See Supplement to *World Trade Union Movement*, No. 7, July, 1957.

Despite the severe repression, the arrest, torture and imprisonment of thousands of workers, the Algerian working class continued, in different forms, to make its contribution to the national struggle. When the FLN (Front of National Liberation) decided at the beginning of 1957 to hold a week of strike action throughout the country to coincide with the United Nations' General Assembly discussion on Algeria, the workers' response was massive:

> ... on January 28, the date set down for downing tools, the whole of Algeria presented a most unusual sight although the authorities had neglected no possibility in their attempt to thwart the movement. Emergency measures were taken such as searches and raids, press-ganging of the workers, helicopters flying at low level over the working class districts, and so on. . . . In spite of this, during the night of January 28 to 29, Algerian employees in the communications services stopped work. In the morning, tradesmen and artisans left their shops closed. There was a general strike throughout industry and the public services. . . . The towns resembled ghost-towns, all activity having come to a standstill. This was particularly noticeable in the working class districts which are usually so lively. The strike continued throughout the week as planned. . . . In spite of the threat of dismissals, in spite of prison sentences ranging up to six months and heavy fines, civil servants and employees deserted the administration and public services unless they were forcibly dragged to work from their homes. Never before in Algeria had a strike been so successful.[1]

The participation of the Algerian workers in the struggle against French imperialism drew down on them the wrath and repressive hand of the authorities. A protest to the ILO made by the World Federation of Trade Unions, on November 29, 1956, after describing the conditions under which trade unionists were being kept in concentration camps at Djorf, Berronaghia, Aflou, Guelt-Es-Stel, Lodi, Bossuet, Ain-Sefra, went on to list "an incomplete list of interned trade unionists", together with a list of those expelled. As a result of these measures, it pointed out, the Secretariats, Bureaux, and Executive Committees had been deprived of all or part of their members not only at the national level but in trades councils of Algiers, Oran, Constantine, Bone, Sidi Bel Abbes, Blida, Philippeville, Djidjella Bougie, Guelma, South Ahram, Tlemcen, and Orleansville. In that same year, Aissat Idir, General Secretary of the UGTA, was locked up

[1] "Whole World Demands a Peaceful Solution to the Algerian Problem", by E Djezairi: *World Trade Union Movement*, April, 1957.

tortured and murdered. An appeal of the UGTA issued in 1958, declared that "76,000 of our leaders and members are in detention camps and prisons".

Admittedly the rural population of Algeria provided the main forces of the liberation army (ALN). But, as the facts above show only too well, the workers in no sense passively acquiesced or accepted the colonial system. They fought it in the towns, in the factories and offices, in the concentration camps and prisons. They suffered economic hardship, persecution and torture in the cause of national liberation. Once again, the facts challenge Fanon's characterisation of the role of the working class in the anti-colonial movement in Africa.

(e) Southern Africa

In Swaziland, too, the national liberation movement experienced a big surge forward in 1963, when workers in the asbestos mines and on the sugar plantations came out on strike in support of demands for higher wages, and in protest against the new Constitution which the British Conservative Government had imposed in May of that year. Some 4,000 workers participated in the strike at Big Bend, 3,400 at the Havelock Mines, and over 3,000 at Mbabane. When other workers came out in June and the strike became general, the British Government air-lifted 700 British troops from Kenya and a State of Emergency was declared. The strikes were suppressed with great severity; several hundred workers were arrested, and, after some months in jail, a number of the leaders who were also significantly enough members of the Ngwane National Liberatory Congress (NNLC) as well as of the Swaziland Congress of Trade Unions, were put on trial, and several given prison sentences. Once again it can be seen how the struggles of the workers were intertwined closely with the wider struggle for national independence.[1]

When one comes to consider those African territories in which struggle is still continuing to end colonialism and white settler rule, one finds once again that Fanon's thesis breaks down in the face of fact. In South Africa, as H. J. and R. E. Simons have described in immense detail,[2] the struggles of the African workers were intertwined with the national liberation over several decades. In the post-1945 period, in which independence struggles throughout Africa took on new

---

[1] This is borne out by the slogan which G. E. Lynd (*The Politics of African Trade Unionism*, New York–London, 1968, p. 927) reports the NNLC adopted during the strike: "One Pound a Day and *Amandla Awethu* (a democratic constitution)".

[2] H. J. and R. E. Simons: *Class and Colour in South Africa, 1850–1950*, London, 1969.

dimensions and significance, this was even more true. The great strike of African gold mine workers in South Africa in 1946 undoubtedly marked a new phase of struggle. Though defeated by police brutality—nine Africans being reported killed and 1,248 injured—the strike served to deepen the understanding of the African people of the nature of their oppression and of the necessity to struggle for liberation. Its result, notes H. J. and R. E. Simons, was "an alliance between communists and African nationalism", and the emergence of the Congress Alliance, an alliance of the African National Congress, the Congress of Coloured People, the Indian National Congress, the South African Congress of Trade Unions, and the Congress of Democrats; and within this alliance, and within each component organisation of it, the South African communists, who had struggled and worked for so many years precisely for such a working unity of all the forces opposed to segregation, discrimination and oppression, played an essential role. It was they, above all, who had laboured for so long to unite the forces of the working class and the forces of African liberation, and who understood, too, that without the strong, and potentially still more powerful, African working class, the national liberation struggle in South Africa could never achieve its final victory over apartheid and tyranny.

In the "Defiance" campaign launched in 1952, the workers' response to the call for a general strike on June 26 was widespread. Again, in March, 1960, following on the massacre at Sharpeville, thousands of workers quit their jobs, took part in demonstrations, and stayed out on strike for several days despite the unprecedented use of force by the Government, which sent in armed forces, with armoured trucks, right into the African townships to force workers out of their homes at bayonet point. When the Verwoerd government inaugurated its apartheid republic in 1961, the workers carried through an heroic three day strike in protest. In answer to the call of the National Action Council of South Africa, led by Nelson Mandela, thousands came out on May 29, 30, and 31, 1961. The strike had been well advertised in advance; it had to be, under the circumstances. The Government was therefore well placed to take measures to prevent it. The Army, armed police and armed European civilians were deployed in African townships and other key areas. *The Government arrested over 10,000 Africans even before the strike began*, in a desperate attempt to intimidate the workers. Despite these strong-arm methods, the workers succeeded in mounting what was undoubtedly the most widespread general strike ever witnessed in South Africa—one, moreover, called on a straight political issue of protest against the new republican constitution. In Johannesburg, the *Star* estimated that between 40 and 75 per cent of the workers stayed away from work. In Port Elizabeth, it was estimated that 75 per cent of the non-white workers were out on May 30. Durban, Cape Town and other centres were also hit severely by the strikes. Thus, in the face of the Government's powerful concentration of armed forces, of arrests and intimidation, the African working class and its allies succeeded by their strike action in turning public attention on "Republic Day" from the inauguration of the new republic to the nation-wide protest against it.

In the Portuguese colonies of Angola, Mozambique, Guinea and Cape Verde, the struggles of the workers have been a component of the independence movement and, in a certain sense, the harbingers of the national struggle. These workers' struggles began in the late 1940's, and were one of the factors which helped to awaken the fighting spirit of the people which has culminated in the widespread actions now embracing all the Portuguese colonies in Africa. Of particular significance were the strikes of dockers in Lourenço Marques in Mozambique, of sugar plantation workers in Cape Verde, of railway construction workers in Tete, Mozambique, of bakers in Luanda, Angola, of the crews of fishing vessels in Guinea. The strikes of plantation workers in northern Angola in 1961 contributed to sparking off the large-scale revolt of that year.

The late Dr. Mondlane has explained that the struggle of the workers in Mozambique not only pre-dated the wider national liberation struggle, but also inspired the intellectuals. "The sufferings of the forced labourer and the mine worker inspired many poems",[1] including Noémia de Sousa's powerful call to revolt written after the strikes of 1947. Moreover, noted Mondlane, "it was among the urban proletariat that the first experiments in organised active resistance took place. The concentration of labour in and near the towns, and the terrible working conditions and poverty, provided the impetus to revolt."[2] Evidently the poor and oppressed workers of Mozambique in reality were far removed from Fanon's picture of the "pampered" and "privileged". It was, wrote Mondlane, the "radical discontent of the labour force" together with political agitation, which produced a series of strikes in the late 1940's in the docks and plantations, culminating in "an abortive uprising at Lourenço Marques in 1948". Again,

[1] Eduardo Mondlane: *The Struggle for Mozambique*, London, 1969, p. 110.
[2] ibid., p. 115.

in 1956, the Lourenco Marques dockers went on strike; this time it ended in the sacrifice of forty-nine dockers' lives. Despite this heavy loss, the heroic dockers of Lourenco Marques, now working more closely with the underground liberation organisation of Frelimo, struck again in a series of actions in 1963. This, too, resulted in a number of deaths and widespread arrests. These experiences led Frelimo to conclude that it was necessary to change its tactics, shift over to armed struggle and to build a base in the countryside. Such a justified change of tactics, however, in no way provides a basis for Fanon to disparage the efforts, the courage and the sacrifices made by the workers of Mozambique who, quite clearly, made a vital contribution to the national liberation struggle. That they still contribute to that struggle and continue to be victims of Government repression is indicated by Mondlane's reference to the mass arrests of "nationalist sympathisers" which have taken place in Mozambique since the armed struggle began. "The majority of these", he wrote, "are peasant and *manual workers*." (Author's italics.)

In Guiné-Bissau, Amilcar Cabral has pointed out that, notwithstanding the difficulties in mobilising some sections of the wage-earners, "there is a majority of them committed to the struggle".[1] Explaining the difficulties of the peasants to comprehend the nature of their exploitation, Cabral stresses that it is easier for the workers to understand this and so, from an early stage, they were drawn into the struggle. In its initial stages, the group of "petty bourgeois who were driven by the reality of life in Guiné, by the sufferings we had to endure, and also by the influence events in Africa and elsewhere had on us"— a group which was to form the nucleus of the African Party of Independence of Guiné and Cape Verde (PAIGC)—began its activities amongst the workers, "and we had some success with this". One important group, notes Cabral, "were the dockworkers; another important group were the people working in the boats carrying merchandise, who mostly live in Bissau itself and travel up and down rivers. These people proved highly conscious of their position. . . . We therefore decided to concentrate all our work on this group. This gave excellent results and this group soon came to form a kind of nucleus which influenced the attitudes of other wage-earning groups in the towns—workers proper and drivers, who form two important groups. Moreover, if I may put it this way, we thus found our little proletariat."[2]

[1] Amilcar Cabral: *Revolution in Guiné*, London, 1969, p. 51.   [2] ibid., p. 54.

Following on these early attempts to organise, Cabral and his colleagues turned to their second phase, that of creating cadres who would be able to go to the countryside to organise the peasants for the phase of armed struggle. This group of cadres, of whom about one thousand were trained at the PAIGC party school in Conakry, included wage-earners, as well as peasants and young people from the rural areas who had come to the towns in search of jobs. It was these cadres who were given "what you might call a working class mentality", who "inculcated a certain mentality into the peasants", and "who are now leading the struggle". Explaining that his party is not a Communist or Marxist-Leninist party, Cabral asserts that "the people now leading the peasants in the struggle in Guinea are mostly from the urban milieux and connected with the wage-earning group".[1]

Thus, once again, when one comes to examine the real course of the national liberation struggle in specific countries, to weigh up the facts as well as the opinions of the national liberation leaders themselves, one finds that Fanon's assessment is invalid and not at all in tune with reality.

THE ROLE OF THE WORKERS AFTER INDEPENDENCE

Nor are Fanon's strictures against the role of the African working class in the post-independent phase borne out by the actual events that have followed. Nowhere in Africa has there taken place the kind of post-independence revolution envisaged by Fanon—an armed uprising against a neo-colonialist puppet government, an uprising which commences in the countryside, based on the armed struggle of the peasants, backed by the *lumpenproletariat* of the towns, with the workers at best as passive spectators or even on the "wrong side of the barricades". Of course, the fact that such revolts have not yet taken place does not theoretically rule out their future possibility.

But Fanon's shortcomings lie not only here. A major factor of post-independence Africa, over the past decade, and one which is basic to our understanding of Africa's present and future, is the development of the class struggle. Fanon sees the African working class after independence as the corrupted and pampered ally of the indigenous bourgeoisie, or, at most, as its economic rival. He does not see or understand the struggle between the workers and the capitalists as being not only over the distribution of the national wealth but increasingly over

[1] ibid., p. 55.

policy. Which way will Africa march—to capitalism or to socialism? One cannot ignore the role that the African working class, whatever its present weaknesses, must play in helping the people to make their choice and to implement it.

Fanon's confused style and method of writing does not assist in gaining clarity. He shuttles back and forth in space and time like a man in a dream. At times it is impossible to tell whether he is referring to the struggle against direct colonial rule or to the conflicts which emerge *after* independence has been won. The transitions of his thoughts, and his means of expressing them, are often hard to follow. A colonial government inexplicably becomes a government of the national bourgeoisie—and the next moment we are plunged right back again into the anti-colonial liberation war.

Even making allowances for this lack of clarity, one is forced to the conclusion that Fanon's assessments as to what would happen to Africa after gaining independence is no more helpful than his judgment as to how that independence was won. Some developments he did point to. Certainly most of the mass national parties fell into disuse after independence, their leading personnel taken up by state and other duties, the organisation at grass-roots level allowed to rust, the cult of the individual leader often becoming a substitute for politically educating the working people. But, despite Fanon, there have been in some countries attempts to strike out in different fashion, as for example, in Tanzania, Zambia, Congo (Brazzaville) and Guinea, as well as in Ghana, Mali and Uganda before the coups. True enough these attempts have themselves been beset with confusion and weakness; but the attempts have been made, and it is this, with all its attendant problems, that one has to build on.

Fanon was correct to draw attention to the role the army was likely to play, and to forecast the reactionary military coups which have been such an alarming feature of Africa in the 1960's and 1970's. But there is no room in Fanon's analysis for an explanation of the quite different and more complex coups that took place in Egypt (1952), or the Sudan (1969 and 1971).

Prior to independence, as we have seen, the fight of the workers for higher wages and better conditions, against racialism and oppression was part of the general anti-imperialist movement. The workers' blows were struck against the big foreign monopolies and the imperialist state. The African bourgeoisie was generally rather weak, did not exercise state power, and in any case sections of it were, to a certain degree, partners in the national struggle. With the winning of independence, and the resolution of the first political phase of the national problem, the African capitalist class has begun to flex its muscles. Utilising the political power of its state functions, it is able to strengthen its economic positions and gain a hold over sections of the national economy. To secure its enrichment and make possible the continued exploitation of the workers on which its own class advancement relies, it finds it necessary to curb the workers' rights and limit their possibilities of resisting this exploitation. In a few countries progressive groups of the petty-bourgeoisie have formed the independence governments; and in these cases there is a basis for an alliance between the workers and the governmental groups in order to weaken the economic grip of the foreign monopolies and make possible the building of a balanced economy and the winning of economic independence. Such a progressive alliance must also rest on the mass support of the majority of the people, the peasants.

In most independent African states, however, the new rulers have been only too anxious to co-operate with the imperialists and to utilise their governmental and state positions for personal and class enrichment rather than for national development and the improvement of the people's livelihood. In such cases, African governments have openly taken an anti-working class stand and have often directed sharp blows against the working class and their trade union organisations.

This was so, for example, in the 1959–60 period, in Niger, Upper Volta, the Ivory Coast, Congo (Brazzaville), and Senegal; arrests, mass dismissals, the banishment of union leaders, the banning of union organisations and other forms of repression were experienced at that time. In some cases, as in the strike called in protest against the expulsion from Upper Volta of Yao N'Go Blaise, General Secretary of UGTAN (Union Générale des Travailleurs Africains Noirs), workers were shot at, in this particular case resulting in one being killed and twenty-three wounded.

But from about 1963 a distinct shift began to take place; the workers and their unions began to take the offensive against the puppet governments, in some cases gaining important successes. This change is of considerable political importance. Up to the early 1960's the main preoccupation of the African people was to end direct colonial rule and win national independence. This achieved,[1] they were prepared to

---

[1] It still, of course, remains the essential task in southern Africa and in a few other territories.

wait, to see how their new African governments would act, what steps would be taken to improve living standards, and to make fundamental economic and social changes. In a very short time, however, in a number of states it has been found that the main benefits of political independence are being reaped by a small upper crust, by the African bourgeoisie, State officials, traders and landlords. The former colonial political structure has been changed, but for the majority of people social and economic conditions have not been seriously altered. The big foreign firms and plantation companies still make huge profits on the basis of cheap African labour. Unemployment is widespread and is growing, and wages climb slowly while prices soar.

If the working people could see a purpose in their having to go short of benefits for a time, if they felt it necessary to sacrifice now in order to put their country on its feet and lay the basis for prosperity in the future, they would probably be prepared to tolerate their difficulties. But in most African states they see on every side waste and extravagance, corruption, bribery and embezzlement, nepotism and selfish careerism. All the worst features of the Western "rat race" are here demonstrated, openly and brazenly, in front of people who are often grievously undernourished, ill-clad and ill-housed. Under these conditions the benefits of independence must seem largely illusory.

In addition to carrying on their backs the burden of foreign monopolies, the African people now find in such states that they are expected to carry an additional load of indigenous rulers who are increasingly coming to be regarded as mere puppets of the big foreign firms and of the former colonial authorities. As a consequence, an ever widening gap is opening up in a number of African states between the African working people and their governments. A second round of struggle has begun; and a key part in it is being played by the workers and their unions who have shown that in African conditions the political general strike can sometimes be the decisive action to pull down an unpopular government.

Pro-imperialist governments have certainly been overthrown, but in ways quite different to what Fanon had expected. In Zanzibar it was a blow struck by a relative handful of resolute militants against a fairly weak state apparatus that toppled the Government; and it was popular support for this action *after it had been carried through* that enabled the new régime to consolidate its position. Significantly, an important group of these militants were trade unionists; and they contributed several members to the Revolutionary Council that was set up after independence.

In Congo (Brazzaville), it was the Congolese Federation of Trade Unions which, by calling out the workers on strike for three days in August, 1963, played the key role in bringing about the downfall of the Youlou government. The workers' strike action and demonstrations in the streets of Brazzaville were followed by a meeting between thirty union leaders in the Presidential Palace on August 15, as a result of which a new provisional government was established. "Having won the day in the capital," explained Leon Robert Angor, a prominent trade union leader who became Speaker in the National Assembly, "the unions sent emissaries to other parts of the country to explain the aims of the revolution and to prepare the people for the National Assembly elections and a referendum on a new, democratic constitution. It was a very difficult but indispensable campaign. We succeeded in winning over the overwhelming majority of the population."

There is no doubt that the unwillingness of the army to act in defence of Youlou was a key factor in the success of his opponents, but there is equally no doubt that the mass action of the workers and others in the capital was a powerful deterrent as far as the army was concerned. Explaining the significance of these events, *Le Monde* (August 17, 1963) commented: "The sudden removal of the President by the people of Brazzaville, led by trade unionists . . . is the first example of an African authority, the direct successor of the colonial system, being overthrown by the masses for fully political reasons."

In Cotonou, the capital of Dahomey, the general strike and mass demonstrations of workers called by the trade unions were key factors in the national protest movement in October, 1963, which toppled the régime—only to see the fruits of their victory snatched from them by the manœuvres of the military and the old corrupt politicians like Apithy and Ahomadegbé.

A valuable lesson was provided by the experience of the Sudan where the military dictatorship of General Abboud was overthrown at the end of October, 1964. The armed forces there were no negligible power, but, when the "moment of truth" came, they proved incapable or unwilling in the face of popular feeling to save the Abboud dictatorship. It was, according to most observers, the general political strike, together with the student demonstrations, which proved to be decisive in both phases of the struggle in October and November, 1964.

At the end of October a widespread protest movement, accompanied by a three day general strike, resulted in General Abboud agreeing to dismiss the military junta and accept a civilian government in its place. Within a week the new Government was facing the danger of a counter-coup by the military. On November 9 the workers of Khartoum went on strike to defend their new Government. People rushed into the streets, surrounded all important buildings and, armed with whatever weapons they could lay their hands on, demonstrated outside the British and United States embassies, shouting "Down with colonialism!" The British and American flags were torn down and burnt by the demonstrators. In face of this widespread protest the Government dismissed General Abboud from the post he still held as commander-in-chief, and shortly afterwards he was compelled to resign as President.

In explaining the demise of the military junta in the Sudan at the end of October, the *Daily Telegraph* wrote:

> The effectiveness of the general strike in Khartoum Omdurman surprised foreign observers. The capital was paralysed for four days. *It was the strike weapon that compelled the generals to give way* in negotiations with the National Front and swallow the insult of exclusion from the new National Government.

Commenting on the fall of Abboud in November, after the second major clash, the *Financial Times* wrote:

> The Khartoum students, Communist politicians and trade union leaders have shown that an unpopular military dictatorship can be broken. *The key to the fall of Abboud was the railway strike which threatened to cut off the capital from its vital oil supplies.* . . . It could happen elsewhere (December 2, 1964).

The overthrow of Abboud did not solve the problems of the people of the Sudan.

By 1965 reactionary political forces had regained dominance in the Government. Eventually, in May, 1969, a group of young officers took power. This was a popular move, and was backed by the workers and the trade unions as well as by the people generally. The significant thing about the experience of the Sudan as far as our examination of Fanon's theories is concerned was that neither in 1964 nor in 1969 did the overthrow of an unpopular government take place in the way envisaged by Fanon. In the overthrow of Abboud it was the mass action of the workers, and especially their use of the strike weapon that was decisive. In the second case, that of 1969, it was the military action that was the key factor. In neither case was it a peasant insurrection from the countryside advancing on the towns, to be supported by the *lumpenproletariat*.

In Libya and Somalia, too, the overthrow of unpopular, pro-imperialist régimes in 1969 was a result of a military seizure of power, evidently with considerable public support.

Fanon, although he was able to foresee reactionary coups in Africa carried out by corrupt military groups in the service of reaction and imperialism, apparently did not appreciate that the military apparatus in the newly independent countries of Africa was also subject to class and political influences, and that progressive forces could grow within it. These forces do not emerge in isolation from surrounding political phenomena. It is the consistent action of the masses, their growing discontent and anger which at times boils over into strikes and demonstrations and riots, which both stimulates the forward-looking officers to act and which provides the mass basis for the consolidation of their new power. The experience of Egypt (1952), and of the Sudan, Libya and Somalia (1969), fully bear out this new possibility.

The subsequent turn to the right in the Sudan by the ruling military officers in 1971 and the drive against the Communists who enjoy the overwhelming support of the Sudanese working class only confirms that progressive phases of the African revolution, if led by non-working class sections of the population, can easily lapse into a period of reaction in which repressive acts are taken against the working class and its Party. Significantly, after the 1969 overthrow of the old régime some of the victorious officers began to talk in lyrical quasi-Fanonist terms about the revolutionary role of the peasants whom they hoped to use as the basis of their political power. The Nimeiry government's move against the Sudanese Communists is a danger not only to the Communists and the long-term aim of socialism but also to the more immediate national interests of the country, especially since the Uganda coup which threatens revived assistance to the rebellion in the South. It is not out of place to note that, in the attempt since 1969 to find a solution to this long-standing problem, an outstanding contribution was made by the Communist Party, particularly by one of its leaders, Joseph Garang, who was Minister for the South in the period 1969–71, and later hanged after Nimeiry's counter-coup of July, 1971.

But to return to the role of the workers in post-independence Africa and Fanon's expectation that they would become conservative defenders of the *status quo*. The experience of Senegal and Nigeria, two West African states with a fairly well-developed bourgeoisie, reveals the growing class differentiation between the working class and the new rulers, and the continuing potentiality of the African working class to shake up those governments which collaborate with imperialism and refuse to carry forward the African revolution.

In Senegal, where, in the words of Majhemout Diop, the "parliamentary and bureaucratic bourgeoisie (in power) was, from the beginning, a reactionary class, an abortion tied, from its very origins, to its colonialist placenta like a foetus",[1] the workers have repeatedly clashed with the Government. The ruling circles in Senegal have frequently resorted to sheer demagogy and sown division between the workers and the peasants by arguing that increases in workers' wages would mean keeping the peasants in poverty. Strikes and demonstrations shook the capital, Dakar, in 1964; and a protest march for the release of political prisoners ended with the tearing down of the prison gates. Four years later, in May, 1968, Senegalese trade unions called a general strike in sympathy with student strikers in Dakar. The army intervened, and the union leaders were arrested, but released not long after when the Government agreed to wage increases, and accepted commitment to the idea of social security. In June, 1969, the unions called a general strike again, this time in support of striking bank employees. A Declaration of a State of Emergency, and divisions in the ranks of the unions, ended the general strike after 48 hours. In commenting on this strike and explaining the basis of Senghor's political power and his ability, up until now, to cope with the workers' struggles, the London weekly journal, *West Africa*, explains that 'apart from French goodwill', Senghor receives support from Islamic religious leaders, from the "rural masses", and from the army.[2] Thus, Fanon's sole "revolutionary class", the peasantry, is, in Senegal, found to be the main social support of the power of the bureaucratic bourgeoisie which is largely dependent on "French goodwill".

In Nigeria, the important role of the working class in the struggle against a pro-imperialist government after the attainment of independence has been even more pronounced. Overcoming previous divisions in their ranks, the trade unions were able to come together in 1964 and conduct one of the most significant general strikes in African history. This action was the biggest and longest-sustained general

---

[1] Majhemout Diop: op. cit., p. 51. (Author's translation.)
[2] *West Africa*, issues of June 14 and 21, 1969; pp. 666 and 709

strike yet held in an independent African state. It brought out almost a million workers and lasted for nearly two weeks, throwing a great shaft of light on the economic and social situation in Nigeria and helping to pin-point the problems facing workers in many other African states.

As noticed earlier, the Nigerian trade union movement has been involved in many industrial actions in the past twenty years, notably the strikes of 1945, 1949, 1950 and 1955–6. All these strikes took place in the period before independence and, being directed mainly against the big foreign firms, went beyond purely industrial disputes and therefore won warm support from other sections of the people who clearly recognised the national significance of these actions. The general strike of June, 1964, was conducted under very different circumstances, nearly four years after the winning of national independence. In that period there had been no basic improvement in wage levels, and the minimum wage in the capital, Lagos, in mid-1964, as stated by the authorities, was only £7. 11s. 8d. a month, and as low as £4 a month in the northern rural areas. While wages had been pegged to these low levels, prices had risen continually and the conditions of life of the workers had actually deteriorated instead of improving as they had hoped.

Already, earlier in 1963, the country had been shaken by a two weeks' nation-wide strike of dockers (February 1 to 14), when 16,000 dock-workers, in seven ports, came out for higher wages and better conditions. On that occasion the Government tried to break the strike by force. The police and the army were brought in, and three strike pickets were beaten to death by the police. But the workers stood firm, and received wide support throughout the country.

On September 27, 1963, the Joint Action Committee, which co-ordinated the three main trade union bodies—the Nigerian Trade Union Congress, the United Labour Congress, and the Nigerian Workers' Council—called a general strike in protest against the Government's wages policy. The strike was led by railway workers, municipal workers and dockers. An estimated 200,000 workers took part in the strike, which was called off after three days on the basis of a promise by the Government to set up a Commission to consider the whole wages position.

This general strike of 1963 helped to reveal more than ever before the deep-seated grievances of the workers. *The Guardian* (September 29, 1963), in an article entitled "Rising Discontent in Nigeria", referred to the "general disillusion about low wages and rising prices, growing unemployment, too much corruption and inefficiency". The journal, *West Africa* (October 5, 1963), pointed out that the September, 1963, strike "showed how widespread is the discontent of Nigerian wage and salary earners". It emphasised that *"Organised wage-earners are now, even if still only a fraction of the population, a significant political factor in Nigeria. . . ."*

As a result of the 1963 general strike the Government set up a Commission of six men—civil servants, business and professional men —under the chairmanship of Chief Justice Adeyinka Morgan. The Commission sat for several months, taking evidence. It finished its work in April, 1964, and presented its report to the Nigerian Federal Government. As the days went by and the Commission Report was not published and neither did the Government present its own proposals, the workers and their unions became increasingly impatient. The Joint Action Committee therefore presented an ultimatum to the Government on May 26—"Publish your proposals within 72 hours or else face a general strike."

On Saturday, May 30, with no report yet published and with no response from the Government, the workers began their strike preparations. At a mass rally that day, called by the Joint Action Committee, the workers expressed their determination to strike. They then began a march over the Iddo Bridge into Lagos, despite the Government's ban on processions. The police attacked the workers, and dozens were injured; in addition, a number of union leaders were arrested, including the veteran Michael Imoudu and the NTUC leader Wahab Goodluck. The workers' feelings were now thoroughly aroused. They were determined to give the Government a powerful and united rebuff. They responded with enthusiasm to the union leaders' appeal and at midnight on Sunday, May 31, the historic strike began.

Three days later the Government published the Morgan Commission Report along with its own White Paper. The facts presented in the Commission Report exposed the poverty of the workers and the corruption, extravagance and feather-bedding in high places. It was, in effect, an indictment of the Government's neglect of the low wages of the workers; and it indirectly revealed the Government's failure to do anything decisive about the cheap labour system bequeathed to Nigeria by the British colonial government.

Despite the Commission's Report, the Government White Paper only recommended a basic minimum of £9. 2s. 0d. a month (seven shillings a day) in the highest zone scale, i.e. Lagos, down to £4. 15s. 4d. a month (three shillings and eight pence a day) in the lowest zone, the Northern rural areas.

The publication of the Government's paltry offer only angered the workers still further. There was then no holding them back. Even those unions which up till then had not joined the strike were compelled to do so by the angry protests of their members. All the decisive sections of the working class, both in Government employ and in privately-owned concerns, and covering all the major centres in the country, came out. Within a few days, a million workers were on strike, and solidly united. On the eighth day the Government tried to break the strike by announcing it would dismiss all Government workers who did not return to work, and that these workers would lose whatever pensions rights they had. The Government thought that in the conditions in Nigeria, with widespread unemployment and no general social security system, the workers would be intimidated by this threat into returning to work in order to safeguard their jobs and pensions. Private employers issued a similar ultimatum.

It was useless. The workers were not to be pressured or divided by such moves. Within a few days it was the Government which had to sue for terms. The two weeks' strike had almost brought it to its knees, and the strike ended on Saturday, June 13. The Government and employers had to agree that there would be no victimisation; all dismissal notices were withdrawn; no strikers were penalised for the period of the strike, and the two weeks' strike period was regarded as leave, for which the workers received full pay without prejudice to any normal leave already taken.

The outcome of the post-strike negotiations was a further success for the workers, albeit a limited one. The Lagos wage was raised to £10 a month (compared with £7. 11s. 8d. previously, with the Government White Paper offer of £9. 2s. od., the Morgan Commission recommendation of £12, and the JAC demand of £20), and the northern rural rate was raised to £5. 4s. od. a month, compared with £4 previously and £4. 15s. 4d. offered by the Government. These wage increases were backdated to January, 1964. In addition, the Government agreed to introduce cheap fares and better transport for the workers, to establish a system of rent control, to accelerate low-cost housing schemes for workers, and to peg prices. The working out of these measures was left to Expert Committees on which the workers were to be represented. Periodic wage reveiws were also promised.

The strike therefore resulted in economic advances for the workers which they could see had been won by their determined and united struggle. The significance of the strike, however, went beyond the immediate gains of the workers. It had a deep political significance. In the three and a half years since independence, the workers had gained pratically nothing; in fact, for most of them conditions had deteriorated. At the same time, they had seen their country become a by-word for corruption and get-rich-quick racketeering. Nigeria had come to be regarded throughout Africa as a classic case of neo-colonialism, with imperialism still holding economic positions and wielding political and ideological influence. It was widely known that there were, in fact, more big British and American monopolies exploiting Nigeria than there were before independence. Barclays Bank, Shell, Mobil Oil, Texaco, Esso, ICI, the United Africa Company, the Dunlop Rubber Company, Amalgamated Tin Mines, and many other British and US firms had been able to extend their positions within Nigeria's economy. Nigerian politicians were competing with one another to get the plums of office, and increasingly becoming the mere pawns of the foreign firms. Submission to neo-colonialism had led to the large-scale squandering of the nation's resources. The Morgan Commission revealed that car allowances to civil servants had amounted to no less than £4,300,000 in the previous three years, while domiciliary allowances had cost £1,200,000. Higher civil servants were paying very little for their luxurious apartments which were mainly being subsidised by the Government.

Comparisons by the workers of their own wretched plight with the extravagance of Nigeria's ruling circles only served to increase their bitterness and their determination to struggle so as to compel the Government to make concessions. At the same time, the workers had been coming more and more to feel that the real default of their rulers was not simply that they had enriched themselves but, more significant still, that they were selling out their country to the highest bidder. The ruling Nigerian politicians and the feudal and trading strata with which they were allied were simply making hay while the sun shines, being able to enrich themselves because they were part of the general pattern of the robbery of Nigeria by neo-colonialist methods.

Nigeria's general strike of 1964 marked a new phase in the struggle of the Nigerian people. In its immediate aim it was an industrial action for higher wages; but in its deeper significance it was a reflection of the gathering of a new storm in Nigeria, and a powerful blow against a government and a system which were becoming increasingly un-popular. The strike undoubtedly shook the whole country. "Nigeria will never be the same again" was a widely held view.

The general truth of these estimates was confirmed within less than six months when Nigeria faced its gravest electoral and political crisis since independence. The strike had had no direct and immediate bearing on the electoral crisis, but it had sharply exposed the most reactionary ruling circles, intensified popular feeling against them, and thus opened the way to the emergence of a wide movement of dissent.

The 1965 General Election and those that followed in the Western Region witnessed a polarisation of the country between two blocs. But reaction was determined to hold on to power. The feudalists and their supporters brazenly declared the nominations of their opponents null and void, arrested candidates, kidnapped them, and in a number of cases killed them. By 1966 the country was on the verge of revolt, and in January the Government was swept away by a young officers' coup. Later coups thwarted the efforts of the people, and then followed the crisis over Biafra, and the two and a half years' war. Opinions may vary as to the causes of this war, and there will no doubt be different estimates as to its outcome. But the crisis into which Nigeria's ruling class was plunged in 1965 was undoubtedly influenced largely by the massive action of the workers in 1964. The major political role in the fight against reaction was that of the organised working class, not that of the peasantry; and this experience of Nigeria's once again calls into question Fanon's thesis.

Algeria, too, in the period after independence, challenges Fanon. The experience here was entirely different from that of the Nigerian workers but once again it reveals how wide off the mark were Fanon's derogatory estimates concerning the role of the working class. As has been noted earlier, the role of the Algerian workers prior to the launching of the armed struggle in 1954 and during the liberation war itself was not at all that depicted by Fanon. In the immediate post-independence period, too, the Algerian workers displayed a significant capacity for leadership and self-sacrifice which refutes the allegations against them of "selfishness", and bears out only too well the necessary role of the working class in advancing from independence to socialism.

During the liberation war the working people, both those in the liberation army and those who struggled in other ways in the towns and the countryside, held continuous and searching discussions about the future of Algeria—what kind of state they would create, the character of the economy to be built in the new Algeria, the social institutions which would be established, and the role to be played by the workers and their unions. Out of these discussions, and out of the experiences of the seven years' war, emerged the new Algeria, with its Tripoli programme, its aim of marching away from capitalism and towards socialism, and its determination to give a new life to the millions of poor peasants and workers.

In addition to the general desire of the people for major social and economic change, there was the terrible disruption and destruction resulting from the war and from the scorched-earth policy of the OAS, especially in the last few months of the war. With the coming of independence, large numbers of former French *colons* fled, leaving their farms and factories without management, without funds, without plans or instructions. To put Algeria back on to its feet, the Government had to introduce quite radical measures which enhanced the role of the workers and the unions. A major innovation was that of workers' management. This was not entirely a new responsibility for the Algerian workers. During the liberation war they had played a part in helping to administer the liberated regions, in managing their own resources, in allocating funds and materials supplied by international solidarity.

In the summer of 1962, after independence had been won, the workers, quite spontaneously at first, found themselves obliged to set up management committees in the abandoned factories and estates, mainly in order to safeguard their jobs. This movement spread, until a country-side network of workers' management committees was in existence. Responding to the responsible mood of the workers, and seeing in their action a necessary step to rescue the country from its state of economic difficulty, the government of President Ben Bella issued three historic decrees in March, 1963, which institutionalised and gave legal sanction to the principle of workers' management which the workers and peasants had begun to put into effect.

The Decree of March 18, 1963, defined vacant property as collective property (thus dealing a blow at those rich Algerians who had hoped to inherit, for their own purposes, the properties left vacant),[1] and extended its provisions to all abandoned enterprises or land, as well as to land not sufficiently cultivated. The Decree of March 22 legalised

[1] In practice things were not quite so simple. Get-rich-quick individuals in the town had already moved smartly into many vacated properties prior to the Decree, and still did so in a number of cases even after the Decree was issued; while in the countryside the *wilaya* leaders and their friends took over many vacant estates.

and institutionalised the principle of workers' management, and clearly defined the forms and functions of the bodies through which the workers were to administer the enterprise.

It laid down that within each enterprise coming under workers' management there should be a Workers' General Assembly (the highest authority in the enterprise or estate), a Workers' Council, a Management Committee, and a President. All were to be elected democratically by the workers of the given undertakings; and, in addition, there was to be a Director nominated by the State. Further, on a national scale, there was to be a body given the task of promoting the growth of the public sector of the economy. This body was to consist of the elected Presidents of the enterprise Management Committees, plus a representative of the FLN, the UGTA and the National People's Army, together with representatives of local administrative authorities.

The third Decree, that of March 28, provided for the distribution of the annual revenue of the farms and other enterprises under workers' management, part of the revenue being used for the general national interest, and to consist of a sinking fund, a national investment fund, and a national fund for the stabilisation of employment; and the other part being for the direct interests of the workers—wages and output bonuses, social security, education, housing, leisure facilities and so on.

On October 25–27, 1963, a Congress of the Socialist Agricultural Sector was held, attended by over 3,000 elected peasant delegates. On March 28–30, 1964, a year after the famous March Decrees, the first Congress of the Socialist Industrial Sector was held, to weigh up the experience of workers' management in the twelve months since the passing of the Decrees and to consider the lines of future activity. The Congress was attended by 1,134 delegates elected by 10,000 workers in approximately 450 industrial units. The Congress, in which members of the UGTA participated, and at which the role of the unions was fully discussed, debated seriously the two-fold task confronting the workers, namely that of assisting the Government and the party, the FLN, to overcome the economic difficulties and lay the basis for economic advance; and secondly, to ensure that within this framework the particular interests of the workers were safeguarded. Production problems, supplies, administration, trading, shortage of spare parts, late deliveries of raw materials, bad management, banking and credits, and direct economic sabotage by interests hostile to the régime—all these were the subject of animated and informed debate. In calling for more effective measures to be taken as a matter of urgency, delegates put special emphasis on the need to extend the public sector of the economy, and urged further nationalisation and the placing of more enterprises under workers' management.

On this latter point it is of interest to note that in his closing speech to the Congress of the Socialist Industrial Sector, Ben Bella, referring to the fact that at that time the public industrial sector accounted for only 12–15 per cent of Algerian industry, stated emphatically that this percentage would be increased as rapidly as possible. The following month, when the Congress of the FLN was held (April 16–29, 1964), demands were made for the nationalisation of foreign trade, banks and transport. Shortly after, enterprises in the food industry, flour milling and aluminium foundries were nationalised and placed under workers' management.

Fanon, it will be recalled, looked with disfavour on the steps taken by newly independent African states to nationalise foreign enterprises. He admitted the absolute necessity to nationalise "the middleman's trading sector" in order to prevent it falling into the hands of "the young bourgeoisie". He argued that in a colonial economy the intermediary market is the most important, and that therefore, "if you want to progress, you must decide in the first few hours to nationalise this sector".[1] Then, with that typically irritating habit of his, he argued contrariwise that "the national middle-class constantly demands the nationalisation of the economy and of the trading sectors"[2] in order that it may transfer "into native hands" the unfair advantages "which are a legacy of the colonial period". Quite apart from his tendency to confuse "Africanisation" of the enterprises with the question of nationalisation, Fanon's hesitations and contrary notions about nationalisation spring from his petty-bourgeois position, his ability, on the one hand, to see the dangers of the new grasping bourgeoisie, and, on the other hand, his failure, or refusal, to recognise that through working-class leadership it would be possible to advance to the building of a publicly owned economy in the interests of the whole people.

Ben Bella's appreciation of the role of the workers was quite different. Addressing the Congress of the Socialist Industrial Sector, in March, 1964, on the important role of the workers' management committees, he declared:

Everyone should know that this form of government was won in a tense struggle by the working people and that it has done more for

[1] *The Damned*, op. cit., p. 144.   [2] ibid., p. 124.

the glory of Algeria than all utterances and speeches about revolution and socialism. Irrespective of all the possible critical remarks—some of them quite legitimate ones—it is thanks to the working people that the land was worked and that operation at enterprises was put back to normal despite the absence of financial, technical and other assistance from the administration, which was completely disorganised at the time.

At this same Congress the delegates were informed of other steps being taken to strengthen the economy, and it was made clear that the workers were to be fully associated with the measures to be introduced. These included the setting up of a Commission on Markets, on which industrial workers would be represented; and the power to appoint a Government Commissioner to take the place of inefficient managements or of managements not conforming to economic regulations. These Commissioners were to be assisted by a works committee elected by the workers.

In giving their support to these measures, the workers were aware that their efforts, in co-operation with the Government, had already resulted in the creation of 400,000 new jobs, each of 24 days a month. They also knew that the question of wages and social security was being treated sympathetically by the Government and the party. With a full sense of responsibility for the tasks confronting the people as a whole, the Congress at the same time adopted resolutions urging the payment of an annual bonus equivalent to a month's pay, the establishment of wage scales and output bonuses on the basis of skill and output (with the ending of the differential wage zones), the unification of wage scales in each branch of industry in both private and socialist sectors, and a unified family allowance scheme for all workers.

Something of the spirit of the Algerian workers and trade unions at that time was captured in the May Day message issued by the UGTA for the 1964 May Day:

On May First this year the UGTA, the organisation of all Algerian workers who understand their part in the building up of their country, is issuing a call under the slogan of the construction of socialism. The two congresses—on industrial and agricultural self-management—confirm the deep hopes and desires of the workers. Indeed, the suggestions put forward have clearly proved the socialist understanding and the mature seriousness of workers in town and country. Working men and women, you hold the future of socialism in your hands; it is an exalting task which demands from all of you

vigilance and great efforts. Today your toil and labour are no longer
in vain. Every worker is assured that the fruit of his work goes to the
nation and its children. To increase production in quantity and
quality is to set the country on its feet again and to prove to the
whole world the vitality, energy, and strength of the will of our
people. Now we are working for ourselves and our country. The
time of the exploiters is gone, a whole page of our history has been
turned. . . .

By August, 1964, Rabah Djermane, the General Secretary of the
UGTA, was able to report that the organisation had a membership of
800,000 organised in fourteen unions, and that between 80 and 90 per
cent of all industrial workers, and a substantial part of workers in the
publicly managed sector of agriculture, were members. Explaining
that the Algerian unions regarded their "principal task" as being that
of "expanding and defending the gains of our socialist revolution",
Rabah Djermane stressed that the unions were playing such a key role
in the life of the country that they could be termed "governing
unions". He referred to the participation of the unions in drawing up
production programmes and economic development plans; to their
role in the workers' management committees in industry and agriculture; to their special efforts to help train technical personnel and
administrators, especially for the enterprises under workers' management, and for which a central trade union school had been opened to
train unionists who would themselves help train further workers at
factory and farm level; to the management by the unions of the social
insurance funds; and the help given to the poor peasants on lands that
had become publicly owned, especially to assist them setting up
agricultural co-operatives.

A copy of *Revolution et Travail* (official journal of the UGTA) of
November 5, 1964, provides two typical examples of the problems
the Algerian unions were then facing and the policy they were adopting. These two examples, one negative and one positive, describe the
situation in two different Algerian factories under workers' self-
management. In one factory, a building concern which had been
nationalised in August, 1963, and left by the previous owner in good
condition, the new director had become a petty dictator; there has
been no real consultation with the workers, and the enterprise had
begun to decline. The journal commented: "There is only one solution:
to restore the workers' legitimate rights by respecting the March
decrees, because there is no room for bosses in Algeria. As President

Ben Bella has said time and again: The workers must be the true masters of their destiny."

In the other factory, SIRAT, the largest coffee-roasting establishment of its kind in North Africa, striking progress had been made. *Revolution et Travail* wrote:

> The workers do not stint their energy and today they proudly show their results. . . . Everything is clean and tidy, well arranged and running smoothly. Good organisation assures a continuous flow of production, and has eliminated the slightest chance of petty pilfering or sabotage. The workers discovered they had many skills they had not known about. . . . Systematic improvements were introduced, raising the workers' living standards. . . . Material incentives correctly applied, team work based on mutual trust, the outcome of fraternal discussion, and firm links between management, members of the management committee and staff, gradually transformed the SIRAT enterprise into one large family united by the shared hardships and joys of workers who know they are the pioneers of a more humane and just society. . . . The experience of SIRAT conveys many lessons, especially for self-management coupled with joint management of the state and private sector. The workers are fully aware of their rights and duties.

This is certainly closer to the real voice of the Algerian working class than are the selfish tones which Fanon wished to attribute to the African workers. Through the words of the Algerian union journal one can detect a voice based on a full sense of responsibility to the nation as a whole, a voice conditioned by "shared hardships", self-sacrifice, and devotion to the people. A voice, in fact, which arose directly out of the experience of the Algerian struggle for liberation.

There can be argument about the significance of the first few years of Algeria's independence under Ben Bella's leadership. There was far more talk about "socialism" than the stage of development Algeria had reached fully justified. There were illusions, a tendency to talk big and to run ahead of developments. Realism and a sober assessment of the situation were not characteristic of Michael Raptis (Pablo) and the Trotskyist group around him who, in their somewhat influential position as advisers and technicians in economic fields, were pushing Ben Bella forward headlong.

But despite all the difficulties the country was clearly travelling away from capitalism; Ben Bella was increasingly understanding the need to encourage the workers to take a responsible and leading share in the management of the economy, and the working class was responding in a way which showed quite clearly that it was not animated by narrow selfish aims but, on the contrary, was ready to struggle and sacrifice for the progressive benefit of the overwhelming majority of the people.

The events in Algeria in 1965 on the eve of the coup—the massive women's demonstration in Algiers on March 8; the preparations for the Congress of the rapidly growing youth section of the FLN (JFLN); the historic conference of the UGTA in March, 1965, when the old leadership were swept out of office; and the growing sympathy between Ben Bella and the Communists—all were, to a considerable extent, the result of the effort of the organised workers, including the Communists. It was precisely this encouraging left trend that caused anxiety in some quarters and led to Ben Bella's overthrow.

The triumphant five mile march through Algiers which followed the UGTA Congress, when Ben Bella and the newly elected leaders of the unions marched arm in arm at the head of the mass demonstration, was an enthusiastic expression of the new mood and feeling. The Congress, according to many observers, was "a watershed of Algeria's socialist revolution".[1] A definite change in the balance of power in Algeria was taking place.

> For the first time, it seemed that the partisans of the socialist revolution were beginning to supplant the generation of Algerian politicians that had been brought to power by the struggle for national liberation. A new political generation was coming to the fore, with its own programme and its own conception of a political alliance.[2]

Within less than three months after the second UGTA Congress Ben Bella had been ousted by a military coup led by Boumedienne, who was "above all concerned about Ben Bella's *rapprochement* with the UGTA and the Algerian Communists".[3]

Since the coup the Communists, who merged with left-wing forces of the FLN to create the Socialist Vanguard Party of Algeria, have been driven underground and suffer constant persecution; while the UGTA has been reduced to a shell of its former self.

Post-independence Algeria in no way conforms to Fanon's pattern His faulty analysis of class forces cannot explain what happened in Algeria. His despised working class was the rock on which the new Algeria could have been erected; it became a victim not because it was "privileged" but because the petty-bourgeois and military leaders o

---

[1] David and Marina Ottaway: op. cit., pp. 141-3.   [2] ibid.   [3] ibid.

the new privileged class were determined to oust the workers from their advanced positions and prevent them eventually assuming the leading position in the State.

POST-FANON

In trying to assess the extent to which Fanon's arguments are valid it has been necessary to examine in some detail the role of different social classes in Africa's national liberation struggles. In particular, a close analysis of the role of the working class has been required. As regards the actual participation of the working class in the national struggle, the examples given here cover Nigeria, Ghana, Guinea, Mali, Niger, Dahomey, Cameroun, Sierra Leone, Gambia, Uganda, Tanzania, Kenya, Zambia, Malawi, Southern Rhodesia, Swaziland, Malagasy, Sudan, Tunisia, Morocco, Algeria, Congo (Kinshasa),[1] South Africa, Angola, Mozambique, Guinea-Bissau—no less than twenty-six different African territories in which, as has been shown, the struggles of the workers were closely intertwined with the whole fight for national liberation. For the period after independence, further examples have been given, covering Senegal, Nigeria, Congo (Brazzaville), Dahomey, Sudan, and Algeria.

It would have been easy to counter Fanon's assertions, which nowhere rest on any foundation of fact, with equally trenchant and sweeping contra-affirmations. But such a form of polemic would prove nothing. Equally, the mere citing of one or two examples would leave one open to the charge of incorrectly generalising on the basis of few untypical cases. It is hoped that the considerable weight of evidence produced here will at least raise doubts about Fanon's analysis of the role of classes in Africa, especially as Fanon himself brings forward no evidence whatsoever but rests content with a powerfully written, emotion-charged "indictment" of the working class in the form of rash generalisations unconfirmed by fact in any African state.

A number of commentators, who do not necessarily share Fanon's anti-colonialist views, have, in different ways, echoed his downgrading of the role of the African workers in the national liberation struggle. Thus, Elliot J. Berg and Jeffrey Butler (the former a United States assistant professor, the latter a South African carrying out research in the United States) have come to the conclusion that "what is most striking about the political role of labour movements in the countries

[1] Now known as Zaire.

of Tropical Africa is their failure to become politically involved during the colonial period, their limited political impact when they did become involved, and their restricted role after independence".[1]

In justification of their view, Berg and Butler claim that "many of the facts remained unrecorded". This may well be so in the sources they have drawn on, but I hope the facts cited above will demonstrate that there is sufficient evidence available to provide a completely different conclusion. What is really incredible about Berg and Butler's thesis is that they admit not only that the African workers had to face frequent repression, but that, especially in the British colonies, they faced persistent pressure from the authorities to prevent them participating in any organised form in the struggle for national independence. Surely this very fact indicates a conscious striving on the part of organised workers to become involved in the national struggle. And if this participation was sometimes restricted this can in no sense be dismissed as a failing by the workers; rather is it a condemnation of the colonial authorities who, in restraining the workers in this way, revealed only too well their class appreciation of the potentialities of the African working class. The constant anxiety displayed by the imperialists towards the African workers, their attempts over the first forty years of the twentieth century to deny them the right to form trade unions, and their subsequent repeated efforts to turn the workers' organisations into tame, non-political instruments of collaboration with the colonial authorities provide additional evidence of the striving of the African workers to play their part in the national movement. What the imperialists feared above all was that the workers would emerge as a leading force in the national liberation struggle, and would thus give it a more radical shape which would threaten the real economic basis of imperialist exploitation.

To bring Fanon up to date, as it were, some New Left writers raise additional doubts as to the ability of the African working class to participate in the further unfolding of the revolution after the achievement of national independence. Pointing to the growth of capital intensive investment in Africa in place of labour intensive investment Arrighi, for example, argues that there is a consistency of interest between international capitalism and what he terms the "labour aristocracy of Tropical Africa". The term itself is misleading, however

---

[1] Elliot J. Berg and Jeffrey Butler: "Trade Unions", in the book, *Political Parties and National Integration in Tropical Africa*, edited by James S. Coleman and Carl G. Rosberg Jr., Los Angeles, 1964, p. 340.

since Arrighi includes within its framework the African "élite and sub-élite".[1]

This élite and sub-élite, according to Arrighi himself, includes teachers, skilled artisans, executive and clerical grades, top civil servants, managers, personnel in public relations, lawyers and doctors. Arrighi lumps all these together with "the proletariat proper" (excluding migrant labour, the main body of workers) to arrive at his grouping of a "labour aristocracy". That there has been an emergence of an élite and sub-élite in Africa is obvious. There has also emerged a stratum of more permanent, skilled and higher paid workers; but this is still a minority of the working class, the main body of which remains largely unskilled and semi-skilled and certainly underpaid. The vast majority of Nigerian workers, for example, were found by the Morgan Commission in 1964 to be living in a state of "penury". The heroic miners of Ghana were shot down like dogs when they struck against their miserable conditions imposed on them after the overthrow of Nkrumah.

Arrighi provides no convincing statistical evidence to justify his argument about the labour aristocracy. Claiming that in most countries of Tropical Africa feudal elements, land-owning classes and national bourgeoisies are either non-existent or too weak to constitute a power base of the State, he comes to the conclusion that "the stability of the system" (this itself, in the light of the series of coups, a most questionable proposition) must be sought in the consistency of interests between "international capitalism" and some other classes which, he suggests, are grouped together in the "labour aristocracy".

To support their view, Arrighi and those who have followed him along this particular line of argument, produce figures and draw conclusions from them which are certainly open to debate. Arrighi provides one table, taken from Doctor and Gallis[2] which gives a total labour force in all Africa of 100 million, of which 19,200,000 are engaged in wage employment, including 5,800,000 in agriculture. Arrighi provides a second table, the source of which is not given, for a limited list of nine countries, covering non-agricultural wage employment, and giving percentages under two headings only, public sector and services sector.

Supporting Arrighi, Ruth First[3] arrives at the strange and un-

---

[1] G. Arrighi: "International Corporations, Labour Aristocracies and Economic Development in Tropical Africa", unpublished paper, 1969.
[2] Kailas C. Doctor and Hans Gallis: "Size and Characteristics of wage employment in Africa: some statistical estimates", *International Labour Review*, February, 1966.
[3] Ruth First: *The Barrel of a Gun*, London, 1970, p. 455.

explained conclusion that there are only eleven out of every 100 members of the labour force in wage employment (cf. Arrighi's 19 out of every 100). She goes on to assert that "everywhere government is the largest employer of labour", and then argues as if all those employed by the government were privileged white-collar workers. She even refers to "the heavy white-collar composition of the working class in Africa", although there is no statistical evidence to confirm this. It is difficult to credit that anyone who has travelled as widely in Africa as Ruth First has done, could argue in this way.

The assumption that "government employment" is "white-collar employment" is fallacious. Doctor and Gallis point out that the public sector in Africa covers not only administration, education, health, etc., but also a whole variety of enterprises which clearly employ manual labour, unskilled, semi-skilled and some skilled labour. These include farms, plantations, mines, factories, public works, construction, utilities, railways, posts, and telegraphs, etc. Nor do their enquiries, for which they provide figures, confirm Ruth First's assertion that "everywhere government is the largest employer of labour". In fact they state categorically that their findings "do not support the assertion that it already accounts for a majority of national wage earners".

We have already noted that agriculture is far and away the largest employer of wage labour; and there is no "labour aristocracy" here. As for the "service" sector used by Arrighi, this includes transport and domestic service. The last named, again clearly not in the "labour aristocracy" sector, is a major component of the service grouping. Doctor and Gallis also find that in eleven out of twenty-six countries examined manufacturing industry was the largest or second largest source of wage employment outside agriculture.

Ruth First, summarising Arrighi, finds two main strata in the African working class. "The first consists of the workers who inherited colonial salary rates and live a middle-class style of life." The second is made up of the lower strata, "the under-employed and under-paid, or the altogether unemployed, of the urban slums".[1] Vanished into thin air are the main contingents of the African working class—the agricultural workers on farms, forests, and plantations, the domestic servants, the miners, dockers, railway workers, and builders. These are the categories among whom in the main are to be found those who have constantly battled against colonialism and neo-colonialism. Africa's major

[1] Ruth First: op. cit., p. 456.

and most bloody strike struggles have been waged precisely by the miners, dockers, railway workers, and plantation workers. These are not white-collar workers. On the contrary, they are the decisive sections of the African working class and no unfounded arguments about a labour aristocracy can ignore them.

New factory production in Africa may allow scope for a small stratum of highly paid, skilled workers to emerge as part of a labour aristocracy. But this is *not* the main characteristic of the African workers today. By over-emphasising a certain trend, Arrighi and his supporters have virtually written off the majority of African workers. Anthony Steel, in reviewing Ruth First's book, approves because she "had not been misled into regarding the paid employees of industry as the proletariat".[1] Change, therefore, argues Steel, will come not from the workers but from those who hang "around street corners with nowhere to go and nothing to hope for".

This is how the Fanon myth works; and because it is based on part of the truth it too easily becomes accepted as the whole truth.

Fanon may not have realised that his attempts to belittle the role of the African working class could become such a source of confusion; nor that, in a different form, they would come to be echoed by cold-war warriors who ignore the main purpose of Fanon's work but, from quite a different standpoint, likewise attempt to cut the African working class out of the living picture of Africa's exploitation and struggle for freedom. But life is a harsh teacher, and the logic of Fanon's argument here, whatever his intentions, is to lend support to all those who wish to foster a stunted form of capitalism in Africa and maintain the working class in a subordinate position. Attempts to minimise the role of the African working class in the struggle for national liberation are part of the ideological and political struggle to keep the workers out of decisive positions of power and influence in the post-war independence period.[2]

If Fanon's assessment of the role of the African working class in the liberation struggle had been demonstrated to be correct it would be idle to ignore it. On the contrary, it would have been essential for the African revolutionary movement to analyse such a phenomenon. But no real evidence has been brought forward by Fanon to justify his case; nor have his followers been able to fill the gap. General assertions

[1] Anthony Steel: "Real Power in Africa", *Tribune*, January 29, 1971.
[2] Cf. for example, Nimeiry's attack on the Sudanese working class and Communist Party and his claim that they were the enemies of the Revolution when, in fact, they were the outstanding and most consistent opponents of imperialism over the past two decades.

that the African working class played no part, or little part, in the national liberation struggle get us nowhere. What is more, all the available evidence, all the facts of the struggles in the different African territories, show the opposite.

What is also striking is that, while Fanon recognises the danger of the *lumpenproletariat*, he calls for reliance on it as an important revolutionary force, and urges the need to win it over. As regards the workers, however, Fanon does not draw attention to their weaknesses in order to overcome them. Nowhere does he urged that efforts must be made to win the workers for the revolution; still less that the alliance of workers and peasants is decisive for revolutionary advance. The workers are simply written off, virtually put on the other side of the line-up as a counter-revolutionary force.

What is the purpose of Fanon's denigration of the African working class? Is it "proletarian messianism" (as Arrighi and Saul[1] term it) to refute Fanon on this point? The independent African states face a new, difficult and complex stage of their struggle. They have to break the grip of imperialism, defeat the manœuvres of neo-colonialism and endeavour to put their countries on a path that will take them away from capitalism and towards socialism. There is a concerted effort by imperialism and its supporters, including sections of the new capitalist forces in the independent states, to drive a rift between the workers and the peasants in order to make it easier to maintain political power in the hands of the collaborators with imperialism. Part of this political and ideological offensive is to deny the role played by the workers in the national liberation struggle as a justification for excluding them from positions of power in the building up of the new system in their countries after independence. Any unthinking acceptance of Fanon's ideas on the African working class assists those who want to keep the working class in a subordinate position in order that they can push their countries along a capitalist path in submission to neo-colonialism and in bondage to imperialism, or even in the vain hope of building an independent capitalist economy. That is why it is necessary to be concerned with this question.

There is no sense in exaggerating or misrepresenting the role either of the workers or of the peasants beyond what their role has actually been. But it is both unscientific and politically dangerous to deliberately minimise the role of the workers, and in no sense can an attempt to

[1] Giovanni Arrighi and John S. Saul: "Nationalism and Revolution in Sub-Saharan Africa", *Socialist Register*, 1969, p. 137.

re-establish the facts of African working-class participation in the national struggle be dismissed as "proletarian messianism".

Unfortunately it is not only the imperialist powers and the collaborating bourgeoisie which benefit from down-grading the workers. Patriotic nationalists, anti-imperialist officers, and other sections of the radical petty-bourgeoisie who genuinely seek to weaken their country's dependence on imperialism, are also often found to be taking steps to restrict the role of the workers after independence. Trade unions are denied an autonomous existence, made subject to enactments which give the State powers over the union, and sometimes turned into a subordinate wing of a national party led by the petty-bourgeoisie. Workers are denied the right to form their own separate working-class party, or, where it exists, pressure is put on them to dissolve their organisation and for its members to act simply as uncritical supporters of the Government and the national leaders.

This has frequently caused grave difficulties for Marxist parties, as in Algeria, the United Arab Republic, Nigeria and the Sudan. Sometimes it has resulted in a Marxist party taking tactical decisions which limit its role and bring harm not only to the further development of national liberation but also to the future prospect of a transition to socialism.

Those, like Fanon, who base their hopes on a peasant revolution ignore the fact that nowhere has the peasantry ever overthrown capitalism except in alliance with and under the leadership of the working class. Nowhere has the peasantry ever created its own permanent social system. The African countries will either become capitalist, in which case they will be led by the bourgeoisie; or they will advance to socialism, which requires a state led by the working class.

To advance to socialism the African people will have to defeat imperialism and carry through a social revolution. Such an immense and complex task, requiring the total transformation of society, cannot be led by the peasantry, and those who assert that it can, and at the same time claim to be Marxists, forget that the essence of Marxist teaching is that to break the power of capitalism political power must be taken by the working people led by the working class. As Lenin remarked, acceptance of the class struggle does not make one a Marxist; what distinguishes a Marxist from a reformist is the extension of one's understanding of the class struggle to the recognition of the need for the dictatorship of the proletariat. This requires the leadership of the working class, expressed in a Marxist philosophy and a Marxist organisation. One cannot build a peasant socialism. Socialism requires an industrialised and technically advanced society, and this presupposes a constantly expanding class of workers and a corresponding diminution of the peasantry, with peasants gradually moving from the country-side to centres of wage labour and changing their class status.

Connected with the whole problem of the advance from independence to complete liberation and the subsequent transition to socialism is the question of democracy. It is a major weakness of many new states and an important cause of setbacks in a number of countries, that the democratic participation of the people is replaced by conceptions of guided democracy, sometimes of a military character, and accompanied often by an excessive adulation of individual leaders; with the masses regarded as passive followers, not as creative thinkers and leaders; with government control of trade unions and a one party system which inhibits or forbids the existence of a party of the working class, that is a Marxist Party.

The cult of the leader springs from the soil of peasant society in which the people have been taught for decades to accept passively what the feudal landlord, the chief, or the marabout has told them. In Africa the democratic activity of the people is a key problem. The masses have been downtrodden for centuries, by patriarchal societies, by feudalism and above all by colonialism. For years they have been told to regard themselves as second class citizens, as inferior beings who are not capable of ruling themselves.

> Often they'll say: We're blacks, we don't even know how to make a safety-match. The whites have guns, aeroplanes. However can we get rid of them?[1]

To awaken these millions, and to create in their minds the conception that they have a role to play as makers of history, not as its victims—this is one of the major tasks facing the national liberation movement today. But this task can only be achieved if the people are led by a clear, scientific body of views, by an organisation embodying these views, by a Party in which at least its leading core is based on Marxism and uses Marxism creatively to tackle the particular problems of its own country, making use of the international experience of revolutionary struggle and socialist construction, but finding its own road to full liberation and socialism in accordance with its own

[1] From a conversation reported to Basil Davidson by Antonio Bana, a political worker of the Party of African Independence of Guiné and Cape Verde (PAIGC); quoted in *The Liberation of Guiné*, op. cit., p. 54.

class structure, history, traditions, institutions, and circumstances.

Those who denigrate the role of the working class in Africa are, whether intentionally or not, striking at the very heart of Marxism, putting up ideological barriers to the spread of working-class influence and assisting the extension of petty-bourgeois conceptions. Fanon nowhere shows any understanding of Marxism. He preaches instead a form of utopian socialism based on the peasantry and other non-working class sections. His projected "solution" is really no solution since it ignores the role of the working class as the only modern class which can organise the struggle, win over other urban strata, including newly arrived peasants and young school-leavers, and build an alliance with the peasants. Of course there will be individuals and groups from among the petty-bourgeoisie and intellectuals who will throw in their lot with the revolution; and some may even play a decisive role in the leadership. But what we are concerned with here is not individuals or groups, but social classes. By rejecting the working class Fanon rejects the main core of Marxism. Yet, strangely enough there are some left-wing thinkers who take these anti-Marxist views as a new contribution to Marxism.

In discussing the views of Fanon and the role of classes in the revolution it is not only a question of taking issue with him as to the extent of participation by each class in the revolution. What is at issue here is a question of ideology. Fanon himself admits that what Africa lacks is ideology, but he fails to face up to the question of ideology related to class. Which ideology is to lead Africa forward from independence to full liberation and socialism? Is it to be the spontaneity of the peasants with their utopianism, their leftist acts born of desperation and their lack of consistent organisation and theory? Is it to be the demagogy of the indigenous bourgeoisie, which indulges in ebullient talk about socialism while extending capitalism and keeping the working class out of power? Is it to be the adventurism and vacillation of the petty-bourgeoisie, which speaks in favour of violent change and socialism while glancing nostalgically over its shoulder at the "lost innocence" of the village before the coming of the European, because of its very fear of working-class power and discipline and the loss of its own status and privilege? Or is it to be the ideology of the working-class movement, Marxism, which alone can guide Africa out of its present difficulties, and create an alliance of the workers, intellectuals, petty-bourgeoisie and the peasants, and even sections of the national bourgeoisie, in order to take Africa along the road to socialism?

It is not so much a question as to who struggled most or longest being the measure of leadership, although the very act of participation and sacrifice in the struggle is part of the process of creating the disciplined, experienced and theoretically equipped force that can exercise a leading role; but rather is it a question as to which ideology must assume leadership, and on what decisive class force must this leadership be built if Africa is to advance from independence to socialism. This requires the creation of the necessary political weapon, the party of the working class. This is the decisive problem. Without its solution no advance to socialism is possible.

Fanon provides nothing to assist this process. On the contrary, his argument can only bring confusion and division to the revolutionary movement. He is right to emphasise the need to turn attention to the rural masses. He is correct to draw attention to the tendency of leaders of national parties and reformist trade unions to neglect the poor peasants. But his presentation, far from helping to build an alliance of workers and peasants, can only have the effect of making the creation of that alliance all the more difficult. His whole thesis discredits the working class and increases the distrust of the peasants towards them. Nowhere does he appeal to the workers, suggest to them, as allies in the revolution, how best to strengthen their links with the peasants. His appeal is to the peasants, petty-bourgeoisie and *lumpenproletariat* to turn their backs on the workers.

Thus, despite his militant language, his passionate denunciation of colonialism, and his plea for radical change, Fanon rejects the main revolutionary class in modern society, and provides ideological cover for an alliance of the élite, the petty-bourgeoisie, the *lumpenproletariat* and the peasants *against* the workers. Such an alliance is the basis of a variety of régimes in Africa, some of which have registered some progress since independence, but all of which are still exploited by imperialism. It is precisely because the African working class (still relatively small in numbers, largely tied to the countryside through the migrant labour system, and not yet a stabilised permanent force based on modern industry, factory production and urbanisation) has not been able to emerge as the leading force, ideologically, organisationally, and politically, that Africa has nowhere yet been able to expel imperialism. And in so far as Fanon's theories stand in the way of the African working class emerging to take that leading role their effect on the further unfolding of the revolution is negative.

This is not what Fanon would have wished. He was, above all else, dedicated to the struggle against colonialism and racialism. He died a comparatively young man. He was cut off in the midst of his development; and his honesty of purpose, if he had lived, might have helped to carry him forward to a clearer appreciation of the revolutionary process.

In view of his experiences, and his having witnessed the results of the appalling tortures and massacres inflicted by French imperialism on the people of Algeria, it would be remarkable if he had not written with bitterness, or developed his ideas with exaggeration and over-emphasis, and even distortion. But there was more to his thinking than hatred of oppression and racialism. His innermost being yearned for an end to the old world of capitalism and the creation of a cleaner, nobler world in which men could live as brothers, even though his vision of that world was blurred and confused.

It was clearly no accident that the title of his best-known book, *Les Damnés de la Terre* (*The Wretched of the Earth*), was a phrase taken from Eugene Pottier's original words for *L'Internationale,* the anthem of the international working class, which ends with the words "L'Internationale sera le genre humain". It was the fate of the "human race" which was really at the core of all Fanon's thinking; and when the theoretical confusions and political inadequacies of his writings have been forgotten, the noble struggle against colonialism to which he devoted his short life will still be remembered.

Debray and the Revolution in Latin America

3

Debray and the Revolution in Latin America

Régis Debray was arrested in Bolivia in 1967, and given a savage sentence of thirty years' imprisonment under the same government that was responsible for the capture and murder of Che Guevara. Debray's dignified and courageous stand in court and the subsequent heavy sentence meted out to him are a double testimony to his sincere commitment to the struggle against imperialism.

His release under a new Bolivian government in December, 1970, and the possibility which then became available to him to seek asylum in Chile are themselves ironic commentaries on the inadequacy of the views he expressed in his writings prior to his capture and imprisonment. The changes brought about in Bolivia following the ousting of the old régime by military forces, backed by popular sentiment, and the election of President Allende in Chile are two important successes registered in Latin America in ways which were certainly not foreseen in Debray's previous analysis.

Even before his capture Debray, though yet a young man, had aroused considerable interest in revolutionary circles through his writings on Latin America and, more particularly, because of his book, *Revolution in the Revolution?*[1] This work, together with his other published writings,[2] have given rise to considerable discussion, possibly as much in Europe and North America as in Latin America itself. Consideration of his views is necessary for understanding the Cuban revolution and its lessons; and especially for their relevance to the revolution in Latin America. Furthermore, despite Debray's own warnings that his theories were intended for Latin America alone, others have tried to extend their significance beyond this and to seek in them justification for their views on revolution in general, for their attitude to the role of classes in revolutions, and to the part played by

---

[1] Régis Debray: *Revolution in the Revolution?*, New York, 1967.
[2] Most of these have appeared in the volume *Strategy for Revolution*, edited by Robin Blackburn, London, 1970.

armed struggle, and justification, too, for their sweeping condemnation of "orthodox" or "traditional" Communist Parties.

> The Latin American revolution is taking a third way, the first stages of which have already been revealed in Cuban experience. Hence the need amounting to a necessity for Latin American revolutionaries to study the Cuban experience, to learn its lessons, and to guide their actions accordingly.
>
> But it is not only Latin American revolutionaries who are concerned. If Debray is right, the "Latin American way" may be of the utmost relevance to other countries around the world which are faced with conditions essentially similar to those of Latin America. And if a third way is possible, then those of us who live in countries where conditions are basically different from those obtaining in Tsarist Russia or Kuomintang China or contemporary Latin America, had better ask ourselves very seriously whether still other revolutionary patterns may not be possible.[1]

It seems to me that Huberman and Sweezy are themselves falling into a new dogmatic mistake in grouping revolutions into types—the Soviet type, the Chinese type, the Cuban type. Certainly there are laws of revolution common to all socialist revolutions and the course of revolution in any particular country is inevitably influenced by world processes and relations of forces. But what is also a law is that each socialist revolution is of its own type, is its own model, and, whilst it may learn and borrow from the experience of other revolutions, whilst it may imitate the spirit, the political essence of all socialist revolutions, it must at the same time proceed according to the specific conditions, class structure, traditions, national characteristics, institutions, experiences of the given people and so on. There has been not just a Soviet "way", a Chinese "way", and a Cuban "way"—there have been socialist revolutions in *fourteen* countries, each with their own particularities and variations; and each future socialist revolution, whether in countries of Europe, Asia, North and Latin America, Africa, or Australasia will have its own distinguishing features. There is no single model of revolution, as Lenin pointed out long ago, nor a continental model.

In his *"Left-Wing" Communism—an Infantile Disorder*, Lenin emphasised the necessity for revolutionaries to take into account the "definite peculiar features" of the struggle in each country, to apply

---

[1] Leo Huberman and Paul M. Sweezy: Foreword to *Revolution in the Revolution?*

the fundamental principles of Communism in such a way that they "*correctly modify* these principles in *certain particulars*, . . . properly adapt, apply them to the national and national-state differences".

He drew attention to the need to "investigate, study, seek out, divine, grasp that which is peculiarly national, specifically national in the *concrete manner* in which each country *approaches* the fulfilment of the single international task"—the overthrow of the capitalist system and its replacement by working-class power and socialism. It is this "single international task" which is common to all—but the road taken and the final forms are different in each case.

In his address to the Second All-Russian Congress of Communist Organisations of the Peoples of the East, November 22, 1919, Lenin told the delegates:

> You are confronted with a task which until now did not confront the Communists anywhere in the world: relying upon the general theory and practice of communism, you must adapt yourselves to peculiar conditions which do not exist in European countries and be able to apply that theory and practice to conditions in which the bulk of the population are peasants, and in which the task is to wage a struggle not against capitalism, but against medieval survivals.[1]

In a letter to Orjonikidze, March 2, 1921, Lenin advised that in Georgia the Communists should "avoid mechanically copying the Russian pattern. They must skillfully work out their own flexible tactics, based on bigger concessions to the petty-bourgeois elements."[2] One month later, in a letter to the Communists of Azerbaijan, Georgia, Armenia, Daghestan, and the Highland Republic, April 14, 1921, he once again stressed "the need to refrain from copying our tactics, but thoughtfully to vary them in adaptation to the differing concrete conditions. . . . Go beyond the letter and apply the spirit, the essence, and the lessons of the 1917–1921 experience."[3]

These warnings of Lenin, apparently, have been ignored by Robin Blackburn who has made the most extravagant claims on behalf of Régis Debray, arguing that the latter's writings "have helped a new style of revolutionary politics to spread from the Third World back to the metropolitan heartlands of imperialism. The sort of immediacy which the *foco* strategy can achieve has also been attained in the actions of the revolutionary movement of Europe and North America

---

[1] V. I. Lenin: *Collected Works*, Vol. 30, p. 161.
[2] V. I. Lenin: *Collected Works*, Vol. 32, p. 137.
[3] V. I. Lenin: *Collected Works*, Vol. 32, pp. 316–18.

—in factory and university occupations, black uprisings, squatters' movements and so forth."[1]

Writing in similar vein in May and June of 1968, a good number of Fleet Street revolutionaries in their Sunday newspaper articles described the seizure of the Sorbonne University and other Paris buildings in terms of an application of Debray's *foco* theory to French urban conditions. And there have been others, including Robin Blackburn himself, who have spoken of the temporary sit-ins or "occupations" at British universities in the same fashion. In so far as students or others have been influenced so as to regard such partial actions as the prelude to, or even as an actual act of "liberation", Blackburns' exaggerated extension of Debray's conceptions harms the revolutionary struggle rather than helps it forward. But to this aspect of the problem I shall return in the next chapter.

Debray himself, incidentally, makes no such claims for his views as are attributed to them by Blackburn. On the contrary, he argues that "it is a ridiculous and aberrant idea to make Cuba into a 'model' or basic type to be brought out in several editions either by reproduction or exact copying. . . . Everyone knows that the irony of 'universal history' lies in its habit of disturbing settled customs and breaking out into the unexpected, advancing from the wrong direction—that is, the direction on which the learned have turned their backs."[2]

Unfortunately not "everyone knows"—and in fact it is above all Debray's most enthusiastic supporters who have tried to make both the Cuban revolution and Debray's writings themselves a new dogma which, to them, has a universal validity.

Despite Blackburn's attempted application of the *foco* to Western European and United States' contexts, Debray asserts quite categorically:

> If this body of new ideas were to be transposed from one specific set of historical conditions to another, for instance from certain Latin American countries where it has its roots to the United States or Western Europe, there would of course be a danger of emptying it of its practical meaning, of reducing what it affirms as a revolutionary policy to something that appears as pantomime or simply romantic radicalism.[3]

[1] Robin Blackburn: Introduction to *Strategy for Revolution*, op. cit., p. 11, footnote.
[2] Régis Debray: "Reply to My Critics" (1969), included in *Strategy for Revolution*, op. cit., p. 232.
[3] ibid., p. 233.

Alas, all too often the pantomime has ended not in laughter but in tragedy and tears.

This underlines once again that the very attempt to give Debray's writings the stamp of universality, and to treat them as having a a general relevance for revolutionary struggle everywhere, is one of the main reasons why it is necessary to treat him seriously, to examine his theories and to consider whether they contain correct conclusions and scientific deductions, or whether Debray has elaborated his ideas too hastily, minimised or ignored or totally rejected facts and experiences where these do not fit in with his theories, or even put forward general concepts which at times he has had to contradict by quite different ones.

Most of Debray's writing has been done in the short space of five years, 1965–70, a time during which his thinking has clearly been going through a process of working out an approach to many fundamental questions of the revolution in Cuba and other Latin American countries. He himself, whatever some of his most fervent supporters may say,[1] has never claimed a scientific exactitude or finality about his views, although regrettably he writes at times with a somewhat arrogant presumption and certitude which would warrant the belief that he is staking such a claim. In examining what he writes, therefore, one should note the modifications taking place in his approach and the apparent inconsistencies that appear from essay to essay.

Secondly, while subjecting Debray's theories to critical analysis, one should never forget his four years in prison and his fervent desire to serve the cause of the revolution. But neither should his recent imprisonment dissuade one from a considered probe into the views he expounds. He himself, as a sincere opponent of imperialism, would doubtless expect that these concepts should be treated seriously and, if necessary, challenged.

Debray disclaims that his articles on Latin America were any more than "simply review articles—rough sketches intended for European readers".[2] He regards them as "light luggage (which) has never pretended, nor could it pretend, to be a body of 'theses', rigorously

---

[1] "Régis Debray has written three closely linked studies of the Latin American revolution. Together, they unquestionably constitute one of the most brilliant examples of Marxist-Leninist analysis to have appeared in recent years." Editorial in *New Left Review*, September–October, 1967, p. 8.

[2] Régis Debray: "Reply to My Critics" (1969), included in *Strategy for Revolution*, op. it., p. 238.

deduced one from the other, an established system of the final definition of a 'blueprint'. With regard to revolutionary action, such terminology is so frightening that it makes one smile." As for *Revolution in
the Revolution?*, this he regards as "simply a political tract . . ." which
attracted attention mainly because of his arrest and trial, and especially
because of "the overwhelming shadow of Che". In his writings
Debray examines experiences in a number of different countries of
Latin America, in the course of which he harshly condemns the Latin
American Communist Parties. No one is challenging Debray's right
to criticise revolutionaries of any country, but in his condemnation of
these organisations Debray makes sweeping judgments that necessi-
tate investigation, not simply because they differ from those of the
Communist Parties on the spot but still more important because they
present views about the past and future course of the revolution in
the Latin American countries which are certainly open to debate if
not to sharp challenge.

Debray's fundamental views arise not only from his examination
of the alleged mistakes and problems confronting Latin American
revolutionaries, but above all from his assessment as to what happened
in Cuba. It is clear that he has given much thought to the lessons
of the Cuban revolution; and he has had the benefit of discussions
with its leaders, in particular with Fidel Castro and Che Guevara,
although the conclusions he draws from these discussions are naturally
his own and naturally, too, he gives attention and emphasis to the things
which he has selected as significant but which do not necessarily add
up to a correct and balanced account of the revolution in Cuba.

In discussing Debray's analysis of the Cuban revolution one is
faced with the problem that there is a certain lack of detailed information available from official Cuban sources. There are, of course, the
speeches of Fidel Castro, which are invaluable as source material.
There are also the writings of Che Guevara, although these understandably concentrate on the mechanics of armed struggle and, in
particular, guerrilla warfare, rather than on the total shape of the
revolution, of the forces involved, its political stages and so forth.
Then there are the views of the leaders of the Popular Socialist Party
(the former Communists of Cuba), such as Blas Roca, Fabio Grobart,
and Carlos Rafael Rodríguez, who have contributed ideas and information which should also be considered if one is attempting to obtain an
all-round and balanced view of the way the Cuban revolution
developed and, above all, the reasons for its success.

Partly as a result of Debray's writings, and partly due to the over-simplified conclusions drawn from them by some of those who make use of the Cuban revolution and of Debray's ideas as weapons in their struggle against the majority of Latin American Communist Parties, a view of the Cuban revolution has grown up which not only flies in the face of facts but which, by the omission of some facts, the exaggeration of others, and the use of deductions which the facts really do not justify, presents an unbalanced picture. This is not of mere academic interest for historians; for false assumptions and conclusions regarding the Cuban revolution have become an important prop of those who are attempting to challenge Marxism in the name of Marxism.

Perhaps more dangerous still, these false conclusions are often used to mislead and confuse those who, now awakening to the need for revolutionary change, are thus being shepherded or attracted along adventurist roads which, despite the heroism and revolutionary sincerity of those so attracted, can lead, and indeed already have led, to disaster and death.

Debray himself has warned about this:

Cuba gave rise—without knowing it—to half a hundred revolutionary organisations on the margin of the Communist Parties, resolved on direct action. Several years of revolutionary action have now made it clear that heroism is not enough, and that ideological maturity and above all political sense, absence of sectarianism and seriousness in preparing armed struggle, were lacking. Too young and too spontaneously formed under the inspiration of Cuba, prisoners of the Cuban model, these so-called Fidelista organisations perished, at least in their initial form—in Colombia, Ecuador, Peru, Uruguay,[1]

What, in essence, is the substance of the ideas which Debray draws from his examination of Cuba's experience?

First, he sees the revolution as having begun with the attack on the Moncada barracks, led by Fidel Castro, on July 26, 1953.

Secondly, he contests the views normally held by Communist Parties in Latin America as to the role of classes in the revolution. He sees the peasantry as initially "passive" but as capable of becoming the main force; the national bourgeoisie as having no role in the revolution; the working class as a force corrupted by city life playing

[1] Régis Debray: "Problems of Revolutionary Strategy", in *Strategy for Revolution*, op. cit., p. 126.

little or no role; and the students and intellectuals as the leading element.

Thirdly, he totally ignores the role of the Popular Socialist Party of Cuba (the Cuban Communists) prior to 1953, during the period of armed struggle to 1959, and in the subsequent transition to socialist construction.

Fourthly, he considers that the armed action of the small group led by Fidel was sufficient to arouse the people against Batista. The "small motor" set in motion the "large motor". He poses the armed actions of the guerrillas as against "pure mass action".

Fifthly, he regards the *foco* (the originally isolated guerrilla group) as the only form of armed struggle likely to succeed in most Latin American countries.

Sixthly, he argues that the military actions of the guerrillas create the revolutionary vanguard, and not vice versa. It is this, above all, which constitutes "the revolution in the revolution".

Seventhly, his emphasis is to depict the revolution almost solely in terms of the overthrow of Batista. The armed struggle was "the revolution". The conflicts between different social forces within the anti-Batista camp are nowhere properly analysed, and he says practically nothing about the changes since 1960 and the struggle to go over to socialism and build a new society. To do this, of course, would have necessitated a new look at the role of the different classes in the revolutionary process, and, in particular, the key role of the working class.

It can be seen at a glance that these propositions of Debray's pose a number of basic problems of the revolution, and especially that of the role of the different classes in the Cuban revolution. The role of the Cuban Communists cannot be so easily dismissed as Debray attempts; their participation before, during and after the armed struggle was an essential factor in the success of the Cuban revolution, as I shall endeavour to show. Debray's thesis also carries one into a consideration of the site of the struggle, town or countryside; into questions of spontaneity and voluntarism versus political organisation and deliberate ideological work; the relations between military and political organisation; armed actions and mass struggle; the *foco* as a particular form of guerrilla warfare.

Nor can we overlook the extent to which the Cuban experience was based on particular Cuban circumstances and history, and the degree to which its success was assisted by positive external factors.

One cannot ignore the question of the attitude adopted by the ruling circles in the White House and the Pentagon towards the Cuban revolution up to 1959, and its contrasting attitude to the armed struggle in the Dominican Republic in 1965 and to other armed struggles in Latin America since the Cuban victory. In drawing lessons from Cuba's experience it would be fatal not to appreciate the new dangers and obstacles which revolutionaries in Latin America now face precisely because of the success of the Cuban revolution. Whilst it would be too sweeping to argue, as some have done, that each successful revolution closes the door to its imitation in form and method elsewhere, no serious revolutionary can fail to take into account that imperialism also draws conclusions from revolutionary actions and successes and, in consequence, sharpens its weapons and adapts its methods to the new dangers threatening it.

Any attempt to analyse the Cuban revolution and deal with the numerous problems listed above can naturally be only tentative. But the attempt must be made, whatever the difficulties and resultant shortcomings, since the constant repetition of incorrect conclusions has gained for them a certain currency. This has led to the consequent adoption of tactics in a number of Latin American countries and sometimes further afield, by revolutionary groups which have thrown themselves prematurely into battle in conditions which have led to their isolation and defeat. Furthermore, these armed actions, however courageous were those who carried them out and however sincere and justified their motives, have been utilised by reactionary régimes to restrict democratic liberties still further, to extend their repression against the democratic and anti-imperialist movement as a whole, and often to inflict heavy damage on the whole course of the revolution.

Revolution is a serious matter. It cannot be solved by subjective wishes or the bold use of revolutionary slogans. And serious revolutionaries have to take a responsible attitude towards the people—the workers, peasants, students, intellectuals and others—who feel on their backs any mistakes made by those who would claim to lead them. The suffering of the people which results from the inability of their leaders to mount an offensive against tyranny can be as great as the suffering meted out to the people following the failure of an offensive. A revolutionary organisation cannot itself flinch from suffering; nor can it hide from the people that the struggle for liberation involves suffering by them too. But at all times revolutionaries must strive to avoid unnecessary suffering and attempt to safeguard the people from having to make sacrifices which arise primarily from the mistakes of leaders.

Central to our understanding of the Cuban revolution and the reasons for its success is a correct grasp of Cuban history and an understanding of what the revolution was about. It is understandable that, with the most dramatic and significant phase of the Cuban revolution commencing in the 1950's, some people, and especially young people, should tend to look at Cuban developments solely in terms of this period.

This, however, is not the view in Cuba—neither of Fidel Castro[1] nor of the Communist Party which he leads. Not only are the patriots, Carlos Manuel de Céspedes, José Martí and Antonio Maceo revered as much as Castro and Guevara but the reorganised Communist Party of Cuba takes pride in the earlier heroes of the original Communist Party as it does in others who, in different ways, worked, fought and sacrificed for the liberation.

The entry of Fidel and Raúl Castro, Che Guevara, Camilo Cienfuegos, Juan Almeida and their colleagues of the Sierra Maestra into Havana in January, 1959, was the climax of a hundred years' struggle, and especially the inevitable outcome of the Cuban people's resistance to sixty years of exploitation by United States imperialism. When José Martí led the Cuban people into revolt against their Spanish oppressors at the end of the nineteenth century, US imperialism utilised the opportunity to declare war against Spain, to move into Cuba and take virtual control. From then on, until January, 1959, Cuba was in reality an American semi-colony, despite its outward formal independence, its possession of a national flag and a national anthem, and its Government of Cuban citizens.

By 1958 the United States owned one-third of all cane land, and had 956 million dollars invested in mining, oil (which it shared with Great Britain), trade, manufacturing, and public utilities which were entirely US owned. Its domination of the sugar industry and the economy as a whole distorted the economic life of the island which had to import rice, tomatoes, onions, chickens, eggs—and to pay valuable

[1] "What does October 10, 1868, signify for our people? What does this glorious date mean for the revolutionaries of our nation? It simply signifies the beginning of one hundred years of struggle, the beginning of the Revolution in Cuba, because in Cuba there has only been one revolution: that which was begun by Carlos Manuel de Céspedes on October 10, 1868, the revolution our people are still carrying forward." (Fidel Castro speech at the commemoration meeting held at La Demajagua, October 10, 1968.)

dollars for these items which the island should have been perfectly capable of producing.

For the people this meant poverty and oppression. Out of a population of some 6½ million, one million never wore shoes. Half a million rural workers never tasted milk or meat; their diet was mainly rice and blackbeans. Out of a working force of 2,400,000 no less than 700,000 were unemployed during the sugar slack season—the full season only lasted for three months—and 200,000 were out of work throughout the year.

An investigation made in 1957 by the Catholic University Association revealed widespread poverty, hunger and disease among peasants and farm workers.

While for the Cuban people it was a system of misery, for the big monopolies of the United States, whose ambassadors virtually told the Cuban governments what they should do, it was a highly profitable system; and to maintain it, and continue their system of exploitation, the US imperialists helped to instal régimes of tyranny.

In his writings Lenin has outlined the conditions which create a revolutionary situation. These are the inability of the ruling class to continue to rule in the old way, the unwillingness of the people to continue living in the old way, and the readiness of a majority of the politically active workers to die in order to change their conditions.

For such a situation to result in a *successful* revolution there must be a leading force, a revolutionary organisation, capable of understanding what has to be done, capable of planning and organising its own forces, and capable of inspiring and leading the people. That is to say, for a revolution to be successful there has to be a combination of objective factors, which arise out of historic development, together with the subjective factor, the organised, conscious force and leadership which seizes the decisive moment to propel the people forward for the assumption of power. Correct guidance by this leadership can react back in turn on the objective factors and hasten their process of maturing.

Ever since 1917, and today even more so, world factors—the balance of power as between imperialism and anti-imperialism (the socialist countries, the international working class and democratic movement, and the national liberation movements)—play a major role.

In Cuba, for sixty years prior to the overthrow of Batista, there was continuous battle against the various US-supported dictators; and in this long struggle, the Cuban working class always participated.

Martí's political party, the Cuban Revolutionary Party, formed in 1892, included representatives of the worker's clubs, and its leadership included Carlos Balino, a Marxist, who, in 1925, became one of the founders of the Cuban Communist Party. As early as 1904 a Workers' Party was formed, to be renamed in 1905, the Socialist Workers' Party. In 1925 the Communist Party[1] was established under the leadership of Carlos Balino and the legendary Julio Antonio Mella who, while still a young man, was murdered in 1939 in Mexico by the secret police of dictator Machado.

By 1946 the Communist Party had a large membership and wide influence, especially among the workers. With its help the Cuban people struggled heroically over many years. Thousands were victims of these struggles—jailed, tortured or murdered.

Nothing can ever dim the glorious memory of the heroes who stormed the Moncada barracks on July 26, 1953, nor of those who attacked Batista's palace on March 13, 1957, and still less of those who sailed in the *Granma* in December, 1956.

But regrettably, Debray's writings, by ignoring the struggles of the Cuban people prior to the 1950's, and even then concentrating almost solely on the armed actions of the last period of Batista's rule, have given rise to a conception of the Cuban revolution which omits many essential facts. Debray, and those who accept most of his main premises, display a certain contempt for or ignorance of the great sacrifices made by the Communist Party and by the Cuban workers, whose struggles were decisive for the overthrow of the Machado dictatorship in 1933, and were one of the factors in the defeat of Batista in 1959, and equally if not more so, in the rapid transition to the Socialist phase of the Cuban revolution.

It was following the formation of the Communist Party in 1925 that the workers' strike movement really began to grow. From 1927 on a number of economic strikes took place—in textiles, the shoe industry, the hat industry and in transport. In the course of these struggles the Communists helped the workers to gain an understanding of the necessity to extend the scope of their actions, and to fight for the overthrow of the Machado dictatorship. In 1925 the Cuban Communists had suffered a triple loss—Carlos Balino had died, the Party general secretary, Miguel Perez, had been deported, and Julio Antonio Mella forced to take refuge in Mexico where Machado' gunmen shot him down. The mantle of Party leadership fell on

[1] It later took the name of Popular Socialist Party (PSP).

Rubén Martinez Villena, who was also a leader of the National Confederation of Cuban Workers.

"At the beginning of 1930", writes Fabio Grobart,[1] "the strike movement plus the authority and trust which the Party enjoyed among the workers reached such a level that it was possible to pass from isolated struggles to actions enrolling all of the working class."

March 20, 1930, had been fixed by the Latin American Union Federation as the date for a continental day of action in support of the demands of the unemployed. The National Confederation of Cuban Workers, which was affiliated to the continental Federation, announced its readiness to participate in this day of action, and began organising "hunger marches". Machado's reply was to outlaw the National Confederation, which answered the challenge by calling a general strike for March 20, now not only for the claims of the unemployed, but also in protest against the banning of the Confederation. This was the first general strike in Cuba's history, and its significance is added to by the fact that it was organised despite the savage dictatorship of Machado.

"The general strike of March 20", writes Grobart, "attained complete success. More than two hundred thousand workers and employees went on strike for twenty-four hours. In Havana and Manzanillo, the cessation of production, trade and city transportation, was complete."[2]

Describing the general strike of March 20, 1930, as "the first mass action directed by the Marxist-Leninist Party of that time", Grobart gives his assessment that it was this general strike, followed forty days later by the large-scale demonstrations on May Day in Havana and other towns, that "changed the panorama of the struggle against Machado", inspiring students and others to take up the struggle, too.

"Encouraged by the victorious actions of the working class, the university students again launched themselves into active combat, followed by the secondary school students. The heroic students' demonstration of September, 1930, in which Rafael Trejo fell, was doubtless inspired by the heroic example of the proletarian actions of March 20 and May First. In this demonstration, in which many workers also took part, Julio Antonio Mella's old idea, expressed in a resolution of the first students' congress in 1923, again crystallised: "the necessity of a close union in struggle between workers and students

[1] Fabio Grobart: "36 Years Since First General Strike Against Machado", *Granma*, March 27, 1966 (English edition).
[2] ibid.

against imperialism and for a social régime that would be more just".[1]

The importance of the students' demonstration of September, 1930, as part of the anti-Machado struggle has often been stressed but, as Grobart rightly comments, "with evident historical injustice, the general strike of March 20 has been ignored, in spite of the fact that, due to its range, content and repercussion, it was the beginning of the great popular movement which put an end to the Machado tyranny and deepened the struggle against imperialism".

The March 20 strike, Grobart points out, also began a process of fundamental change within the workers' movement itself. "The working class began to be transformed into an active and independent revolutionary force, with its own program and its own policy." The Party extended its work beyond the confines of Havana and other towns; it went to the countryside to work amongst the peasants, set up "peasant leagues"[2] and to organise the workers employed on the sugar plantations and in the sugar factories, for it understood that this section of the Cuban working class was the most important, being the numerically largest, among the most exploited, and being employed in Cuba's major industry. The Communists organised the sugar workers and led them into struggle for the eight-hour day, for wage increases, for trade union rights, for unemployment insurance, for the right to strike. "In a short time", writes Grobart, "the communists had become the soul of the great strike movement of these workers."

It was the strike movement of the Cuban sugar workers which, in unity with the struggle of the workers and students in the towns, culminated in the second great general strike, that of August, 1933, which finally led to the overthrow of the Machedo dictatorship.

The year 1933 opened with a strike of sugar workers in Las Villas Province. They quickly took over a number of sugar mills, demanding the eight-hour day and improvements in wages. The United States, afraid of the imminent fall of Machado, whose rule had been steadily weakened under the impact of the people's growing struggles, tried to intervene. Its hope was that the US ambassador to Cuba, Sumner Welles, would be able to effect a compromise agreement with the bourgeois opposition which would make it possible to bring about the

---

[1] Fabio Grobart: "36 Years Since First General Strike Against Machado", *Granma*, March 27, 1966 (English edition).

[2] In the period after the downfall of Machado the peasants, under PSP leadership, seized land in several places and formed their own "Red Guards" to defend the land. Outstanding was the liberated commune "Realango 18" in Oriente Province, where steps were taken to improve the people's livelihood and diversify agriculture.

peaceful removal and replacement of Machado, without having to make any significant concessions to the people.

This attempt at US interference met with widespread opposition, as expressed in the stand of the National Confederation of Cuban Workers, the Communist Party, the Students' Revolutionary Directorate, the Students' Left Wing and the Anti-Imperialist League. In July, 1933, bus drivers came out on strike in protest against sackings. In the same month, the Second National Conference of the National Sugar Workers' Trade Union was held in Camagüey. Attended by seventy delegates from sugar mills and plantations, along with representatives from the National Confederation, the International Workers' Defence, the Anti-Imperialist League, the Young Communist League and the Communist Party of Cuba, the conference worked out its tactics for struggling for the workers' demands during the coming harvest.

On August 1, *El Trabajador*, the organ of the Central Committee of the Communist Party, called for an extension of the strike movement and for massive struggle "against the bloodthirsty Machado" and against the attempted "mediation" of the United States. The strike spread rapidly, and extended to the interior of the country through a network of strike committees, backed up by aid committees. Machado tried to drown the strike movement in blood. Spreading a rumour on August 7 of his resignation, he enticed thousands of people out on to the streets of Havana where his troops were waiting to mow them down with machine-gun fire. This barbarous reprisal boomeranged against the Machado régime. The strike movement became a national uprising under the slogan of "Down with Machado", and the dictator fell on August 12.[1]

In the following two decades the Cuban Communists were to the fore in organising the workers in town and countryside. A *Report on Cuba*, prepared in 1951 for the International Bank of Reconstruction and Development, refers to the "superior industriousness, devotion, training and tactical skill" of the Communists, which enabled them to establish decisive influence in the Cuban labour movement. A Christian Reformist, Felipe Zapata, has described how the Communists won the support of the workers by their "superior capability, integrity of principle, and moral strength".[2]

---

[1] See Pedro Luis Padrón: "The people's revolutionary action overthrew Machado", *Granma*, August 23, 1970 (English edition).

[2] Felipe Zapata: "Esquemas y notas para una historia de la organización obrera en Cuba", Unidad Gastronómica, June–November, 1948, p. 13. Cited by Prof. O'Connor 1 *The Origins of Socialism in Cuba*, Ithaca, 1970, p. 180.

A key role was played by the sugar workers throughout the 1930's, 1940's and 1950's, as well as after the overthrow of Batista; and the decisive influence amongst this important section of the Cuban proletariat was that of the PSP.

Outstanding was the Communist trade union leader, Jesús Menendez. Fired and thrown out of the Constancia Mill where he had been born, for the double "crime" of being a Communist and a Negro, Jesús Menendez became one of Cuba's greatest labour leaders and a constant target of the sugar companies who engineered his murder on January 22, 1948. From this same sugar mill came Abel Santamaria, who later was to become one of the martyred heroes of the battle of Moncada.

When the American journalist, Joseph North, visited Cuba just after the victory of 1959, he was shown a stack of literature produced by the Cuban Communists and their youth sector during the Batista régime. The stack consisted of one copy of each item, for the archives— and it was six feet high. It contained leaflets and pamphlets on wages, lower rents, housing, health, democracy.

"All these had been written secretly, printed secretly, distributed secretly, in the millions, during the reign of terror of the dictator whose uniformed and plain-clothes police were searching high and low for anybody engaged in this perilous work. And woe to those they captured."[1]

Such was the situation in which the young Fidel Castro appeared in the early 1950's and in which he planned the attack on the Moncada Barracks, of July 26, 1953.

With these events we are yet to deal, but at this stage we are seeking to establish the fact that the revolution did not begin on July 26, 1953, nor in December, 1956, but that the events of the 1950's were the culmination of a century-long struggle, and especially over the six decades prior to 1959, a struggle in which the Cuban workers participated consistently and to which the Cuban Communists for over three decades contributed both leadership and heavy sacrifice.

Even more important, it was precisely because there had been this long and arduous struggle, mainly led by the Cuban Communists, that the situation in Cuba had matured by the 1950's to the extent that it was possible for the actions of Fidel Castro and his heroic colleagues to receive an increasing response from the people. Those who subsequently attempted, on the basis of a superficial understanding of the Cuban revolution, to imitate the "Cuban example" elsewhere

[1] Joseph North: *Hope of a Hemisphere*, New York, 1961, p. 22.

(going up to the mountains to start armed struggle, or even starting it in the towns) and who came unstuck, failed to appreciate that one of the main reasons for Castro's success—and for their own failure—was that a mass sentiment for anti-imperialist revolution and for socialist change had been created in the minds of the Cuban people over several decades, due largely to the work of the Cuban Communists who were one of the most powerful Communist Parties in Latin America.

Lenin's conditions of a revolutionary situation had ripened over the years in Cuba. The Batista régime found it increasingly difficult to carry on in the old way, and apart from the opposition it faced from the very beginning from some strata of the bourgeoisie, other sections of the Cuban ruling class, too, began to desert it. The majority of the working people increasingly manifested their unreadiness to go on living in the old way, and a section of them, as shown in the armed actions that began with the attack on the Moncada Barracks in 1953, were prepared to give their lives for the revolution.

Slovo,[1] in his valuable analysis of Debray's theories, draws attention to Che Guevara's formulation in his book *Guerilla Warfare* that the Cuban revolution had shown that "one does not necessarily have to wait for a revolutionary situation to arise: it can be created". Che's conclusion is that Cuba's experience refutes "those who feel the need to wait until, in some perfect way, all the required objective and sub-jective conditions are at hand, instead of hastening to bring these condi-tions about through their own efforts". Slovo cites the interesting commentary by Glezerman[2] that "Determined action of the revolu-tionary forces, supported by the masses, can be merely the impetus which speeds the maturing of the revolutionary situation, but only if sufficient combustible material has accumulated in a country, if there are objective conditions creating a revolutionary situation. The idea that the boldness and determination of the revolutionary vanguard are sufficient to rouse the masses to revolution, is a dangerous illusion."

Che was right that a revolutionary must not wait until all the conditions have matured and that a revolutionary's own activity can hasten the process of the revolution; but Glezerman is correct, too, to point out that the determined action of the vanguard helps forward

---

[1] Joe Slovo: *The Theories of Régis Debray* (African Communist Pamphlet, London, 1968), p. 8.
[2] Dr. Grigory Glezerman: *Voprosi Filosofi*, No. 11, 1967.

the entire revolution "only if sufficient combustible material has accumulated in the country". Such combustible material had accumulated in Cuba, and this fact, together with the pioneering work carried out by Martí and later by the Cuban Communists, had produced a situation in which the heroic actions initiated by Fidel proved to be the vital spark to start the combustion. In other Latin American countries where the same degree of "combustible material" has not matured—or where other factors, not present in Cuba, act as heavy obstacles in the path of the revolution—mechanical attempts to emulate Castro's guerrillas have suffered setback.

Fidel Castro, in his speech of December 2, 1961, declared that "among the small peasants in the Sierra Maestra we encountered active members of the Popular Socialist Party" (the Cuban Communists). Castro has more than once remarked on the high degree of political understanding and organisational capacity he found amongst the peasants and rural workers in the Sierra Maestra.

Thus the developing revolutionary situation in the country and the years of patient and self-sacrificing work by the Communists and others had helped to produce conditions in which the armed actions of the 1950's fell on fertile soil. When the guerrillas came down from the hills the people in the cities rose in response and Havana was taken without firing a shot, for the working people were solidly on the side of the revolution. And if the rapid switch to socialism was made so relatively smoothly in 1960 this, too, was due not only to the swift changes sweeping over the people—for in days of revolution people learn more than they do in years of more normal peaceful conditions—but also to the years of socialist propaganda and political work carried out by the Cuban Communists.

Writing on the forty-fifth anniversary of the Cuban Communist Party, *Granma* has given the following significant and splendid testimonial to the early founders:

> Amidst the difficult conditions posed by the necessity to operate in secret, that small group of men making up the Communist Party of Cuba launched into the task of spreading and popularising Marxism-Leninism among the workers and peasants, and exhorted the people to struggle against imperialism and for national liberation and socialism. . . . The Communist Party of Cuba worked tirelessly to organise the workers and peasants and was the guiding light in the struggle for social gains and the final triumph of socialism. . . . The fruits of the effort begun by that handful of men on August 16,

1925, are now found in our victorious Revolution and in the awareness with which all our people today are tackling the gigantic task
of winning the battle against underdevelopment and of building a
socialist, communist society.[1]

Thus the united Communist Party of Cuba of today—in which the
July 26 Movement, the Revolutionary Directorate and the Popular
Socialist Party have merged their forces—recognises the continuity
of their fight, and the historical role played by the Cuban Communists
in the struggle against imperialism and for socialism.

Debray, in contrast, asserts: "The Party is the same age as the
Revolution, it will be fourteen on July 26th, 1967."[2] This assertion,
it will be noted, contradicts both Fidel's view that the Revolution
began nearly a hundred years before Moncada, as well as the official
view of the Communist Party led by Fidel which sees the present
Communist Party as a continuation of the Party first formed in 1925.
On both these points, therefore, Debray has no claim to be representing
the opinions of Castro.

It is, however, with the period of 1953 to 1959, and the conclusions
drawn from that, that most of Debray's argument is concerned. And
in examining his ideas here we come right up against his appraisal
of the role played by the different classes in the Cuban revolution
and by the Cuban Communists, as well as his theories concerning
armed struggle, the relation of politics to guerrilla war, questions of
ideology and questions of tactics.

Debray claims that "the Cuban Revolution has established that
in the insurrectionary phase of the revolution, while it is indispensable
to have some sort of organisation and a firm political leadership
(July 26th Movement) it is possible to do without a vanguard Marxist-
Leninist Party of the working class".[3] Such a claim, however, ignores
entirely the fact that at the time of the insurrectionary phase of the
Cuban revolution there was in existence "a Marxist-Leninist Party
of the working class", which increasingly won and organised widespread popular support for the Rebel Army, especially in the ranks
of the workers; and without this support the armed struggle could
not have succeeded. It can be argued that the PSP did not act as a real
vanguard in that phase, since it did not lead the armed struggle itself.

---

[1] *Granma*, August 23, 1970 (English edition).
[2] *Revolution in the Revolution?*, p. 106. The date reference here is to the 1953 attack on
Moncada.
[3] Régis Debray: "Castroism: The Long March in Latin America", see *Strategy for
Revolution*, op. cit., p. 53.

Nevertheless, despite this failure, one cannot sweep aside the role of the PSP in this way. Whatever may have been its shortcomings, and whatever its mistakes (which we shall come to later), the Popular Socialist Party was essential for the victory of the revolution, and, as we have seen, its leaders and heroes are regarded by Fidel Castro and the existing leadership of the Communist Party of Cuba as part of the Party's history.

It is significant that Fidel Castro, in his speech in Havana, October 3, 1965, when he announced the formation of the Central Committee of the new united Communist Party of Cuba, declared: "There is no heroic period in the history of our Revolution that is not represented here." In illustrating this point, he began by citing "Comrade Fabio Grobart, who was a founder of the first Communist Party".

It is, of course, true that the decisive leadership of the armed struggle was that of Fidel and the July 26 Movement. The same forces are also the dominant section of the Cuban Communist Party leadership today; but they act in combination with the leaders of the former PSP now merged into the single Communist Party. Debray's simplified presentation would give the impression that the emergence of such a Marxist-Leninist Party was *solely* the outcome of the armed phase of the struggle. As we shall see later, this was not how it really happened.

STUDENTS AND WORKERS

Thus far we have seen that the Cuban working class and its party, the PSP, consistently fought against tyranny, helped to pull down the dictator, Machado, in 1933, and continued to inflict blows against his successors over the two decades following his downfall and prior to the attack on Moncada. These actions by the workers, moreover, helped to create the conditions in which Fidel's historic act of taking up arms could expect to meet with support and eventual victory.

All this, however, seems to be a closed book to Debray. He has no faith in the workers and warns that "the city can bourgeoisify the proletarians".[1]

Elsewhere[2] he refers to the "illiterate peasants . . . suffocated by centuries of 'social peace' under a feudal régime. . . ." Such peasants,

---

[1] *Revolution in the Revolution?*, op. cit., p. 77.
[2] "Castroism: The Long March in Latin America", see *Strategy for Revolution*, op. cit., p. 57.

he writes, "cannot be awakened or acquire political consciousness by a process of thought, reflection and reading".

So who is left, according to Debray, to lead the revolution? "The irony of history", he asserts, "has willed . . . the assignment of precisely this vanguard role to students and revolutionary intellectuals, who have had to unleash, or rather, initiate, the highest forms of class struggle."[1] And again he writes; "The students are in the vanguard of the revolution in Latin America."[2] It is, according to Debray, the students and intellectuals who initiate the revolution by taking up arms, thus arousing the illiterate peasants who, incapable of reaching political understanding on their own, are shaken out of their feudal torpor by the example of the guerrillas. The total result of Debray's views on the role of classes in the Cuban revolution (and other Latin American revolutionary struggles) is to denigrate the working class, and to elevate the peasantry as the main potential revolutionary force which can be won only by the efforts of the students and intellectuals. No one would deny that in Cuba the rural population became the backbone of the revolutionary army; nor that revolutionary intellectuals such as Fidel Castro and Che Guevara played a key role in the leadership of the struggle (though it should not be overlooked that Lenin, and a number of other Bolshevik leaders in 1917, were revolutionary intellectuals; as were Mao Tse-tung and Chou En-lai; and Gramsci and Togliatti). It is also true that sections of the Cuban working class, under the influence of Batista's agent Mujal and other reformist trade union leaders who were imposed on the labour movement, tended to be economist and were reluctant to be drawn into the political struggle against Batista. But it would be entirely wrong to draw from these facts the kind of generalised conclusions drawn by Debray.

One must give full recognition to the key role played by such intellectuals as Fidel, Raúl and Che. It is a fact that amongst those who took part in the attack on the Moncada barracks, as well as those who sailed in the *Granma*, was a group of intellectuals who initiated and planned the actions, and took the original decision to commence the phase of armed struggle. But it would be entirely wrong to give the impression or to draw the conclusion from this that it was *all* an affair of the intellectuals and students, and that the workers, "bourgeoisified by the city", stood on the side-lines, too indifferent, too corrupted

[1] *Revolution in the Revolution?*, op. cit., p. 21.
[2] "Castroism: The Long March in Latin America", see *Strategy for Revolution*, op. cit., p. 44.

or too afraid to take part. (In any case, it would be dangerous to draw conclusions about the behaviour of entire social classes simply because the best-known participants in these actions happened to be intellectuals. No one would claim that the Russian Revolution of October, 1917, was led by intellectuals even though Lenin and other leading Bolsheviks were from the intelligentsia. It is not individuals we are concerned with, but classes—and the leading class in October, 1917, was the working class.)

A scientific examination of the social and class composition of those who took part in the heroic acts of Moncada and the *Granma* provides a picture somewhat different from that which Debray's followers take to be true. Debray himself is, perhaps, not to be blamed too much for what his followers have assumed or declared, but neither can he be absolved entirely from responsibility for the currency of these beliefs since he has never bothered to contest them.

Herbert Matthews, who first wrote up Castro's guerrilla forces in the *New York Times*, has claimed that those who took part with Fidel in the attack on Moncada were "nearly all students".[1] This has been repeated by Huberman and Sweezy—"Most of them were students or graduates",[2] by O'Connor[3] and, surprisingly, by Gil Green[4]—"The student youth that started the guerrilla war were mainly from the middle class." In such fashion myths are made. In fact, it can now be taken more or less for granted that in most left-wing circles this assertion concerning the prime role of the students is believed.

But what are the facts? Hugh Thomas, on the basis of a careful social study of the actual participants in the attack on the Moncada Barracks, claims that "The only organised group of students who took part in the assault on Moncada were five who withdrew at the last minute."[5] Among those who did take part he names one student, Ramiro Váldes, who became Minister of the Interior in 1965, and Raúl Castro, who had just left university. Of the other 165 men who took part, Thomas records that only seven, apart from Fidel Castro himself, "appear to have had any higher education, and probably most had had no secondary education. Certainly a majority of Castro's followers

[1] H. L. Matthews: *The Cuban Story*, New York, 1961, p. 144.
[2] Leo Huberman and Paul M. Sweezy: *Cuba, Anatomy of a Revolution*, New York, 1960, p. 28.
[3] James O'Connor: *The Origins of Socialism in Cuba*, Ithaca, 1970, p. 38.
[4] Gil Green: *Revolution Cuban Style*, New York, 1970, p. 69.
[5] Hugh Thomas: "Middle-Class Politics and the Cuban Revolution", see *The Politics of Conformity in Latin America*, ed. by Claudio Velíz, Oxford, 1967, p. 259.

were at this time lower class in origin, however that phrase is understood."

Thomas' analysis of those participants about whom he could obtain the necessary information shows 10 factory workers, 8 shop assistants, 8 other urban workers, 5 agricultural workers, 9 intellectuals (made up of students, lawyers, accountants, a doctor, a dentist, a cartographer), 1 farmer, and several artisans or small businessmen (butcher, baker, sweep, watchmaker, tanner, photographer). Of the fifty occupations listed by Thomas, over thirty cover wage work of one kind or another, and these constitute by far the largest group.

This analysis is well borne out by the seventy-two memorial photos of the Moncada martyrs published in *Granma* on August 2, 1970 (English edition). In addition to the seventy-two whose photos appear, *Granma* also lists four more names of martyrs for whom apparently no pictures were available but for whom details of employment are given. The captions under the photos (and of the other four) indicate only too clearly the class composition of those who fell at Moncada: teacher, medical worker, sales clerk, driver, electrical worker, physician, employee in a funeral parlour, driver's assistant, construction worker, clerk, employee and photographer, mason, carpenter, accountant, centrifuge operator, small farmer, oyster vendor, milkman, worker in a tile factory, parking lot attendant, bartender, stevedore and butcher, carpenter, clerk, sheet metal worker and flower vendor, mason as well as baker and pastry cook, farmhand, clerk, worker and athlete, shoe-maker, construction worker and student (killed later in *Granma* landing), market-stall holder (killed later in *Granma* landing), teacher, clerk, bakery worker, shipping agent, photographer, meatpacking worker, dairy worker, bank clerk, restaurant worker, docker, amateur boxer, travelling salesman, construction worker, messenger, cultural worker, agricultural worker, mason, student, farmer, cabinetmaker, mason's apprentice, florist, manufacturing industry worker, quarryman, kitchen helper, cook, construction worker, construction worker, typist and farmer, brewery worker, sugar mill worker, driver, worker in cattle industry, farmer, tanner (killed later in *Granma* landing), painter (killed in *Granma* landing), store clerk (killed later in Sierra Maestra), travelling salesman (killed later in Sierra Maestra), parking lot attendant (killed later in the underground struggle), refrigeration mechanic (killed in the underground struggle), and radio technician (killed in the underground struggle).

Some of the facts provided by *Granma* show a slight discrepancy with those presented by Hugh Thomas, but these differences are quite minor, and in no sense change the conclusions drawn by Thomas. Of the seventy-six names and occupations of the Moncada heroes listed by *Granma*, only two are listed as students, and a mere handful could be classified as intellectuals. Although there is a sprinkling of artisans and other non-proletarians of a lowly character (florist, oyster vendor, bartender, flower vendor, etc.), the overwhelming majority are wage workers of one kind or another, and of these about thirty are manual or industrial.[1]

And yet the myth spread by Herbert Matthews, and repeated by others, that those who took part in the attack on Moncada were "nearly all students", persists; and Debray, by his tendency to downgrade the role of the workers and emphasise the role of students and intellectuals, helps to perpetuate this myth. Given Debray's sincere commitment to the anti-imperialist struggle, it is to be hoped that he will not be unwilling to re-assess some of his views in the light of the actual facts.

For it is not only amongst the martyrs of Moncada that one finds mainly workers, but also, according to Hugh Thomas, much the same picture is revealed of those who took part in the *Granma* landing. "Most", notes Thomas, "were again not of middle-class origin."

The attack on the Presidential Palace, and the seizure of Radio Relój, carried out by the Revolutionary Directorate, on March 13, 1957, was a more emphatic expression of student participation in the Cuban revolution, but even here, as *Granma* points out (March 22, 1970, English edition) "the group of revolutionaries" who fell that day were "composed mainly of young students *and workers*" (own italics). Once again the facts are that the workers were not absent from the struggle.

It is not out of place to note that Castro himself, in describing the role played by different classes in the Cuban revolution, has said:

[1] Later, in his book (*Cuba*, London, 1971), Hugh Thomas provided, in an appendix, details of 154 people who had taken part in the attack on Moncada and Bayamo on July 26, 1953. His list, he claims, accounts for 90 per cent of those involved, which was 170. The social origins of the 90 per cent which he provides show quite clearly that the overwhelming majority of the participants were workers or others of lowly origin and occupation. The biggest single category were wage workers; there were only six students and only about twenty could be classified as professional or "white collar" (see pp. 1546–7). Thomas notes: "Those who followed Castro in 1953 were almost entirely men of the lower middle class or working class" (p. 824). In a footnote he adds: "To Lockwood Castro said that 90 per cent of his followers were 'workers and farmers'. He seems to have been right."

"All the participants . . . were young men with a modest, working-class background; workers and peasants, the sons of working people, employees."[1] O'Connor claims that this assessment is incorrect, but he provides no evidence at all for his assertions that students, intellectuals and professionals were the main protagonists.[2]

THE CUBAN COMMUNISTS AND THE ANTI-BATISTA STRUGGLE

But what of the role of the workers as a class, and of their party, the PSP, during the period of armed struggle? Is Debray justified in writing as if the workers played little role, and the PSP still less?

We have already noticed the considerable role which the Cuban Communists played in the long struggle of the Cuban people prior to 1953, and the view of Fidel and the present leaders of the Communist Party that there was a continuity between the activity and role of the Cuban Communists throughout the whole period of struggle against Batista.

The period of 1953 to 1959 is more complex to deal with if one is to strike a correct balance. When the *coup d'état* was carried out by Batista on March 10, 1952, the PSP was the first political party in Cuba to condemn it. It brought the masses out on to the streets in protest on March 10 itself, in Oriente, Camagüey and Las Villas provinces, and revealed the role of US imperialism in the coup. This was important because, at that time, there were some opponents of Batista who had illusions that they could win US backing in their efforts to overthrow the Batista tyranny.

The PSP did more than oppose Batista and expose the role of the United States. It advanced and popularised a complete programme for setting up a democratic and popular government to achieve national sovereignty, establish democratic rights for the people, carry through land reform, encourage working-class unity and trade union democracy, end racial discrimination, nationalise the public services, and carry through industrialisation in order to facilitate the country's economic independence. It called for a purge and reconstitution of the armed forces[3] so that they could become a real instrument for the protection of national sovereignty and of the people's gains. The main directions of this programme—for a real popular democracy, for national

---

[1] Radio interview with editors of *Pravda* and *Izvestia*, January 29, 1962.
[2] James O'Connor: op. cit., pp. 42–4.
[3] In practice, of course, the question of the army was solved differently. Batista's army dissolved to be replaced by the popular Rebel Army and the creation of a new state.

sovereignty, for radical changes in the state, and for economic and social reconstruction—provided an orientation for the people's struggle against Batista so that it did not become confined simply to his overthrow but opened the way to revolutionary transformation.

This programme of the PSP, which was known as the Democratic Solution of the Cuban Crisis, was further elaborated and completed in 1957 by the PSP National Committee which saw in it an instrument of struggle not just for immediate demands, important as these were, but for basic change.

Explaining this to the Eighth National Congress of the PSP, in August, 1960, after Batista's overthrow, Blas Roca, the General Secretary, declared:

> Today we can have a better appreciation of the importance of these plans. And they were an effective and powerful contribution to the development and extension of the national realisation that the elimination of the tyranny of Batista could not be limited to a change of personalities, but that the reality of the Cuban situation called for a change of régime, a profound change in its system and institutions. They were effective in showing that the changes that had to be undertaken were not only political and administrative, but were principally social and economic in nature; that the struggle against the Batista government could not be separated from the struggle against the semi-colonial structure and the imperialist rule that had produced and sustained that régime. . . . A correct position with respect to immediate demands and basic solutions . . . was a very important factor in defeating the attempt to limit the struggle against the tyranny to mere political changes and in cancelling the influence of the pro-imperialists, of those who hoped that the new government that would follow the tyranny would continue, like the tyranny itself, to be subordinate to imperialism.[1]

On the day of the attack by Fidel Castro and his followers on the Moncada barracks, July 26, 1953, the PSP was declared illegal and had to go underground where it carried on its heroic struggle right up to the overthrow of Batista in January, 1959. This work, as Blas Roca rightly asserts, "required great courage, firmness of principle, and ability and foresight, since all those that were captured were tortured, humiliated, molested, and many a one cruelly assassinated. The immense majority of those who found themselves in this position behaved like heroes,

[1] Blas Roca: *The Cuban Revolution*, Report to the Eighth National Congress of the Popular Socialist Party of Cuba, New York, 1961, pp. 13–14.

showing that the education and temper that the Party had given them was effective."[1]

The PSP was particularly active in developing a variety of actions by different sections of the Cuban people, and, in the first place, by the workers. This reached outstandingly high and militant levels in December, 1955, and again in August, 1957, when the actions of the workers went beyond the demands for immediate economic improvements. The national sugar strike of December, 1955, was promoted by the large-scale agitational work carried on by the illegal PSP and by the committees set up by the workers to defend their conditions. The strike was remarkably militant and embraced all the sugar refineries.

Many sections of the workers outside the sugar industry joined it immediately. The towns near the sugar refineries or connected with them declared themselves dead cities. In Santa Clara and other places, the emboldened masses blocked traffic on the Main Central Highway. In some sugar towns of Camagüey and La Habana provinces, the masses practically took over the situation and dominated it, even though they were unarmed. When they went into the struggle, the masses not only demanded payment of the differential[2] but also called for the defeat of the tyranny. "Down with the criminal government" was the slogan repeated by the masses who took part in the struggle on the streets.[3]

Describing this strike, Lazaro Peña, an outstanding militant trade union leader and General Secretary of the Confederation of Workers of Cuba until removed from that position by the Batista Government and compelled to go into exile, wrote:

At the end of December 1955 Fulgencio Batista, the dictator of Cuba, cowered for six fearful days in the biggest military barracks of the country which were locked and defended against the anger of the working people, while the US Ambassador cut short his holiday and flew back to the island in great haste to resume his behind-the-scenes control of the situation.

The reason for this upheaval was the six-day general strike in the sugar industry which lasted from December 26 to 31 and swept into action not only sugar workers but distributive workers, tobacco

[1] ibid., p. 16.
[2] The demand for payment of the so-called "differential" was the main economic demand of the strike.
[3] Blas Roca, op. cit., p. 24.

workers, railwaymen, students, small shopkeepers, and professional people as well.[1]

In sixty municipalities out of 126 the area was declared "dead", in other words all economic and social activity ground to a halt. In some of them the towns were practically taken over by the workers. The strikes were accompanied by mass demonstrations, to which the government replied with armed force. Several workers were reported to have been killed by the soldiers and armed police.

Following this action the workers began to struggle more and more under direct political slogans, protesting against the terror and the maltreatment of political prisoners. In this way the mass anger of the workers spilled over following the assassination of Frank País and Raúl Pujol on August 1, 1957, and a massive strike broke out in Santiago. From there it spread to the entire Oriente Province, and then to Camagüey, Las Villas and Pinar del Rio. "On the 5th it embraced practically the entire country, when many working-class sections of Havana answered the call and took part in the strike."[2]

THE FAILURE OF THE 1958 GENERAL STRIKE

A very different fate overtook the strike of April, 1958—and its failure has been used by Debray to push his argument concerning the relative roles of "the mountain" and "the city" in the Cuban revolution—and, by implication, in most Latin American revolutions in general. The facts about the 1958 strike, however, by no means serve Debray's arguments on this point. On the contrary, they tend to refute them.

Developing his theory that "the mountain proletarianises the bourgeois and peasant elements and the city can bourgeoisify the proletarians",[3] Debray seeks to find in the failure of the 1958 strike proof that the failure lay at the door of the "bourgeoisified" urban population.[4] And since his analysis of this strike is made in the context of his argument about the relative roles of workers and peasant it is understandable if his readers draw the conclusion that the failure was, in part, a failure of the working class.

[1] Lazaro Peña: "General Strike Wins Workers $6\frac{1}{2}$ Million Dollars", *World Trade Union Movement*, May, 1956, p. 16.

[2] Blas Roca, op. cit., p. 25.

[3] *Revolution in the Revolution?*, op. cit., pp. 76–7.

[4] It seems to me that Louis Althusser is right when he comments that Debray is "tempted to insert a class frontier between the mountain and the city" (letter to Régis Debray March 1, 1967).

Admittedly, Debray does not write this; furthermore he points to the heavy responsibility for the failure which must be borne by the petty-bourgeois leaders in the town. But Debray's lack of scientific clarity when dealing with the role of classes in the revolution is such that what he sets down on paper often gives rise to utterly false conclusions concerning the part played by the workers and by the peasants. In his downgrading of the workers and his rather romanticised hope that the mere act of taking up arms and fighting in the countryside will create the revolutionary forces and leadership, Debray shares an obvious affinity with Fanon.

The 1958 strike, which according to Debray was urged by "the city dwellers", was supported by Fidel. Debray states that this was because Fidel acted on the basis that "it was for the city dwellers to decide what was to happen in the city". By the use of the non-class term "city dweller" Debray clouds the issue; for, as the events were to show, only some of the "city-dwellers" apparently decided on this action; it was certainly not an independent initiative of the workers in the towns.

Debray argues that the strike was crushed because "the ruling class possessed all the means for repressing and crushing" it. But he goes further than this, and asserts that the revolution was "imperilled by the city" which prompted the strike because it was anxious to secure a *coup d'état* in the capital and so ensure a "civilian" government to replace Batista, instead of a government led by the Rebel Army.

To make his point Debray quotes rather extensively from Che Guevara. The argument is important enough to justify reproducing Che's words:

Why was the April strike called? Why was there a series of controversies within the movement between what we called *"the Sierra"*,[1] and *"the Llano"*,[2] which manifested themselves in diametrically opposed interpretations of the elements judged to be of prime importance in making decisions concerning the armed struggle?

The *Sierra* was ready to engage the army as often as necessary, to win battle after battle, capture arms, arriving one day at the total seizure of power, with the Rebel Army as its base. The *Llano* favoured generalised armed struggle throughout the country, culminating in a revolutionary general strike that would drive out

[1] "Mountain range".
[2] "Plain" (literally), but, in guerrilla terminology, meaning "the city".

the Batista dictatorship and establish a government of "civilians"; the new army would then become "apolitical".

. . . The April strike was prepared and ordered by the *Llano*; this was done with the agreement of the *Sierra* leadership, which did not consider itself able to prevent it (even though it had serious doubts concerning its outcome) and with the stated *reservations of the PSP which warned of the danger in time* (own italics—author). . . . These differences go deeper than tactical divergences. The Rebel Army is already ideologically proletarian and thinks like a dispossessed class; the city remains petty-bourgeois, contains future traitors among its leaders, and is very much influenced by the milieu in which it develops.[1]

Che's contrast between city and *Sierra* in no sense explains the class essence of what was involved. "Future traitors", after all, were found not only "in the city" but also in "the mountain", in the Rebel Army, vide Hubert Matos and Pedro Díaz Lanz; and the workers of "the city", of Havana, rose in their might in January, 1959, and staged a four-day general strike which helped Fidel and his heroic comrades to take the capital without firing a shot. The workers of Cuba had already shown, in their great strike of 500,000 workers in 1955, and in the strike of 1957, that they could sacrifice and die for the revolution, and that they could organise effective protest actions against the Batista dictatorship, actions which helped to develop the people's fighting spirit, stimulated their anger against the régime and provided them with necessary experience in the struggle. It is of little value, therefore, for Debray to quote Guevara or to use the failure of the 1958 April strike to elevate his "theory" of the countryside, the mountain, the guerrilla versus the city, the plain, the worker. Once again it seems as if Debray, in his anxiety to develop his thesis, ignores or overlooks some facts, or draws conclusions from them which cannot really be justified. Perhaps if he had overcome his apparent reluctance to turn his critical eye on some of Che's opinions he would have been less confident in his own theories.

In fact, Che himself, on a different occasion, spoke quite differently about "the city". Speaking on November 30, 1964, to commemorate the uprising in Santiago de Cuba, in November, 1956, intended to coincide with the landing of the men from the *Granma* (bad weather delayed the arrival until December 2), and also in memory of the later heroic action in 1957, when Frank País met his death, Che Guevara declared:

[1] Che Guevara: Preface to *El Partido marxista-leninista*.

The martyrs whose deaths we recall today are but links in the long chain of martyrs who died during the two years of the revolution in the city of Santiago. Every day, men of the people gave their lives here, around this city and in the ranks of the Rebel Army, which they swelled with their sons, for the freedom of Cuba.[1]

Che noted that most of the first group of men who came to join the guerrillas "came from Santiago de Cuba, sent by Frank País". Che then made these eloquent remarks about the people of Santiago which completely belie Debray's contention that the city corrupts and "bourgeoisifies".

We often thought [declared Che] of the dangers faced by the people in the city, of how difficult it must be for a known revolutionary to keep up the clandestine struggle, with a permanent death sentence imposed by the Batista henchmen hanging over his head. This is why, on a night in late July 1957, at a moment when two columns of the Rebel Army were formed, all the officers wrote a letter of gratitude to Frank País and the city of Santiago for their heroic, firm and prolonged action in support of the revolutionary struggle. The letter, however, was never received, for Frank País gave his life, as well, in the insurrection against the Batista dictatorship.
This city has won the plaudits of the entire nation.

The general strike proposed for April 9, 1958, was no normal strike. It was intended to be accompanied by armed actions, by the seizure of the armoury and other activities. In a sense the strike itself was planned rather as the accompaniment to a military attack, but an attack which appears to have been singularly badly organised. The critical comments of Huberman and Sweezy in themselves indicate a certain lack of clarity as to what kind of action was intended—strike or coup, or a combination of both?
"Faustino Pérez," they wrote, "in charge of the strike operation" (a single individual "in charge" of a strike is in itself a most quaint conception), "kept the time so secret that many workers weren't informed; some underground operators who had bomb-throwing assignments didn't get the bombs on time. Running a general strike under the best of circumstances is extremely difficult, and in this one serious errors were made. . . . It succeeded, temporarily at least, in Matanzas, Santa Clara, Camagüey, Holguín, and Santiago; but in the key city of Havana it was only partially successful so that troops from

[1] Reproduced in *Granma* (English edition), December 6, 1970.

Camp Columbia were available to be flown to the other towns where the rebels had momentarily seized power."[1]

Torres and Aronde are even more critical:[2]

> A few days before April 9, when the *Llano* leadership met in Havana with those in charge of Action and Sabotage, the latter were clearly opposed to a strategy that condemned them not only to political defeat but to death. When the plan was explained to them one thing was evident: beyond providing armed support for a strike, they were being assigned to carry out a putsch in which, to make things worse, there were no arms (only hundreds of waiting men) and they had to begin by obtaining them . . . in the end, going to a sure death was accepted for *reasons of discipline*. . . . On the 9th April, 1958, Marcelo Pla was to lead to their deaths a group of militants in order to carry out an action (the assault on the armory) in which it had no faith. Within a few days over one hundred fighting cadres of Action and Sabotage were murdered by the police.

This failure, it should be recalled, was not a failure of the Cuban working class, for whom Debray shows little understanding. The workers of Havana never took the decision to strike—the decision was taken for them. The Party which had the greatest claim to represent their interests and their outlook, the PSP, openly stated its grave reservations about the whole operation. The failure of the strike cannot therefore be laid at the door of the "city" (which Debray often implies is the working class); rather it was a failure of those who decided on it —and that includes the petty-bourgeois leaders in the town as well as those in the Rebel Army, in the "mountain", who agreed. As for the failure of the armed actions which accompanied the "strike" of April 9, these, too, cannot be laid at the door of the urban masses, but at the door of the leaders, in the city and in the Rebel Army, who planned or endorsed such actions.

April 9, therefore, in no way upholds Debray's theory concerning the necessity to stake all on the "proletarian" mountain and to distrust the "bourgeois" city. If it proves anything, it is that decisions about strikes must be taken in consultation with the working class itself; any attempt to organise a strike from outside the ranks of the workers themselves, without taking due regard to the feelings and estimates of

[1] Leo Huberman and Paul M. Sweezy: *Cuba: Anatomy of a Revolution*, op. cit., p. 62.
[2] Simon Torres and Julio Aronde: "Debray and the Cuban Experience", *Monthly Review*, July–August, 1968.

the workers and their organisations, is a desperate gamble, as April 9th turned out to be. Perhaps if more heed had been taken of the warnings of the PSP this setback could have been avoided. But Debray cannot bring himself to consider this as he is bent on presenting things in terms of his pre-conceived theory to which he tries to fit the facts. This, of course, is the very reverse of Marxism.

Debray's idealisation of the peasants and his hostility to the "city" and its "treachery" is a curious and interesting echo of the views of the Ukrainian anarchist, Makhno, who contrasted the "natural simplicity" and "anarchist solidarity" of the peasants to the "political poison of the cities" which "always give out a smell of lying and betrayal".[1] Fanon, too, shared Debray's preference for the peasantry, and dislike of the town. Cohn-Bendit, who has more than once indicated his hostility to the mass organisations of the French workers, greatly admires Makhno. In all three instances, the petty-bourgeois intellectual apparently finds it easier to identify with the peasant (who is basically petty-bourgeois, too) than with the working class. Subjectively, of course, such intellectuals are expressing their opposition to the *status quo*. The upholders of the *status quo*, however, as we have noted above when discussing Fanon, share this same sympathy for the "unspoilt" peasant, whom they always contrast with the "Westernised" and "corrupted" town-dweller, and especially the allegedly "privileged" wage-worker. Neither Fanon nor Debray had any intention of giving comfort to the "establishment". But ideas and theories are not luxuries. They are weapons of struggle. And if they are pointed in the wrong direction it is no consolation to the victim to be told: "I meant to shoot the other fellow."

THE PSP'S ATTITUDE TO ARMED STRUGGLE

Given the clear understanding by the PSP leadership of the need to develop the struggle against the Batista tyranny, and its understanding, too, of the role of the United States, and of the necessity to work out and make widely known a programme for revolutionary change to follow the overthrow of Batista, the question remains as to its attitude to *armed* struggle and to the actions initiated by Fidel Castro and his comrades, especially after the *Granma* landing.

Does Debray's contention—that the town softens up a revolutionary

[1] Nestor Makhno: *La Revolution Russe en Ukraine, Mars 1917–Avril 1918*, Paris, 1927, pp. 297-9. Cited by E. J. Hobsbawm in *Primitive Rebels*, Manchester, 1959.

leadership and makes it reluctant to embark on armed action—really stand up? Or what of his alternative suggestion—that the town is too completely held down by the repressive apparatus of the tyranny to enable the urban population to initiate armed struggle? It seems to me that neither of these propositions can be said to provide a satisfactory explanation as to the role of the PSP in relation to the armed struggle.

The unspoken implication in all that Debray has written is that the PSP played no part in the armed struggle—and that it was solely orientated on other forms of struggle which were not very effective. In the entire pages of *Revolution in the Revolution?* Debray mentions the PSP once—in a footnote, in relation to the failure of the strike of April 9, 1958.

Certainly Fidel Castro's historic contribution to the overthrow of Batista was that he grasped that the essential thing was to take organised steps to commence armed struggle, and that he seized the correct time for starting the armed actions—correct, that is, not in the sense of the correct year or month but in the historic sense that he appreciated that things had reached a stage in the 1950's which necessitated bold armed action in order to precipitate the further unfolding of the revolutionary process.

But for the PSP the situation was not at all easy or simple. Its first experience of the consequences of the attack on the Moncada Barracks —an action on which it had not been consulted—was increased repression by the Batista régime against the PSP itself and against other sections of the working class. In fact, the PSP was outlawed the very day of the Moncada attack, its newspaper offices wrecked and one of its leaders, Lazaro Peña, arrested along with hundreds of others.

One cannot ignore the fact that the experience of the working class throughout the world over a period of at least one hundred years prior to Moncada had taught it to be cautious over actions by small groups of people which led to attacks by the ruling class against the workers and their organisations. Some understanding, at least, even if not endorsement, should be accorded the Cuban Communists if they did not show immediate and complete support for the actions begun by the July 26th Movement. The caution displayed by the Cuban Communists in these circumstances is not difficult to understand, especially as some of those connected with the Moncada attack had links with the bourgeois opposition parties.[1] This latter fact gave rise to the initial belief that the

---

[1] Fidel Castro himself was a member of the Orthodoxos, although he did not share all the official views of that organisation.

attack was simply a bourgeois putsch intended to displace Batista by the former President Prio Socarras; and the World Federation of Trade Unions, in campaigning at that time for the release of Lazaro Peña, Carlos Fernandez, and Joaquín Ordoqui, did in fact characterise the attack on Moncada as "this adventurous action organised and led by some sections of the bourgeois opposition tied to the former dictator Prio and serving interests which have nothing in common with those of the workers".[1]

The initial statement of the PSP after the attack on Moncada contained the same estimate:

> We repudiate the putschist methods, peculiar to bourgeois political factions, of the action in Santiago de Cuba and Bayamo, which was an adventurist attempt to take both military headquarters. The heroism displayed by the participants in this action is false and sterile, as it is guided by mistaken bourgeois conceptions.[2]

And again:

> The entire country knows who organised, inspired, and directed the action against the barracks and knows that the Communists had nothing to do with it. The line of the PSP and of the mass movement had been to combat the Batista tyranny and to unmask the putschists and adventuristic activities of the bourgeois opposition as being against the interests of the people. The PSP poses the necessity of a united front of the masses against the government for a democratic way out of the Cuban situation, restoration of the 1940 Constitution, civil liberties, general elections, and the establishment of a National Democratic Front Government, with a programme of national independence, peace, democracy, agrarian reform, which will give land free to the peasants, and of the demands of the workers. . . . The PSP bases its fight on the action of the masses, on the struggle of the masses, and exposes adventuristic putschism as contrary to the fight of the masses and contrary to the democratic solution which the people desires.[3]

That the PSP should emphasise the need for mass action was absolutely correct. What it did not yet see was that a combination of armed activities together with other actions by the people in town and countryside was now on the order of the day and that it was necessary

[1] *World Trade Union Movement*, October 16–31, 1953, p. 17.
[2] See *Daily Worker*, New York, August 5, 1953 (cited in Scheer and Zeitlin, p. 126).
[3] See *Daily Worker*, New York, August 10, 1953 (cited in Scheer and Zeitlin, op. cit., p. 122).

to press ahead on both fronts. Instead it posed the armed actions as against mass action, and characterised the former as "putschist" and "adventurist".

In a certain sense the initial reaction of the PSP was similar to that taken by some sections of the international working-class movement to the Easter Uprising in Ireland in 1916. At that time the *Berner Tagwacht*, the organ of the Zimmerwaldists, including some of the Left sections of that trend, characterised the Easter Uprising as a "putsch". Lenin described this view as "monstrously doctrinaire and pedantic" and then went on to give this valuable definition of a putsch.

> The term "putsch", in the scientific sense of the word, may be employed only when the attempt at insurrection has revealed nothing but a circle of conspirators or stupid maniacs, and has aroused no sympathy among the masses. The centuries-old Irish national movement, having passed through various stages and combinations of class interests . . . expressed itself in street fighting conducted by a section of the urban petty-bourgeoisie and *a section of the workers* after a long period of mass agitation, demonstrations, suppression of the press, etc. Whoever calls *such* an uprising a "putsch" is either a hardened reactionary or a doctrinaire hopelessly incapable of picturing a social revolution as a living thing.[1]

For Lenin, it will be noticed, what was decisive was the attitude and relation of the masses towards the armed actions, not necessarily the limited extent to which the overwhelming mass of the people initially participated. In the Easter Uprising only some 3,000 people took part. But the "sympathy among the masses" was far wider and it was this, and the aims of those who took up arms, that determined Lenin's attitude. Lenin emphasised that there is no such thing as a "pure" social revolution. The 1905 Revolution in Russia, he pointed out, embraced people "imbued with the crudest prejudices, with the vaguest and most fantastic aims of struggle; there were small groups which accepted Japanese money, there were speculators and adventurers, etc." But—and this for Lenin was of key importance—"Objectively, the mass movement was shattering tsarism and paving the way for democracy; for that reason the class-conscious workers led it."[2]

The PSP's mistaken estimate of the July 26th Movement as being essentially "putschist" prevailed in the ranks of the Communists for a

[1] V. I. Lenin: "The Irish Rebellion of 1916", see *The Discussion on Self-Determination Summed Up*, July, 1916, *Collected Works*, Vol. 22, pp. 354–5.
[2] V. I. Lenin: ibid.

considerable time, and found expression again in some circles even after the landing from the *Granma*. But once again it is essential to see what were the circumstances which led to this mistake, without in any sense condoning it or attempting to play it down.

The landing of Fidel and his comrades from the *Granma* in December, 1956, was followed once more by ferocious attacks by Batista on the working people. On Christmas Day, 1956, twenty-two citizens, most of them trade union leaders and workers, were dragged from their homes and murdered by Batista's thugs. In the following few weeks many other active trade unionists suffered the same terrible fate. In the face of this savage persecution Lazaro Peña wrote:

> The armed movement, led by Fidel Castro, who landed in Cuba from Mexico, and the wave of acts of terror committed in this connection, have served as a pretext for the recent fierce crimes which have aroused the indignation of all. Ever since this armed uprising, repression has become worse. Vigilance measures have been pressed to extremes—thousands of homes are raided during the night by police squads. Hundreds of citizens have been arrested, imprisoned and tortured.[1]

Peña, at that time, considered that the armed actions by Fidel and his comrades were "doomed to failure". Before the end of 1958, however, Peña had reassessed the position, and was referring positively to the partisans in the hills as "patriots" who, together with the growing "vast popular campaign", would "end by overthrowing Batista's despotic regime".[2]

Lazaro Peña's initial assessment of the *Granma* landing and of the actions which followed was not identical with the official position of the PSP, as we will see below. The differences in estimate only serve to point to the complexity of the situation and help one to understand how the PSP viewed the launching of the armed struggle.

The PSP made two mistakes. The first, that of being slow to recognise the historical correctness of the actions begun by Fidel and his comrades. Secondly, a mistake of omission—that of not having commenced the armed struggle itself. As for the first of these, we have tried to explain the circumstances in which the mistake was made; nevertheless, as will be seen below, the PSP, despite its initial caution, increasingly rallied to the side of Fidel. As for the second mistake, this, too, was not so simple as some followers of Debray tend to think.

[1] *World Trade Union Movement*, April, 1957, p. 17.
[2] *World Trade Union Movement*, December, 1958, pp. 16–18.

In a self-critical passage in his report to the Eighth National Congress of the PSP, Blas Roca, the General Secretary, gives his explanation as to the reasons for the second of the PSP's mistakes:

> We had correctly planned, far in advance, for the prospect that the mass struggles, under the conditions created by the tyranny, would develop until they reached the phase of armed struggles or armed popular insurrection. But over a long period we did not take practical steps to promote these prospects. The prospect that such struggles, including the prolonged general strike, would end up in general armed insurrection, was envisaged as something that could take place spontaneously. We did not prepare properly, we did not organise or instruct or arm cadres far enough in advance for them to prepare and develop the prospect. That was our failure.[1]

It seems to me that this explanation is not entirely satisfactory. Even after the events of 1956 to 1959 Blas Roca is still talking in terms of the "general armed insurrection", as if his mind were rather set on the pattern of October, 1917, or the Paris Commune, and ignoring other ways in which the taking of power might be possible and was in fact achieved.[2]

Certainly he does not attempt to explain why the PSP itself did not take organised steps towards preparing not just for armed struggle in general, but for the particular form of guerrilla struggle commenced by the July 26th Movement. As in the case of Algeria, there was not only an underestimation of the necessity for the Party itself to organise armed actions but also an initially incorrect estimation and attitude towards those who had boldly set about organising such armed struggle.

[1] Blas Roca: op. cit., p. 26.

[2] There seems to have been a certain rigidity and dogmatism, a clinging to formulae, in the thinking of the leaders of the PSP that was to find later expression. This not only influenced its views on armed struggle and its expectations of a classical insurrectionary situation, but also some of its positions in the post-Batista period. It was probably slow in recognising the possibility of a quick change-over from the democratic to the socialist phase of the revolution. Blas Roca, for example, in his report to the Eighth National Congress of the PSP in August, 1960, emphasised that the main character of the Cuban revolution at that stage was that it was "anti-imperialist and anti-latifundist". This was correct; but the big question, how to make the transition from this phase to that of socialism, was not really dealt with in the report, although this was already becoming the central task of the revolution. And was not Escalante's later sectarianism and intrigue in part due to a tendency, connected with past dogmatic habits and thinking, to interpret the "leading role of the Party" in the narrow terms of controlling key positions rather than winning people by political persuasion and activity? Blas Roca, to his credit, already warned against this in his speech to the Congress, characterising sectarianism as being fed by subjective thinking that "nobody outside the familiar group is any good for anything". He rightly launched the slogan: "Sectarianism is division" (see *The Cuban Revolution*, op. cit., pp. 125-6).

In analysing the extent of the PSP's mistake, however, one should also consider what would have happened if the PSP itself had launched the armed actions in 1953 or 1956. Would it have enjoyed the same popular support that Fidel Castro, with his less obvious socialist commitment prior to 1959, was able to win in the course of the struggle?

This point, in fact, is made by Fidel himself:

> Naturally, if we had stood on the top of Pico Turquino (the highest point in the Sierra Maestra—author) when we had only a handful of men and said that we were Marxist-Leninists we might never have got down into the plain.[1]

Would a PSP-led guerrilla force have met with the same response as Castro did from the United States, which certainly underestimated or wrongly estimated his purpose and never sent a single US soldier to fight against him although, of course, it backed Batista and provided the dictator with economic and military aid including a military mission? (This was in marked contrast not only to the US aggression in far-distant Vietnam but also to the direct and massive armed intervention carried out by the United States in the Dominican Republic in 1965.)

Morray may be correct when he claims:

> Had he (Castro) been a member of the Communist Party, doubtless the Revolution would not have come so soon. The United States would have frustrated him short of power, either by deterring him with an effective threat of intervention, or, if necessary, by an actual intervention, as in 1947 in Greece, in time to keep the advantages of office from a Latin American Communist. Castro was the one kind of revolutionary who could succeed in the given historical situation.[2]

This is also underlined by O'Connor:

> The fact is that the State Department had little reason to believe that the Cuban Revolution posed any danger to the United States. United States policy-makers were taken completely by surprise when the revolutionary leadership launched a programme of deep-going economic and social reform, pressed on with it in the face of State Department and Congressional opposition, nationalised industry and agriculture, tore the island away from the world market

[1] Speech of Fidel Castro, December 20, 1961: cited in Goldenberg, op. cit., p. 169.
[2] J. P. Morray: *The Second Revolution in Cuba*, New York, 1962, p. 33.

system, and transformed a national, democratic revolution into a socialist revolution.[1]

Che Guevara made the same point when he remarked that "North American imperialism was disorientated and failed to fathom the genuinely far-reaching aspects of the Cuban Revolution."[2] Che added this significant explanation:

> The monopolies, as is common in these cases, began to think of a successor to Batista precisely because they knew that the people were opposed to him and were looking for a leader of revolutionary mind. What more intelligent stroke than to depose the unserviceable dictator and replace him with the new "boys" who would, in good time, serve the interests of imperialism? Imperialism repeatedly played this card from its continental deck, and lost pitifully. Before our triumph they suspected us, but they did not fear us. Emissaries of the State Department went several times, disguised as reporters, to penetrate into the depths of the mountain Revolution, *but they failed to diagnose any symptoms of imminent danger.* (Author's italics.) When imperialism was ready to react, when it realised that the group of inexperienced young men who marched in triumph through the streets of Havana had a clear view of their political duty and an unrelenting will to fulfil that duty, it was already too late. And thus, in January of 1959, the first social Revolution of the Caribbean and the most profound of all the American revolutions was born.

Even Che, perhaps, was oversimplifying things then, for by no means all of those who marched into Havana "had a clear view of their political duty". The Rebel Army included forces which were not yet won for socialism—and even some who subsequently came out against the turn to socialism and, in particular, against co-operation with the Communists. For the United States, too, although by January, 1959, it was historically speaking, "already too late", there might well have still been the hope in Washington and Wall Street that with the aid of men like Hubert Matos, Roberto Agramonte, Pedro Díaz Lanz and President Urrutia,[3] Cuba could yet have been saved for imperialism.

[1] James O'Connor: op. cit., p. 2.

[2] Che Guevara: "Cuba—Exception or Vanguard!", *Verde Olivo*, April 9, 1961 (see *Venceremos: Speeches and Writings of Che Guevara*, ed. by John Gerassi, London, 1968 p. 133).

[3] Urrutia, as President, and Roberto Agramonte, as Foreign Minister, were two of the members of the first post-Batista government who wanted to restrict the changes to minor adjustments in the direction of bourgeois democracy without any fundamental revolutionary transformation in the economic, social and political structure. In June 1959, Urrutia began a public anti-Communist campaign. He was joined by Pedro Día

In fairness to Debray, he, too, recognises the unique situation that faced Fidel and his comrades who went up to the Sierra Maestra not with the red flag of socialism (still less of communism) but with the patriotic and democratic flag of Cuba.

> The historic fortune of the Cuban revolution was to have been able to win the material and moral aid of (the) old liberal politicians whom Fidel and Raúl Castro, Camilo Cienfuegos, Ernesto Guevara and Almeida, young men without a political past but with élan and honesty, were soon to sweep away. . . . In the most intense moment of the clandestine struggle the July 26th Movement could collect funds in New York in the name of "The Rights of Man"; accept the material aid of Pépé Figueres, president of Costa Rica, for the defence of democracy; receive official monetary aid from Venezuela which had recently been liberated from the Pérez Jiménez dictatorship, as well as the plane-load of armaments from Larrazabal, president of the Democratic Junta; and assure itself of a world-wide protective publicity thanks to the capitalist press, *Life* and *Paris Match*.[1]

What Debray recognised in 1965 he appears to have largely forgotten when he came to write *Revolution in the Revolution?* in 1967. Out of the particular circumstances of the Cuban revolution he has tried, despite his warnings against a "Cuban model", to urge Latin American revolutionaries almost everywhere to emulate Fidel and his comrades by retreating to the countryside and raising the standard of armed revolt in the form of the small guerrilla creating the *foco*. He berates the Communist Parties of Latin America because of their reluctance to act in this way, although he himself is forced to admit that a Communist Party raising the banner of armed struggle would face a very different reaction, both internally and internationally, from that which initially (and almost to the end) met Castro. Of course, it should not be lost sight of that the Communist Parties' attitude as to whether or not to commence armed struggle is based on far more fundamental questions than the character of the response they might receive from liberal politicians, and reformist presidents, or even from non-communist sources in the imperialist countries (though, naturally, they would not entirely ignore these factors).

The fact that Castro was able to secure the support, or in some cases

anz, Chief of the Revolutionary Air Force, and Hubert Matos, Military Commander of Camagüey Province.
[1] *Strategy for Revolution*, op. cit. See essay, "Problems of Revolutionary Strategy", p. 133–4.

the neutrality, of forces which would normally be opposed to socialist change, in no way lessens the historic significance of his initiative in commencing the armed struggle but it partially explains the dilemma which has faced Communists before—in Algeria and Cyprus, for example—when other forces or groups have commenced armed actions against imperialism not as part of an anti-imperialist alliance including the Communists but as an initiative quite independent of the Communist Party.

> It is a historic merit of Fidel Castro [declared Blas Roca][1] although at that time he did not give enough attention to other aspects of the struggle—that he prepared, organised, trained and developed the fighting elements needed to begin and carry on the armed struggle as the means of overthrowing the tyranny and opening the way to the Cuban revolution. The armed struggle, begun by a little nucleus of guerrillas and by the action of armed groups in Santiago de Cuba, developed from that of small guerrilla bands which grew into columns and then into the Rebel Army, and became the decisive means for overthrowing the tyranny and establishing the revolutionary power.

Blas Roca rightly comments that "even though the armed struggle was a decisive means for achieving the overthrow of the tyranny and the triumph of the revolution, we should not underestimate the role played by the other forms of struggle, which co-operated in achieving these ends. The constant struggles, large and small, which were carried on in the cities and fields, outside of the field of military operations, and the agitation which went along with them, kept the repressive forces of the government in check, prevented them from concentrating against the guerrillas, politically influenced many members of the army and the police, disorganising these forces and tending to paralyse them. The actions and mobilisations of every type, in city and country, co-operated effectively in helping the Rebel Army to defeat the offensives of the army of the tyranny and finally to win the battle for revolutionary power."[2]

The PSP did not limit itself to such parallel actions to the armed war being waged by the guerrillas. It directly helped the armed struggle, too. Blas Roca claims that "as soon as the first combat groups were established in the Sierra, we tried to give them all possible aid. One outstanding and widely publicised case was a letter we sent to all the opposition parties, shortly after the *Granma* landing, asking them to

---

[1] *The Cuban Revolution*, op. cit., p. 26.   [2] ibid., pp. 26–7.

carry out joint or separate actions 'to hold back the murderous hand of the government and prevent it from using its superior force to exterminate Fidel Castro and his comrades'. . . . Practical aid grew and broadened in the course of the struggle. The co-operation included the organisation of supplies, communications, medical attention and the diffusion of propaganda, and went up to the recruiting of combatants."[1]

According to Torres and Aronde[2] "in Mexico some contacts were also made with leaders of the PSP, an organisation that had influence over the sugar workers, in order to synchronise the arrival of the *Granma* with the political struggles of the labour sector".

Goldenberg[3] writes that Che Guevara's fighting unit in the Sierra Maestra "was largely supplied by the Communist Party organisation in the town of Bayamo".

"By the end of the war", notes Morray,[4] "some Communist guerrillas, notably those commanded by Felix Torres in Las Villas Province, had been incorporated into Rebel Army columns; and individual Communists had been accepted as volunteers without discrimination. But these were a very small percentage of the rebel forces."

For their participation in this way three of the volunteers of the PSP who took part in the fighting emerged as *Comandantes*—three out of the Rebel Army's total of seventeen, chosen by the troops and the commanders because of their capacity and courage. Among the members of the PSP who went up to the mountains to serve under Fidel Castro was Carlos Rafael Rodríguez, former editor-in-chief of the Communist paper, *Hoy*, and today a leading figure in the united Communist Party. Rodríguez, in fact, was an official representative of the PSP at Fidel Castro's headquarters in the Sierra Maestra from June, 1958, to January, 1959.

Joseph North reports that when, shortly after the liberation, he interviewed Che Guevara in Cuba, Che angrily rounded on a correspondent of the *Chicago Tribune* who had asked a provocative question about the Communists.

"I will tell you this," declared Che, "though I am no Communist, I did not see your newspaper or you when the Communists were fighting and dying at our side in the Sierra Maestra."[5]

[1] ibid., p. 27.
[2] Simon Torres and Julio Aronde: "Debray and the Cuban Experience", op. cit.
[3] Boris Goldenberg: *The Cuban Revolution and Latin America*, London, 1965, p. 161.
[4] Morray: op. cit., p. 60.
[5] Joseph North: op. cit., p. 16. Note, this was before the united Communist Party was formed.

When the crisis arose in Camagüey province in October, 1959, after Batista's downfall, a crisis precipitated by the mass resignation of Rebel Army officers headed by Hubert Matos who called for a purge of Communists, Fidel and Raúl Castro both appeared as witnesses in the ensuing trial of Matos and "defended the government's respect for the Communists *as earned in the civil war* . . ."[1] (Author's italics). The whole country, wrote Morray, now heard the Communists "lauded and defended by Camilo Cienfuegos and by Fidel Castro".

Of course, there was misunderstanding on both sides between the July 26th Movement and the Communists from 1953 onwards—and some of the July 26th supporters kept their suspicions of the Communists after the overthrow of Batista and fell prey to the anti-communism of those who did not want Batista's defeat to be followed by revolutionary change. Eventually their anti-communism led some of them into the camp of the enemy.

Fidel Castro himself has explained why the Communists were at first suspicious of himself and his comrades.

> This suspicion was quite justified because we guerrilla fighters in the Sierra Maestra were still full of lower middle class ideas in spite of our Marxist courses. We lacked ideological clarity and only wanted to destroy tyranny and privilege with all our strength.[2]

With the same revolutionary honesty Fidel has explained the nature of the doubts which he had towards the Communists.[3]

> Did I have prejudices about the Communists? Yes. Was I ever influenced by imperialist and reactionary propaganda against the Communists? Yes. What did I think about the Communists? Did I think they were thieves? No. Never. I always regarded the Communists—at the University and elsewhere—as honourable and honest people. . . . Why did I have such opinions about the Communists? Simply, I am absolutely convinced that the ideas I have about the Communists, not about Marxism, about the Communist Party, were like the ideas of many people, a product of propaganda and prejudices inculcated in my mind ever since I was a little boy, almost from my schooldays. . . . In short, I was prejudiced against the Partido Socialista (PSP), prejudices stemming fundamentally from the (political) campaigns. I admit it with the honesty one ought to have when admitting such things. . . . On certain occasions, on certain occasions early in the revolutionary process, there was some

[1] J. P. Morray: op. cit., p. 66.
[2] Interview with *Unità* correspondent, January, 1961. Cited in Goldenberg, op. cit.
[3] Speech on December 1, 1961. Cited in Scheer and Zeitlein, op. cit., p. 223.

friction between us, probably due to different conceptions of certain things, but, basically, because we did not discuss matters. . . . I believe that one of the errors of those first days was the lack of any major exchange of views between the different organisations. Each of us was acting more or less on his own account. It was the revolutionary struggle itself which brought us more and more into contact, more and more into common discussion, more and more into an exchange of views, and steadily promoted our unification.

From the side of the PSP members, too, there were sectarian errors and grave mistakes arising out of tendencies on the part of such PSP leaders as Aníbal Escalante to establish a monopoly position and control for themselves after the decision had been taken to merge the July 26th Movement, the PSP and the Revolutionary Directorate into a single united organisation. In the summer of 1961 the first phase of this process was set in motion with the establishment of the Integrated Revolutionary Organisation (ORI)—the initial form of what was intended to be the United Party of the Socialist Revolution. By March, 1962, it had become necessary for Fidel to denounce Escalante publicly and to expose the serious nature of his attempt to place his favoured members into key controlling positions in the new body.

The denunciation of Escalante was supported by the overwhelming majority of members of the PSP; Blas Roca and Carlos Rafael Rodríguez fully associated themselves with the criticism of Escalante, and the latter's brother, César, was among the Communist leaders who voted for the decision to remove Aníbal Escalante from his post.[1]

Despite these difficulties, the members of the PSP played their part in assisting the unification of the three revolutionary organisations which culminated on October 3, 1965, with Fidel's announcement of the formation of the Central Committee of the Communist Party of Cuba. Included in the Secretariat were Blas Roca and Carlos Rafael Rodríguez.

POST-BATISTA—THE TRANSITION TO SOCIALISM

Debray's claim that the revolutionary Party was born in 1953 completely belies the past record of the Cuban communists which Castro and other present leaders have fully recognised. Further, it fails entirely

[1] A few years later Aníbal Escalante was accused of serious factionalism and plotting against the leadership of the Party, and was sentenced to fifteen years' imprisonment. It has been reported that shortly afterwards he was released and allowed to work on a farm, under some form of supervision.

to recognise that the PSP was an essential component of the new unified Party, and that this became possible only because of the role which the PSP played in assisting the carrying through of the revolutionary changes after the defeat of Batista. Debray presents his arguments as if the revolution was solely the physical overthrow of the former existing régime. Such a presentation ignores the main purpose of the revolution, which was to build a new society—and for this task the work of the PSP was of key importance.

One of the most striking and telling indications of the inadequacy of Debray's analysis of the Cuban revolution is that he virtually stops short with the military defeat of Batista. The problems of building socialism in Cuba, the role and relations of classes in the post-Batista period, finds practically no treatment in Debray's writings.

The period, 1959 to 1961, was a critical one for Cuba. Not so far away, in terms of modern communications and military equipment, was the United States, breathing fire like an angry and desperate dragon. Inside Cuba itself there were at first forces which sought to replace Batista with a bourgeois reform government which would leave the capitalist system basically intact. Such elements were to be found in the first post-Batista government—notably Urrutia and Agramonte—and even in the Rebel Army (Pedro Díaz Lanz and Hubert Matos).

Their main weapon to divide the revolutionary forces and prevent fundamental revolutionary change was anti-Communism. Castro and his colleagues defeated this attempted counter-revolutionary move, defended the Communists and initiated steps to unify all the revolutionary forces into a single Marxist-Leninist party.

Such a development was necessary to safeguard the revolution and to advance to socialism; and the PSP members themselves, by the patient but principled way in which they worked after the overthrow of Batista, made it easier for Castro to win over the majority of the Cuban people to head for socialism and to establish a unified Communist Party for this purpose.

> With the collapse of Batista, the Revolution entered a new phase; in its advance it made new enemies and tested its ranks with a new kind of trial. The Communists, long prepared for such a struggle began to stand out for their loyalty and understanding.[1]

As Morray explains, once the post-Batista struggle was faced with the task of advancing from the bourgeois-democratic phase of the

[1] Morray: op. cit., p. 33.

revolution to the socialist phase—a transition which, in Cuba, happened in a few short months (as, indeed, it did in Russia in 1917)—reliance on the working class was essential, and to obtain this support the Communists were indispensable. ". . . the solidarity of the proletariat became a life-and-death question for the Revolution. But where the proletariat were, there also were the Communists."[1] It was Castro's revolutionary understanding that helped him to see his way clear in this situation and to unite with the Communists. But some credit must surely go to the Communists, too, for conducting themselves in a responsible manner and so facilitating the growth of this unity.

> One of the creditable sacrifices of Cuban Communists has been their ungrudging support for the non-party man who arrived late to pre-empt the honor of leading the country into the promised land. Castro knew how to appreciate their unselfishness. The historic marriage of the Mountain with the proletariat has been made easier by the magnanimity of leaders on both sides.[2]

Debray, however, does not seem to understand this. For him the whole process of the revolution can be explained as the action of a few hundred guerrillas who swept down from the mountains, liberated the towns and proceeded to build socialism. How they were sustained, how the people were won to support them, how the people and especially the working class was won for socialism, how the alliance was forged between the workers and the peasants, how the enemies of revolutionary unity, the protagonists of anti-communism, were defeated at large, and how their marionettes were overthrown in the trade union movement whose official organisations had been dominated for several years by the US backed *Mujalistas*[3]—all this appears to be a closed book to Debray. But these problems go right to the heart of the revolution. Without their solution there could have been no defeat of Batista, still less the transition to socialism.

As Eqbal Ahmad has commented:

> A thousand or so guerrillas did not make possible Cuba's transition from liberation to socialism; the post-liberation alliance with the

[1] ibid., p. 48.
[2] ibid., p. 49.
[3] Supporters of Eusebio Mujal, trade union leader under Batista; Mujal was supported by ORIT (the ICFTU's American continental organisation, backed by the US State Department and the CIA). After Batista's downfall Mujal fled from Cuba, taking his ill-gotten fortune with him.

Communists probably did. Today the spectre of a stagnant, bureau-cratising Algeria under the Liberation Army haunts us.[1]

Even Goldenberg, no friend of the Communists, has had to admit that the growing role of the Cuban Communists after the downfall of Batista was due not only "to the radicalisation of the revolution" but also to the fact that "they (the Communists) alone possessed a disciplined organisation".[2]

Max Clos[3] has written:

> In the middle of the remarkable anarchy which exists in Cuba, one occasionally meets islands of some orderliness, for example in the political police and also in land reform. Every time one can detect the presence of communist cadres. Another example is the people's militia. . . . The militia had to be provided with cadres and this is where the communists came in, not for ideological reasons but because they were the ablest people available.

O'Connor explains that the PSP was well placed to play an important role in helping Castro to carry through important changes after Batista's overthrow. "The PSP had a large reservoir of goodwill in many sections of the working class, especially the sugar workers, oil workers, and bank employees. . . ."[4] The sugar workers, especially the mill-workers, were regarded by Castro and his colleagues as a most reliable force for revolutionary change. O'Connor points out that the 100,000 mill workers, not being confined geographically, were able to exert their revolutionary influence on a national scale. Che Guevara called them the "most combative, class-conscious working group".[5] Castro called on the mill workers to join the militia and to become the "best organised, trained and disciplined";[6] by the middle of 1961 over a half of the 122,000 members of the cane co-operatives were members of the militia, comprising no less than a third of the total strength of the militia at that time.

It was not only that the PSP provided capable and devoted cadres who helped to bring about the transition to socialism. Their years of patient and self-sacrificing work had been a vital factor in developing the political understanding of the workers who supported "socialis

---

[1] Eqbal Ahmad: "Radical But Wrong", an essay in *Régis Debray and the Latin American Revolution*, special number of *Monthly Review*, July–August, 1968.

[2] Goldenberg: op. cit., p. 298.

[3] *Figaro*, June 15, 1961.

[4] James O'Connor: op. cit., p. 192.

[5] Speech on June 18, 1960: *Obra Revolucionaria*, No. 11, 1960.

[6] Quote in *Havana Post*, March 19, 1960.

and Communist ideas, owing to three decades of PSP education and propaganda work in the cities and countryside".[1]

Even after the purging of Escalante and his sectarian supporters Castro once again stressed the positive role of the members of the former PSP at the same time as he emphasised their need to display "modesty".

> What must our attitude towards the old Communists be? It must be an attitude of respect, of recognition of their merits, of recognition of their militancy.[2]

And this praise, it should be remembered, was made in the midst of a difficult situation when Escalante's sectarian behaviour had led to the fully justified criticism made by Castro of such PSP attitudes. (Even the later intrigue and mischief-making of Escalante failed to shake Fidel's appreciation of the "old Communists".)

It has been necessary to deal at some length with the role of the Cuban PSP because of Debray's attempt virtually to expunge the PSP from the record of the revolution and, on that basis, to develop his theory regarding the creation of the revolutionary party by the guerrilla units. Debray quotes Castro as saying:

> Who will make the revolution in Latin America? Who? The people, the revolutionaries, with or without a party.[3]

Debray comments:[4] "Fidel Castro says simply that there is no revolution without a vanguard; that this vanguard is not necessarily the Marxist-Leninist party; and that those who want to make the revolution have the right and the duty to constitute themselves a vanguard, independently of these parties."

It is quite incredible that these lines could have been penned in 1967. They might have been excusable in the first flush of 1959–60, though even then by no means valid. But to put these ideas forward in 1967 only betrays the limitations of Debray's understanding of revolution in general, and of the Cuban revolution in particular; and no reference to Castro alters this. What is this "revolution" which is being referred to? A revolution, in Lenin's words, is a change of *class* power. It requires a fundamental change in the whole political, social and economic structure. Such a revolution has certainly been carried out in Cuba, but it neither began in July, 1953, nor did it end in January, 1959, with the flight of Batista. This was only the first essential step; for the revolution

[1] James O'Connor: op. cit., p. 302.   [2] Fidel Castro: speech, March 26, 1962.
[3] See *Revolution in the Revolution?*, op. cit., p. 98.   [4] ibid., p. 98.

to be completed the struggle had to be conducted against the enemies of the revolution who hid behind anti-Communist slogans—in the Government, in the Rebel Army, in the July 26th Movement, and in the trade unions. The revolution required sweeping measures of nationalisation and land reform; it necessitated the building of a new state apparatus. And the revolution had to be defended against US imperialism which launched its counter-attack from outside as well as utilising the forces inside Cuba who were opposed to socialist change.

All the facts show only too clearly that to follow up the overthrow of Batista by carrying through the Cuban socialist revolution it *was* necessary to have a "Marxist-Leninist party", that this was precisely the form of vanguard that was needed; and that it was in no way created "independently" of the existing Marxist-Leninist party. One would not think, from reading Debray's *Revolution in the Revolution?*, that the activity of the PSP right up to January, 1959, had any relevance to the defeat of Batista, nor that the role of the PSP *after* the overthrow of the tyranny was equally essential for the new phase. One would not ever guess from Debray that the united vanguard which arose in 1961 included the PSP as an essential element.

In an attempt to answer this argument, Debray writes:

It has been said with dismay that the party, the usual instrument for the seizure of power, was developed *after* the conquest of power. But no, it already existed in embryo—in the form of the Rebel Army. Fidel, its commander-in-chief, was already an unofficial party leader by early 1959. . . . Just as the name of socialism was formally applied to the revolution after a year of socialist practice, the name of the party came into use three years after the proletarian party had begun to exist in uniform. . . . The first party leaders were created on July 26, 1953, at Moncada. The party is the same age as the revolution; it will be fourteen on July 26, 1967.[1]

The Communist Party, argues Debray, was formed by "other political forces" being able to come together and unite around the political-military leadership of the Rebel Army. Somehow Debray cannot bring himself even to mention that among the "other political forces" was the PSP which produced for the Cuban revolution such outstanding figures as Carlos Balino, Julio Antonio Mella, Rubén Martínez Villena, Fabio Grobart, Lazaro Peña, César Escalante, Jesús Menendez, Blas Roca, Carlos Rafael Rodríguez and many, many others. No! declares Debray, "what is today the Communist Party of

[1] See *Revolution in the Revolution?*, op. cit., p. 106.

Cuba" is a party in which "both the base and the head continue to be made up of comrades from the guerrilla army".

Among the guerrilla army, as we have noticed, there were already members of the PSP; but further, PSP members in the towns and the countryside who, in a number of ways assisted the overthrow of Batista, loyally stuck by Castro in the difficult years of 1959–61, and rallied to the battle for socialist change and construction, also became members of the new united Party and are to be found in "both the base and the head". This is entirely hidden by Debray. It cannot be that he did not know of the role of the PSP, both before and after 1959. One can only assume that because its presence and role does not fit in with his theory of the "revolution in the revolution" he simply eliminates it from the whole discussion.

It would, of course, be entirely wrong to claim for the PSP a pre-eminent role. All three elements—the July 26th Movement, the PSP and the Revolutionary Directorate—had important achievements to their credit, and their co-operation was vital for the formation of the united Communist Party in which there is no longer any distinction as regards the original basis of one's membership. All three trends have equal status in the Party and enjoy equal recognition for their share in the revolutionary struggle.

It may well be that in arguing against Debray, and in trying to correct the historical record by restoring the role of the PSP as an essential part of the Cuban revolution, the impression may have been given that the mistakes of the Cuban communists are being overlooked. There is no intention of doing this.[1] The PSP, like any other responsible party which is concerned with the whole fate of the revolution and with the well-being of the working people, had at all times been motivated by what it regarded as the best interests of the Cuban working people. If it made mistakes—and its failure to prepare properly for armed struggle was recognised by itself as a major mistake—it made them neither out of cowardice (as I am sure Debray would be among the first to recognise) nor out of any deliberate opportunist desire to hold back the struggle, but, as Blas Roca has explained, by an incorrect political estimate as to how the path of the revolution would develop in Cuba. But the mistake having been made, the PSP leadership was

---

[1] No Communist Parties claim infallibility. The PSP, like other Communist Parties, had its share of mistakes. One can, for example, question its tactics at times towards the Machado régime, the periods of Grau San Martín and Prio Socarras, and the first period of Batista's rule, 1940 to 1944. The attitude of a revolutionary Party towards its own mistakes is all-important. The PSP drew the correct conclusions in 1959 and thus helped to make possible the revolutionary change of 1959–61.

principled enough and sufficiently wise to appreciate where it had gone wrong and increasingly to rally behind the banner of Fidel Castro to which it has given sincere, devoted and disciplined service.

No attempt to reassess the role of the PSP, however, should be allowed to diminish in any way the decisive part played by Fidel Castro. It was, above all, he and his colleagues who had the revolutionary audacity and courage to defy seemingly overwhelming odds, and to seize the correct revolutionary moment for commencing the armed struggle.[1] And they had the guts, too, to continue it in the face of initial setbacks of a character that would have convinced lesser men that they had made a ghastly blunder and should seek different tactics.

Fidel Castro is one of Latin America's greatest sons. Too often his achievement has been depicted in terms of the heroic man who led the guerrillas in the mountains and overthrew the Batista dictatorship. Castro's contribution, however, was not limited to that phase of the struggle. His physical bravery has been matched by an intellectual courage which has enabled him to keep in step with history. When the testing time came after January, 1959, Fidel grew with the revolution. At every bitter challenge he moved forward, learnt, assimilated lessons, grasped the next key link in the chain and so helped to pull forward the whole revolutionary movement. At no time did he waver or let himself be engulfed by the surging complexities of the situation; nor did he weaken and succumb to the frantic and dangerous efforts of the counter-revolution. He kept close to the people, strove to capture and at the same time kindle their spirit, while elevating their political understanding as to what had to be done at each decisive stage of the revolution.

As he himself explained, he became a Marxist-Leninist in the process. Not that he was a stranger to the works of Marx or Lenin prior to 1959. But it was in the course of those critical years of the late 1950's and early 1960's that he matured, step by step with the revolution; and it was this maturity that led him to understand the role of the PSP, to ally himself with the Cuban Communists, and to make possible the creation of a united Communist Party of Cuba. This is not in accord with Debray's presentation; but it is in accord with historical fact, and is more in accord with Castro's own understanding of what took place than in Debray's treatment in *The Revolution in the Revolution?*

[1] It seems to me that Edward Boorstein (*The Economic Transformation of Cuba*, New York, 1968) is fully justified in citing, in reference to Castro and his colleagues, Engels' well-known quotation from Danton: *de l'audace, de l'audace, encore de l'audace.*

SOME CHARACTERISTIC FEATURES OF THE CUBAN REVOLUTION

In his account of the Cuban revolution Debray tends to pay insufficient attention to the particular characteristics of Cuba, of its history, of its class structure.

More than one commentator has noted Debray's lack of economic analysis in his studies of Cuba and of Latin America in general. Althusser has remarked:

> One looks in vain in your text for an analysis or the outline of an analysis, or the indication of the absolute necessity of an analysis which *goes to the depth of things*, that is to say which recognises that politics are only, as Lenin said, the "resumé" of economic conditions. You mention somewhere the necessity of analysing specific combinations of modes of production which exist in Latin America, but you do not go any further than this mention and this is a shame, for this precisely is the absolutely decisive point.[1]

As far as Cuba itself is concerned, of particular importance is the question of the rural population. General reference to "the peasants" is not really of much help here to our understanding. Unlike the majority of countries in Latin America the countryside in Cuba was characterised not by peasant small-holdings and primitive methods of subsistence agriculture but by plantation wage labour. Cuba's *latifundia* before the revolution were not feudal but capitalist. In his famous *History Will Absolve Me* speech, Fidel Castro referred to the main body on the land as five hundred thousand farm labourers who worked for four months in the year and starved for eight. After them, came the 100,000 smallholders who lived and died working on land which was not theirs. (Some estimates have given a smaller figure for these tenants and sharecroppers.) Baran[2] has emphasised that "the overwhelming majority of the *campesinos* . . . was composed of agricultural labourers working in sugar, tobacco, and coffee plantations, earning a mere subsistence wage in the few busy months of the harvest season." Thus, he points out, the rural population in Cuba consisted mainly of "proletarians wholly alienated from their means of production (and subsistence) and having nothing to sell but their labour power". Consequently they "longed and fought not for the soil which they tilled, but for essentially working class

[1] Louis Althusser: op. cit.
[2] Paul A. Baran: *Reflections on the Cuban Revolution*, New York, 1961, p. 11.

objectives: steady employment, more human working conditions, and more adequate wages". They were also organised to a remarkable degree, both in sugar and tobacco, where the early Communist pioneers and their followers in later years had developed considerable trade union organisation. (This situation on the land was later to facilitate Cuba's transition to socialism in the countryside since there was no question of first having to satisfy the land hunger of a mass of poor and middle peasantry whose main aspiration was to own a plot of land for themselves.)

Plotting this "proletarianisation of the land" in Cuba, Wood[1] has noted that it developed rapidly as a consequence of the US takeover of Cuba after 1898. The old slave plantation gave way not to feudalism but to the capitalist plantation which squeezed the small farmer out of existence and created a large army of wage workers. Ortiz observed in 1947:

> The small Cuban landowner, independent and prosperous, the backbone of a strong rural middle class, is gradually disappearing. The farmer is becoming a member of the proletariat, just another labourer, without roots in the soil, shifted from one district to another.[2]

This process was most marked in sugar, which dominated Cuba's economy; but it was also characteristic of tobacco where the number of independent growers fell from 11,000 in 1925 to 3,000 in 1949.[3]

Analysing this fact that "in the majority of districts of Cuba the peasant had been progressively proletarianised by the demands of large-scale, semi-mechanised, capitalist farming and had entered upon a new level of organisation which gave him greater class consciousness",[4] Che Guevara adds that in the area where the survivors of the *Granma* first found support the peasantry were mainly composed of smallholders, peasants who had gone to the Sierra Maestra "to find a new parcel of land which they snatched from the state or from some voracious landholder in the hope of making a little money". These smallholders, however, although imbued with a petty bourgeois spirit,

---

[1] Dennis B. Wood: "The Long Revolution: Class Relations and Political Conflict in Cuba, 1868–1968", *Science and Society*, Spring, 1970, p. 7.

[2] Fernando Ortíz: *Cuban Counterpoint*, New York, 1947, pp. 53–4. Cited in Dennis B. Wood, op. cit.

[3] See James O'Connor: "The Foundations of Cuban Socialism", *Studies on the Left*, IV, Fall, 1964, p. 98.

[4] Che Guevara: "Cuba—Exception or Vanguard?", see *Venceremos!*, op. cit., pp. 133–4.
Note: Che correctly understands here that what "proletarianises" the peasant is not the ᵍraphical factor of "the mountain" but fundamental socio-economic transformation.

soon found that it was necessary to destroy the capitalist landholding system; and that in such a struggle the proletariat was its ally.

These specific features of Cuba's rural economy are not generally paralleled in most other countries of Latin America where, despite the onward march of capitalism, there is still a considerable weight of semi-feudal structures to be destroyed, and consequently where the question of organising the rural population presents a number of quite different problems.

Blas Roca has pointed to a further distinguishing feature of the Cuban revolution, namely that it was the last Latin American country to wrest independence from Spain. As a result, he notes, "the struggle for independence in our country had an extensive social background; it was headed, not by owners of sugar-cane plantations, but by radical revolutionary leaders from among the peasants and the middle urban strata who not only fought against Spanish colonialism but also opposed the emerging imperialism of the United States".[1] Fidel Castro, by taking up the national banner of anti-US imperialism and combining it with the banners of democracy and economic and social change, was able to place himself well within Cuba's national tradition, in line with Maceo and Martí, and thus gather to his standard the overwhelming majority of the Cuban people.

Cuba was also favoured by the fact that there were no linguistic diversities, and cultural differences were limited. Cuba had no Indian problem. Many Latin American countries have considerable indigenous Indian populations,[2] and in some the majority in the countryside are Indians, living often outside the money economy, subject to semi-feudal forms of exploitation, wrapped in their own language and age-old cultures and beliefs. Cuba, however, has a large Negro population, about 25–30 per cent. Though subject, in practice, to considerable discrimination before the revolution, this Negro population was to a large extent integrated into the normal culture and economic and social life of the Cuban people. Cuba's traditional heroes were the white Martí and the black Maceo. Among the top leaders of Fidel's Rebel Army was the Negro, Juan Almeída. Among the outstanding leaders of the trade union movement were the martyred sugar worker, Jesús Menendez, and the tobacco worker, Lazaro Peña—both Negroes.

Two of the main forces of conservatism and counter-revolution

[1] Blas Roca: "Historic Significance of the Cuban Revolution", *Cuba Socialista*, No. 29, 1964.
[2] Three-quarters in Bolivia and half in Peru.

in Latin America, namely the Church hierarchy and the army, which have traditionally been linked in most Latin American countries with the landed oligarchy, played a limited role in Cuba. As we have already noted, it was the US-controlled capitalist plantations that dominated the Cuban countryside, not the Cuban landowners. As for the Church, it never played the role in Cuba that it did elsewhere in Latin America.[1] The Cuban church took no part in the struggle for independence. Most of the priests were Spanish, and continued to be drawn from Spain even after 1898. They easily became identified with Spanish colonialism and thus were regarded as the enemies of the nation. They were numerically small—only about one priest for every 10,000 inhabitants before the revolution—and their social support was limited. The Cuban church hierarchy was thus not in a position to influence wide strata against the Rebel Army, and after the victory it was in a still weaker position to do so, especially as most of the priests were not Cuban.

Since neither the Church nor the landed oligarchy were strong in Cuba, the army, unlike the traditional armies in other Latin American countries, could not base itself on these twin pillars. Batista's army was largely his own personal instrument. It was, writes Wood, "politically and socially isolated, since it possessed no real roots in class needs".[2] The middle strata did not trust it, and its venal behaviour led to its general alienation from most sections of the population.

Following Batista's example, his officers were mainly preoccupied in amassing huge fortunes for themselves and leading a life of opulence and pleasure. They were involved in every money-making racket, in smuggling, drug traffic, prostitution, gambling and bribery. "As uncouth *parvenus* who acquired riches through a lucky strike", writes Andreski,[3] "they were lazy and dissolute. Having risen through treachery, they felt neither loyalty to their chief nor to each other, whilst the possession of big funds in foreign banks undermined their will to undergo dangers for the sake of retaining power." Naturally enough, the soldiers who fought under them increasingly felt reluctant to give up their lives for such a corrupt crew. Morale was on the side of the Rebel Army which month by month won ever wider support from the people. Comparatively limited military success by Fidel's men—limited not in their significance for the revolution nor in the

[1] See Dennis B. Wood: op. cit., pp. 33–4.
[2] ibid., p. 35.
[3] Stanlislav Andreski: *Parasitism and Subversion*, London, 1966, pp. 247–8.

skill and dedication of the guerrillas, but in the scale of the fighting—were eventually enough to bring about the disintegration of Batista's army which found itself facing the hostility of almost the entire nation.

Cuba's particular history and resultant class and social structure had its consequences for the national bourgeoisie, which was very small and weak. Boorstein[1] has pointed out its limited basis in national industry and commerce. The upper classes of Cuba were, in the main, closely tied to US imperialism. They embraced sugar magnates, owners of the sugar centrals and *latifundia*, the big importers (described by Boorstein as "the core of the urban oligarchy"), bankers and real estate operators and the majority of retail stores. The owners of the small shops and factories, often family concerns, were not in the same league as the dominant bourgeoisie. They were, notes Boorstein, too weak and numerically too small "to make them in the aggregate into a force that could worry imperialism and its local partners".

As O'Connor has commented, Cuba's middle classes were relatively large in comparison to those of many other Latin American countries but were "small in comparison with Cuba's urban and rural proletariat and small farmers. Fragmented, dependent, and demoralised, the middle classes were unable to systematically employ state power for their own ends. Cuban governments and the state bureaucracy were made up of time-servers, opportunists, and thieves. For these reasons, there was no significant organised resistance to the rapid socialisation of the Cuban economy."[2]

As a consequence the attempt, after Batista's overthrow, to switch Cuba on to a path leading away from socialism failed. Not that there was no danger, for in the first post-Batista period there was a rapid increase of class conflict within the anti-Batista camp; and if the forces of the revolution had not been able to unite to overcome this threat, there could have been a merging of all sections of the bourgeoisie to maintain the capitalist system in Cuba. The task of the revolution was undoubtedly aided by the fact that the top ranks of the bourgeoisie were discredited by their past service to US imperialism, and by the fact that the national bourgeoisie was too weak to replace them or to take over the leadership of the revolution.

One should not ignore, however, the positive role of the national bourgeoisie in the struggle against Batista. Even sections of the big

[1] Edward Boorstein: *The Economic Transformation of Cuba*, New York/London, 1968, pp. 12–13.
[2] James O'Connor: op. cit., p. 280.

bourgeoisie fell away from his side, retaining, of course, their hope that his removal would merely mean a change of government and not of the system itself.

> We do not believe [wrote Che Guevara] one can consider exceptional the fact that the bourgeoisie, or at least a good part of the bourgeoisie, favoured the revolutionary war against the tyranny at the same time that it supported and promoted movements to find negotiated solutions which would permit them to replace the Batista government with elements disposed to put a brake on the Revolution . . . neither is it exceptional that some big land-owning elements adopted a neutral attitude, or at least a non-belligerent attitude, towards the forces of the insurrection.
>
> It is understandable that the national bourgeoisie, oppressed by imperialism and by a tyranny whose troops pillaged their holdings, should look with sympathy when young rebels of the mountains punished the armed servants of imperialism who composed the mercenary army.[1]

After Batista's downfall, as has been noted, sections of the national bourgeoisie were opposed to co-operation with the Communists and to going over to socialism; and a sharp political struggle ensued until they were defeated. But this inevitable clash in no way negates the correctness of Fidel and his colleagues making full use of the anti-Batista trend of the national bourgeoisie and maintaining the alliance with it as long as it continued to march in the ranks of the revolution.

THE ENEMY ALSO LEARNS

Whatever lessons may be derived from the experience of the Cuban revolution, it would be foolish to ignore the fact that the imperialists have also drawn their conclusion. As Hobsbawm has noted,[2] one consequence of Fidel's victory (and the manner of it), is that "the forces which are now mobilised against Latin American guerrillas are immeasurably more effective, determined and backed by the USA than was believed necessary before 1959". Hobsbawm himself cites examples of the new counter-insurgency techniques which draw heavily on technological and strategic-tactical innovations—the helicopter, the systematic encirclement and separation of guerrillas

[1] Che Guevara: "Cuba—Exception or Vanguard?", *Venceremos!*, op. cit., p. 133.
[2] E. J. Hobsbawm: "Guerrillas in Latin America", *Socialist Register*, 1970, London, p. 52.

from their political and supply base by the forced removal of the peasants to concentration camps, the isolation of the guerrillas within a confined space and then tracking them down with specially trained and equipped Rangers. As an alternative to removing the peasants, counter-insurgency forces are sometimes stationed in the villages where terror and intimidation is employed alongside political propaganda in order to wean the villagers away from supporting the guerrillas. Debray himself has noted the new counter-insurgency techniques:

> . . . channels of communication are increasing; airports and landing fields are being built in the most remote areas, heretofore inaccessible by land routes. . . . As for North American imperialism, it has increased its forces in the field and is making every effort to present itself, not in repressive guise but in the shape of social and technical assistance.[1]

Among the forms used in connection with the latter, Debray mentions sociological projects, the Peace Corps and Christian missionaries.

Within two years of the overthrow of Batista President Kennedy had begun to organise the US counter-insurgency apparatus. Robert Kennedy and Richard Bissell of the CIA were apparently additional "enthusiasts of counter-guerilla warfare".[2] A special Counter-Insurgency Committee was set up in late 1961, under the chairmanship of General Maxwell Taylor. It is reported that since 1960 over 20,000 officers from Latin American armies have been to the special US training courses in Panama in order to learn how to cope with guerrilla warfare. Special Forces (Green Berets) have seen action in a number of Latin American countries, and have played their part in actions against guerrillas in Guatemala, Bolivia, Venezuela and Nicaragua. US officers have not limited their role to that of training: they have been on "active military and intelligence missions throughout Latin America".[3]

In Guatemala, acting on US advice, the government combined ruthless military action with the "Plan Piloto"—a Pilot Plan for social and economic development, aimed at weaning the peasants away from supporting the guerrillas by providing a minimum of welfare. In 1967 the Guatemalan vice-president, Marroquín Rojas, revealed that US pilots had flown planes from bases in Panama to drop napalm on suspected guerrilla haunts in Guatemala. In addition

[1] Régis Debray: *Revolution in the Revolution?*, op. cit., p. 52.
[2] Richard Gott: *Guerrilla Movements in Latin America*, London, 1970, p. 360.
[3] ibid., p. 361.

to these direct military actions, the United States forces, he said, were "co-operating in plans for Civic Action in the countryside, the distribution of food-stuffs such as dried milk and medicines and the execution of simple jobs of public works".[1]

In Peru, too, the guerrilla force led by Luis de la Puente Uceda, came up against US intervention. "At least one United States army counter-insurgency expert was said to have helped plan and direct"[2] the attack that resulted in the defeat of de la Puente's guerrilla force. In that short battle the guerrillas had to face merciless bombing by napalm and high explosives.

In Bolivia, where the Americans sent in helicopters, advisers and intelligence officers to help the Government track down Che Guevara and his group a significant new refinement in counter-guerrilla warfare was introduced. The inhabitants of villages which had been visited by the guerrillas and to which the latter were expected to return, were taken away by the military and the whole area sown with informers dressed as peasants. As Gott has commented:

> Nor should one underestimate the United States' contribution to intelligence work within Bolivia. The guerrillas' urban network was not discovered by the unaided efforts of Bolivian intelligence. Nor did the Bolivians think up the idea of sowing the guerrilla zone with soldiers dressed up as peasants.[3]

It is probably Colombia which, more than any other Latin American country, has experienced the full weight of the new United States tactics. Describing the US-organised "Operation Marquetalia" of 1964, when 16,000 troops were used to attack the peasant guerrilla base of Marquetalia, Gilberto Vieira, the general secretary of the Communist Party of Colombia, has outlined the five phases of the new tactics.[4]

> *Phase one: preparation and organisation:* Once the troops have been trained in anti-guerrilla action, spies are sent into the area and informers recruited. For this purpose, "civil-military action" is organised, in which the army appears under the guise of a benefactor, bringing presents to the peasants (clothes, medical supplies,

---

[1] An interview in *Latin America* (Interpress Newsletter), September 15, 1967. Cited in Gott, op. cit.
[2] Richard Gott: ibid., p. 276.
[3] See Richard Gott, ibid., p. 355.
[4] Gilberto Vieira: "La Colombie a l'heure du Marquetalia", *Democratie Nouvelle* July–August, 1965.

American food from Care and Caritas), medical and dental services, bridge-building, roads and schools.

Phase two: A larger-scale programme of psychological action is then put into operation, using the factor of surprise. Measures are taken to control the civil population. This is the first stage in setting up a blockade of the area.

Phase three: The next operations try to isolate the armed rebel groups in order to destroy them.

Phase four: The armed rebel movement is systematically divided, using psychological techniques. Advantage is taken of internal splits, resulting from political differences, the ambitions of the leaders, human weaknesses, or mistakes by the guerrilla command. This is an attempt to win over those who would be likely to carry on the guerrilla struggle.

Phase five: The final stage is the economic, political and social "reconstruction" of the zone of operations, using the American aid that was previously used to destroy the area.[1]

There is no doubt that these new methods played an important role in tracking down Che Guevara in Bolivia. New technical improvements were also utilised. It has been alleged that one of the new devices used by the American-trained Bolivian helicopter forces to detect Che's presence measured the heat coming from his outdoor stove. The stove, it is said, was a smokeless model, specially designed in order to avoid the tell-tale signs of smoke being seen from the air. With the new techniques, however, to see the smoke was not necessary. The stove could be "seen" just the same. Sam Nujoma, President of the South West African People's Organisation (Swapo), has reported[2] that the US has sold to the South African Government radar and heat detection devices which were developed in Vietnam and which can detect the body heat of troops on the ground. A press report on the 1971 invasion of Laos refers to "electronic devices that monitor movement on the trail".[3] The war in Vietnam has been, for the United States, a veritable experimental station as regards methods and techniques of counter-insurgency operations. In addition to all the additions to the armoury of destruction and murder (napalm, cluster bombs, various anti-personnel bombs, laser guided bombs and so forth), the US military now has at its disposal view scopes that see the enemy in the dark, "people sniffers" or chemical detectors which react to enemy body odours, thermal images which react to body heat, and

[1] Cited by Gott, op. cit.   [2] Reuter report, August 26, 1970.
[3] *Guardian*, February 23, 1971 (requoting *Washington Post*).

seismic registers which pick up the thump of trucks or troops on the move.[1] Methods used in Latin America to discover whether guerrillas have been in a given locality include an analysis of the type of branches or twigs used to make an open fire,[2] and an examination of cigar or cigarette ends (the type of tobacco used in supplies arriving from the cities being markedly different from that contained in the kinds usually available in the village).

The new counter-revolutionary techniques should in no sense act as a deterrent to guerrilla warfare. But revolutionary movements should certainly take them into account and adjust their methods accordingly. Failure to do this—and the almost inevitable amateurishness of most of the early guerrilla groups—has undoubtedly caused serious losses.

It has been necessary to argue at some length with Debray's presentation of the main characteristics of the Cuban revolution since, in the absence of any authentic overall analysis of this historic event, his depiction has gained a certain acceptance in some New Left circles, and beyond; and, on this basis, very debatable general conclusions have been drawn.

No serious revolutionary would ignore the terrific impact which the Cuban victory has had, especially in Latin America. A leading Venezuelan Communist has written:

> The Cuban Revolution challenged everything, upset everything, stripped the sacred sham-truisms from the altar and subjected everything to criticism (not always correctly let it be said) and gave rise to doubts, confusion and over-simplification. But out of this chaos would come ultimately the Latin American theory of revolution.[3]

One may have reservations as to what is meant by "the Latin American theory of revolution", but there can be no doubt that a full assimilation of the lessons of the Cuban revolution will be of enormous assistance to all the countries of Latin America. To draw such lessons, however, needs, in the first place, a correct appraisal of the Cuban events themselves. Such an appraisal, I have tried to show, has not been made by Debray. Secondly, to make use of the lessons of the Cuban revolution does not mean to take it as a model, to attempt

---

[1] Paul Dickson and John Rothschild: "Automated Battlefield", *Washington Monthly*, reproduced in *Sanity*, September, 1971.

[2] Guerrillas, not from the locality, take the nearest twigs and branches; the local people take those they know burn best.

[3] Francisco Mieres: *World Marxist Review*, No. 11, 1967.

to do the same everywhere else. Cuba, as we have seen, had many quite specific features which are not repeated in other countries of Latin America. Moreover, the revolution took place under conditions which are unlikely to be repeated elsewhere in the same form; and this is particularly so as regards the reaction of the United States, more anxious now to avoid "another Cuba", and yet, as a result of Cuba and the spread of the revolutionary process in initial and different forms to Peru and Chile, and as a result, too, of world reactions to US imperialism's aggression in Indochina, confronted now with greater difficulties if it desires to intervene massively and directly with military forces in Latin America.

Debray does not limit himself to "explaining" Cuba. On the basis of what appears to be a distorted picture of Cuban reality, he draws theoretical conclusions which are themselves open to challenge; and he attempts to grapple with the problems of the revolution in other Latin American countries in a way which subsequent developments have often shown to be shallow.

Among these theoretical conclusions are his treatment of the national bourgeoisie and the character of the revolution in Latin America; the question of armed struggle, and the relation between military and political leadership; and the role of ideology.

THE NATIONAL BOURGEOISIE

A highly interesting article by Carlos Rafael Rodríguez[1] which was published in February, 1970, touches on the first of these questions. In the section dealing with the bourgeois-democratic revolution in Cuba he makes an important distinction between the content of a bourgeois-democratic revolution and the introduction of a capitalist stage of development. As he rightly points out, the main tasks of a bourgeois-democratic revolution, including anti-feudal land reform, the ending of foreign domination, and the building of an independent economy, are sometimes left to a socialist revolution to complete. This was certainly so in Russia in 1917, as it was in China after 1949, and in Vietnam and Korea after 1945. (Even in an advanced capitalist country like Britain the ending of such feudal relics as the monarchy and the House of Lords, which in their present form, of course, serve capitalist interests, will, almost certainly, have to be effected after the working people have come to power.)

[1] Carlos Rafael Rodríguez: "Lenin and the Colonial Question", *Casa de las Americas*, supplement, February, 1970.

In Latin America, argues Rafael Rodríguez, there is a basic difference between the social and economic developments that have taken place there and those in most countries of Asia and Africa. This difference, he writes, lies in the fact that in Latin America many bourgeois-democratic goals have already been reached a long time ago and capitalism is the dominant characteristic of the economic and social structure, even though some semi-feudal features still remain. Not to understand this means that the revolutionary movement runs the risk of entering into alliance for electoral and other purposes with sections of the bourgeoisie on a basis which results not in a neutralisation of the bourgeoisie but in the proletariat itself becoming neutralised.

At the same time, he argues, it would be wrong to conclude from this that there is no national bourgeoisie and no bourgeois-democratic phase of the revolution. He makes this interesting point:

> The concept of "national" . . . does not arise from the "origin" of its ownership, but from the *political position* to which this ownership has led a section of the bourgeoisie. It is a political and not a geographical conception. (Author's translation, based on a French version of the original text.)

A correct understanding of this whole problem enables a revolutionary movement to avoid the mistakes of revolutionary impatience which desires to avoid the bourgeois-democratic phase and march directly to socialism. Such an attempt flies in the face of the teachings of Marx and Lenin; and is in contradiction, moreover, with what has happened in all the socialist revolutions. Calling on the Russian working class in the pre-1917 period "not to keep aloof from the bourgeois revolution"[1] Lenin, at the same time, urged the Russian workers to take over the leadership of this bourgeois-democratic revolution in order to make it possible to pass to the socialist phase.

> From the democratic revolution we shall at once, and just in accordance with the measure of our strength, the strength of the class-conscious and organised proletariat, begin to pass to the Socialist revolution. We stand for uninterrupted revolution. We shall not stop half way.[2]

This transition between the two phases in Russia lasted from February to October, 1917, although even after October, as we have

---

[1] V. I. Lenin: *Selected Works*, Vol. 3, p. 77.
[2] V. I. Lenin: "Attitude of Social Democrats to the Peasant Movement", *Selected Works*, Vol. 3, p. 145.

already noted, certain tasks of the bourgeois-democratic revolution remained to be completed. In Cuba, affirms Rodríguez, the bourgeois-democratic phase lasted until August, 1960, when the commencement of the socialist phase was marked by Fidel's dramatic proclamation to the fighters en route to the defence of Cuba at the Bay of Pigs: "Long live our Socialist Revolution!"

Debray understands the necessity of including the national bourgeoisie in the anti-imperialist front. He believes that since the Cuban revolution "it is much more difficult . . . to integrate any sizeable fraction of the national bourgeoisie" into such a front, but nevertheless, he argues, this "can and must still be the prime objective".[1] At the same time he argues that because, unlike in Asia and Africa, political independence has been enjoyed in Latin America over a long period, the struggle against imperialism there "does not take the form of a front against foreign forces of occupation, but proceeds by means of a revolutionary civil war: the social base is therefore narrower, and the ideology consequently better defined and less mixed with bourgeois influence. . . . While in Africa and Asia the class struggle and national struggle may be blurred by the tactical implications of the national front, or delayed until after liberation, in South America class struggle and national struggle must, in the final analysis, go together. The path of independence passes by way of the military and political destruction of the dominant class, organically linked to the United States by the co-management of its interests."[2]

While Debray rather one-sidedly, sees only "revolutionary civil war" as the means, as regards the class question it seems to me he is correct to pose the problem of turning the edge of the struggle against the internal class ally of imperialism as part of the anti-imperialist struggle; although this should not mean—and the Cuban experience helps us here—neglecting to make use of every potential ally against imperialism, no matter how unstable, wavering and temporary that ally may be. Above all, it is important not to confuse stages of a revolution, even though they are linked and often merge into one another.

In a later exposition on this question,[3] Debray warns that "it is perilous to count on the 'national bourgeoisie' . . . to make a bourgeois-democratic revolution, since it is well aware of the process which it

---

[1] Régis Debray: "Castroism: The Long March in Latin America", op. cit., p. 72.
[2] ibid., pp. 75–6.
[3] Régis Debray: "Problems of Revolutionary Strategy", Strategy for Revolution, op. it., p. 147.

would be unleashing". He argues that if the national bourgeoisie is allowed to secure the leadership of this phase of the revolution then there will be an evolution into what he terms "demo-bourgeois fascism".

While it is true that revolutionary working-class leadership is necessary if the bourgeois-democratic revolution is to pass to the socialist phase, it would be wrong to accept Debray's thesis that leadership by the national bourgeoisie (which is sometimes expressed by the petty bourgeoisie) must inevitably lapse into "demo-bourgeois fascism". The recent experience of Peru indicates that there can be a phase, under national bourgeois leadership, during which positive steps are taken to weaken imperialism and its semi-feudal and bourgeois allies, and which gives the working class and its allies a certain breathing space in which they can consolidate their forces, strengthen their organisation and political influence, and so prepare the way for their assuming the leadership of the revolution. To see only simple alternatives—leadership by the national bourgeoisie resulting in disaster or leadership by the revolutionary working-class movement—and not to see transitional phases within which the working class can advance towards the leadership, can result in a certain tactical rigidity which would create unnecessary problems for the revolution.

In a much more recent and strangely neglected essay,[1] Debray develops still further his ideas on the national bourgeoisie.

Starting with an analysis of the differences between the recent developments in Peru and Bolivia, he argues that in Bolivia the Revolution of 1952, despite the check it suffered later, has more or less completed the main goals of the bourgeois-democratic revolution. In Peru, on the other hand, where such a stage has not yet been reached, the bourgeois-democratic character of the revolution does not prevent it from playing a positive role. Further, he believes, Peru has a more substantial industrial bourgeoisie, in Lima and on the coast, which is capable of supporting and exploiting an anti-feudal, anti-

[1] Régis Debray: "Notes". These were first distributed on February 17, 1970, by *Prensa Latina* and subsequently published in the February, 1970, issue of the Cuban journal, *Pensamiento Crítico*, although they had been written originally in October, 1969. In these "Notes", written while Debray was still imprisoned in Bolivia and shortly after General Ovando took power in Bolivia and began to take anti-imperialist measures Debray quite clearly modified a number of his views—not only on the national bourgeoisie, but also on the role of the working class, the question of theory, mass political activity, models of socialism, and the role of the socialist countries. Neither the *New Left Review*, an early champion of Debray, nor the *Monthly Review*, the first English language publishers of *Revolution in the Revolution?*, has seen fit even to mention this essay, let alone publish it.

imperialist revolution. In Bolivia, however, "the extreme weakness of capitalist development has created a national bourgeoise which is markedly timid, pusillanimous, with no confidence in its own strength, and economically and ideologically dependent on imperialism". As a consequence, in Bolivia, the revolution can no longer be led by the petty bourgeoisie or those who claim to be the national bourgeoisie, since these classes fulfilled their historic role during the 1952 Revolution and subsequently demonstrated during the ensuing decade their inability in practice to live up to their historic task and carry through national construction.

Subsequent developments in Bolivia, despite the coup against the Torres government in August, 1971, by no means bear out Debray's assessment of the Bolivian petty bourgeoisie and national bourgeoisie. The Bolivian revolution has gone through a very complicated process in the past few years. Following the death of the dictator Barrientos in 1969, General Ovando pushed aside the official Vice-President and assumed power. Despite his reactionary past and his role, as Commander in Chief, in the war against Che Guevara's guerrillas, Ovando after taking power embarked on a path of anti-imperialist actions, carrying through the nationalisation of the Gulf Oil properties, establishing a state monopoly over the export of all minerals, opening up diplomatic relations with socialist countries and making economic agreements with them with a view to hastening the industrialisation and economic independence of Bolivia.

Attempts to "freeze" this process did not succeed. A right-wing coup in October, 1970, failed, and the result was the replacement of Ovando by General Torres, Ovando's Commander in Chief of the Army. Under Torres, Bolivia continued on her path of anti-imperialism and democratic change, being kept to this path by popular pressure and because a section of the Bolivian national and petty bourgeoisie were ready to follow this road. For the first two years each attempted coup by reactionary sections of the bourgeoisie and the army, backed by the United States, was followed, in fact, by a further political lurch to the left.

This, in itself, naturally created additional tensions in the country. The Bolivian working-class movement was neither politically clear as to how to proceed, nor was it sufficiently united to be the decisive driving force and leadership of the revolutionary process. Some organisations on the extreme left were pushing the movement into positions which alienated sections of the national and petty bourgeoisie, and even of the peasantry which had been, to a large degree, a political base for the former dictator, Barrientos. Torres and the military group around him began to vacillate, pushed forward by mass pressures on one side and pulled back on the other by those who feared that the revolution was going too fast. In these conditions, the right wing struck. Patriotic forces in the army were insufficient to defeat reaction; the miners, armed but insufficiently so, were many miles distant from the main centres of struggle; workers and students in the towns were virtually unarmed and were not yet a sufficiently cohesive force to rally mass resistance.

There were two kinds of illusions at work in Bolivia. There was the illusion of those who believed in a tidy, liberal path of progress and who assumed that the Torres government would be allowed by internal reaction and by the United States to continue along that path. The result of this illusion was that the Torres government was ill-prepared when the blow struck. The other illusion was that of those on the left who mistook their own revolutionary positions for that of the masses, and who, in consequence, voiced slogans and demands and pursued actions which far from widening and deepening the basis of the revolution narrowed it and caused divisions, anxieties and hesitation among its potential supporters.

Any tendency to draw the conclusion that the Ovando–Torres phase was a farce, that the revolutionary movement should have lent no support to these governments, and that the only question then, and now, was that of preparing armed struggle, should be resisted. Not in the sense that the people of Bolivia should not prepare for armed struggle; for if one learns anything from the stormy history of this country it is that non-armed ways forward are extremely difficult, and the democratic processes and institutions appallingly fragile. Yet to see arms as the only answer is to draw a very over-simplified conclusion from the Bolivian tragedy.

If Lenin and the Bolsheviks had drawn the conclusion after the defeat of 1905 that arms was the only answer there would have been no armed victory in 1917. For Lenin the answer was certainly arms, if necessary; but the *main* conclusion he drew was: widen and deepen the base of the revolution, unite the workers, win the majority of them over to revolutionary positions, convince the peasants that they needed to ally with the workers if they were to obtain the land and defeat their poverty and hunger, and unite all the various streams of class, social, economic and national discontent into one powerful torrent of revolutionary struggle that would topple the Tsar, tear down feudalism and open up the way to working-class power and the advance to socialism.

The Bolivian revolutionaries, too, will undoubtedly draw political conclusions from their experience, conclusions which do not confine themselves to deciding what forms of struggle they should embark on, armed or otherwise, but which place emphasis on how to unite their own forces and how to win and unite the workers, peasants, students and others who want to end this sordid history of coup after coup after coup which has been Bolivia's sad fate for over a hundred years.

Debray, in his "Notes", also attempts to arrive at general conclusions regarding the national bourgeoisie in Latin America. Thus he writes:

> However wavering and weak it may be, this class can no longer support its subordination to North American imperialism, it can no longer grow and develop without first ending its national independence, and in this sense there exists an objective contradiction between it and imperialism. In the most developed countries of the continent, Christian democracy ("revolution in freedom") constitutes the first attempt to solve this contradiction. . . . In the less-developed countries, neo-militarism constitutes the answer (Peru, Bolivia). But equally, this national bourgeoisie or middle class as it is called, has on the other hand, its specific contradiction with the proletariat, as the antagonistic and challenging class. As a result it is compelled to fight on two fronts:
>
> —on the one hand, to recover the wealth and above all to recover its right to exploit the national wealth in its own interests and profit—and in this is expressed its "anti-imperialism";
>
> —on the other hand, to defend its ambitions as an exploiting class against the working classes, to defend its ideological leadership, to defend its political positions—and in this is expressed its anti-communism, repression, utilisation of "Rangers", etc.[1]
>
> It is a paradoxical situation because this ruling class, in order to consolidate its rule, has to lean on one of its adversaries in order to defeat the other and vice versa; that is to say, it needs on the one hand the support of the imperialist structure, political and military, in order to face an eventual armed struggle [evidently to Debray

[1] Debray's reference to the logic of the "neo-militarist" solution in Bolivia and Peru is not at all borne out by recent developments. The internal policies of the Torres government in Bolivia and the Peruvian military government can in no sense be characterised as "anti-communism, repression, utilisation of 'Rangers', etc." Ironically, Debray owes his release from jail to precisely an internal turn towards democracy made by the military government of Torres in Bolivia.

this is still the only revolutionary way forward] . . . but, on the other hand, to make full use of its rights against imperialism it needs to group together all the popular forces in a national anti-imperialist front. It is this which explains its steps forward and its steps back, its duplicity, its traditional swinging back and forth, etc. . . .

The second premise which goes with it is that the Army represents, as an institution and social force, not the interests of the oligarchy (especially in a country like Bolivia) but the middle class as we have defined it. That is to say, in those countries which historically are less developed, the Army represents the economic and political interests of the intermediate strata, hemmed in between two opponents, externally imperialism, and internally the forces represented by the front of the proletariat, the poor peasantry and the revolutionary intelligentsia. (Author's own translation from a French text. See *Nouvelle Critique*, June, 1970, p. 25.)

It will be seen here that Debray has come close to a Marxist position as to the role of the national bourgeoisie, as already examined in relation to Fanon (pp. 94–101); and yet, at times, he is still somewhat schematic and rigid. It is not enough to understand that the national bourgeoisie faces two ways and consequently vacillates. In revolutionary practice what counts is the ability to assess correctly the given direction of the national bourgeoisie *in each phase*, to make use of its positive potential, and at the same time to be alive and vigilant towards its tendency to turn against the revolution. In short, to unite with the national bourgeoisie against feudalism and imperialism; and to struggle against the national bourgeoisie whenever it vacillates, tries to halt the revolution or even turn against it. In this process the working class can come to oust the national bourgeoisie from leadership and to assume that role for itself.

REVOLUTION IN THE REVOLUTION?

At the heart of Debray's theories, and arising from his own particular conception of the way the Cuban revolution developed, and from his views as to the role played by the different classes and political forces in the Cuban struggle, is his whole approach to the question of armed struggle, and the politics of armed struggle.

Marxists have no quarrel with Debray as regards the right and often the necessity of the working people to adopt forms of armed struggle in order to overthrow tyranny, to defeat imperialist domination and foreign rule, or to end capitalism and introduce socialism

"Marxism", as Lenin remarked, "positively does not reject any form of struggle."[1] On the contrary, "Marxism demands an attentive attitude to the *mass* struggle in progress which, as the movement develops, as the class-consciousness of the masses grows, as economic and political crises become acute, continually gives rise to new and more varied methods of defence and attack."[2]

Neither do Marxists oppose guerrilla warfare as a legitimate and often effective form of armed struggle. In fact, as Lenin wrote, "Guerrilla warfare is an inevitable form of struggle at a time when the mass movement has actually reached the point of an uprising and when fairly large intervals occur between the big 'engagements' in the civil war."[3]

But Lenin also emphasised that Marxism demands that the question of forms of struggle must be treated in relation to the concrete historical situation.

> At different stages of economic evolution, depending on differences in political, national-cultural, living and other conditions, different forms of struggle come to the fore and become the principal forms of struggle. . . . To attempt to answer yes or no to the question whether any particular means of struggle should be used, without making a detailed examination of the concrete situation of the given movement at the given stage of its development, means completely to abandon the Marxist position. . . . A Marxist bases himself on the class struggle, and not social peace. In certain periods of acute economic and political crisis the class struggle ripens into a direct civil war, i.e. into an armed struggle between two sections of the people. In such periods a Marxist is *obliged* to take the stand of civil war.[4]

Che, too, while arguing against those "who sit down to wait until in some mechanical way all necessary objective and subjective conditions are given without working to accelerate them", takes pains to point out that nevertheless one must take into account the concrete historical situation; "Where a government has come into power through some form of popular vote, fraudulent or not, and maintains at least an appearance of constitutional legality, the guerrilla outbreak

[1] V. I. Lenin: "Guerrilla Warfare", *Collected Works*, Vol. 11. First published in *Proletary*, September 30, 1906.
[2] ibid.
[3] ibid. Lenin was referring here to the particular form of mainly urban guerrilla warfare that developed in Russia in the wake of the unsuccessful 1905 revolution.
[4] ibid.

cannot be promoted, since the possibilities of peaceful struggle have not yet been exhausted."[1]

For Debray, the armed struggle is everything. "The socialist revolution is the result of an armed struggle against the armed power of the bourgeois state," he writes, claiming that this is an "old historic law".[2] Even more so does he see armed struggle as the decisive and only way forward for Latin America.

"In Latin America today a political line which, in terms of its consequences, is not susceptible to expression as a precise and consistent military line, cannot be considered revolutionary."[3]

Subsequent developments in Peru, Bolivia and Chile in no sense fit into this categoric prognosis. Furthermore, Debray himself shows a striking lack of consistency on the question of armed struggle in Latin America, and a considerable lack of clarity in the way he presents his views. In contrast to the above quotation from *Revolution in the Revolution?*, for example, he wrote two years earlier that "Armed struggle absolutely cannot be brandished in Latin America as a categorical imperative or a remedy in itself: armed struggle conducted by whom, one may ask, when, where, with what programme, what alliances? These are concrete problems which no one in the world can resolve abstractly—only the national vanguard which alone can carry the weight of the political responsibilities. In other words, the *Foco* cannot constitute a strategy in itself without condemning itself to failure. It is a moment of struggle whose place can only be defined within an overall integrating strategy."[4]

In Uruguay, notes Debray, there are no conditions for armed struggle. This opinion is in keeping with that expressed by Castro in his speech in Havana after the Tri-Continental Conference of January, 1966. On the question of Chile, however, notwithstanding the opinion of the Cuban Delegation to the Organisation of Latin American Solidarity (OLAS) Conference in August, 1967, that it would be "foolish and absurd" to talk about guerrilla warfare in Chile, Debray includes the Communist Party of this country among a list of Parties which he criticises for their "frank hostility to armed

---

[1] Che Guevara: *Guerrilla Warfare*, US, 1961; London, 1969, p. 14.
[2] Régis Debray: *Revolution in the Revolution?*, op. cit., p. 19.
[3] ibid., p. 24. Note how this idea becomes part of current thought in some left circles. Writing about Luis Turcios Lima, the Guatemalan guerrilla leader, Maya Campios has written: "His audacious actions led him to discover the path that the Cuban Revolution had already proved to be *the only revolutionary path* for the American continent: the path of guns and dynamite." (Emphasis added.) See *Turcios Lima*, Havana, 1970, p. 167.
[4] Régis Debray: "Latin America: the Long March", op. cit., pp. 49–50.

struggle",[1] and he denounces, as "irrational optimism" the view expressed in the programme of the Communist Party of Chile as endorsed at its Twelfth Congress in March, 1962, that "The present correlation of national and international forces has increased the possibility of achieving revolution[2] without armed struggle."[3]

To read, today, the section on Chile in Debray's essay, "Problems of Revolutionary Strategy", is, in a sense, painful reading. Debray in no way probes the reality of the Chilean scene. He starts not from Chile, but from his theory on the impossibility of any other way forward than that of armed struggle. He derides the role of the Chilean Communist Party and Allende's Socialist Party in the 1964 Presidential elections, not only because of the way they conducted their electoral campaign, and not even because of their defeat at the polls. It was widely known, he claims, that even "an electoral victory for Allende would have brought no fundamental change in the structure of the State apparatus, and that neither the Chilean ruling class nor the imperialist forces were going to be cast into oblivion by popular action".[4]

It would, of course, be idle to claim that the eventual electoral victory of the Popular Front of Unity in 1970, with the establishment of Allende as President, has automatically brought about "a fundamental change in the structure of the State apparatus"; and no one would seriously pretend that the Chilean ruling class and the imperialist forces have yet been "cast into oblivion by popular action". But it would be foolish not to see that the 1970 electoral victory and the events since then have been an important and necessary stage in the advance of the working people in Chile towards the full exercise of their power. What would Debray have had the Communist Party and the popular forces do? It is clear that he had no confidence that the Front could win an election. In commenting on the 1964 election, he stresses that against the Front were overwhelming factors—"the decisive importance of the Catholic Church . . . the total control of the large newspapers and all the propaganda media by the dominating class", the possibility for the "charity organisation", Caritas, to buy up working-class votes by the free distribution of foodstuffs supplied by the Alliance for Progress, the US anti-Cuba campaign. All these, he believed, "guaranteed the electoral supremacy of the bourgeoisie from the outset".

[1] ibid., p. 53.
[2] i.e., in Chile.
[3] See Régis Debray: "Problems of Revolutionary Strategy", *Strategy for Revolution*, op. cit., p. 139.
[4] ibid., pp. 136–40.

In arguing thus, Debray was using the same kind of arguments that were used again in 1970 by all the ultra-left groups in Chile (Maoists, Trotskyists, etc.), and who were thrown into disarray not only by the results but also by the ability of the Front to maintain itself as the Government and by its inauguration of a number of radical measures ("... the losers are (together with the oligarchy) the ultra-left and those who favoured the path of insurrection. ... Events moved differently than anticipated, throwing most of the above mentioned groups into crisis: they do not know what to do in the immediate future").[1]

If, as the Cuban Party delegation to the 1967 OLAS conference rightly asserted, it was "foolish and absurd" to talk of armed struggle in Chile, then why does Debray believe it was "irrational optimism" for the Chilean Communists to state that it was possible to achieve revolution *without* armed struggle? If the people of Chile are not to advance by non-armed forms of struggle, including electoral struggle, then what else is left? Of course, the working people of Chile have not yet established their full power; they still live under a capitalist system; their resources are still subject to imperialist exploitation. Moreover, the attempt to pass on from the present stage and to begin digging up the very roots of the system may be met by violence from internal and/or external reaction; and therefore the people may have to use armed force to defend their gains, or to press on to further changes. They might even be defeated, and have to turn to armed struggle in order to overturn their temporary victors.[2] But this is not what is being argued. What Debray was claiming in 1965 was that an unarmed way forward for Chile was impossible, and that an electoral victory for the popular forces could not open the way to major transformations.

His interview with Allende in March, 1971, indicates that he (Debray) still retains something of his dogmatic distrust of any form of struggle other than armed action. In his replies to Debray, Allende draws attention to the interesting dedication in one of Che Guevara's books: "For Allende, who is trying to obtain the same result by other means."

Debray, however, is not so confident, as the following extracts from the interview show:

[1] "Chile: September 4 to November 5", by Special Correspondent, *Monthly Review*, January, 1971, pp. 21–2.

[2] If any of these situations were to arise, the working people of Chile would know that they had pushed peaceful, legal forms of struggle to the limit and therefore would be more ready to resort to and support armed action if this became necessary. Furthermore, the social and political gains won since Allende's election will have given them something worth defending.

Debray: With you in government, the Chilean people has chosen the road of revolution, but what is revolution? It is the transfer of power from one class to another. Revolution is the destruction of the machinery of the bourgeois State and the replacement of it by another, and none of this has happened here. What is happening then?

Allende: Indeed, the people of Chile chose the road of revolution and we have not forgotten a fundamental principle of Marxism: the class struggle. During the electoral campaign we said that the purpose of our struggle was to change the régime, the system, in order to obtain the power to carry out the revolutionary transformation which Chile needs, to break the nation's dependence: and you say nothing has happened? What country do you think you're in? During the few months we've been in power we've . . .

Debray: Done a lot of things?

Allende: Yes, we've done quite a lot. The people are in government, and from this position they are struggling to gain power through the programme of the Popular Union.[1] This is a working-class government because the predominant ideology is that of the working class. The interests of the exploiting class are not represented in the Government—on the contrary, there are wage earners in the Cabinet, four of them workmen. As for the bourgeois state at the present moment, we are seeking to overcome it. To overthrow it!

Debray: But bourgeois democracy remains intact here. You, in fact, hold the executive power, but not the legislative nor the judiciary, nor the apparatus of police power. The law, the institutions, these were not the work of the proletariat; the bourgeoisie formulated the Constitution to suit its own ends.

Allende: Of course, you're right, but what did we say during the electoral campaign? We said that if it was difficult, not impossible, to win the election, the stage between victory and taking government was going to be very difficult, and it would be yet more difficult to make a new road for Chile. . . .

---

[1] Luis Corvalán, the General Secretary of the Communist Party of Chile, puts it in these words: "The Left parties have formed a government, are in control, that is, of the political-power mechanism. But the oligarchy still holds strong positions in the legislative and judicial branches, controls the communication media and, as partner of US imperialism, dominates the economy. The outlook, therefore, is for a series of clashes between the people and their government, on the one hand, and imperialism and the oligarchy, on the other. . . . We should not, therefore, preclude the possibility of the people having to resort to one or another form of armed struggle. To ward off any such situation the popular forces must immobilise the enemy, straitjacket him, drive him into a corner and thus spare the country the civil war the opponents of reform would so gleefully welcome. ("Chile: the People take Over", *World Marxist Review*, December, 1970, pp. 2–3.)

Debray: It is interesting that instead of the traditional falling away of a "government of the Left" once it has got into power, in this case, support is growing. Do you envisage a time when there will be a genuinely popular revolutionary majority?[1]

Allende: We haven't been around long enough to show a loss of support, but of one thing I am sure and that is the reaction, the Right, and even a lot of people on the Left, first of all didn't believe we would win, and then they didn't think we could carry out what we had said we'd do. Then, we hit back hard at reaction. Persistently. We hit them, they don't lie down, and we let them have it again. For example, the Constitutional Reform for nationalising copper, the expropriation of an important textile company in Concepcion, the nationalisation of steel, the nationalisation of coal, the Bill to nationalise the banks. Now then, Régis, are we or are we not looking for the road to Socialism? . . .

Debray: I come back to my earlier question, comrade Allende: the workers behind you have voted you into office, but if I ask you how and when you are going to win real power, what is your answer?

Allende: We shall have real power when copper and steel are ours, when nitrates are genuinely ours, when we have put far-reaching Land Reform measures into effect, when we have collectivised a major portion of our production. . . . Now then, if these things—affirming our national sovereignty, recovering our fundamental wealth and attacking monopolies—do not lead to Socialism, I don't know what does. . . .

Debray: Comrade President, allow me to look ahead a little. How can the transition from a bourgeois system to another more democratic, more revolutionary, more proletarian system be achieved without a break? Doubtless I am over-generalising, but basically my question is: "Who is using whom? Who is taking whom for a ride?". That's putting it brutally and perhaps a little provocatively... there are those who say I'm a professional "agent provocateur", comrade President.

Allende: I shall not allow myself to be provoked.

Debray: The question is important.

Allende: And the answer is short: the proletariat.[2]

I have thought it necessary to quote this interview at some length in order to enable the reader to understand how Debray approaches the question of power. Basically, of course, he is correct to draw attention to the problems that still remain to be solved by the Chilean working

[1] Since the time of this interview, the municipal elections in Chile, held on April 4 1971, gave the parties of the Popular Unity front 50·86 per cent of the votes, compared with the 36·3 per cent won in the election of Allende in September, 1970.

[2] *Sunday Times*, March 14, 1971.

class and people if they are to complete their taking over of political power. But one cannot help feeling that there is something of a romantic yearning on the part of Debray to witness a sudden dramatic change, the fanfare of trumpets, the whistle of bullets, the crash of explosions, the violent armed overthrow of the present "bourgeois" state of Chile.

In his report to the Central Committee of the Chilean Communist Party, in November, 1970, Luis Corvalán said:

> The people have taken over governmental power and thus a part of political power. This achievement must be defended and consolidated so that the entire political power, the whole state apparatus goes into its hands. Moreover it is necessary to push imperialism and oligarchy out of the centres of economic power, to put the entire political and economic power into the service of national progress. . . .[1]

Allende, in the interview quoted above, does not fully deal with the question raised by Debray concerning the state apparatus, and makes no comment on the question of the armed forces. As president he may, of course, have regarded Debray's question as provocative, especially at a time of great political complexity and danger. It is interesting, however, to note how Corvalán approaches the question of the armed forces. As he points out, the Programme of the Popular Unity front advocates the provision of the necessary material and technical equipment to the army that will enable it to fulfil its main tasks, namely "the defence of national sovereignty and performance of other specific duties". The programme proposes a democratic system of army pay, promotion and pensions, which will provide all ranks, from top officers to privates, with sufficient material means for their period of service and after retirement, and with realistic opportunities for promotion solely on the basis of ability.

Corvalán comments:

> As repeatedly pointed out by President Allende, the Popular Unity parties came to power not as a result of grappling with the armed forces or any part of them. The armed forces did not take part in the fight for power, and when the people triumphed, with the National Congress confirming their victory, the armed forces publicly recognised the government. They retained their spirit of professionalism,

[1] See *New Age* (India), January 3, 1971.

their respect for the Constitution and the law. For this approach it was that the Ultra-Right elements assassinated the army's commander-in-chief General Schneider.

To be sure, we should not overlook the circumstances in which the armed forces were formed, and especially the fact that their professional training was in recent decades influenced by the Pentagon. This does not go to say, however, that they are loyal servants of the imperialists and the upper classes. Our ground troops and navy were constituted in the fight for independence. Privates and non-commissioned officers in all the three arms come from a poor social background and nearly all the officers from the middle strata. The oligarchy and the prosperous bourgeoisie have long ago stopped choosing a military career for their sons. It should be borne in mind, however, that these days no social institution is indifferent to the social storms raging all over the world and the tragedy of the hundreds of millions of poverty-stricken people.

The attitude of the armed forces of the Dominican Republic during the US invasion and the progressive nature of the military government in Peru show that a dogmatic approach to the army is no longer valid. The military establishment, too, needs change, but that change should not be imposed on it. It must be initiated by the military and based on their awareness of its imperatives.[1]

The novelty advanced by Corvalán lies in the conception, based on an analysis of the social and political changes taking place in the army, that the further progress of these changes and the resultant qualitative character of the transformation, will come about as a result of the efforts of the progressive elements in the armed forces themselves, helped, no doubt, by the Government and the parties of the Popular Unity front, but not imposed by them against the wishes of the army.

There is in Debray's writings no preparation for such a development, and even his later interview with Allende indicates that he has a rigid and fixed view as to the armed forces in Chile.

Nor are Debray's views on Argentina any more helpful. He evidently has no time for the slogan launched by the Communist Party of Argentina at its Twelfth Congress in 1963: "Towards the conquest of power through the action of the masses."[2] And yet he has nothing serious to offer as a practical revolutionary way forward. Slovo,[3] it seems to me, penetratingly pointed up Debray's failure here:

[1] Luis Corvalán: "Chile: the People Take Over", op. cit., p. 5.
[2] See "Castroism: The Long March in Latin America", op. cit., p. 32.
[3] Joe Slovo: *The Theories of Regis Debray*, op. cit., p. 10.

His general formula has no validity here, for Debray himself concedes that in Argentina, with its urban concentration of 75 per cent of the population, a rural insurrectionary centre "can only have a subordinate role", that nothing can be achieved without the active participation of the urban workers, that a general strike, short of insurrection, "tends to be broken by violence". There are generalised clichés about armed struggle and preparation for such struggle. But if, as he emphasises repeatedly, urban insurrections have become a virtual impossibility; if "pure mass action" is spurned, what future is there for the Argentinian masses? What is the answer to the crucial question of the strategy for the transfer of power in Argentina? Debray sheds little light on this.

Debray's views on Bolivia, in the light of developments there in the past five years, appear equally to be out of tune with reality. In 1965 Debray was of the opinion that "Bolivia is the country where the subjective and objective conditions are best combined. It is the only country in South America where a socialist revolution is on the agenda, despite the reconstitution of an army which was totally destroyed in 1952. It is also the only country where the revolution might take the classical Bolshevik form—witness the proletarian insurrection of 1952, on the basis of 'soviets', which 'exploded' the state apparatus by means of a short and decisive armed struggle."[1]

Since those lines were penned, Bolivia has been through three important phases. The first, when the struggles of miners and others in 1965 were crushed in bloody massacre by the army. The second, the guerrilla campaign led by Che Guevara, 1966-7. Thirdly, the new anti-imperialist path followed by the military government under General Torres, who came to power in October, 1970, and, within three months, released Debray himself from jail.[2] None of the above events demonstrates the likelihood of the revolution in Bolivia taking "the classical Bolshevik form". Presumably by this term Debray means the rapid armed taking of power in the main cities by the working class in alliance with sections of the army (peasants in uniform) which had ceased to uphold the system and had gone to the side of the revolution.

Debray himself, shortly after the defeat of 1965, apparently had second thoughts. In *Revolution in the Revolution?*, written in 1967, he gives a vivid description of the way in which the US-organised Rangers launched their savage attack on the miners after the Trotskyists

---

[1] Régis Debray: "Castroism: The Long March", op. cit., p. 38.
[2] This third phase came to an end with the coup against Torres in August, 1971.

had initiated an unlimited general strike. Debray draws the conclusion:

> If there were a combined general insurrection at several mines, plus
> La Paz and certain rural areas, and if this insurrection brought to
> completion a long war of attrition carried on elsewhere by other
> means, miners organised in revolutionary unions could play a deci-
> sive role. But one thing appears to be impossible: that a spon-
> taneous insurrection should be able, in a few days, to defeat a
> modern army, trained and reinforced by a well-equipped North
> American military mission, equipped with shock troops, few in
> number but aggressive.[1]

Here, Debray, embracing the concept of "a long war of attrition",
had clearly abandoned the idea of a Bolivian revolution in the "classical
Bolshevik form". Two years earlier he had written:

> The theory of the *foco* is thus in Bolivia, for reasons of historical
> formation which are unique in America, if not inadequate at any
> rate secondary.[2]

In 1967 the *foco* was to be attempted in Bolivia—by Che Guevara,
with tragic results. Debray was to be arrested in that period, in Bolivia
itself; and there is sufficient evidence to indicate that he had high hopes
of Che's attempt. Thus, in two years Debray had abandoned his idea of
a "classical Bolshevik" insurrection in Bolivia in favour of protracted
war; now he was to place his stakes on the *foco* which he had previously
regarded as "if not inadequate at any rate secondary". The defeat of
Che Guevara does not, of course, by itself disprove the validity of
Debray's argument concerning the *foco* in general, nor does it invalidate
his support for the *foco* in Bolivia. But neither does it lend any powerful
support to his theory.

After another two years, and following on the defeat of the *foco* in
Bolivia, Debray once more attempted to explain the path of the revolution in that country, denying the possibility of the national bourgeoisie
and petty-bourgeoisie breaking out of their dependence on imperialism
and pursuing an anti-imperialist policy.[3] Yet once again life calls into
question Debray's theories.

Already, under the government of General Alfredo Ovando, which
came to power in 1969, a number of important steps were taken to

---

[1] Régis Debray: *Revolution in the Revolution?*, op. cit., p. 34.
[2] Régis Debray: "Castroism: The Long March", op. cit., p. 38.
[3] See above, pp. 244–8.

weaken the economic stranglehold of the US monopolies, to strengthen the national economy, and introduce democratic reforms.[1] After Ovando's replacement by General Torres further democratic and anti-imperialist measures were inaugurated and political prisoners released. Perhaps even more significant, the government of General Torres found it necessary to lean for support more decisively on the workers and their unions, and on the peasants; it was, after all, the actions by the workers and others which were decisive in enabling General Torres to defeat the first two right-wing coups against him.

There is plenty of room for debate as regards the character of General Torres' government and of the social and economic changes that were introduced into Bolivia after Barrientos. Certainly no revolutionary should have had any illusions that the Torres government would be adequate to end the grip of imperialism and backwardness, still less to commence the construction of socialism. But once again, as in the case of Chile, no serious revolutionary would ignore the new possibilities for advance which were open in that period or abandon them in favour of armed struggle against a government which had inaugurated extremely important reforms; it is, in any case, fairly certain that the majority of people would not have supported such armed action in those circumstances, especially as it could have played into the hands of the oligarchy which was down, but not out.

Debray, himself, seems to have abandoned his perspective of armed struggle in Bolivia—either in the form of the "classic Bolshevik insurrection", or in the form of a protracted war climaxed by a widespread insurrection in the mines, the capital and the countryside, or in the form of the *foco*. What he now holds out for Bolivia, or, indeed, for Latin America in general, is not yet clear, although his "Notes", published in 1969, and constituting his most comprehensive analysis since *Revolution in the Revolution?*, provide evidence of some new thinking on his part.

Two key ideas in *Revolution in the Revolution?* and in Debray's other earlier writings are that the form of armed struggle in Latin America must be the *foco*, and that instead of the political vanguard forming the military instrument it is the latter which gives rise to the political vanguard.

Debray believes that it is determined action by a group of militants that can itself produce the revolutionary situation in Latin America, and that the action required is the armed action of creating the *foco*, or nucleus, which spreads like "an oil patch . . . through the peasant

[1] See above, p. 245.

masses, to the smaller towns, and finally to the capital".[1] At a first glance, this idea—"from the countryside to the towns"—appears remarkably similar to the views both of Lin Piao and other followers of Mao Tse-tung, and of Fanon. Unlike Fanon, however, Debray, at least in this earlier essay, does not write off the workers, neither does he look in the towns to the *lumpenproletariat* as the basic ally of the peasants. The surge from the countryside to the towns, according to Debray, is a two-way process, "since from the towns themselves there comes a movement of mass strikes, demonstrations in defence of public liberties, fund-raising campaigns, and an underground resistance movement galvanized by the exploits of the rural guerrilla".[2] The guerrillas will find support among the workers, "the agricultural workers of the plains: the cane workers of Northern Argentina . . . the unemployed from the market towns of Falcon; the wage-labourers from the coast of the Brazilian north-east." All these, asserts Debray: "form a social stratum which is far more receptive and better prepared for the struggle, because of its concentration, its chronic unemployment, its subordination to the fluctuations of the capitalist market". And finally, in the nearby towns, "there will be convergence with the small groups of political workers" for whom there will be no "need for the slow preliminary work which is indispensable in the mountains". Later, Debray was to be far less emphatic and confident about the role of the "politicised workers".

Debray is convinced that the essential motor to move the masses into action must be the armed *foco*, established in the countryside, and which grows eventually into the people's army that will liberate the towns in conjunction with the organised urban movement, where the universities will play a key role.[3] In pursuit of his theory, Debray argues on the one hand that those who stay in the towns become soft, become in essence "bourgeoisified", and so incapable of leading the struggle—and indeed unwilling to do so. At the same time, in that strange contradictory way that he argues (a habit which he shares with Fanon), he equally affirms that the revolutionary struggle cannot be initiated in the towns because of the weight of the repressive machine there, which renders it dangerous for the revolutionary leaders, who should retreat to the countryside where it is safer to commence and organise the struggle. As he himself points out, the casualty lists of dead and

[1] Régis Debray: "Castroism: The Long March in Latin America", op. cit., p. 39.
[2] ibid.
[3] ibid., pp. 44–5.

imprisoned in Latin America are mainly Communist Party leaders—
"the militant communists have carried the principal burden". This
hardly squares up with his contention that militants in the towns have
an easy life and have become softened.

There are too many contradictions here for a clear conclusion to be
drawn from Debray's argument. But the essence of his plea is that the
struggle in most Latin American countries must commence in the
countryside, and that it must take the form of the *foco*. He rejects other
forms of armed struggle based on the political mobilisation of workers
and peasants, as was carried out in China or Vietnam, arguing that this
experience, while correct for these countries, does not apply to Latin
America—although his case for such an assertion is in no way convincing. Similarly, he rejects other forms of armed struggle such as armed
self-defence[1] (used in Colombia), armed propaganda (used in Vietnam,
China and the Philippines), or the establishment of firm guerrilla bases
(as in China). Only the small *foco* is, according to Debray, suitable for
Latin America; and this small unit, in his view, must start on its own,
deliberately isolated from the peasants who will mistrust it and might
betray it.

What of the political leadership required for such a struggle? On the
basis of his false analysis of the course of the Cuban revolution Debray
argues that the political leadership or vanguard organisation only
arises *after* the taking of power, and that it emerges as *a result of armed
struggle*. In his scheme of things the military leadership takes priority
over political leadership.

> *The guerrilla force is the party in embryo.* This is the staggering
> novelty introduced by the Cuban Revolution.[2]
> Any guerrilla movement in Latin America that wishes to pursue the
> people's war to the end . . . must become the unchallenged political
> vanguard.[3]
> *The people's army will be the nucleus of the party, not vice versa.* The
> guerrilla force is the political vanguard *in nuce* and from its develop-
> ment a real party can arise.[4]

This concept, in brief, is Debray's theory of the "revolution in the
revolution".

[1] For a refutation of Debray on this point see Wilfred G. Burchett: "'Self-Defence'
Centres in a People's War", cited in *Guerrilla Warfare and Marxism*, edited by William
J. Pomeroy, London, 1969, pp. 225–9.
[2] Régis Debray: *Revolution in the Revolution?*, op. cit., p. 106.
[3] ibid., p. 109.
[4] ibid., p. 116.

The experience of modern guerrilla movements and armed struggles in other continents does not at all bear out this contention. In China it was the political vanguard, the Communist Party, which created China's "Red Army", later changed to "The People's Liberation Army". In the Malayan war of resistance against the Japanese it was the Communist Party which, in conjunction with other political forces, created the Malayan People's Anti-Japanese Army; as it was the Malayan Communist Party which created the Malayan National Liberation Army after the outbreak of the fighting with British imperialism in 1948. In Vietnam, it was the Communist Party which created the liberation forces which fought the French, the Japanese, again the French and now the United States forces of intervention. In the South it was the National Liberation Front which created the liberation army, not vice versa. On the occasion of the 25th anniversary of the founding of the Vietnam People's Army, December 22, 1969, the daily paper *Nhan Dan* carried an article by Lt.-General Song Hao, Head of the General Political Department of the army, which was significantly entitled: "Party leadership: source of strength and victory of our army." General Vo Nguyen Giap has said: "All the great successes of our people originate from the correct revolutionary line and the clever leadership of our Party. . . . The soundness of the revolutionary and military lines of our Party has been demonstrated by the successes recorded on the battlefield. *These lines are the very source of our indomitable strength and of all our victories.*" [1]

In Angola, Mozambique and Guinea-Bissau, it has been the political party which has built the armed forces, and not vice versa. Amilcar Cabral, who can certainly speak on the basis of both experience and success, has explained the relationship between the political and military leadership in Guinea-Bissau in these words:

> The political and military leadership of the struggle is one: the political leadership. In our struggle we have avoided the creation of anything military. We are political people, and our Party, a political organisation, leads the struggle in the civilian, political, administrative, technical, and therefore also military spheres. Our fighters are defined as armed activists. It is the Political Bureau of the Party that directs the armed struggle and the life of both the liberated and unliberated regions where we have our activists. Within the Political Bureau is a War Council composed of members of the former who

[1] Vo Nguyen Giap: *Vietnam People's War Has Defeated U.S. War of Destruction*, Hanoi, 1969, p. 22 and p. 29.

direct the armed struggle. The War Council is an instrument of the Political Bureau, of the leadership of the armed struggle.[1]

Debray's attempts to bring forward exceptionalist conceptions to justify his claim that in Latin America it is necessary to have a "revolution in the revolution", to set up the guerrilla force first from which the political party will emerge, are not confirmed by actual events. As has been already noted this is not the way things developed in Cuba, whatever Debray may assert to the contrary. It was, after all, a highly politically motivated group which began the armed struggle; the Cuban guerrillas were increasingly sustained and supported by the people in the countryside and the towns, who were organised by political movements, including that of the Cuban Communists, the PSP; and it was the coming together of these political forces and the armed fighters which created the present Cuban Communist Party.

In other Latin American countries a major cause of the defeats of many guerrilla movements has been precisely this attempt to set up *focos* without either adequate political preparations or links with political organisations in key centres capable of rallying popular support, and material aid, and capable of taking advantage of the situation created by the guerrillas to hasten the political crisis for the government. It is not too much to say that acceptance of Debray's theory on this point has been an important factor contributing to conflicts between guerrillas and political organisations, as well as within the guerrilla forces themselves and also within the political organisations, including some Communist Parties.

It is not without significance that the longest established and most powerful guerrilla force in Latin America, that in Colombia, came into existence in the early 1950's (before the commencement of the armed struggle in Cuba), and that it was created by the Communist Party. Jacobo Arenas, a member of the Executive Committee of the Communist Party of Colombia and of the General Staff of the Revolutionary Armed Forces of Colombia (FARC), has explained, in considerable detail, the role played by the Communist Party of Colombia in helping to build the guerrilla movement, emphasising that it is the Communist Party which "leads and guides the liaison with the masses, puts forward the policy, the military and political line, that the guerrilla movement will follow".[2]

---

[1] Amilcar Cabral: "Practical Problems and Tactics", interview published in *Tricontinental* magazine, No. 8, September, 1968: see *Revolution in Guinea*, op. cit., p. 118.
[2] Jacobo Arenas: *Colombie: Guerillas du Peuple*, Paris, 1970, p. 112.

The example of Colombia is not easily explained away by Debray or those who, to a considerable degree, accept many of his arguments. The Colombian Communists fought alongside the peasants during the terrible period of *La Violencia* (1949 to 1953), helped them to establish the first guerrilla groups (1954 to 1957), and after 1957 set up and led the self-defence zones which defeated a government attack by 7,000 troops in 1962, and a further attack by 16,000 in 1964. This latter attack compelled the guerrillas to give up territory in the self-defence zone of Marquetalia, but the Government forces failed in their main objective of destroying the guerrillas, which in April, 1966, established the Revolutionary Armed Forces of Colombia (FARC). In 1967 the FARC successfully resisted another attack—this time by 25,000 Government troops. To this day the Government has been unable to destroy this Communist-led guerrilla army.

Despite this outstanding record, the Colombian Communists are not without their detractors. Richard Gott claims to detect a certain lack of "enthusiasm for the armed struggle" among Colombian Communists. To prove his point he even misrepresents what the Colombian Communists have said. Thus, in reference to the Tenth Congress of the Party, Gott writes:

> The Tenth Congress emphasised that the guerrilla struggle in Colombia had preceded the development of a revolutionary situation . . . guerrilla resistance was not the most important factor in the revolutionary process. "Mass struggle" was more crucial in the eyes of the orthodox Communists.[1]

In fact, the Tenth Congress said something quite different, as Richard Gott could have noticed if he had read the text from the Tenth Congress which he reproduces in an appendix to his own book. As he presents it in the passage quoted above it could certainly give the impression that the Colombian Communists lacked enthusiasm for the armed struggle. But this is what the Congress Report actually said:

> 1. The armed resistance against the attack on Marquetalia, El Pato, Guayabero, Rio Chiquito, Southern Tolima and other sectors proves that a guerrilla movement which arises from the masses, expresses their needs and is guided by Marxist-Leninist principles is invincible, however powerful the enemy forces and even if conditions are not ripe for making fighting the main form of struggle.
> 2. The armed struggle has been going on in Colombia, in its peasant

[1] Richard Gott: *Guerrilla Movements in Latin America*, op. cit., pp. 193–4.

guerrilla form, since even before there could be said to be a revolutionary situation in the country. It would be negative and fatal for the Colombian revolutionary movement to stand by and watch the destruction of this force while waiting for a revolutionary situation to mature before beginning the armed struggle. The armed aggression of the enemy must be met by guerrilla resistance and armed struggle in the countryside. When conditions permit, this should be spread to the cities and working class areas.

3. There is no conflict between mass struggle and armed guerrilla struggle. Guerrilla is one of the highest forms of mass struggle and it only flourishes and spreads where it has mass characteristics, where it springs from the masses, where it is the faithful expression of their immediate and historical interests. The experience of revolutionaries who tried to begin armed struggles in the last few years without counting on the peasant masses, with their passive and active support, shows that idealist plans give easy victories to the army, the police or the bandits controlled by the local authorities and landowners.[1]

Gott is misleading when he writes that the Colombian Communists regard "mass struggle" as more important than guerrilla resistance. Where he sees a conflict between mass struggle and guerrilla struggle, a choice of one or the other, the Colombian Communists see the two as indissolubly linked—"There is no conflict between mass struggle and armed guerrilla struggle." Moreover, they stress, "guerrilla warfare is one of the highest forms of mass struggle".

Like Debray, Gott is anxious to play down the role of the Communist Parties in Latin America; and like Debray, who is scornful of the slogan "Towards the conquest of power through the action of the masses", Gott, too, apparently cannot accept the idea that it is *mass* struggle that is required, whatever weapons are used.

Debray's élitist approach also colours his attitude to theory and ideology. He apparently does not accept the Marxist concept that "without a revolutionary theory there can be no revolutionary movement". Instead, he embraces spontaneity, the idea that people spontaneously become revolutionaries and acquire revolutionary understanding from practice alone; and this practice, in his view, must be military practice. These ideas, which are linked with his attempt to play down the role of a political and ideological leadership of the struggle, and which include the concept that the military *foco* will give rise to the political vanguard and not vice versa, arise from his belief that the mass of

[1] See Richard Gott: op. cit., pp. 381–2.

people are passive and inert and will only come alive when the active few show the way by their own heroic armed actions.

Debray evidently ignores Lenin's warnings as to the dangers of looking upon guerrilla warfare as the decisive weapon, and especially the danger of neglecting ideology. Defending the guerrilla fighters in tsarist Russia against their traducers in 1906, Lenin nevertheless argued that:

> . . . the party of the proletariat can never regard guerrilla warfare as the only, or even as the chief, method of struggle; it means that this method must be subordinated to other methods, that this method must be commensurate with the chief methods of warfare, and must be ennobled by the enlightening and organising influence of socialism. And without this *latter* condition, *all* methods of struggle in bourgeois society bring the proletariat into close association with the various non-proletarian strata above and below it and, if left to the spontaneous course of events, become frayed, corrupted and prostituted.[1]

There are several examples in history to demonstrate this, including the fate of some of the guerrilla groups in the Philippines, which eventually lapsed into banditry.

Debray's views on theory and the role of ideology are, in a way, one of the most astounding things about him. He has gone to great lengths to work out and present his own set of views and theories on Latin American revolutions—even though he disclaims, as we have noted, any intention of presenting a body of theory. Whatever term he might wish to give to his ideas, the fact remains that he has written them down and obtained their publication presumably because he thinks it is necessary for his ideas to be accepted and used for the Revolution. There is nothing wrong with such an act. On the contrary, any sincere revolutionary would do the same. But few would be so contradictory as to present their ideas as to how to develop the revolution and simultaneously argue as if ideas about revolution are really of little significance.

Repeatedly he plays down the role of theory:

> The sending of cadres to schools for political studies and the flanking of the military cadres with "political commissars" is bound to hamper the natural emergence of popular leaders, of well-rounded military-political leaders.[2]

[1] V. I. Lenin: "Guerrilla Warfare", op. cit.
[2] Régis Debray: *Revolution in the Revolution?*, op. cit., p. 90.

The best teacher of Marxism-Leninism is the enemy, in face to face confrontation during the people's war. Study and apprenticeship are necessary, but not decisive. There are no academy-trained cadres.[1]

It is quite remarkable that Debray should attempt to denigrate the role of theory in this way and to spread the illusion that the mere act of participating in struggle, even revolutionary struggle, can by itself produce a socialist consciousness. Debray himself, in a lengthy footnote (p. 20) in *Revolution in the Revolution?*, gives considerable detail of the reading and study carried out by Castro even *prior* to the armed struggle. Among the authors he cites are Marx, Engels, Lenin, Martí; and, later, Mao Tse-tung. Thus, it is clear that Fidel saw the need for theoretical and ideological study as an essential part of revolutionary struggle, even though Debray minimises the role of ideology.

Jacobo Arenas has described the political role of the guerrilla in these words:

The guerrilla fighter today is a professional revolutionary who must ceaselessly raise his political and cultural level. We (the Party) have never lost an occasion to get together with our armed units, to organise educational meetings, and intensive study courses on the basis of a simple and straightforward plan of studies. The central journal of our Party is for us a valuable instrument of education. Each article, each item of news, each report is studied and tasks fixed accordingly.[2]

Manuel Marulanda, the commander of the FARC, has elaborated further on the political activity of the Colombian guerrillas:

The guerrilla fighter, and everyone taking part in the revolutionary movement, must be prepared in every way, above all as regards political and military matters, in order to become an exemplary *guerrillero* and a political cadre capable of explaining the policies of the revolutionary movement, and must not allow himself to be misled by the demagogy of the enemy who will use all manner of guises in order to fool the people. It's our duty to train ourselves politically so that the guerrillas may be in a position to win over the people to join the struggle. Not only the peasants, but all the people. Otherwise victory for the revolution is not possible.[3]

Criticising Debray's contempt for theory, Slovo rightly comments: This competitive contrast between revolutionary theory and

[1] ibid., p. 111.   [2] Jacobo Arenas: op. cit., p. 49 (Author's translation).
[3] ibid., p. 60 (Author's translation).

revolutionary practice; this rejection of the true role of theory and its place in a revolutionary struggle, stems from the quite incorrect assumption that the scientific principles of Marxism-Leninism grow naturally and almost spontaneously out of struggle. A clue that this is what Debray believes is contained in the following statement:

> "There is a further reason why Fidelism lays a greater stress on revolutionary practice, when it is honest and sincere, than on ideological labels: this is the belief that in the special conditions of South America the dynamism of nationalist struggles brings them to a conscious adoption of Marxism." ("Latin America: The Long March", *New Left Review*, No. 33, p. 54.)

I emphasise this because if Debray is correct in his contention that the acceptance of correct ideology and scientific socialism will arise, in the special conditions of Latin America from the very process of struggle, then indeed, it is not vital to start off with a theoretical grasp of scientific principles nor a vanguard party to propagate them. The struggle will create all this.

But the belief that a people or a class which is engaged in honest and sincere revolutionary practice will of necessity arrive at the correct ideological termini, is an old illusion advanced in the revolutionary movement not for the first time. It was at the nub of the thesis of the Russian "Economists" and their German Revisionist counterparts.[1]

Slovo quotes here the very relevant passage from Kautsky cited by Lenin in *What is to be done?*, in which Kautsky writes that "There can be no talk of an independent ideology being developed by the masses of the workers themselves in the process of the movement. . . . There is a lot of talk about spontaneity but the spontaneous development of the working-class movement leads to its becoming subordinated to the bourgeois ideology."

Slovo pointedly adds:

> And if it is true of workers in direct conflict with their class enemy that, left to themselves, they tend towards bourgeois rather than proletarian ideology, how much more true is this of a struggle whose main content is national in character.

This, of course, is borne out by the experiences of liberation struggles both in Asia and Africa, where intense political and ideological work has been carried out both prior to and during phases of armed struggle. The examples of China and Vietnam are too well known for it to be

[1] Slovo: op. cit., p. 16.

necessary to cite them here. As I know from my own experience in Africa, the guerrilla forces now engaged in liberating Guinea-Bissau went through an intense training period in preparation for the armed struggle; the training included both guerrilla practice and ideological and theoretical study. And political study continues to be an essential duty for these guerrilla fighters.

Debray's attempts to ignore international experience cannot be explained away by references to the specific conditions in Latin America. There are, admittedly, characteristics in each Latin American country which have to be taken into account by the revolutionary movements; but none of these particular features are of a type which could justify in any way a reliance on the theory of spontaneity. Hobsbawm[1] points out that "Marulanda, writing as a Colombian peasant guerrilla commander, has no doubts that organisation, discussion and education are essential for the morale of the guerilleros if only to keep them occupied between action." ("That's why in camp we must have a political instructor at all costs.")[2]

URBANISATION AND THE WORKING CLASS

As already noted, Debray fails to make any basic analysis of classes and social phenomena in Cuba or in Latin America in general. But no serious attempt to understand revolutionary processes in this continent is possible unless one starts from the basis of factual reality. There are, of course, considerable differences, for a start, between one Latin American country and another; but taking the continent as a whole there are certain major characteristics that need to be taken into account.

The proportion of wage workers to the total population is far higher than it is in most countries of Asia and Africa; moreover, the total labour force in industry, trade, clerical work, etc., is now greater than in agriculture. (See table, page 270.)

In the last decade the trend has continued. The labour force in the countryside declines, while in industry, etc., it increases. Luis Corvalán has stated (in 1967) that as many as 40 million people—or more than half the gainfully employed population between the Rio Grande and Cape Horn—earn their living by selling their labour power. Some estimates give a figure for 1968 as high as 50 million. Changes are also revealed by the growth of urbanisation. Urban population in Latin America rose from 61,369,000 in 1950 to 119,362,000 in 1965—a rise

---

[1] *Socialist Register*, 1970, p. 60.   [2] Jacobo Arenas: op. cit., p. 118.

	1940	1950	1960
Total labour force (in thousands)	42,810	52,950	68,630
In agriculture	24,830	28,160	32,260
Per cent.	58·0	53·0	47·0
In industry, trade, clerical work, etc.	17,980	24,790	36,370
Per cent.	42·0	47·0	53·0

from 33·5 per cent of the total population in 1950 to 50·3 per cent in 1965.

While in Central America, the rural population still tends to be in the neighbourhood of 60 per cent, for a number of other territories the weight of the working class in the population and the growth of urbanisation is really considerable.

Even in the early 1950's it was estimated that wage-earners comprised 70 per cent of the total labour force in Cuba, Chile and Argentina; over 60 per cent in Uruguay; and more than 50 per cent in Brazil, Venezuela, Ecuador and El Salvador. The factory proletariat in Argentina grew from 876,000 in 1948 to 1,700,000 in 1958, almost 100 per cent in ten years; in Brazil, from 669,000 in 1939 to 2 million in 1956, a 200 per cent increase in 17 years; in Mexico, from 379,000 in 1945 to 1 million in 1958, a 150 per cent increase in 13 years; and in Uruguay, from 90,000 in 1936 to 263,000 in 1958, an increase of nearly 200 per cent in 22 years.

Already, by 1961, Argentina had an urban population of 62·5 per cent, Brazil (1960) of 45 per cent, Chile 66 per cent, Colombia 46 per cent, Mexico (1960) 50·71 per cent, Peru 48 per cent, Uruguay 82 per cent, and Venezuela (1960) 62 per cent. The population of Santiago, the capital of Chile, rose from 1 million in 1930 to nearly 2·5 million in 1960—or one-third of Chile's total population.

Brazil has two cities of over 5 million inhabitants, and three of over 1 million. It is true that a large proportion of the populations of such cities in Latin America today are peasants who have flocked to the towns in search of work, and that many remain unemployed, a section falling into the ranks of the *lumpenproletariat* proper. This presents its own problems for the revolutionary movement; but, in any case, it in no way invalidates the argument that the rural population is declining.

The above figures show quite clearly how decisive are the urban centres and the aggregates of wage workers in an important grou

Latin American countries. The growing proportion of workers within the total labour force also expresses itself in the increased strike movement over the past two decades. In the 1950's the number of workers engaged in strikes in Latin America rose from $2\frac{1}{2}$ million to 6 million by 1954, to 9 million in 1957 and over 11 million in 1958. In the first half of the 1960's the annual average of strikers had reached 20 million. In the last few years there have been immense mass movements in the towns, general strikes, huge demonstrations, barricade fighting, clashes with police and troops. These actions have involved hundreds of thousands of workers on each occasion, notably in Mexico City on the eve of the Olympic Games, in the upheavals and barricade fighting in Cordoba in Argentina in 1969 and again in 1971, and in the series of general strikes and huge demonstrations in Uruguay in 1967.

One should not ignore, however, certain other features of the Latin American working class. While it already represents a substantial force, its main core, namely the industrial proletariat, is still comparatively small, totalling only some 7 million,[1] or less than a quarter of the continent's total urban wage earning class. There are other characteristics of the working class in Latin America which should not be overlooked, either, and which help to explain why in a number of countries it has not yet emerged as the leading class. Past emphasis by Communist Parties in Latin America that the vanguard role belonged to the working class was not always accompanied by the concentrated work necessary to ensuring this in practice. This work is now being tackled more effectively and more account is being taken of particular features of the working class, including the fact that its rapid growth between 1940 and 1955 meant the influx of large numbers of newcomers, both from the countryside and from the urban petty-bourgeoisie, who lacked experience of working-class struggle.

Sections of the higher paid workers have been influenced by reformism and social demagogy and have tended to hold back from militant struggle. Others are influenced by the preponderantly *lumpenproletarian* or petty-bourgeois environment from which they have come. Their conditions of life, their pressing social problems, appalling housing, and the constant threat of unemployment make them an important contingent of the revolutionary movement of protest. But they are also characterised by a certain instability, a readiness to swing from one political position to another, and a tendency to accept too easily general adventurist slogans. Thus sections of the working class of Latin America

[1] Some estimates indicate it is nearer 9 million.

which in the earlier stages of its formation sometimes produced moods of anarchism, have, in the more recent period, expressed feelings of impatience and ultra-leftism. In some cases this has led to forms of guerrilla warfare (kidnappings, assassinations, bank robberies, the burning or blowing up of buildings)[1] which have not assisted the growth of the mass movement itself.

This is not the place for a detailed examination of the Latin American working class; but any serious attempt to examine Debray's theory of the *foco* and all that goes with it cannot ignore the main trends in social life—the increasing urbanisation, the growth of the working class, and the relative decline of the rural population. This trend continues to make itself felt and cannot but influence the form and the scene of the revolution in most countries of Latin America.

Both demographic trends as well as the increased ability of the United States and its client governments in Latin America to challenge more effectively the activities of guerrillas in the countryside clearly must have an important bearing on the strategy and tactics of revolutionaries. The simple proposition—"from the countryside to the towns"—will not suffice. The towns, in fact, are becoming increasingly the major scene of class confrontation and liberation struggle in a number of countries of Latin America. At the same time in no sense can it be argued that there is no longer any place for guerrilla warfare in Latin America countryside today. In a number of countries such struggles are still being pursued; in others the necessity for mounting them might arise. Under certain conditions, where sufficient "inflammable material" has been accumulated, their role can be indispensable. In other cases, guerrilla warfare, even when temporarily defeated, can be one of the factors giving rise to significant advances achieved by other forms of struggle. There is no doubt, for example, that even though the guerrillas in Peru and Bolivia were defeated on the battlefield, and despite the mistakes they may have made—and after all, which heroic struggle has ever been carried through without errors?— and despite the amateurishness which often marked their efforts (sometimes but not always inevitable)—their clashes with the military and the noble aims of their proclamations were certainly among the influences which gave rise to changes within the armed forces of these two countries, resulting in the installation of progressive anti-imperialist governments in both cases.

[1] It should be appreciated that most of these actions are not carried out by industrial workers.

It has been said that although the defeated guerrillas in a number of Latin American countries were brave men who fought for just aims, they had no right to throw away their lives so easily nor to fight under conditions which led to such defeats, since this can only discredit the idea of armed struggle and bring about a certain discouragement and even demoralisation to the working people, including to the revolutionary movement itself. On the other hand, it can be argued equally that the courage and self-sacrifice of these heroes, of men such as Che Guevara, Turcios Lima, Camilo Torres, Luís de la Puente, Carlos Marighela, Guillermo Lobatón, Hector Bejar, Inti Peredo, Coco Peredo, Tamara Bunke, and many others has contributed to deepening the crisis in Latin America and has helped to open up the way, in several countries, to important democratic changes even though this has not taken place in the way these martyred guerrillas had anticipated.

The advances have not arisen directly out of armed struggle, out of a process of "*foco* to Liberation Army", "countryside to town", as envisaged by Debray. Nevertheless one can say that the guerrilla actions in Latin America, which many people so often equate with the ideas of Debray, have had, even if often in indirect fashion, an important effect on the great movements for change which are now shaking the continent. But this in no way confirms Debray's theories concerning the *foco*, his emphasis on armed struggle, his preference for the countryside over the town, his attempt to play down the role of theory and ideology, his strictures against the Latin American Communist Parties, his tendency to write off the working class in preference to the students, intellectuals and peasants, his scorn for mass political activity, and his belief that it is the armed guerrilla force which gives rise to the political vanguard.

The growth of Latin American Communist Parties in recent years should not be ignored. These parties now have a combined membership of some 300,000 and, in several countries, represent a major political force. The working-class composition is heavily accented in a number of these parties, notably in Uruguay where workers constitute 78 per cent of the Party membership, in Chile (70 per cent), and in Argentina (63 per cent).

Non-Marxist writers often describe Debray as a Marxist; but at the heart of Marxism is the necessity for the working class to replace the capitalist class as the ruling force in society, in order that all exploited people can be liberated and the new socialist society created. Debray's supporters are perfectly within their rights to discard this central thesis of Marxism; but, doing so, they cannot at the same time claim Debray to be a Marxist. If the working class is not to be the leading class in Latin American societies, if it has become "bourgeoisi-fied" and must surrender its leading role to intellectuals and peasants, how then is the new socialist society to be created? And to what role is the working class to be assigned?

If Debray is simply arguing that, *at present*, the working class in most Latin American countries is not fulfilling its role as the vanguard, then one would expect him to devote considerable attention to the problem as to how this temporary weakness of the working class can be over-come. But (and we have seen the same above in the case of Fanon) the weaknesses of the working-class movement, even in their exaggerated form, are not brought forward here by Debray in order to remove them, but rather as a justification for turning away from the working class.

No Marxist would argue that the Latin American peasantry (though one must define this in more precise class terms) is not a vital force for the revolution. Nor would any Marxist deny that the students and intellectuals have played an exceptional role in many Latin American countries; this, in fact, has been a particular feature of the struggle in most Latin American countries for some decades, even though it is now more marked than ever. Debray, however, in search of justifications for his theory, has ignored many facts, and exaggerated others. Thus, he has arrived at conclusions, sometimes contradictory, which are not confirmed by real fact, and which, if accepted without question, and followed in practice, can only bring confusion and defeat to the efforts of those struggling for revolutionary change.

POSTSCRIPT ON DEBRAY

One hopes that Debray can still learn from his own mistakes and acquire a more scientific approach to the questions of Latin America. Certainly he has the ability to make a contribution. His interview with Allende, and his "Notes" of 1969, both show that he has shifted his ground somewhat in the light of actual developments, even though he obviously retains some of his dogmatic and sectarian illusions.

Nevertheless, in his "Notes", there are signs of a certain modification of some of his earlier ideas. Commenting on events in Bolivia, Debray asserts that "it is only if the workers, allied with the revolutionary intellectuals, play the leading role that the national interest can be full-defended". This new emphasis on the need for the working class to exercise its leading role is certainly welcome. So is his fresh approach to the question of theory. "Populist rhetoric like nationalism is an ephemeral support, and good intentions, sincerity, a genuine and respectable patriotic emotion, do not take the place of social forces organised and *guided by a scientific theory of social development*." (Author's italics.)

In his "Notes", Debray develops at some length his new ideas on theory, mass work and the role of classes in the revolution. Referring to the critical support given by the popular forces to the Ovando Government of Bolivia, he comments that this support "must always be accompanied by ideological clarity and an exact knowledge of the class nature of this or that political trend, of the relation of forces between the different classes in the country and the changes in these relations brought about by further developments. It is necessary to mount a strong ideological and political struggle against the illusions and hesitations of the petty-bourgeoisie. . . . Clearly all this ideological work can only take place in the course of daily political struggle, social practice, the defence of the people's economic interests. . . . In brief, it is necessary to struggle for the ideological leadership of the popular forces over those of the bourgeoisie. . . . Unity with the petty-bourgeoisie, yes. Under its direction, no."

Interesting, too, is his stress on the necessity for each country to find its own way to revolutionary change. The people of Bolivia, he writes, need to find "their own forms, their own path to socialism based on their traditions, their national characteristics, their history and their values. Today there is no longer a model, a fatherland or universal centre of socialism. Each people must seek out and take the road which suits it, without however forgetting the experience of other peoples which previously took this road (to socialism) or are taking it now."

This reference to each people finding its own road to socialism, however, is not put forward by Debray in any spirit of isolationism. On the contrary, he writes: ". . . the only way that a semi-colonial country can maintain and develop its independent national existence is by relying on the solidarity of the socialist camp and of the world revolutionary movement. The principle basis of support of a popular national régime must be the exploited classes, and, on the international plane, the socialist countries and the friendly or neighbouring countries sharing the same status."[1]

---

[1] All the above quotations from Debray's "Notes on the Political Situation in Bolivia" have been translated by the author from the French version, published in *Nouvelle Critique*, June, 1970 (No. 35), pp. 24–30.

This new recognition by Debray of the need to link the struggles in Latin America with those of the rest of the world, with an emphasis on the role of the socialist countries, represents a further positive development in his thinking. Debray's "Notes" from prison would justify one hoping that, now that he is free to continue his theoretical work and to learn more about the actual course of revolution, he would make a new assessment of his earlier writings and publicly discard everything which can be harmful to the revolution in Latin America.

Regrettably his first work published since his release[1] does little to fulfil that hope. As we have noted above, Debray's discussions with Allende on the events in Chile indicate that he has not shrugged off that tendency to arrogant dogmatism which is typical of his writings prior to his imprisonment. Neither has he abandoned his antipathy to the Communist Parties. In his long introduction to *Conversations* Debray cannot bring himself to making any positive reference to the key role of the Communist Party of Chile, which has struggled for thirty years to unite the working class and popular forces and achieve a government, such as the present Popular Unity government, which represents these forces. References in *Conversations* to the working class of Chile indicate, too, that Marcuse's views have had an impact on Debray who believes that the political system in Chile has been able to "absorb the impact and destructive force" of the workers' movement, and that participation in Parliamentary struggle has resulted in "defusing and sublimating the direct action of the working-class forces" (see pp. 35–6). Debray clearly remains an intellectual outsider of the struggle, a "teacher" who, from his theoretical armchair and without direct participation in mass activity, tries to teach those who are striving to carry through revolutionary change. This divorce from the real live movement of the people undoubtedly contributes to his dogmatic and often voluntarist assertions. Yet, Debray could still make a worthwhile contribution to revolutionary theory; but this he will never do while he retains his hostility to the Communist Parties and his lack of understanding of the working-class movement.

[1] Régis Debray: *Conversations with Allende—Socialism in Chile*, London, 1971.

Marcuse and the Western World

4

Marcuse and the Western World

In the last decade the principal political ideas of Herbert Marcuse have become widely known in many circles of the political movement in the Western world. Marcuse's intellectual career has not been a narrowly political one. He has made his mark as philosopher, psychological theoretician, and sociologist. Born in Berlin in 1898, he was a member of the Social Democratic Party from 1917 to 1918, but broke with it after the murder of Rosa Luxemburg and Karl Liebknecht. He attended the universities of Berlin and Freiberg, where he studied with Heidegger. Later he was associated with the Frankfurt Institute of Social Research. After the Nazis came to power Marcuse went to Geneva, where he taught for a year, and then emigrated to the United States. From 1934 to 1940 he worked in the Institute of Social Research which had been transferred to Columbia University from Frankfurt. Working with him at the Institute in the United States were Max Horkheimer, Fromm and Adorno, all of whom are regarded as having, at that time, rather overshadowed Marcuse. During the second world war he was employed by the Office of Strategic Studies. After having worked with the Office of Intelligence Research in the State Department, where he was finally acting Head of the Eastern European Section, he took up research at Columbia University in 1950, working in its Russian Institute. He also worked at Harvard's Russian Research Centre, and then, from 1954 to 1967 he was at Brandeis University. He has spent periods as director of studies at the École Pratique des Hautes Études in Paris. From 1967 he taught at the University of California where he became Professor of Political Thought at the San Diego campus.

It is, in particular, his political theories with which we are concerned, since these have a bearing on the main subject matter of this book—namely the role of classes in the revolution; and it is his views on this question above all which have gained for him considerable popularity in intellectual and student circles in the Western world. His political ideas have undoubtedly matured in his mind over a number of years, inevitably influenced by his earlier experiences in Germany and the rise of the Nazis (though strangely enough his later, more directly political writings have practically nothing to say about this), and by his thirty-seven years in the United States. It was only after the publication of *One Dimensional Man* in 1964, however, that his political theories first acquired wide currency. His views have been further expounded in *An Essay in Liberation* (1969) and *Five Lectures* (1970). Some of the sharpest and most direct expositions of his theories have appeared in slighter form, in interviews, lectures, speeches, and in participation in seminars and conferences.

As in the case of both Fanon and Debray, Marcuse's writings have been widely published by bourgeois publishing houses, translated into several languages, and become the subject of discussion and analysis in circles not confined to those of the left wing. Again, as with Fanon and Debray, his writings are not without their inconsistencies. It is not so much that his writings show a development of thought over the years—such "inconsistencies", after all, would be perfectly natural and indeed welcome if, at the same time, they revealed a positive maturing of ideas. Marcuse's inconsistencies, however, are not of this nature. Rather they reflect a certain muddle in his thinking, a tendency to ignore unpalatable fact or to select and emphasise those facts and trends which argue in his favour and neglect those that do not, no matter how essential they may be for arriving at a balanced and scientifically based conclusion.

All this is notwithstanding his avowed purpose of studying modern capitalist society, and his seeming ability to grasp what is new. To a considerable extent he helps us to extract from the complex phenomena of twentieth-century capitalism some of the decisive trends which enable one to see more clearly the shape and character of the coming revolution. He undoubtedly does turn his own attention, and ours, to many important new aspects of current development; and, in a sense, even his unbalanced emphasis on some points, as well as his regrettable and unjustified generalisations on others (virtually distortions in some cases), helps to focus our thoughts on a number of essential problems which relate very much to the big questions of the strategy and tactics of the socialist revolution in the major imperialist countries today. But his failure to grapple scientifically and comprehensively with the concrete realities of this epoch—and certainly a view which virtually excludes all treatment of the modern struggles of the working class cannot claim to be scientific—results in his having to make confused attempts to justify his "new thinking" by introducing modifications in his views when he finds that reality has, after all, overtaken him and rendered his previous bold assertions manifestly inadequate. His unsatisfactory attempts to grapple with the 1968 events in France are, as we shall see, a case in point.

In discussing Marcuse's political theories it is intended to concentrate on three major questions which have been the subject of wide discussion in radical circles.

First, the role of students in the capitalist world: what factors have brought them to the fore of the political scene, how they differ from previous generations of students, what is the nature of the contribution which they make to the revolution, to what extent can they be considered as a leadership of the revolution, what is the theory of "Red Bases" in the universities.

Secondly, the experience of France in May–June, 1968, which, to some radicals, is to a large extent a confirmation of Marcuse's views on the leading role of the students, the alleged lack of capacity of the working class, and the failure of the Communist Party. These views, in my opinion, are refuted by the real facts of the crisis in France in 1968, which, far from confirming Marcuse's analysis, reveal its superficiality and, what is more important to the working-class movement, the dangers to the revolution which flow from attempting to act on the basis of Marcuse's approach.

Thirdly, the role of the modern working class in the West: the question of the impact of the scientific and technological revolution on the structure and outlook of the workers, the question of the labour aristocracy, the role of reformism in the working-class movement, the new scientific and technical sections of the working class, the policies of the Communist Parties in the capitalist countries, the position of "the outsiders and outcasts", the poor, the unemployed, the Black people.

MARCUSE'S VIEWS OF MODERN CAPITALIST SOCIETY

The basis of Marcuse's political thinking is his critique of what he calls "industrial society", sometimes identifying this with modern capitalism but not always making such a clear distinction. *One Dimensional Man* (1964) and his speech to the Korcula Conference (1964) are among the most comprehensive expositions of his approach to the question of the role of class forces in the revolution in the industrialised

Western world. An examination of these two works quickly reveals the main themes which dominate Marcuse's political thinking. These themes raise a number of the fundamental questions of the modern capitalist world, questions which must be examined if one is to find satisfactory answers to the problems facing the socialist revolution in the advanced capitalist countries. Some of these questions have already been discussed in the first chapter of this book; others are, in some ways, an echo of certain ideas of Fanon and Debray which I have attempted to analyse in the second and third chapters.

One dimensional man, as presented by Marcuse, has been aptly described by one commentator[1] as a "well-fed semi-zombie, shallow in his emotions, impoverished in his human relationships, a philistine puppet, controlled from the cradle to the grave by expert manipulators". Basing his ideas largely on developments in the United States, Marcuse sees a society in which domination over individuals becomes ever greater; society grows richer and more powerful; scientific and technological progress has produced a tremendous increase in efficiency and a high and constantly rising material standard of living. All opposition forces are restricted, subdued or absorbed into the system. All man's needs and his very freedom are manipulated by the mass media which have themselves been transformed and become all-powerful opinion-forming factories.

This society, according to Marcuse, is based on an alliance between big business and the working class which has been brain-washed into chasing an ever expanding flow of goods and inessential gadgets that their relative affluence enables them to purchase. Caught up in this "consumer society", the working class has become corrupted and tamed, has lost its political bearings, no longer retains its revolutionary potential but, on the contrary, willingly acquiesces in its own exploitation and becomes a staunch and conservative defender of the *status quo*. All existing democratic institutions, the democratic rights won by the people, and the social and political organisations they have set up, including trade unions, and political parties (and not excluding the Communist Parties), have become integrated into the system. The working class, and its organisations and parties, is no longer the "negation" of this society, no longer the main antagonist but a major collusionist.

These ideas, as set out in *One Dimensional Man*,[2] are not easily

---

[1] W. Thompson: *Morning Star*, July 26, 1968, in a review of Marcuse's book.
[2] Herbert Marcuse: *One Dimensional Man*, London, 1964.

grasped at first reading, but their meaning is inescapable. In his Introduction, Marcuse writes:

> The capabilities (intellectual and material) of contemporary society are immeasurably greater than ever before—which means that the scope of society's domination over the individual is immeasurably greater than ever before. Our society distinguishes itself by conquering the centrifugal social forces with Technology rather than Terror, on the dual basis of an overwhelming efficiency and an increasing standard of living.[1]

Technical progress, he argues, has extended to the whole system of domination and coordination, creating forms of life and power which seem to "reconcile the forces opposing the system and to defeat or refute all protest in the name of the historical prospects of freedom from toil and domination. Contemporary society seems to be capable of containing social change. . . . This containment of social change is perhaps the most singular achievement of advanced industrial society."[2]

Looking at the two main antagonists of modern capitalism, the bourgeoisie and the proletariat, Marcuse admits that they are "still the basic classes". He claims, however, that "capitalist development has altered the structure and function of these two classes in such a way that they no longer appear to be agents of historical transformation". On the contrary, he asserts, "An overriding interest in the preservation and improvement of the *status quo* unites the former antagonists in the most advanced areas of contemporary society."[3]

Marcuse seems to appreciate that this thesis might appear overwhelmingly pessimistic and, right at the outset, indicates that there is an alternative, although even about that he is not over-confident:

> *One-Dimensional Man* will vacillate throughout between two contradictory hypotheses (1) that advanced industrial society is capable of containing[4] qualitative changes for the foreseeable future; (2) that forces and tendencies exist which may break this containment and explode the society.[5]

But once again his defeatism asserts itself:

> I do not think that a clear answer can be given. . . . The first tendency is dominant, and whatever preconditions for a reversal may exist are being used to prevent it. Perhaps an accident may alter the situation, but unless the recognition of what is being done and what

[1] ibid., p. 9.   [2] ibid., p. 11.   [3] ibid., p. 11.   [4] i.e. holding in check.
[5] *One Dimensional Man*, p. 13.

is being prevented subverts the consciousness and the behaviour of man, not even a catastrophe will bring about the change.[1]

Again and again his deep lack of faith in the people and his virtual awe of the apparently omnipotent system under which he lives break through his critique of this system and his expressed desire to see it abolished.

(i) Independence of thought, autonomy, and the right to political opposition are being deprived of their basic critical function in a society which seems increasingly capable of satisfying the needs of the individuals through the way in which it is organised.[2]

(ii) Under the conditions of a rising standard of living, non-conformity with the system itself appears to be socially useless, and the more so when it entails tangible economic and political disadvantages and threatens the smooth operation of the whole.[3]

(iii) The distinguishing feature of advanced industrial society is its effective suffocation of those needs which demand liberation—liberation also from that which is tolerable and rewarding and comfortable—while it sustains and absolves the destructive power and repressive function of the affluent society. . . . Under the rule of a repressive whole, liberty can be made into a powerful instrument of domination.[4]

(iv) We are again confronted with one of the most vexing aspects of advanced industrial civilisation: the rational character of its irrationality. Its productivity and efficiency, its capacity to increase and spread comforts, to turn waste into need, and destruction into construction, the extent to which this civilisation transforms the objective world into an extension of man's mind and body makes the very question of alienation questionable. The people recognise themselves in their commodities; they find their soul in their automobile, hi-fi set, split-level home, kitchen equipment. The very mechanism which ties the individual to his society has changed, and social control is anchored in the new needs which it has produced. . . . Mass production and mass distribution claim the *entire* individual. . . .[5]

(v) The highest productivity of labour can be used for the perpetuation of labour, and the most efficient industrialisation can serve the restriction and manipulation of needs. When this point is reached, domination—in the guise of affluence and liberty—extends to all spheres of private and public existence, integrates all authentic opposition, absorbs all alternatives.[6]

[1] *One Dimensional Man*, p. 13.   [2] ibid., p. 19.   [3] ibid., p. 19.
[4] ibid., p. 23.   [5] ibid., pp. 24-5.   [6] ibid., p. 31.

In the face of this constantly repeated warning of defeat and sub-mission, it is not strange to find throughout this book no real examina-tion of the struggle against the system and its effects. Marcuse is often hailed by his supporters as a Marxist—and indeed makes the same claim himself; but the class struggle lies right at the heart of Marxism, and, in the advanced *capitalist* societies (Marcuse tends to use the non-class term, "advanced *industrial* societies"), the role of the working class, as the decisive social force to end capitalism and introduce socialism, was repeatedly stressed by Marx and Engels, as it was later by Lenin and other Marxists. As has already been pointed out, Lenin emphasised that "the main thing in the teaching of Marx is that it brings out the historic role of the proletariat as the builder of socialist society".[1]

Of course, Marcuse is perfectly free to challenge this central thesis of Marx—and to bring forward evidence to prove his point (like Fanon and Debray, he relies more on sweeping generalised assertions than on a scientific examination of reality). But if he rejects the central core of Marxism in this fashion he cannot, at the same time, claim to be a Marxist or be termed so by others.

MARCUSE'S REJECTION OF THE WORKING CLASS

When he examines the working class, Marcuse can only see "the collusion and alliance between business and organised labour".[2] We cannot ignore that in the United States this collusion between the big monopolies and reactionary labour leaders, such as George Meany, head of the AFL–CIO, is very real. It is also very marked in all capitalist countries. Moreover, this collusion is carried through on the basis of the continuing reformist illusions of large sections of workers, and the ability of right-wing leaders to mislead them, while not excluding intimidation, pressure and force, aided by the State, against those who challenge such compromised leaderships. But to see only this collusion, or, to emphasise it at the expense of any treatment of the workers' struggles, presents an unreal picture of modern capitalist society, as I shall attempt to show below.

Marcuse includes the Communist Parties, too, within his condemna-tion. He falsely alleges that "the strong Communist Parties in France and Italy . . . bear witness to the general trend of circumstances by adhering to a minimum programme which shelves the revolutionary seizure of power and complies with the rules of the parliamentary

[1] See above, Chapter One, p. 18.   [2] *One Dimensional Man*, op. cit., p. 32.

game."[1] Minimum programmes, partial demands, the fight for reforms, the use of Parliament as one of the necessary forms of struggle—those have always been a vital part of Marxist and Communist theory and practice. One need only recall, for example, Engels' pregnant remarks concerning the electoral gains made at the end of the nineteenth century by the Social Democrats in Germany and his characterisation of the important role of Parliamentary elections. Lenin urged the Russian workers to enter even the restrictive and farcical Duma (Parliament) of the Tsar, dubbing it a "pigsty", which nevertheless had to be used in the interests of the revolution.

If in countries which have a long-standing democratic and Parliamentary tradition, a relatively powerful working-class movement and the basis for a wide alliance of forces alongside the working class, the Communist Parties have put special emphasis on the use of Parliament, backed up by various forms of extra-Parliamentary mass action, to weaken the power of big capital, diminish its control and ownership of the national economy and restrict its role in the various institutions of the State in order to open up a road to fundamental socialist change, this is fully in conformity with the actual possibilities within these particular countries and of the present-day world relation of forces. The example of Chile, mentioned in the previous chapter, indicates that important progress can be registered in this way, whatever may be the further obstacles met with in the effort to carry through basic transformations of Chilean society. For Communist Parties in some other countries—such as France, Italy, Great Britain or Japan—to have somewhat similar perspectives in no sense justifies Marcuse's accusation that such Parties "play the historical role of legal opposition parties 'condemned' to be non-radical".[2]

Elsewhere, Marcuse has charged the French and Italian Communist Parties as being the "doctors at the bedside of capitalism".[3] Marcuse seems to be unaware of his contradictory argument. All his writings are directed to present an almost frightening picture of the all-powerful capitalist society which "absorbs all alternatives" and which is evidently enjoying good health. It is therefore inexplicable why the French and Italian Communist Parties are suddenly to be found tending to a capitalist society which, in the new context, is presumably at death's door.

In explaining his critique of the working class and the Communist Parties Marcuse gets into really deep waters. He argues thus:

[1] *One Dimensional Man*, p. 33.   [2] ibid.   [3] *Praxis*, Zagreb, 1965.

No analysis in depth seems to be necessary in order to find the reasons for these developments. As to the West: the former conflicts within society are modified and arbitrated under the double (and interrelated) impact of technical progress and international communism. Class struggles are attenuated and "imperialist contradictions" suspended before the threat from without. Mobilised against this threat, capitalist society shows an internal union and cohesion unknown at previous stages of industrial civilisation. It is a cohesion of very material grounds; mobilisation against the enemy works as a mighty stimulus of production and employment, thus sustaining the high standard of living.[1]

According to this argument the Communist Parties in the West, in the face of the "threat from without", namely "international communism" (whatever that may mean in this particular context), rally behind their own capitalist class, assist in attenuating and modifying the class struggle and help, in the face of this external enemy, in bringing about a quite unprecedented degree of class collaboration—and all this in order to defend the country against communism! It is difficult to credit that Marcuse really believes this. One can only conclude, that his determination somehow to demonstrate the alleged incapacity of the Communist Parties and their downright betrayal of the struggle against capitalism so blinds his judgment and sense of reality that he is no longer quite aware of what he is writing.

Utilising certain aspects of the scientific and technological revolution and their impact on the structure of the working class and on the role of workers in production, Marcuse argues that "the labouring classes in the advanced areas of industrial civilisation are undergoing a decisive transformation". The main factors of this transformation he lists as follows:[2]

(i) "Mechanisation is increasingly reducing the quantity and intensity of physical energy expended in labour." In place of the "physical pain and misery of labour", which accompanied the extraction of surplus value in the earlier stages of capitalism when the worker was a "beast of burden", mental effort and technical skills are now employed more, and the worker shares more in enjoying the riches he creates, instead of, as previously, "living in filth and poverty" while creating society's wealth. Thus the worker becomes "incorporated into the technological community of the administered population".

---

[1] ibid., p. 33.   [2] ibid., pp. 35–52.

(ii) The number of manual ("blue-collar") workers tends to decline in relation to the number of white-collar workers, and the number of non-production workers increases.

(iii) The changes in the character of work and the instruments of production change the attitude and the consciousness of the worker, "which become manifest in the widely discussed 'social and cultural integration' of the labouring class with capitalist society".

(iv) The new "technological work-world" enforces a "weakening of the negative position of the working class: the latter no longer appears to be the living contradiction to the established society". This trend is strengthened by the effect which the technological changes allegedly have on management and control. "Domination is transfigured into administration. The capitalist bosses and owners are losing their identity as responsible agents; they are assuming the function of bureaucrats in a corporate machine. Within the vast hierarchy of executive and managerial boards extending far beyond the individual establishment into the scientific laboratory and research institute, the national government and national purpose, the tangible source of exploitation disappears behind the façade of objective rationality. Hatred and frustration are deprived of their specific target, and the technological veil conceals the reproduction of inequality and enslavement."

One cannot ignore the profound effects which flow from the scientific and technological revolution, and the impact which they have on the whole scope and character of the struggle against capitalism. And Marcuse is correct to draw our attention to the need to study these new phenomena and to draw the necessary conclusions from them. But the deductions he makes in the fourth point listed above show quite clearly his complete divorcement from the modern working-class movement and his total lack of knowledge of the daily industrial struggles of workers and the way in which they regard these conflicts.

Far from the "tangible source of exploitation" disappearing, with the workers being "deprived of their specific target", and a "technological veil" hiding the continuation of inequality, workers in the developed capitalist countries are increasingly becoming only too aware of the source of their exploitation and of the nature of their target, and are more and more coming to see the connection between their own particular boss, the multifarious ramifications of the international firms, the role of the capitalist class as a whole, including the monopoly press and the other mass media, and the function of Government policies which lead to attacks on trade unions, attempts to hold down wages and other measures to lower the standard of living.

It is not intended as a jibe to say that Marcuse has clearly never taken part in a strike; but the real point is that millions of workers have done so, and in the course of these battles have advanced their political understanding and acquired a deeper appreciation of the nature of their struggle and of their opponent.

One should not exaggerate how far this process has gone. If the overwhelming majority of the workers had reached a stage of advanced political class consciousness in the United States, Western Germany, Britain, France, Japan, and Italy, then capitalism would certainly be nearer its end than it is today. But the process of political education is clearly not going backward as Marcuse's theories would suggest, but forward, as we shall examine later in more detail.

The denial that the working class in advanced capitalist societies has a revolutionary role to play is central to Marcuse's thought. This is not only a dominant theme of *One Dimensional Man*. In one form or another he repeats this idea in nearly all his writings and speeches. In the paper he read to the conference at Korcula, in Yugoslavia, in the summer of 1964, he elaborates this idea at considerable length, repeating in essence the ideas contained in *One Dimensional Man*. Arguing that the system is "absorbing all revolutionary potential", he asserts that "the very classes which were once the absolute negation of the capitalist system are now more and more integrated into it".[1] He admits that capitalist society is still a class society, "but it is a class society in which the working class no longer represents the absolute negation of the existing order".

Taking up Lenin's theory of the labour aristocracy, Marcuse contends that this theory, as formulated by Lenin, is no longer appropriate to the situation in the advanced capitalist countries. It is, he claims, "not just a small fragment of the working class which has been integrated but, as in the United States today, its vast majority".[2] Changes in the process of production and method of work, together with rising standards of living "have transformed the majority of the organised working class into a labour aristocracy, whereas in Lenin's day this was still no more than a small minority". He argues that the

[1] Herbert Marcuse: "Socialism in the Developed Countries", paper read at Korcula. See *International Socialist Journal*, April, 1965, p. 140.
[2] ibid., p. 145.

changes in the form of work associated with the technological revolution and the development of automation "make the worker more passive than before", although he provides no proof for this very categoric assertion. What he terms the "homogenisation of white- and blue-collar workers" leads, in his view, to the workers becoming "politically apathetic", while the white-collar workers "are reluctant to organise". Again, no proof or convincing examples are brought forward to sustain this argument. Certainly in Britain the readiness of different sections of white-collar workers (teachers, civil servants, bank clerks, technical and managerial staffs, etc.) to join trade unions has been an outstanding feature of the past decade and has led, too, to their increased participation in collective action, including strikes.

"In my opinion", states Marcuse, "there is a definite tendency for political opposition—working-class opposition—to grow weaker in less advanced industrial countries, as well as in the United States."[1] Marcuse is knowledgeable enough to appreciate that in some of the major capitalist countries there has been a consolidation and growth of support for the Communist Party, as in France, Italy, and Japan, as well as in less developed countries such as Spain. He is aware, too, that in many quarters this would certainly be regarded as a sign that the "political opposition—working-class opposition" was becoming stronger, not weaker as he contends. To prove his point, therefore, he charges the French and Italian Communist Parties with "moving towards Social Democracy. It seems that these communist parties, in the changed conditions of capitalism, see themselves in the historical position of Social Democracy. With one crucial difference: apparently there is no real power to their left. In the countries concerned, the reduced effectiveness of the strike as a political weapon runs parallel with growing apathy within the working-class movements."

All this, of course, was stated four years before the French events of May–June, 1968, and before the great strike movement of 1968–70 in Italy, indicating therefore the inadequacy and really the superficiality of Marcuse's argument. In the same way, the big upsurge of industrial struggle in Britain in 1970 and 1971, in opposition to the Tory Government's proposed anti-trade union legislation, even though it was not sufficient to halt the Government processing the Bill through Parliament, was a clear refutation of Marcuse's argument that the working class is becoming more apathetic, more passive, and weaker as political opposition.

[1] ibid., p. 148.

Marcuse concluded his paper at Korcula by discussing whether the working class is any longer "the historic subject of the revolution", the "absolute negation of the existing order".[1] He evidently thinks not. The changes in society which he has attempted to explain have resulted, in his view, in the working class being "no longer capable of creating a qualitatively different society", which, presumably, would be socialism. In fact, he goes further and asks "whether it is possible to conceive of revolution when there is no vital need for it"—the question of need, in his scheme of things, not being related to the fundamental contradictions of modern capitalism but only to an alleged satisfaction of the workers' consumption aspirations.

After all this, it is not surprising to have Marcuse's own wry admission that what he has put forward is "a deeply pessimistic analysis".[2]

In a paper, "The Obsolescence of Marx", which he read in April, 1966, Marcuse continues to express his lack of faith in the working class, finding that "in the advanced industrial countries where the transition to socialism was to take place, and precisely in those countries, the labouring classes are in no sense a revolutionary potential".

In an interview in 1967[3] he expressed the opinion that "in the capitalist countries of the European continent the pre-condition for the efficacy of a serious opposition remains the political revitalisation of the working-class movement on an international scale". Here his indictment of its political apathy and passivity remains, otherwise it would not be necessary to "revitalise" it.

In a paper[4] written just before the May–June events in France, in 1968, Marcuse returns to his attack on the industrial working class which he finds is no longer "a subversive force" although "still the potential agent of a possible revolution". In accepting the revolutionary potentiality of the working class Marcuse is contradicting his own denial of this possibility, cited above from his paper "The Obsolescence of Marx". At the same time, he has little faith in the possibility of the working class rising to its potential, since he sees it as "the prisoner of its own integration and of a bureaucratic trade union and party apparatus supporting this integration". He fears that unless the working

[1] ibid., p. 150.
[2] Peter Sedgwick has also noted the later Marcuse's pessimism, referring to his One Dimensional Man as an expression of "a grandiose journalism of doom" ("Natural Science nd Human Theory", Socialist Register, 1966, p. 166).
[3] Herbert Marcuse: "The Question of Revolution", interview in New Left Review, September–October, 1967, p. 4.
[4] Herbert Marcuse: "Re-Examination of the Concept of Revolution", Diogenes, Winter, 1968, No. 64.

class is able to effect an alliance with the forces of the "new opposition" which stand outside the ranks of the industrial proletariat, the latter may become "in part at least, the mass basis of a neo-fascist régime".[1]

Marcuse draws the conclusion that "*the Marxian concept of a revolution* carried out by the majority of the exploited masses, culminating in the 'seizure of power' and in the setting up of a proletarian dictatorship which initiates socialisation, is '*overtaken*' *by the historical development*". The new stage of capitalist productivity, with its ever-increasing ability to satisfy the material needs of the people, its "productivity of destruction" and the immense concentration of the instruments of indoctrination in the hands of the ruling powers, constitutes the historical development which, according to Marcuse, precludes the industrial proletariat from fulfilling its function as the main agent of social revolution.

In 1969, after the previous year's events in France, Marcuse was still advancing his thesis regarding "the integration of the organised (and not only the organised) labouring class into the system of advanced capitalism".[2] Once more he finds that "the majority of organised labour shares the stabilising, counter-revolutionary needs of the middle classes, as evidenced by their behaviour as consumers of the material and cultural merchandise, by their emotional revulsion against the non-conformist intelligentsia". The working class, because of its role in production, its exploitation and its numerical strength, is, he concedes, "still the historical agent of revolution"; but because it shares the stabilising needs of the system "it has become a conservative, even counterrevolutionary force".[3]

In an interview in July, 1969,[4] long after he had had the opportunity to reflect over his past views and to relate them to the big class struggles of 1968-9, especially in France, Italy, Japan and Spain, Marcuse showed no inclination to abandon his theories. Despite all the evidence which reality was daily placing before him, he persisted in his views regarding the industrial working class in the most advanced industrial countries.

The Marxian proletariat no longer exists in the developed industrial countries ... the role which Marx ascribed to the proletariat of that

---

[1] ibid., p. 21.
[2] Herbert Marcuse: *An Essay in Liberation*, London, 1969, p. 14.
[3] ibid., p. 16.
[4] Herbert Marcuse: "Revolution Out of Disgust", interview in *Der Spiegel*, July 28 1969: English version, *Australian Left Review*, December, 1969.

time cannot simply be transferred to the working class of these countries.[1]

This proletariat, avers Marcuse, is becoming increasingly bourgeois. The working-class movement itself, including both the trade unions and the political parties, has developed in a way which renders it incapable of "struggling against the contradictions rending capitalism".[2] The trade unions, and the "Soviet-orientated communist parties" [sic] have played into the hands of the capitalists. Strangely enough the capitalists themselves do not think so, as any militant Communist shop steward in Fords factory in Dagenham, England, or in the Renault works at Billancourt, France, or in the Fiat plant in Turin, Italy, could explain on the basis of his own very concrete experience.

As recently as 1970 Marcuse was still finding Marx out of date as regards his view that the industrial proletariat is the decisive revolutionary class. "Today in large parts of the most highly developed capitalist countries that is no longer the case."[3] The working class, he argues, "no longer represents the negation of existing needs". This view is still central to his approach although he is prepared to agree that in Europe there may be some sections of the working class "which have not yet fallen prey to the process of integration".

From the foregoing it can be seen that in all his writings, interviews and speeches since he wrote *One Dimensional Man* in 1964, Marcuse has been consistent, almost to the point of repetition, over one essential aspect of his political theories and that is that the working class in the most developed capitalist countries is no longer an agent of social change. Although at times he admits that it is a *potentially* revolutionary force, his admission is made rather grudgingly, and usually accompanied by such reservations as would virtually preclude this potentiality ever reaching fruition and finding revolutionary expression. In particular, it is clear that he does not believe that the working class and its organisations, which have become "integrated" and "absorbed" into the capitalist system, can ever fulfil the role set out

---

[1] ibid., p. 42.

[2] This itself is a strange formulation. A revolutionary movement does not struggle *against* the contradictions in society. The contradiction between the workers and the capitalists is ended by the workers ending the rule of the capitalists and commencing to build a classless society. The contradiction between the social character of production and the private appropriation of its profits is ended by the workers ending the private ownership of the means of production and introducing the system of socialism based on public ownership.

[3] Herbert Marcuse: *Five Lectures*, London, 1970, p. 70.

for the proletariat by Marx and Lenin, namely acting as the leading class in the overthrow of capitalism and the construction of socialism. For this reason, he logically rejects the Communist Parties in these countries, accusing them, too, of having become part of the system. Presumably the revolutionaries in whom Marcuse places his faith will have to act against these Parties if they are to change this system. Marcuse's anti-communism, like that of Debray, may not arise from a subjective desire to aid the capitalist class; but objectively it has the same result. As I have already commented in another context, it is no comfort to the victim to be told "I meant to shoot the other chap".

THE NEW OPPOSITION

If, then, as Marcuse so repeatedly argues, the working class is no longer the decisive agent of social change, to whom then does he turn?

There is a certain difference in emphasis in the way in which Marcuse answers this question at different times. In *One Dimensional Man* he expresses the view that:

> . . . the struggle for the solution has outgrown the traditional forms. The totalitarian tendencies of the one-dimensional society render the traditional ways and means of protest ineffective—perhaps even dangerous because they preserve the illusion of popular sovereignty. . . . However, underneath the conservative popular base [*sic*] is the substratum of the outcasts and outsiders, the exploited and persecuted of other races and other colours, the unemployed and the unemployable. They exist outside the democratic process; their life is the most immediate and the most real need for ending intolerable conditions and institutions. Thus their opposition is revolutionary, even if their consciousness is not. Their opposition hits the system from without and is therefore not deflected by the system; it is an elementary force which violates the rules of the game, and, in doing so, reveals it as a rigged game.[1]

Here, then, is his bold rejection of the organised working class, of its trade unions and parties, and of its forms of struggle, and his equally bold claims on behalf of the "outsiders" who owe no allegiance or commitment to existing organisations and institutions, and who refuse to "play the rigged game" of utilising traditional forms of struggle.

These "outsiders", however, are not the limit of Marcuse's alterna-

[1] Herbert Marcuse: *One Dimensional Man*, op. cit., p. 200.

tive to the working class. First, he adds the great mass of millions of "outsiders" in Africa, Asia and Latin America. Secondly, he includes in his "revolutionary" alliance strata which are, in no sense, "outcasts and outsiders"—namely, the students and intellectuals.

Marcuse's argument concerning these different strata is not always consistent. It is therefore necessary to first set out what he has argued on different occasions, carrying through his argument from *One Dimensional Man*, in 1964, up to *Five Lectures*, in 1970.

Thus, in "Socialism in the Developed Countries" (1964), he writes:

> . . . the masses are integrated and marshalled within the framework of a democratic pluralism. Outside, or rather beneath, this democracy, there are whole sectors who are not integrated into it, who perhaps never will be: racial and national minorities, the permanently unemployed, the poor. They are the living negation of the system. But neither their organisation nor their consciousness are sufficiently developed for them to be the subjects of the transition to socialism.[1]

Marcuse's championing of the "outsiders" has sometimes resulted in the belief that he is hailing the *lumpenproletariat* in the industrialised capitalist countries, although nowhere does he directly assert this.

His "outsiders" are listed as "the exploited and persecuted of other races and other colours", the "unemployed and the unemployable", "racial and national minorities", "the poor", and "the inmates of prisons and mental institutions".

It would be stretching the meaning of words to lump these various categories together as constituting the *lumpenproletariat*. Certainly there may be elements of the *lumpenproletariat* in these strata, but they would only represent a part. Marcuse's reference to racial and national minorities, and to those of other colours who are exploited and persecuted, does not specifically exclude those who are workers, whether they be Black, Chicano, Puerto Rican or American Indian. Unemployment is certainly terribly heavy among these sections of workers, especially among the Black youth, and it is amongst them in particular that one finds the major dynamic force behind the ghetto revolt.

Yet one of the additional factors leading to the upsurge of just anger and organisation among the Black people in the United States in the last thirty years has surely been the big shift from the south into the industrial regions and towns of the north, with the resultant proletarianisation of millions who were formerly sharecroppers or poor

[1] Herbert Marcuse: "Socialism in the Developed Countries", op. cit., p. 143.

tenant farmers. One cannot ignore the millions of Black people who work in industry in the United States today. In many industries they are now a major force, sometimes a substantial minority of those employed, sometimes close to a majority. Are these to be regarded as "integrated" by the system? Is Marcuse throwing aside a major part of the Black people themselves? Or is he arguing that White workers are "integrated" but not Black workers?

There is a danger in the way in which Marcuse has developed his ideas, a danger to the Black, Chicano and Puerto Rican people whose champion he may appear to be. By attempting to persuade them that their real class ally, their essential ally, the White workers, are their potential enemy, or, at the very least to be discounted, he is throwing a terrible burden on the backs of the oppressed national minorities themselves, pushing them into a position where they would have to bear the brunt of the struggle and so court disaster. The students, the intellectuals, the poor whites—these, allies as they may be in the struggle against capitalism, can in no sense make up for the weight and potential collective power of the sixty million American wage workers who, irrespective of their present restricted political outlook, must be won for the revolution for which they, and they alone, can provide the firm bedrock on which the whole movement must rest if it is to overcome capitalism.

Marcuse, as we have noticed, finds the main fault in the capitalist system not in the realm of production relations—which is the Marxist position—but in the field of consumption. In this connection Gil Green makes the following penetrating comment:

> The revolt of middle-class white youth was not against material lack; it was against spiritual void. They felt loathing for society's stress on material possessions in direct proportion to their ability to have them. . . . Thus Marcuse's attack on "consumerism" as the vise by which the ruling class puts the squeeze on individuals and makes the working class impotent, found ready response among these young people. It fed both their dislike for the system and their élitist feelings of superiority to the working class. By shifting the concept of oppression from the arena of production relations to that of consumption, the men and women who work to meet their material needs are downgraded, while the nonworking and non-producing strata are upgraded.[1]

For Marcuse to reject the workers on the one hand, and, on the other,

[1] Gil Green: *The New Radicalism: Anarchist or Marxist?*, New York, 1971, pp. 110–11.

to embrace the poor, the unemployed, the oppressed nationalities, and those in prison, betrays a confusion regarding the nature of social classes. As Gil Green rightly points out: "To see the working class as composed only of those who have jobs, or only of those in the higher wage brackets, or only of whites, is to create a working class out of one's prejudices, not as it really is."[1]

The question of those in prison, especially the Black, Chicano and Puerto Rican prisoners in the United States, constitutes a special question. Among the thousands of prisoners in the United States a very heavy proportion is Black; but one must understand why this is so. Angela Davis has written:

> At least 30 per cent of Black youth are presently without jobs. In the context of class exploitation and national oppression it should be clear that numerous individuals are compelled to resort to criminal acts, not as a result of conscious choice—implying other alternatives—but because society has objectively reduced their possibilities of subsistence and survival to this level.[2]

Many of the Black prisoners are innocent even of the petty crimes they are sometimes alleged to have committed; or sometimes they receive heavy sentences for trivial offences and are then forced into a position of being subject to constant harassment and persecution with the result that they acquire a "criminal record" and become frequent inmates of the jails.

Dr. W. E. DuBois, who was arrested in 1951 in his ninth decade because of his peace activities, became aware of this through his experience of prison and court at that time. Referring to the "thousands of innocent victims" in jail because they had "neither money nor friends to help them", he wrote:

> They daily stagger out of prison doors embittered, vengeful, hopeless, ruined. And of this army of the wronged, the proportion of Negroes is frightful.[3]

But alongside these victims of capitalist society in the jails of the United States is another category of prisoners, the conscious political fighters. In the United States, where there is no official category of political prisoners, political victims are always jailed on an alleged criminal charge. Sometimes the charge is a frame-up; sometimes it

[1] ibid., p. 113.
[2] Angela Davis: *If They Come in the Morning*, London, 1971, p. 35.
[3] Cited in Angela Davis: op. cit., p. 33.

arises out of an act which, prompted by deep political motives, is, on a technicality, classified as criminal.

Angela Davis has noted that "There is a distinct and qualitative difference between breaking a law for one's own individual self-interest and violating it in the interests of a class or a people whose oppression is expressed and particularised through the law. The former might be called criminal (though in many instances he is a victim), but the latter, as a reformist or revolutionary, is interested in universal social change. Captured, he or she is a political prisoner."[1]

Today, in the jails of America there are hundreds of such political prisoners. Their impact, writes Angela Davis, has been "decisive" on the prison populations. Inside the prisons they have carried on their political education work, their propaganda, their agitation, and their organising. They have helped to focus public opinion on the appalling conditions in the jails and stimulated mass movements of protest outside. These, in their turn, especially where they have involved large numbers of Black, Chicano and other oppressed communities themselves, have increased the response of the prisoners and turned them more and more towards politics. In this way, as Angela Davis points out, convicts originally sent to jail for criminal offences, have been transformed into "exemplary political militants".

No one who has read the Folsom Prisoners' Manifesto[2] or the appeal and clear demands of the prisoners of Attica can fail to comprehend the political understanding that is growing fast in the jails of the United States. It is significant that a major demand of those who led the Attica prison revolt was for the right to read political literature. This is no longer the voice of the *lumpenproletariat* but the growing articulateness and awareness of a people rising in revolt.

After such clear declarations of political intent, can one simply refer to the inmates of America's jails as *lumpens*—and leave it there? On the contrary, is it not proof that sections of the people, even if they had previously sunk into a *lumpen* state, can be won for revolutionary change and play a valuable role in the struggle? This, it seems to me, once again confirms what Marx had noted and what we considered in connection with Fanon; namely, that while the *lumpenproletariat*, or sections of it, can be used by reaction to uphold their system, many of them can equally be won over by conscious political workers to the side of the revolution. The fact that they have to be won by those who

[1] Cited in Angela Davis: op. cit., p. 29.   [2] Quoted in Angela Davis: op. cit., pp. 57–66

are more politically aware indicates once again that the *lumpenproletariat* cannot play a role as the leadership of the revolution but can be won to the extent that it begins to desert its *lumpen* outlook and, in fact, fights against it.

While Marcuse, like Fanon, appears to be championing the *lumpenproletariat*, he, too, doubts whether revolutionary theory and understanding can be provided by those at the lowest rungs of society. And so, in élitist fashion, Marcuse turns to the intellectuals and the students.

In a commentary he made in the course of the discussion at the Korcula conference, he drew special attention to these strata, which he termed "humanist". These, he explained, are "intellectuals who are not content just to sit behind a desk, but are even now risking their lives in the Deep South, fighting for bourgeois rights, the elementary civil rights of the Negro". Pleading for the role of the intellectual not to be "underrated", he drew attention to other strata in whom he found "the same kind of combative humanism"—namely the students.

Presumbly "combative humanism", in his view, is not a characteristic of the working class. It is difficult to remain quiet in the face of this élitist arrogance and open display of contempt for and obvious ignorance of the working-class movement. The daily struggle of the working class is itself an assertion of a humanism higher than that of the petty-bourgeois whose views are expressed by Marcuse. Self-sacrifice, solidarity, honesty and integrity, the subordination of one's own individual interests to the collective interests of the group and the class, the desire to end injustice—all these qualities are regularly displayed by the workers in struggle, in strikes, on demonstrations and on picket lines. When the Ford workers on strike in Dagenham collected money to assist postal workers on strike was this not an act of humanism as well as of class solidarity? When London taxi-drivers pay from their own pocket for poor children to go on an outing to the seaside, is this, too, not an act of humanism? When the British postal workers on strike made the exception of keeping counters open to pay out pensions to the old people, was not this an act of humanism? When workers from numerous countries went to Spain in 1936–8 to lay down their lives to defeat fascism, was not this, too, a supreme act of "combative humanism", based on class understanding?

Whatever courageous and humanist actions may be performed by individual students and intellectuals, or by groups of them (I would be among the last to minimise the bravery and integrity of the young white students who risked their lives in the Deep South), the fact remains that the main humanist demands of our time are to be found in the programmes and policies of the working-class organisations and parties. An examination of the resolutions and policy pronouncements of the trade unions and of the Communist Party in Britain, for example, brings one into immediate association with such major humanist concerns as the struggle for peace and against war, the ending of class distinctions in education, equal pay for work of equal value and the ending of the unequal status of women, radical measures to deal with inadequate housing, low wages, and miserable pensions, an end to racial discrimination, solidarity with the national liberation struggles in the Third World, the fight against pollution, and above all, the struggle to end the anti-human system of capitalism and to replace it by socialism which places the material and spiritual satisfaction of man's needs at the centre of its philosophy.

Marcuse, however, all of whose writings betray an appalling lack of knowledge of the working-class movement, evidently prefers to accept the bourgeois "Andy Capp" version of the working class which he then contrasts unfavourably with the students and intellectuals whom he claims have been "casually neglected" by Marxists. Whatever sectarian mistakes may have been made by this or that Communist Party at any particular time, the important role of intellectuals and students and the part they can play in the revolutionary struggle has always been recognised, both in theory and practice. After all, a movement which places such emphasis on its distinct philosophy and on ideological work could not behave otherwise.

In "The Question of Revolution" (1967), Marcuse, dealing more specifically with the United States, places his main emphasis on the youth whom he finds "free from ideology or permeated with a deep distrust of all ideology (including socialist ideology); it is sexual, moral, intellectual and political rebellion all in one. In this sense it is total, directed against the system as a whole."[1]

The reasons which Marcuse puts forward to explain this revolutionary potential of the young people are their disgust with the "affluent society",[2] and the vital need which they feel to "break the rules of a

---

[1] Herbert Marcuse: "The Question of Revolution", op. cit., p. 6.

[2] One of Marcuse's powerful arguments in *One Dimensional Man* is the extent to which the ruling circles have maintained their domination by utilising language itself as an instrument of control, developing habits of thought which uphold the system by the very terms which are invented and used to hide reality. By his uncritical use, on more than one occasion, of the term "affluent society", Marcuse reveals how much he himself has become a victim of this same semantic trickery. Or, perhaps, a practitioner. The same unfortunate habit is shown in his frequent use of the term "Vietcong"—first coined by the CIA—and never the correct term, National Liberation Front of South Vietnam.

deceitful and bloody game—to stop cooperating any more". Building on his own rather obsessive rejection of the allegedly "affluent society", which he appears to regard as the more objectionable aspect of the capitalist system rather than its direct exploitation of the working class and its private appropriation of the surplus value which they create (and all the social, political and cultural consequences which flow from that basic fact and which require the "expropriation of the expropriators"), Marcuse hails the youth as the vital social agent of change:

> If these young people detest the prevailing system of needs and its ever increasing mass of goods, this is because they observe and know how much sacrifice, how much cruelty and stupidity contribute every day to the reproduction of the system. These young people no longer share the repressive need for blessings and security of domination—in them perhaps a new consciousness is appearing, a new type of person with another instinct for reality, life and happiness; they have a feeling for a freedom that has nothing to do with, and wants nothing to do with, the freedom practised in senile society. *In short, here is the "determinate negation" of the prevailing system. . . .*[1] (Author's own italics.)

At the same time he notes that this "determinate negation" is "without effective organisation and is in itself incapable of exercising decisive political pressure". He further warns these young people that they can only become the new "avant-garde" in alliance with the forces which are resisting the system "from without".

In his other writings and speeches he spells out more fully the nature of these "forces from without". In "Re-examination of the Concept of Revolution" (1968), he draws special attention to the national liberation struggles in the Third World, claiming, quite unjustifiably, that while Marxists had paid attention to the "colonial and backward areas", they had looked upon the colonial peoples only as adjuncts or allies of "the primary historical agent of revolution".

On this latter point, Marcuse is misrepresenting the basic position of Marxism.[2] The very concept of allies is based on the understanding that the same forces of monopoly capitalism exploit both the working class in the metropolis and the people in the Third World, that as allies they face a common enemy and therefore share a common interest in assisting one another to overthrow this opponent. There is

---

[1] Herbert Marcuse: "The Question of Revolution", op. cit., p. 7.
[2] It was never the position of Marx or Lenin, but rather of Stalin who developed the theory of the colonial "reserves" of the proletarian revolution.

no question of the national liberation movements being regarded as "adjuncts"; on the contrary, Marxists regard it as one of the special obligations of the working-class movement in the imperialist countries to render direct and effective material assistance to the national liberation movement, as is being done today in Western Europe, for example, in relation to Vietnam and to the struggle in southern Africa. It can, with justice, be argued that this assistance is in no sense sufficient; but this shortcoming in no way supports Marcuse's argument on this point. In the same way, the socialist countries render direct and all-round material and political assistance to the national liberation struggles throughout the Third World. The building up, in this epoch, of a world-wide alliance of the national liberation struggles, the socialist countries, and the international working class, is itself the practical outcome of the correct Marxist approach to this question.[1]

Marcuse correctly warns against the "tendency to regard the national liberation movement as the principal, if not as the sole revolutionary force", but he then lurches right into his particular concept of the character of the world revolutionary process, and of the classes and forces which will act as the determinant forces. In place of the decisive world conflict between capitalism and socialism he sees "a *tripartite division* of historical forces which *cut across the division into the First, Second and Third World*. The contest between capitalism and socialism divides the Third World, too, and as a new historical force, there appears what may be called . . . an alternative to the capitalist as well as to the established socialist societies, namely the struggle for a different way of socialist construction, a construction 'from below', but from a 'new below' not integrated into the value system of the old societies—a socialism of co-operation and solidarity, where men and women determine collectively their need and goals, their priorities, and the method and pace of modernisation."[2] Here, as in all his expositions, Marcuse is very vague about the character of the new society to which he looks forward. The anarchist trends which find expression in many circles of the New Left (worship of spontaneity, in theory if not in practice; opposition to working-class organisations; and rejection of existing socialist societies) are never entirely absent from Marcuse's thoughts.

[1] For a more detailed exposition of the appreciation by Marx and Lenin of the role of the national and colonial struggle as an essential component of the world socialist revolution see: Jack Woddis: "Marx and Colonialism", *Marxism Today*, May, 1965; "Marx and National Liberation", *Marxism Today*, June, 1965; "Lenin on the National Liberation Struggle', *Marxism Today*, April, 1970.
[2] Herbert Marcuse: "Re-examination of the Concept of Revolution", op. cit., p. 20

Having himself warned against regarding the national liberation movements as mere "adjuncts" of the struggle in the advanced capitalist countries, Marcuse yet advances the opinion that "in spite of the apparent evidence to the contrary, the fate of the revolution (as global revolution) may well be decided in the metropoles". Marcuse, of course, is correct in so far as it remains a fact that the main base, the economic, political and military foundation of the imperialist powers, remains their own metropoles. The roots which imperialism has put down in the countries of the Third World are extensions from the base; and even if these extensions are cut off (as they have been, for example, in North Vietnam, China, North Korea and Cuba), the main struggle still remains, that is to finish off the monster in its lair. But this latter task, to be performed primarily by the working class and its allies in the metropolis, is, of course, greatly assisted by the struggles in the Third World. After all, the blows struck against US imperialism by the heroic struggle of the Vietnamese people (together with those of Laos and Cambodia) are undoubtedly a major cause of the rising movement of the people in the United States; they have not only brought military defeat to the US but weakened her economy and financial structure too, and have produced new currents of radical political thinking among wide sections of her people.

Marcuse sees the struggle in the metropolis in terms of the "outsiders" in alliance with the intellectuals and students.

The character of the opposition in the centre of corporate capitalism is concentrated in the two opposite poles of the society; in the ghetto population (itself not homogenous), and in the middle-class intelligentsia, especially among the students.[1]

Marcuse claims to find common characteristics in these varying strata which make up his "opposition". All of them, no matter their differences, share in the "total character of the refusal and rebellion". Elaborating this point, Marcuse identifies the refusal and rebellion in these three points:

1. Insistence on a break with the continuity of domination and exploitation—no matter in what name, insistence not only on new institutions, but on self-determination.

[1] ibid., p. 20. Marcuse's "opposite poles of the society" are not scientifically correct. The topmost pole, which strangely receives no examination in Marcuse's work, is that of the big monopolies. And their main antagonist in objective fact is the working class.

2. Distrust of all ideologies, including socialism made into an ideology.[1]

3. Rejection of the pseudo-democratic process sustaining the dominion of corporate capitalism.[2]

He understands that neither of his two groups—the "ghetto" and the middle-class intelligentsia, including the students—"constitutes the 'human basis' of the social process of production", which he considers was for Marx "a decisive condition for the historical agent of the revolution". These groups do not make up the majority of the population. They find no support, and indeed resentment, in his opinion, among the organised workers who "are still the potential agent of a possible revolution". And neither on a national nor on an international level are they effectively organised.

How, then, does Marcuse escape from this problem he has set himself? For, admitting that "this opposition cannot be regarded as agent of radical change", he adds that it can become such an agent of change "only if it is supported by a working class which is no longer the prisoner of its own integration and of a bureaucratic trade union and party apparatus supporting this integration". But he has already rejected this possibility of the working class in the industrialised capitalist countries breaking out of this "integration". Where, then, is the essential ally of "the ghetto" and the intelligentsia? Marcuse finds this ally in the Third World.

> The revolutionary proletariat becomes an agent of change where it still is the human basis of the social process of production, namely, in the predominantly agrarian areas of the Third World, where it provides the popular support for the national liberation fronts.[3]

Outlining how he sees the relationship between the national liberation struggle and the revolution in the metropolis, he asserts that "the 'negating' forces abroad must be *'synchronised'* with those at home". Under the rather immediate impact of the events in France earlier in

---

[1] An echo, here, of Debray and his disdain for ideology. Marcuse, again like Debray, presumably excludes his own ideology from this collective distrust. One has no right to blame him for the exaggerated claim on his behalf, made on the cover of *One Dimensional Man*, that he has "emerged as the dominant intellectual force behind the present wave of Student Revolutions"; but it is unlikely that Marcuse would have persisted so frequently in developing his ideological concepts unless he had hoped to gain some acceptance for them. Certainly if they are to be distrusted and rejected together with other ideologies by his student disciples the whole point of the exercise would be useless.

[2] Herbert Marcuse: "Re-examination of the Concept of Revolution", op. cit., p. 21.

[3] ibid., p. 22.

the year in which the above thoughts were expressed, Marcuse has had to modify some of his earlier statements and admit the metropolitan working class, or at least part of it, into his revolutionary opposition. But he cannot bring himself to face up to the reality of May–June, 1968, which saw the organised power of the French working class in action. He still rejects the "traditional classes" as "historical agents of change", and, at best, can accept an allliance only between "*working-class groups*" and the "militant intelligentsia". Later he refers to "the politically articulate and active *groups* among the working classes". Thus, the class is still rejected. The most "politically articulate and active", the five million members and supporters of the French Communist Party, are apparently also rejected as they, too, are regarded as "absorbed" and "integrated" by the system.

Is one, therefore, not justified in drawing the conclusion that, to Marcuse, "politically articulate" workers are not those who have created their own, proletarian-based Communist Party, but rather those small ultra-left groups which follow the ideas and leadership of the middle-class intelligentsia and students who, in their turn, base themselves to some extent on the theories of Marcuse himself?

Marcuse's writings after the May–June events in France reveal his attempt, in the face of this upheaval, to cling nevertheless to the main tenets of his theories and, at the same time, to introduce into them a new element to explain why the majority of the French working class, despite his theories of "integration", gave such a solid display of class strength and challenge. This new element in his theoretical exposition is the idea of the political catalyst, the force outside the ranks of the proletariat which, by teaching and example, triggers off the movement of the masses. Thus, in *An Essay in Liberation* (1969), while commencing by defining his "opposition" as the "diffused rebellion among the youth and the intelligentsia, and in the daily struggle of the persecuted minorities" supported by the armed struggle waged outside by "the wretched of the earth",[1] he states that "It is of course nonsense to say that middle-class opposition is replacing the proletariat as the revolutionary class, and that the *lumpenproletariat* is becoming a radical political force. What is happening is the formation of still relatively small and weakly organised (often disorganised) groups which, by virtue of their consciousness and their needs, function as potential catalysts of rebellion within the majorities to which, by their class origin, they belong. In this sense, the militant intelligentsia has indeed

[1] An echo of *L'Internationale* or of Fanon?

cut itself loose from the middle classes, and the ghetto population from the organised working class."[1]

But such a separation does not mean that they are acting in a vacuum. "Their consciousness and their goals make them representatives of the very real common interest of the oppressed."

Marcuse recognises that such a proposition will be challenged by "Marxian theory", but he persists in his argument that the changes in advanced capitalist society are producing transformations of a depth and character which are "far beyond the expectations of traditional socialist theory". Referring to "the slow formation of a new base" which brings to the fore "the new historical subject of change", he draws attention to the changes taking place in the structure of the working class itself. He notes "the declining proportion of blue-collar labour, the increasing number and importance of white collar employees, technicians, engineers, and specialists", which leads, he believes, to the intelligentsia obtaining "an increasingly decisive role" in the process of production. He asserts that this "new working class", because of its position, "could disrupt, reorganise, and redirect the mode and relationships of production"—but he sees no revolutionary role for this stratum of the working class; it, too, is "well integrated and well-rewarded".

Thus, he reverts back to his main "subjective factor", namely the "nonconformist young intelligentsia", the "ghetto population", and the " 'underprivileged' sections of the labouring classes in backward capitalist countries". These factors, he finds, concide with developments in the Third World where "the guerrillas fight with the support and participation of the class which is the base of the process of production, namely, the predominantly agrarian and the emerging industrial proletariat".[2]

In depicting the situation of the "ghetto" in the United States, Marcuse advances ideas which could reinforce the wilder dreams of the Weathermen and other such extremist groups.

> Confined to small areas of living and dying, it can be more easily organised and directed. Moreover, located in the core cities of the country, the ghettos form natural geographical centres from which the struggle can be mounted against targets of vital economic and political importance; . . . their location makes for spreading and "contagious" upheavals.[3]

[1] Herbert Marcuse: *An Essay in Liberation*, op. cit., pp. 51–2.   [2] ibid., p. 56.
[3] ibid., p. 57.

Even the exploited white people, according to Marcuse, have become "partners and beneficiaries" of the brutal suppression of the black people, and "class conflicts are being superseded or blotted out by race conflicts". Consequently, he argues, "at present in the United States, the black population appears as the 'most natural' force of rebellion".

This force, however, is seen by Marcuse as requiring the support of "the young middle class opposition". The student population, a large part of which is "prospective working class", is not expendable, is in fact vital for the growth of the existing society, and is thus able to hit "this society at a vulnerable point". Revolutionary in its theory, instincts and goals, according to Marcuse, the student body is nevertheless assessed by him as "not a revolutionary force, perhaps not even an avant-garde so long as there are no masses capable and willing to follow". Yet, "it is", he proclaims, "the ferment of hope in the overpowering and stifling capitalist metropoles: it testifies to the truth of the alternative—the real need, and the real possibility of a free society".[1] Implicit here is Marcuse's expectation that the students will become the eventual vanguard of the revolutionary struggle.

This élitist streak in Marcuse, which he shares to some extent with Fanon and Debray, is no subordinate theme, but occurs in more than one context. It is, after all, but a logical corollary of his rejection of the leading role of the working class.

Later in 1969, in his interview with *Der Spiegel*, he returns to the question of the new technical intelligentsia which he previously (see above citation from *An Essay in Liberation*) regarded as too "well integrated and well-rewarded" to be able to play a revolutionary role. Modifying his earlier view, he now considers that "the technical intelligentsia can become radical potentials"; even though it lacks power "in relation to all vital social questions" it nevertheless performs "the deciding role . . . in the production process".[2] Its awareness of this contradiction, he believes, can lead it into playing an important part in the ranks of the opposition. Its participation is likely to grow because of "the constant growth in the number of highly qualified employees, engineers, specialists, scientists, and the relative decline of the so-called blue-collar workers".

In this interview, Marcuse also re-emphasises once more the role of the younger generation, especially the students.

[1] ibid., p. 60.
[2] Herbert Marcuse: "Revolution Out of Disgust", op. cit., p. 42.

I believe that the concept of the new sensibility takes up again a central concept of Marxian theory, namely that the socialist revolution can be brought about only by a class whose needs and interests are no longer those of class society, that is a class which represents a new type of man and a radical revaluation of all values. I believe that beginnings of this revaluation, and this on a very deep basis, exist in the young generation and particularly among the militant students.[1]

Marcuse may claim to be speaking in the name of "Marxian theory", but the scientific Marxist definition of a social class has nothing in common with the Marcusean muddle of first equating social classes with generations (which include all classes) and then singling out from this category the students, who once again are not a social class, but, in the advanced capitalist countries to which Marcuse refers, comprise sons and daughters of the bourgeoisie, the petty-bourgeoisie, the professional strata, and, in some cases, the workers. Marcuse, however, is so concerned to carve out this special niche for the students that he abandons the Marxist theory of class struggle, and turns the students into a social class in whom he claims to find the embodiment of the aspiration for basic social change.

The fifty years' consistent, patient, self-sacrificing (tragically too often in the real sense of the term) endeavours of the Communist Parties in the capitalist countries, their constant spreading of Marxist ideas and the resultant creation of a politically class-conscious, revolutionary section of the working class, as the spearhead to lead the majority of the class and their allies in the conquest of political power in order to end the capitalist system and commence the construction of socialism—all this is entirely set aside by Marcuse. Nowhere, at any time, does he give any recognition to this essential activity. Here, again, his essential élitism reveals itself.

Even more than a year after the massive working-class struggles in Europe in 1968, Marcuse is still placing his main emphasis on the students.

Today this still seems remarkable to us, but one needs only a little historical knowledge to know that it is certainly not the first time in history that a radical historical transformation has begun with the students. That is the case not only here in Europe but also in other parts of the world. The role of students today as the intelligentsia out of which, as you know, the executives and leaders even of

[1] Herbert Marcuse: "Revolution Out of Disgust", op. cit., p. 46.

existing society are recruited, is historically more important than it perhaps was in the past.[1]

And then, grudgingly, and with obvious reservations, he agrees that "probably, here in Europe we should add those parts of the working class that have not yet fallen prey to the process of integration". His lack of certitude about the role of the working class in the revolution —the term "probably" expresses his clear reluctance to go any further —can nevertheless no longer be so emphatic after the events of 1968; and so he is compelled to include "parts of the working class" which elsewhere he usually refers to as groups of "young workers". Nowhere, however, does he ever contemplate that even these groups of young workers could be the leadership of the struggle rather than the students. Questions of leadership are not specifically discussed by him, but all the implications that the hegemony is to be exercised by the students and intellectuals are there, and repeatedly so.

Thus, to sum up Marcuse's views on the role of class forces in the revolution in the industrialised capitalist countries:

1. The majority of the working class has become an aristocracy of labour, "integrated" into the system, passive, conservative, and even counter-revolutionary. The only sections which may be won over are the young workers, and the new technical cadres.
2. The decisive new opposition in the metropolis is composed of (a) "the outsiders", the unemployed and the unemployable, the Black people and other persecuted minorities, acting in unison with (b) the students and intellectuals in whom resides the inspiration and the accumulated understanding of the nature of the changes to be made. The essential proletarian ally of these forces is (c) the exploited masses in the Third World.

Linked to these concepts is another major element in Marcuse's thinking—the inadequacy, uselessness and even danger of the traditional forms of struggle and the traditional institutions and organisations of the working class. Parliamentary elections serve no purpose other than to confuse the masses and keep them in submission. Strikes, even political strikes, have outlived their usefulness. Trade unions collaborate with big business, and have themselves become part of the machinery of capitalist rule. (That, presumably, is why the British Tory government is so determined to rob the unions of their powers, and to limit the possible use of the strike weapon.) Even the Communist

[1] Herbert Marcuse: *Five Lectures*, op. cit., p. 71.

Parties are regarded as part of the establishment. The whole range of democratic rights and institutions won by the working class through decades, and even centuries, of struggle, are deemed to be worse than futile; in fact, a snare and a delusion, a means of entrapping the working people into accepting the *status quo*.

More than one critique of Marcuse has drawn attention to the dangers behind these views. In the present period of state monopoly capitalism, with the steady increase of mergers taking place between giant companies, the growth of multi-national firms and the growing concentration of immense economic power in the hands of a relative handful of very rich and powerful men, there is a natural tendency for these economic forces to find a parallel political expression. As Lenin once expressed it: free competition equals bourgeois democracy, monopoly equals a turn to tyranny, a strengthening of reaction all along the line. Hence the many-sided attacks on democratic rights and institutions in the Western world. Even national Parliaments in the European Common Market countries are expected to surrender much of their powers to a handful of faceless, international bureaucrats sitting in Brussels.

For these reasons the defence of democratic rights and institutions, not as embodiments of working-class power, but as footholds for continuing the struggle for power, is a key aspect of the struggle for socialism today. Marcuse's attacks on these democratic institutions, even though made from an apparent "left" standpoint, play right into the hands of those on the right who are assailing these very same institutions. Marcuse hints and suggests that modern capitalism is travelling down the road to fascism. But he should know, from his own experiences in Germany, that one of the factors which facilitated the rise to power of the Nazis was the sectarianism of some sections of the anti-fascist movement which, too late in the day, grasped that the defence of democracy, and the winning of the widest possible alliance for that purpose, was the way to bar the road to fascism. If Dimitrov's historic speech at the Seventh World Congress of the Communist International in 1935 had been made five years earlier, and the invaluable advice it contained then been acted upon, fascism might well have been checked. Marcuse completely discounts this bitter experience, which cost the world so much. In failing to emphasise the defence of democratic gains against those who are only too anxious to whittle them away, he is betraying that brave new world for which he appear to yearn so much. Surely he has lived long enough, been through sufficient experiences and acquired enough knowledge to appreciate the danger of his argument?

He also spreads confusion by his treatment of the socialist countries. Understandably enough, if he has rejected the leading role of the working class in the anti-capitalist revolution, and along with it the leading role of the Communist Party, he cannot embrace the new societies created under such leaderships. He claims to find similarities between the socialist countries and the advanced capitalist societies— both are "advanced industrial societies". The fact that one society is based on public ownership of the means of production and working class political power, while the other is founded on private ownership of the means of production with political power decisively in the hands of the big monopolies, is evidently unimportant to Marcuse, even though he acknowledges this. Questions of class power, of the nature of the state, of ownership of the means of production find little place in his treatment. Yet, he claims to speak in the name of Marxism.

Having rejected socialism where it has already been built, or is in process of construction, he is hard put to it to delineate the new society for which he is appealing. When describing what is to take the place of his "advanced industrial society" he is nebulous to the extreme. General references to Cuban guerrillas and the Chinese cultural revolution do not tell us very much; nor do such general terms as "liberation", "solidarity", "co-operation", and the "construction of a free society".

Attempting to explain this new society, Marcuse writes:

> The anarchic element is an essential factor in the struggle against domination: preserved but disciplined in the preparatory political action, it will be freed and *aufgehoben*[1] in the goals of the struggle. Released for the construction of the initial revolutionary institutions, the anti-repressive sensibility, allergic to domination, would militate against the prolongation of the "First Phase", that is, the authoritarian bureaucratic development of the productive forces. The new society could then reach relatively fast the level at which poverty could be abolished (this level could be considerably lower than that of advanced capitalist productivity, which is geared to obscene affluence and waste). Then the development could tend toward a sensuous culture, tangibly contrasting with the grey-on-grey culture of the socialist societies of Eastern Europe. Production would be redirected in defiance of all the rationality of the Performance Principle;[2]

[1] Surpass itself, be raised to a higher level.

[2] Who would have this task of the redirection of production? Marcuse does not tell us. But if the "performance principle"—"from each according to his work"—is to be abandoned, then on what basis will distribution of the products be effected?

socially necessary labour would be diverted to the construction of an aesthetic rather than repressive environment, to parks and gardens rather than highways and parking lots, to the creation of areas of withdrawal rather than massive fun and relaxation. Such redistribution of socially necessary labour (time), incompatible with any society governed by the Profit and Performance Principle, would gradually alter society in all its dimensions—it would mean the ascent of the Aesthetic Principle as Form of the Reality Principle: a culture of receptivity based on the achievements of industrial civilisation and initiating the end of its self-propelling productivity.[1]

This vague conception is most unlikely to inspire the working class to take to the path of revolution; but, after all, that does not appear to be Marcuse's intention. His appeal, because of its language and presentation, as well as its content, can only find a response in part of his new-found agent of social change. It is not the outsiders who will read, let alone understand and follow, his argument; nor will it be the proletariat in Africa, Asia and Latin America. Only the third element in his opposition, the students and intellectuals, or at least a section of them, will be seduced by his rhetoric and false tone of new discovery.

But even for the students Marcuse's message cannot be lasting, for it is neither grounded on a scientific examination of modern capitalism (even though it throws light on some aspects of it), nor does it express a real appreciation of the position of the students themselves, of their situation in capitalist society, and of the necessary contribution which they can make to the further unfolding of the socialist revolution. Flattery, after all is said and done, is no substitute for political guidance and leadership; and it is the latter which students will increasingly seek, rather than the assurance that they are the hope of the future.

YOUTH AND THE REVOLUTION

So emphatic has been the revolt of young people in the 1960's, in country after country, that it seems unnecessary to emphasise the point. But for serious revolutionaries it is not enough to be aware of this revolt, nor even of its extent; what is more important is to probe into its causes, to assess correctly its character, to be fully conscious both of its great potentialities and of its limitations.

Marcuse is fully justified in drawing our attention to this pheno-

---

[1] Herbert Marcuse: *An Essay on Liberation*, op. cit., pp. 89–90.

menon even though we cannot accept most of his conclusions. It is perhaps not out of place to recall that young people have always played a prominent part in all revolutionary movements, and this is certainly so for the twentieth century. It was true in 1905 and in 1917. It was true in Spain in 1936–9, both for the Spanish people who took up arms to oppose Franco, and for the International Brigades which came to their defence. (The twenty-eight members of the British Young Communist League who died in Spain tell only part of the story, for many of the British Communist Party members, as well as Labour Party and non-Party people who laid down their lives for Spain, were also young people.) Young people were prominent, too, in the war-time resistance movements in Europe. The same was true of the guerrilla forces which fought Japanese fascism in Asia; those who can recall the Malayan People's Anti-Japanese Army representatives who marched down the Mall in the Victory Parade in 1945 will remember the youthfulness of these heroic fighters; similarly those who met Aung Sang and the other liberation fighters of Burma after 1945 will have been struck by their remarkably young age and appearance. In China, too, alongside the veterans of 1925 who marched in the victorious armies of 1949 were to be found thousands of youngsters. And so in Cuba, and again in Vietnam—when it came to the crunch, young people, girls as well as boys, threw themselves into the struggle and generously gave their lives for the revolution.

In this respect, the present revolt of young people in the industrialised capitalist countries and their participation in modern revolutionary movements is no new departure. Yet it would be wrong to consider this participation as a mere repetition of past patterns of behaviour, for the present revolt has many new features and arises from new circumstances.

Many adult workers, when they reflect on their present conditions of life, consider they have secured significant material gains. Television, a washing machine, perhaps a car and holidays abroad, the children attaining a higher educational standard than themselves—a number of such material advances are weighed up and compared with the past. Not that life for adult workers has become adequate. Many do not enjoy these improvements. Those who do have to work overtime: the intensity and strain of work increases: the threat of unemployment or premature retirement hangs over them. Yet they feel, despite the difficulties and strains, that life is better than it was twenty or thirty years ago, and certainly better than what *their* fathers enjoyed.

But for the younger generation in the West the material changes of the past thirty years do not have the same significance. What the adult worker often regards as an achievement, the young worker sees as his starting point; he is eager to press forward and win still more. He is scarcely aware of the long, dogged and bitter struggles his father had to wage to reach his present level of livelihood. When he looks around him he sees the same rich class at the top of the pyramid, a class which becomes more powerful every day, accumulating immense wealth by exploiting all the new techniques of production, by swallowing up lesser firms, and by finding ever new ways of separating people from the money they have earned.

Young people in the West today awaken to adulthood more early, mature earlier, both physiologically and emotionally, have access to better information, stay on at school longer, and live in a society which generally requires more educated people. It is an age of scientific and technological revolution, with a whole series of dramatic changes in methods of work, in man's mastery over nature. As man's horizons of knowledge expand, so he travels further out into space to probe ever deeper into the mysteries of the universe. Schoolboys trace space vehicles on their tracking equipment. They carry out mathematical calculations which are completely alien to the knowledge of their parents. They study subjects which their parents are not even aware of. The television cameras have opened up an entirely new world of knowledge, along with a torrent of rubbish. There is an immense speed of change, both physical and political. New scientific breakthroughs are attained with ever shorter passages of time—and each breakthrough opens up another new world to be explored, and the opportunity for the new knowledge acquired to be applied. And the time gap between each discovery, as well as the gap between its discovery and its application in production, becomes shorter and shorter. The spirit of slow, seemingly static conservatism, has gone.

But with all this rapid change, the young person of today is also increasingly aware of the faults of this society. The wars in Indochina and Biafra, the flood disaster in East Bengal, the genocidal massacres in Bangla Desh—all vividly portrayed on television screens—bring home to him that millions of people live in conditions of incredible deprivation, hunger, poverty and disease. He is mindful of the hazards of nuclear fall-out—and the greater threat of a nuclear war. On every side he witnesses the destructive results of unbridled capitalism—luxury flats, offices, hotels, car parks, when millions are in need of a decent home of their own. The rich grow richer, while the poor become poorer. The noise of our cities becomes more and more unbearable, and the very air we breathe becomes more poisonous. Daily he is told that we are on the verge of an ecological disaster, that the blind greed of this system is destroying our very resources of life.

It begins to dawn on him that the ostentatious wealth which his own rulers enjoy is based on the misery and exploitation of millions of people in the Third World as well as on the speed-up and exploitation of the workers in the metropoles, and the creation of new oceans of poverty.

He becomes aware, too, of the struggles of the people to end these appalling conditions. Significantly he finds it easier to identify himself with Ho Chi Minh, Che Guevara and Angela Davis, than with Nixon, Heath, Wilson or Pompidou who represent all the negative values of modern capitalist society—its smugness, hypocrisy, greed, conservatism, philistinism and destructiveness.

He lives in an age of transition from capitalism to socialism. The influence of the great ideas of socialism, of Marxism, spreads wider and deeper all the time.

Of course, it would be absurd to pretend that all this is part of the conscious make-up of the majority of young people today, or that the majority are actively opposed to the system. As Marcuse and other commentators have rightly noted, the ruling establishments in the imperialist countries have perfected a whole array of propaganda methods and instruments with which to bamboozle the people, including the youth and the students. Monopoly control of the major newspapers, control over radio, television and films, control over the education system—all is bent in the service of the rule of monopoly capitalism. The scale of this propaganda, as well as the sophistication of its methods, enables the real problems to be distorted and the real enemy, capitalism, to be partially hidden from most people. An immense service in this work of obfuscation is rendered by the Harold Wilsons of this world who endeavour, not without success, to divert the wrath of the working people away from their real targets, to blunt their struggles, and to persuade them to accept a reformed *status quo*.

But to see only, or mainly, this immense ideological power in the hands of the capitalist class, and not to see the countervailing forces, is to present an unbalanced and distorted picture of reality. The very awakening of important sections of young people today is itself proof of man's ability to break through the barrage of lies and confusion.

The wave of struggle of the 1960's is but a portent of the tidal wave that is yet to come. And proof, moreover, of the ability of the people to smash through the walls of Marcuse's "integrated society".

Marcuse, and those who base themselves very much on his ideas, speak and write as if they had discovered something entirely new when they draw attention to the revolutionary role of young people. Marx and Engels repeatedly drew attention to the importance of this role, stressing, on the one hand, the dangers that could attend the movement if the young people were neglected, and on the other hand, the successes that were to be won by their incorporation in the struggle. Writing on the 1848 revolution in Paris, Marx stressed that the bourgeoisie, being unable by itself to cope with the working class, resorted to the only way out: "to play off one part of the proletariat against the other".[1] To this end, the bourgeoisie organised 24 battalions of the mobile guard of young people from 15 to 20 years of age. Though many of them came from the ranks of the *lumpenproletariat* their commanders, noted Marx, were "young sons of the bourgeoisie whose rodomontades about death for the fatherland and devotion to the republic captivated them".[2] Marx did not allow this experience to mislead him as to the role played by the working youth as a whole who, in the battles of 1848, fought side by side with their fathers on the side of the revolution. Marx was fully justified in writing that "the most advanced workers fully realise that the future of their class, and, consequently, of mankind fully depends on the education of the rising workers' generation".[3]

Engels, too, noted that the students had their role to play alongside the young workers. In his message to the International Congress of Socialist Students, held in Geneva in December, 1893, he wrote:

> May your efforts lead to the development among students of awareness that it is from their ranks that there should emerge the proletariat of mental labour called upon, *shoulder to shoulder and in the same ranks with other working brothers* engaged in manual labour, to play a substantial part in the oncoming revolution.[4]

Lenin, also, was only too aware of the importance of winning young people to the side of the revolution, and of their readiness to join the struggle and make sacrifice. This, he saw, was particularly

[1] K. Marx and F. Engels: *Selected Works* (two volumes), Moscow, 1950, Vol. I, p. 142.
[2] ibid.
[3] K. Marx and F. Engels: *Works*, Vol. 16, p. 198 (in Russian).
[4] K. Marx and F. Engels: *Works*, Vol. 22, p. 432 (in Russian).

the case with the young workers. "The youth", he wrote, "the students and still more so the young workers—will decide the issue of the whole struggle."[1] Lenin regarded it as only natural that young people predominated in the Party since, he declared, "We are the party of the future, and the future belongs to the youth. We are a party of innovators, and it is always the youth that most eagerly follows the innovators. We are a party that is waging a self-sacrificing struggle against the old rottenness, and youth is always the first to undertake a self-sacrificing struggle."[2]

Today, as we have already noted, the youth generally speaking plays an even more weighty role than hitherto, including in the imperialist countries. Within this general activity of young people, students have been very prominent.[3] This is not the first time that students have made an important contribution to the revolution. We have already referred to the way in which Marx and Engels assessed this. It would be strange if they did otherwise, since it was as young students that the founders of Marxism first entered the revolutionary movement, and many of their early collaborators and co-workers came from the ranks of the young students and intellectuals. Lenin, in his well-known article, "The Student Movement and the Present Political Situation", described the students' strike at St. Petersburg University in 1908 as "a political symptom ... of the whole present situation brought about by the counter-revolution. Thousands and millions of threads tie the student youth with the middle and lower bourgeoisie, the petty officials, certain groups of the peasantry, the clergy, etc."[4] Lenin saw the great importance of this strike and gave it his full support, calling on "the party of the working class" to make use of this action "however weak and embryonic this beginning may be". Yet, although this student action came at a time when the working-class movement itself was temporarily at low ebb, Lenin, unlike Marcuse, never allowed himself to form an unbalanced judgment; and, in words which remain valuable advice to this very day, he wrote:

The proletariat will not be behindhand. It often yields the palm to the bourgeois democrats in speeches at banquets, in legal unions,

[1] V. I. Lenin: *Collected Works*, Vol. 8, p. 146.
[2] V. I. Lenin: *Collected Works*, Vol. 2, p. 354.
[3] One should never ignore the fact that the struggles of young workers receive far less attention than the somewhat more sensational activities of the students; nor that in all the big working-class actions large sections of young workers take part. A recent notable example in Britain was that of the young girls during the postal strike of 1971.
[4] V. I. Lenin: *Collected Works*, Vol. 15, p. 218.

within the walls of universities, from the rostrum of representative
institutions. It never yields the palm, and will not do so, in the
serious and great revolutionary struggle of the masses.[1]

In Asia, too, the students have been very prominent in the revolutionary movement throughout this century. In the aftermath of the
1905 revolution, students in Persia were to the fore in the great upheaval which culminated in the Shah being forced to introduce a
new constitution allowing parliamentary government. The struggle
had begun in December, 1905, with a general strike by the workers
in Teheran; but the students soon joined in. In the Turkish Ottoman
Empire too, students and young intellectuals supported the revolutionary Young Turk movement led by Mustafa Kemal after 1905,
a movement which won supporters in Cairo, Damascus and Salonika
as well as in the capital.

Under the impact of the October Revolution of 1917, huge waves
of struggle swept over Asia. Students, in a number of countries,
played an important part in these events. This was notably so in
the May 4th Movement in China in 1919. This time the students
acted as catalysts for the mass movement; more, they acted as direct
initiators of mass action, following up their own demonstrations
and other activities with a call for a general strike which won an
immediate response from every corner of the country. In later years
in China, right up to the overthrow of Chiang Kai-shek, the students
played a key role in the struggle, notably in Shanghai where many
became martyrs to the revolution.

In India, student participation in the anti-imperialist struggle
began at the beginning of the twentieth century. By the 1930's this
had become a marked feature of the political scene in India, notably
in Bombay.

The Bombay Students' Union entered the broader political movements of the city. Students became active in labour organising and
worked with the Communists and, after 1934, with the Congress
Socialists. The students were a valuable source of active cadres to
the trade union movement. Students were an active element in the
Congress. Moreover, the student movement publicly demanded
complete independence before the Congress had officially adopted
this policy in January of 1930.[2]

[1] V. I. Lenin: *Collected Works*, Vol. 15, p. 219.
[2] Philip G. Altbach: *Student Politics in Bombay*, London, 1968, p. 76.

Students in India have continued to take part in the political movement, and have provided cadres for all the main parties. In Burma and Korea, too, students have traditionally played an important role in revolutionary struggles. In Latin America and in the Middle East, especially since the second world war, students have been prominent in the national liberation struggles.

Even in the West student activity in the past decade has not opened an entirely new page. It is true that in Britain the 1926 General Strike witnessed students—sons of the bourgeoisie in the main—playing the ignominious role of strike-breakers. But already by the 1930's there were signs of a significant change. John Cornford and other Communist students spoke at trade union meetings, organised solidarity for the unemployed marchers, and developed a conscious socialist movement in the universities. The young Communist, Richard Freeman, was flung into a Brazilian prison when he visited Brazil to express his solidarity with the imprisoned Communist leader, Luis Prestes. When the International Brigades were set up in Spain, a number of British students and young intellectuals went out to fight and amongst those who sacrificed their lives were John Cornford, David Guest, Lorimer Birch and Christopher Sprigg (better known as Christopher Caudwell)—all four of them young communists.

In the United States, too, as Bettina Aptheker has reminded us,[1] ". . . there is ample evidence of massive student protests in the late 1920's and throughout the 1930's. By 1939 more than one million college and high school students participated in student strikes for peace. Students of past generations utilised many of the same tactics which are used today—petitions, referendums, sit-ins and strikes. And the college and university administrations responded in like manner: suspensions, expulsions and arrests."

STUDENTS AND SOCIETY

Nevertheless, widespread and often dramatic activities of students in Western Europe and the United States in the past decade, as expressed particularly in the great upheavals of 1967 to 1969 in Japan, West Germany, Italy, Spain, France, Great Britain and the United States, cannot be regarded as a repetition or continuation of these earlier struggles. Student actions in the West in the 1960's are distinguished

[1] Bettina Aptheker: "The Student Rebellion", *Political Affairs*, March, 1969.

by a number of particular factors connected with changes in the system of monopoly capitalism itself: and, as a consequence, these student upheavals are having a significant influence on the general struggle against the domination of monopoly capitalism.

> Intellectuals and students, because of their social origin and position, exercise a tremendous influence on the middle strata, who are generally paralysed by deep-rooted conservative prejudice, who are embedded in the social system and constitute the firmest mass support for the ruling policy and ideology. The experience of Spain in the recent period has shown us that the students and intellectuals, by their struggles, are disturbing the complacent calm, the conformism, the smug satisfaction of the functionary who thinks he is at the summit of society because he is one of the cogs of the system; they are jolting the tranquillity of the petit and middle bourgeois, making him realise that this society is not immutable. They have penetrated into the technical machinery of the capitalist State, the judiciary, even the Army and the forces of public order. They are shattering the conformity of the traditional intellectual circles, the *established ones*.
>
> The students and intellectuals are destroying the influence of bourgeois policy and ideology from inside the social strata which were its support. By so doing they are completing the action of the working class, in the front line of the class struggle, with a flanking movement tending to isolate the supporters of capitalist society, fundamentally to reduce its influence and power, and to help smash this society from both inside and out.[1]

This assessment by the General Secretary of the Communist Party of Spain of the impact of the student movement in his country has a considerable relevance for the students in other Western countries.

As Marcuse and many other commentators on the student movement have rightly emphasised, the role played by students in politics today is clearly connected both with the scientific and technological revolution and with the growing domination by the military-industrial complex of modern state monopoly capitalism over all aspects of life and social activity in the capitalist countries.

The growth of productive forces in the major capitalist countries, and the development of the scientific and technological revolution has had a profound effect on both the scale of higher education and on its function. Science has become a direct productive force; there is an increasing demand for scientific and technical cadres, for engineers

[1] Santiago Carrillo: *Problems of Socialism Today*, London, 1970, pp. 125–6.

and specialists of every kind to play their part in modern industry. In addition to those directly geared to production there is an entire army of ideological specialists—sociologists, personnel managers, economic advisers, industrial psychologists, market researchers, public relations personnel and a whole range of other experts who are engaged in helping the monopoly firms run smoothly, mystifying the workers, providing the arguments and the public case for employers in dispute, and persuading the people to purchase the goods and gadgets produced so that the monopolies are able to realise their profits.

The swollen state bureaucracy, too, needs its growing army of technically trained people. The army, the security organs, the police rely more and more on modern equipment, on an ever increasing array of sophisticated weapons and instruments—and these, in their turn, require thousands of specialists, including in the upper echelons of control. Overseas interests of the big monopolies and their State demand a further host of advisers and practitioners—irrigation experts, geologists, economists, agronomists.

Radio and television commentators, journalists, "expert" commentators—these, too, are needed to sell the policies of the monopolies and the monopoly capitalist state to the people. And to train up this vast army of experts of all kinds, the universities proliferate and expand, and in their turn demand a bigger and bigger supply of professors, lecturers, research workers, many of whom double up their function on behalf of monopoly capitalism by their lofty opinions which they hand out over TV and radio networks or in the press.

This technological progress and the new needs of modern capitalism have called for ever higher educational standards among those drawn into all spheres of production and social activity. In the United States, for example, the number of jobs requiring sixteen years or more of education has gone up by 67 per cent in the last decade, while jobs requiring secondary education have increased by 40 per cent. United States estimates indicate that by 1975 the number of "white-collar workers" will form 48 per cent of labour requirements in the US.[1]

As a consequence there has been a remarkable expansion of the student population, and, at the same time, a change in its social composition. Alongside this, the institutions of higher education have become more closely tied up with big business and the state; their functioning, their curricula, their administration are all subordinated

[1] See P. Reshetov: "The World of Capital and the Alienated Youth", *The Youth and Contemporary Society*, Moscow, 1970, p. 85.

to the interests of the monopolies and the state, including in particular the military.

The explosion of the student population has been really phenomenal. In the United States it has increased from 2 million to 7 million in the ten years 1958-68. In the fifteen years from 1950 to 1964 the student population in France, West Germany and Belgium trebled, and in Sweden it increased almost four times. In the ten years up to 1968 the number of students in West Germany went up from 110,000 to 500,000, in France from 200,000 to 680,000, in Britain (which had only 70,000 before the war) from 216,000 to 418,000. Today there are more than 3 million students in Western Europe and 1 million in Japan. And the figures are still soaring upwards. Clearly, what we are confronted with is a new mass social force of rapidly growing dimensions—a force, moreover, which as Lenin noted, is tied by "thousands and millions of threads . . . to the middle and lower bourgeoisie", and we might add today to a growing yet still limited degree, to the working class as well.

One result of this quantitative leap is a certain change in the physical character of universities and other institutions of higher education. While the more traditional, comparatively quiet and cloistered conditions of the older universities remains, the new colleges acquire a mass character, and become more like factories of study. The large student canteen, with cheap subsidised meals, plain tables and chairs, cheap utilitarian crockery and cutlery, the noise of hundreds eating simultaneously—all seems very similar to a factory canteen, and very far removed from the sedate High Table atmosphere. The superficial and somewhat juvenile atmosphere of the old debating societies makes way for the mass meeting and the serious discussion intended to lead to some specific decisions and action, and no longer to be terminated simply by a vote to express an opinion in general principle. In this new mass atmosphere students acquire a greater sense of cohesion, and of their collective power. It is a situation which is more conducive to propaganda, to organisation and to speedy mass action.

The development of communications, too, has had its effect. Students, being mainly single men and women, are naturally less home-tied than other adults; but now there is an increase in mobility and communication. News and personal contact between one college and another take place in a matter of hours, even of minutes; and the speed up of international transport and communications, and the greatly increased habit of young people to travel abroad, means that there is a great increase in the international mobility of students too. As a result, ideas flow from one country to another very rapidly; solidarity actions are more easily organised; personal contacts between students of one country with those of another takes place more frequently and with greater ease. There is no doubt that this international mobility was one of the factors leading to the outcrop of big student actions in 1967–9 in Western Europe, aided, of course, by the news coverage of these events which also helped to spread ideas of student revolt across the globe.

But the student population is not simply larger; its social composition has undergone changes, too. This is a natural outcome of the changed function of the university, of its becoming more directly a servant of big business, the army and of other sections of the State. Formerly students were mainly sons of the bourgeoisie, trained in the arts and in law, to become administrators, leaders of the bureaucracy, higher civil servants, colonial administrators, teachers and professors, even Tory MP's. Such categories are still required; but with the growing need for trained personnel demanded by developed capitalist society, the scientific and technological revolution, and the militarised state, it has become necessary to reach out beyond the families of the rich and the aristocracy, and to scoop up the sons and daughters of the small and middle bourgeoisie, and even from the working class. The latter still remain a minority, ranging from some 26 per cent in Britain to about 12 per cent in France, 5 per cent in West Germany and 3 per cent in Spain.[1]

These new armies of students, no longer drawn mainly from the upper ranks of the establishment, face entirely new problems. They have to make their way without rich parents; even in countries like Britain where they receive State grants, these are so inadequate as to face students with permanent financial worries throughout their student careers. Their wardrobe is limited and their clothes utilitarian rather than fashionable; their meals are modest and their general pattern of life tends to be frugal. Work during vacations,

[1] Britain's lead over other capitalist countries as regards the percentage of working-class students is challenged in a recent report (*Statistical Supplement to the Eighth Report*). Universities Central Council on Admissions, September, 1971), which argues that the basis on which figures are calculated in Britain place in the category of "working class" a number of students who are not so classified in other countries. By adjusting the figures to make them more comparable, the report arrives at a set of figures which do not alter Britain's percentage of working-class students but which increase those of other countries, and in consequence place France, West Germany, Norway, Sweden and Denmark all above Britain.

in order to pick up some extra cash—and the work is usually unskilled and low-paid (postal sorting, holiday camp waitresses, harvesting, deck-chair attendants at seaside resorts, etc.)—is now a common practice amongst British students. And at the end of it all is the uncertainty and the insecurity. Even with qualifications, the student knows he will have to enter the capitalist rat race—and is not even certain that he will find a job to which his qualifications entitle him.

Above all, he becomes more and more aware that he is being trained to become a cog in the capitalist machine, serving the interests of the big international companies, of the military-industrial complex and its imperialist State.

How far this has gone was revealed, for example, during the crisis at Warwick University in 1970.[1] The connection between this university and big business is revealed by a look at the personnel who make up the Council of the University. It includes directors of Hawker Siddeley, Phoenix Assurance Co., Lloyds Bank,[2] Courtaulds, Reed Paper Group, Barclays Bank, Portland Cement, Rootes Motors, Jaguar Cars, British Leyland Motor Holdings. A veritable roll call of major British monopolies, many of them connected with the car industry whose interests the University is expected to serve. Noticeable also, as pointed out by E. P. Thompson, at least three of the companies concerned have interests in South Africa. All these representatives of big business generally dominate the Council of the University, determine its policies and administration. "When it comes to the crunch," declares Thompson, "they win."[3]

Under these circumstances it is really not surprising to find that Warwick University was urged by the Vice-Chancellor in 1966 to place "automobile engineering . . . high in the University's priorities". Nor that the University has been carrying out research on metal fatigue (Massey-Ferguson), fuel-injection system (Rover Company), vehicle instrumentation (Rootes and Ford Motor Company), and fatigue in tyres (Dunlop). Thompson correctly draws attention to "the danger that some local industrialists might see the University largely as a laboratory for their own research and development".[4]

But the University was not only pressured to act as a technological

[1] See E. P. Thompson (editor): *Warwick University Ltd*, London, 1970, for an excellent analysis of these developments.

[2] E. P. Thompson: op. cit., notes that at least thirteen of the thirty-one directors of Lloyds Bank are governors, pro-chancellors, etc., of universities and colleges (p. 31).

[3] ibid., p. 61.

[4] ibid., p. 72.

aid (and a very economic one, at that) for the motor monopolies, but also to assist in training its management personnel. Consequently, "at some point the Institute of Directors' Professor of Business Studies (Houlden),[1] the Pressed Steel Professor of Industrial Relations (Clegg),[2] Barclays Bank Professor of Management Information Systems (R. I. Tricker) and the Clarkson Professor of Marketing (J. D. Waterworth) were brought together in a single Jumbo Pack as the School of Industrial and Business Studies".[3]

A brochure produced for the University in 1967 in order to explain the general nature of the management courses proposed by this "Jumbo Pack" included the following:

> Basic concepts of profitability, risk and uncertainty in relation to investment, the management and evaluation of assets, capital budgeting under certainty, the incidence of taxation, capital replacement decisions. The choice of finance, the new issue market, institutional leaders, leasing, capital gearing and the cost of capital, taxation and company policies, take-overs, long-term financial planning.

After all this, one is not surprised to find Vice-Chancellor Butterworth claiming that "industrialists whom we have consulted about the proposed course have been enthusiastic as soon as the content of the course has been explained to them". And well they might. So keen did the monopoly-dominated University Council become on the business role of the University, that they called in a firm of industrial consultants, John Tyzack and Partners, to advise on the administrative structure of the University. Their report found the University "inefficient by *normal commercial or industrial standards*" (Author's italics). To overcome these deficiencies they suggested an increase in the ratio of students to staff, and expressed their serious reservations as to the place of democracy in the University. "Sooner or later", they advised, "the university of Warwick will have to come to terms with the age-old conflict between democratic principles and effective government."[4]

We have taken Warwick University as an example, but the trend is noticeable elsewhere, not only in Britain but throughout the capitalist world, and especially in the United States, where the tie-up between the campus and the military-industrial complex is far more advanced. In a speech at a Parents' Convocation in 1961, John A. Hannah, at

---

[1] He is also Operational Research Consultant for NATO.
[2] Formerly of the Prices and Incomes Board, and the Donovan Commission.
[3] E. P. Thompson: op. cit., p. 74.
[4] ibid., pp. 80–1.

that time President of Michigan State University, urged: "Our colleges and universities must be regarded as bastions of our defence, as essential to the preservation of our country and our way of life as supersonic bombers, nuclear-powered submarines, and intercontinental ballistic missiles."[1]

Building on the developments of World War Two, when US universities in the words of Gerard Piel, "transformed themselves into vast weapons development laboratories",[2] the US military authorities expanded this co-operation after the war as part of their world strategy for "containing communism" and pursuing the Cold War. For this purpose the Defence Department was prompted to "establish military research centres at selected universities, to enlist the help of university administrators in the creation of independent research organisation (as in the case of the Institute for Defence Analyses), and to offer financial incentives to universities which agree to adopt an existing facility (as witnessed in the University of Rochester's agreement to administer the Centre for Naval Analyses). Where direct university participation has not proven feasible, the Pentagon has found it expedient to create a network of para-universities—independent research organisations which boast a 'campus-like environment' and adhere to the many rituals of academic life (the most famous example of this kind of institution is the RAND Corporation)."[3]

It is not only military weapons that arouse the military interests, and neither therefore do they limit their university links to questions of science and technology in their most direct and practical sense.

> . . . even the humanists, who had previously been confined to such servile chores as consulting on official histories of the last war, have found more positive assignments in "area and language training for military personnel and studies of certain strategic peoples". With funds abounding for projects in every field of learning, the university campus has come to harbour a new kind of condottieri, mercenaries of science and scholarship with doctorates and ready for hire on studies done to contract specification.[4]

[1] Cited in *The University-Military-Police Complex* (compiled by Michael Klare: North American Congress on Latin America, New York, 1970). This unique study is a startling exposure of the extent to which US institutions of higher education have been made to serve the interests of the US military.

[2] US House of Representatives, Committee on Government Operations, *Conflict Between the Federal Research Programs and the Nation's Goals for Higher Education*, Washington, 1965, p. 362.

[3] *The University-Military-Police Complex*, op. cit., p. 3.

[4] Gerard Piel: Talk to the American Philosophical Society, 1965.

As one would expect, the military tie-up of the universities and research institutes also serves the interests of big business. Technological spin-offs from military research are sheer profit for private industry, especially when they do not pay for the research itself. And how substantial this research is is indicated by the fact that the Lawrence Radiation Laboratory and the Los Alamos Scientific Lab., which come under the University of California, have a combined staff of no less than 11,850 scientists, technicians and support personnel, and an annual budget in 1968 of 288 million dollars.

> . . . as one penetrates further and further into the military research network, the more the distinction between academic and non-academic functions disappears. The trustee or administrator of a university research institute is more than likely the executive of a spin-off company located in the nearby industrial park, and at the same time a consultant to the Pentagon bureau which monitors contracts in his field of research. . . . Defence industry corporations, whose executives often dominate the boards of trustees of the research institutes and think-tanks, gain access to classified information and have the opportunity to "evaluate objectively" the projects they are trying to sell to the government. The universities, in return for their participation in the consortia, receive large research contracts and lucrative consulting fees for their professors. Examples of this arrangement can be found in most university communities, and are especially prevalent at the large research-oriented campuses like MIT, Stanford and Johns Hopkins.
>
> The spirit of co-operation that unites the components of America's military research network is not surprising when one discovers that more often than not the universities themselves are governed by men representing the corporations that stand to profit most from the university's research activities.[1]

Among the Trustees of Columbia University are directors of Lockheed Aircraft Corporation and General Dynamics, the first and third largest contractors for the US Defence Department for the year 1969. Of the top 75 contractors for the year 1968, directors from 19 are represented on the governing body of the Massachusetts Institute of Technology. If one takes multiple directorships into account, the total reaches 41.

In addition to the links built up between the universities, the military and the monopoly firms, the military have established their special

[1] *The University-Military-Police Complex*, op. cit., pp. 4–5.

science panels which draw on university personnel. These panels, in their turn, encourage the setting up of non-governmental advisory bodies which do research jobs for the military network. One such group, the Jason Division of the Institute of Defence Analyses, consists of some 40 leading university scientists who, we are told, "devote as much of their available time as possible to studies in the vanguard of the defence problems".[1] In 1964 its attention was switched to "such problems as counter-insurgency, insurrection and infiltration".[2] Consequently it held a secret conference in Thailand in 1967 for the purpose of mobilising university social scientists for US counter-insurgency operations in that country; and the 1967 Annual Report of the Institute of Defence Analyses reveals that it was also engaged in "work on technical problems of counter-insurgency warfare and systems studies with relevance to Vietnam".

Thus, the traditional idea of universities as independent centres of knowledge and research completely unconnected with sordid questions of war and politics, has completely gone. Not that it was ever true; but in the past two decades the university, especially in the United States, has tended to become completely subservient to the plans of big business and the military.

Senator J. William Fulbright has lamented:

> The universities might have formed an effective counterweight to the military-industrial complex by strengthening their emphasis on the traditional values of our democracy, but many of our leading universities have instead joined the monolith, adding greatly to its power and influence.[3]

The Senator may have liberal illusions as to the capacity of the universities in capitalist America acting on their own to resist the domination of the military-industrial complex, yet he is correct to point out that, as a consequence of their surrender to these forces, the funds they receive will result in them following activities likely to attract a continuation of such funds; and such activities, he points out, "unfortunately do not include teaching undergraduates and the kind of scholarship which, though it may contribute to the sum of human knowledge and to man's understanding of himself, is not saleable to the defence Department or the CIA".[4]

[1] Institute for Defence Analyses, *Annual Report*, 1964.
[2] ibid., for 1966.
[3] *Congressional Record—Senate*, December 13, 1967, p. S18485.
[4] ibid.

It is not only the military and the CIA which have a big stake in the US universities. In recent years the police, too, have strengthened their connections with these institutions. More than 750 American colleges now offer courses in "police science"—a five-fold increase since 1960, which is partly explained by the deepening crisis within the United States, and also by the new turn towards taking an interest in the police forces of Latin America in view of the recent tendency for military officers in some Latin American countries to adopt anti-imperialist positions. Police training and instruction by US personnel in Third World countries has become normal routine, and the universities are increasingly being involved in such enterprises. The well-known operation carried out by the Michigan State University in South Vietnam, in the 1950's to train, equip and finance the police apparatus of the dictator, Diem,[1] became in a sense a pilot scheme which has since been adopted by the US authorities in other countries.

On the grounds of making the police more expert and more professional, the Law Enforcement Assistance Administration (LEAA) and the US Department of Justice have pumped money into the American colleges, 257 of which now offer associate degrees in law enforcement, and 44 of which offer bachelor's degrees. "Both police and military officials", writes Webb,[2] "believe that sophisticated systems and weapons being introduced require manpower with more than high school education. . . . New 'command and control' systems, communications equipment, 'night vision devices', and computerised intelligence systems can only be operated by skilled and trained personnel. A college education is now being viewed by top police officials as yet another weapon for controlling insurgent groups within the population." As a consequence, over 65,000 police are being trained in this way in the American colleges.

This massive invasion by the military and the police, alongside the subordination of the universities and the colleges to the plans and programmes of the big monopolies, has been one of the most powerful factors generating the wave of revolt among US students. Such army and police interference has not yet reached the same proportions in British institutions of higher education, but no one should

[1] For more detail, see Jack Woddis: *An Introduction to Neo-Colonialism*, London, 1967, pp. 78–80: and Robert Scheer: *How the United States Got Involved in Vietnam*, California, 1965.

[2] Lee Webb: "Training for Repression", *The University-Military-Police Complex*, op. cit., p. 63.

doubt that the same process is taking place. A recent report reveals that a secret and heavily guarded department in one British college of art turned out to be producing military maps, allegedly for the US military authorities in Britain.

The new requirements which US monopoly capitalism demands from the universities affects their whole structure, curricula and administration. In the big mass universities the small, quiet, intimate tutorial retreats in the face of large-scale education. The ratio of students to tutors mounts. In the worst cases in the US hundreds of students, packed in lecture halls, are taught via closed-circuit television, with the professor simultaneously lecturing to them all. The state departments and private monopolies which provide funds for different disciplines in the colleges demand an ever narrower specialisation. Physical and biomedical sciences, chemistry and engineering receive the major preference, and the humanities hardly anything. At a time when wide sections of people are insisting on more control over their own destinies, on greater participation in decision-making in all institutions, and an extension of democratic rights, the military-industrial complex seeks more and more stringent and authoritarian domination over all aspects of university life. The centralised bureaucratic State demands the centralised bureaucratic university.

> The university and segments of industry are becoming more and more alike. As the university becomes tied to the world of work, the professor—at least in the natural and some social sciences—takes on the character of an entrepreneur. . . . The two worlds are merging physically and psychologically.[1]

Elsewhere Clark Kerr has described the university of today as "a mechanism held together by administrative rules and powered by money".[2]

In the face of these developments it is not surprising that students have rebelled. It would be strange if they had not done so. They have revolted against the function of the university as an annexe of big business and the military. They have protested against the lack of democracy. They have struck for higher student grants. They have organised sit-ins and other actions in defence of freedom of speech, against the keeping of secret files on students, to change their curricula,

---

[1] Clark Kerr: "The Frantic Race to Remain Contemporary", *Revolution at Berkeley*, edited by Michael V. Miller and Susan Gilmore, p. 14.
[2] Clark Kerr: *The Uses of the University*, New York, 1963, p. 20.

in protest against bureaucratic administration or, sometimes, against particular bureaucratic and reactionary administrators or chancellors. But they have acted not only in connection with their own problems at the universities; they have taken part, too, in major political manifestations, demonstrating against Greek fascism and apartheid or in support of Bobby Seale, and, above all, against the war in Vietnam.

The importance of these developments should not be minimised. Where formerly, in the major capitalist countries, the radicalisation of students was confined to a relative handful who broke away from their original environment, and joined the revolution, now we are witnessing a mass phenomenon. Whole sections are beginning to cut away, to protest against the defects in the university system, and to question and challenge the system of society itself.

One should not over-estimate how far this process has gone. It still embraces only a minority of students. But the fact that students are turning towards the revolutionary movement not individually but as part of a growing mass trend is in itself a significant victory for the revolution which is only to be welcomed.

It is only natural that in this process students should bring with them, into the revolutionary movement, a variety of ideas which are often not fully worked out. At times they take up quite contradictory positions. Anarchist tendencies are not absent, nor Maoism, Trotskyism, and ultra-left ideas in general. And naturally enough, the ideas of Fanon, Debray and Marcuse have found support in some circles.

The working-class movement, in its early stages (and now in countries where the working class is still in a process of formation, or is being largely replenished with former peasants or ruined artisans), suffered from similar problems, expressed for example in anarcho-syndicalism.[1]

Those who, in common with Marcuse, claim the leading role for the students, seem to forget that the students are not a social class in the Marxist sense of the term. They are of mixed class origin and therefore reflect the contradictory views of the different social classes

---

[1] It is interesting to note that the early attempts of the Luddites to destroy machines had a strange echo in the attempt of ultra-left students in Paris in 1968 to persuade the Renault workers to let them into the factory so that they could help them wreck the machinery. The workers, led by the Communists and the Confederation Générale des Travailleurs, refused to let the students into the factory. In a firm display of discipline they guarded the machines, oiled them constantly, kept them in running order, aware of the fact that they would have to work when the strike was over; and confident, too, that eventually they would own the factory and the machines.

and backgrounds from which they come, not in a mechanical and direct sense but indirectly in the way they sometimes approach the questions of the revolution. Students are over-whelmingly non-working class in origin. They are not, as students, direct victims of capitalist exploitation; they produce no surplus value by the expenditure of their labour power, although they suffer from the effects of the capitalist system which pays them small grants, limits their democratic participation in college life, gives them a narrow functional education and tries to make them servants of the system.

The education students receive is preparing them to play a part in the capitalist system, but many of them are likely to do so in jobs that link them with management rather than with the workers. In fact, students when they have graduated, are far more likely to be "integrated" into the system, to use Marcuse's terminology, than are the workers who have fundamental contradictions with the system of private ownership of the means of production.

Some writers in their arguments directed at minimising the role of the working class in the revolution, have attempted to elevate students, or youth as a whole, to a quite preposterous degree. Thus, an editorial in *New Left Review*[1] written in the wake of the events in France, May–June, 1968, referred to "the contradictions in modern capitalist society which have made the university into the weakest link in the chain, the most vulnerable point". One wonders whether the person who penned that remark in 1968 still stands by it today.

Others have tried to develop a theory that youth as a whole is a new "class". John and Margaret Rowntree,[2] although they take issue with Marcuse on some questions, accept his main thesis regarding the role of the working class and, at least as far as the United States is concerned, try to prove that the new decisive revolutionary class is the youth.

> We argue that the amelioration of the lot of the workers in the United States in the 1940's is a result of "class-shifting" inside and outside the United States. As a result of this "class shifting", the new potentially revolutionary exploited class is no longer the workers as a whole within the United States; instead the new proletariat is (1) the masses in the backward countries; and (2) the young of the United States.

This emphasis on the young does not, however, relate to the young

[1] No. 52, November–December, 1968, p. 5.
[2] "Youth as a Class", *International Socialist Journal*, No. 25, February, 1968, pp. 25–58.

workers. In a strange display of ill-digested pseudo-Marxism full of bits and pieces of Marxist concepts without any real understanding of what they are about, the Rowntrees commence by arguing as if they understood the relation between classes and productive forces. They ignore the central fact, however, that social classes are determined by the relations of *ownership* of the means of production. It is therefore not surprising that they get themselves into a frightful muddle, referring to the alleged "crucial pivotal class position" of the youth in the United States, and then admitting that the "youth class [*sic*] is drawn from all of the diverse income, social, ethnic, etc., strata in the US society", which results in "intra-class conflicts" within the "youth class". So the "youth class" after all is not a class, but a category of different classes.

Elaborating their "theory" the Rowntrees argue that the American economy is "dominated by two industries that are large, public and rapidly growing—defence and education". Subsequent elaboration of their argument shows that when they talk about "defence" as an industry the Rowntrees are not referring to the arms industry but to the army itself. Thus the army and the educational institutions become classified as *economic* factors. Utilising the facts that three-quarters of the US army are under 30, that the younger soldiers are the least well-paid, that the average military pay is lower than the average civilian government employee's wage, the Rowntrees classify young soldiers as a key section of the "youth class". Next come the unemployed youth, who, it is stated, face unemployment rates three times those of the labour force of those of 25 and over. Thirdly, come the students. The Rowntrees make a calculation which, they claim, shows that 52·1 per cent of all US young men between 18 and 24 are either in school, the armed forces, or unemployed. This is the force to which they give the name "youth class".

As regards the biggest single section of the youth, the young workers, the Rowntrees are virtually silent. Presumably they place them in the category of the working class, which, like Marcuse, they have written-off as far as the revolution is concerned. The "revolutionary role", they write, which was "traditionally that of the industrial working class, has fallen to the youth. . . . By the end of the second world war, the proletariat had 'disappeared' because production had shifted from manufacturing to the administration of world imperialism, and a shift had taken place in class exploitation in the United States from the working class as a whole to the youth."

Marcuse cannot be directly blamed for such theoretical confusion (although, as we have seen above, he has defined the students as "a class") but there is no doubt that his consistent condemnation of the working class and his unbalanced presentation of the role of young people and of students has contributed to lines of thought in "New Left" circles, the outcome of which in some cases is the elaboration of non-scientific theories about a "youth class".

RED BASES IN THE COLLEGES

Another "theory" which has arisen largely as a consequence once again of Marcuse's exaggerated elevation of the role of students is that of "red bases in the colleges".[1] This concept had a particular vogue in 1968 and 1969, but because it was not limited to the realm of theory, attempts being made to put it into practice—in France, Japan, and elsewhere—it is important to devote some attention to it.

The student movement of the 1960's and 1970's has been very much preoccupied with two major questions. How to change the system of higher and further education so as to bring it into conformity with the democratic aspirations of the students and ensure that it serves their real interests; and how to make a contribution to changing society itself by participating in the wider revolutionary struggle to overcome capitalism, break the power of the big monopolies and construct socialism.

No militant student regards his struggle as being one that is confined by the walls of his college or university: still less does he consider that his efforts to bring about changes on the campus is the final aim of his activity. In fact, one of the most heartening and significant things about the student movement today is that it sees beyond its immediate demands and aspires to a fundamental change in society itself.

There is, of course, a relationship between these two tasks. It is in the course of the battle to bring about changes in the colleges that the majority of students (as distinct from the advanced minority who have already rejected capitalism) can be won for a wider understanding of the issues involved, and can learn to take their place in the more fundamental struggle for socialism itself. In fact, the very struggle to effect changes in the colleges poses problems for the government and the ruling class which touch on key questions of democracy

[1] Marcuse himself has criticised this concept.

and government policy and assist students to see more clearly the role of the state and political power in relation to educational institutions, as well as their connection with the struggle for socialism.

It is important at all stages to see these two aspects of the student movement and to see them on their right relationship. Furthermore, it is necessary to understand, Marcuse notwithstanding, that no revolution is possible in the major capitalist countries without the mass movement of the many-millions strong working class: it is, above all, this massive force, this "collective power" of the working class, which must move into action against the capitalist system if the political state power of the big monopolies is to be ended.

One of the main objectives of the student upsurge in the 1960's and 1970's has been to bring about radical and long-overdue changes in the structure and function of the colleges, in the methods of administration, the content of teaching, the examination system, and the control of discipline. Other questions, such as the financing of students, university and college entry, and the admission of a far greater percentage of working-class students are also being raised.

In general, this whole range of problems has been involved in many of the student conflicts of recent years in Britain, France, Italy, Spain, Japan and other countries. In the United States, too, these questions have been very much to the fore, although sometimes other questions have taken precedence such as the right of free speech and association on the campus, opposition to the use of colleges by the military (for recruitment, for research, etc.) and the demand for Black Studies.

The experience of the student movement in the past decade underlines the need for students to give serious thought as to how to make their struggles, spirited as they are, still more effective.

This requires consideration of the *forms* of struggle, as well as being clear as regards its *aims*. These two are clearly related to each other since the forms of struggle decided on in any given situation should be chosen in order to facilitate the achievement of the specific aims set; and conversely, the use of incorrect forms, of forms which are either insufficient, or, alternatively, too extreme, can jeopardise the very achievement of the aims of the struggle.

The majority of students who are concerned to bring about changes in the colleges undoubtedly see their task as one which involves bringing pressure to bear on the university and college authorities and on the government and local educational authorities by various forms of mass activity, and a readiness to negotiate with such authorities from a position of strength based on the degree of involvement and militancy of the students in the campaign to effect changes. Just as industrial workers will rightly use varying forms of action, including strikes, to force realistic concessions from reluctant employers or governments, so will students quite correctly utilise different forms of mass activity to force realistic concessions from stubborn and conservative college administrations, government departments and local educational authorities.

Just as British miners used "stay-down" strikes in the 1930's to defend their wages and conditions, the French workers used "stay-in" strikes in 1926 and again in 1968 to force major concessions from the employers, and the United States workers did the same through their "sit-down" strikes of 1937, so the students of today, following in the workers' footsteps, have found the tactic of the "stay-in" or "occupation" an effective and fully justified weapon to be used when other methods have failed to produce the necessary result.[1] The *temporary* occupation of parts or the whole of a college building by students, based on the wishes of the majority, as a form of struggle to win concessions or to focus attention on grievances (as was done, for example, at the London School of Economics, Hornsey and Guildford Colleges of Art, Manchester University and other places), is a justified and effective weapon when used correctly and with popular backing.

Some students, however, and some commentators on student affairs, do not look upon the occupation of college buildings as a *temporary* action to win concessions, but rather as a means of establishing what the ultra-left section of students in France in 1968 termed "student soviets", and what the Revolutionary Socialist Students' Federation in Britain have called "red bases in our colleges".

According to some advocates of this theory, student action can "liberate" the colleges from capitalist control, establish oases of "socialism" within the capitalist system, and use these as "red b es" to inspire the workers to "liberate" one factory after another until the whole system has been overthrown. The idea of "red bases" in the colleges is, in one sense, Debray's *foco* theory applied to the university. In discussion, some advocates of these ideas have even envisaged the

---

[1] According to Bethell (Nicholas Bethell: *Gomulka, His Poland and His Communism*, London, 1969, p. 12), the "occupation strike" was first used by Polish workers at the end of the 1920's—and Gomulka was one of its early exponents. Factory occupations had also been an outstanding feature of the great protest movement of Italian workers after the first world war.

"liberated" college being a base from which the students sally forth to extend their "liberated area" and so bring about the revolution.

Describing the dreams of such "revolutionaries" amongst the French students during the events of May–June, 1968, Patrick Seale and Maureen McConville (two observers who are generally most sympathetic to Trotskyist and other ultra-left trends among the French students) write: "They wanted to march, Red Flag flying, from the rubble of the university, on society itself."[1]

The result was quite otherwise. As far as the Sorbonne "Soviet" itself was concerned, let the following comments of Seale and McConville suffice:

> The last days of the student Soviet were as mad as the first had been heroic . . . the halls and corridors grew filthy with the shuffling of a thousand feet. Here, too, tramps moved in, and beatniks, and people who had nowhere else to sleep. Rats moved up from the sewers; police spies came through the front door. Some youngsters took hash and needed daily treatment. The infirmary became a scandal. About thirty thugs, petty criminals, ex-Foreign Legionnaires, deserters—calling themselves "the *Katangais*"—moved into a Sorbonne basement and spread uncertain terror about them. They, too, in their way hated society, and had come to help the students, but they brought disrepute. They had a couple of small-bore sports rifles, some ugly looking knives, a few sticks and bars, some lengths of chain, and a painted girl or two. . . .[2]

Such was the sordid end of an extremist movement which falsely claimed the proud and honoured name of "soviet".

The theory of "red bases in our colleges and universities" received a certain impetus in Britain after the second conference of the Revolutionary Socialist Students' Federation in November, 1968, which adopted a manifesto in which the building of "red bases" was set forth as one of the main aims. In the wake of this manifesto the *New Left Review*, in its issue of January-February, 1969, published a number of articles elaborating on this concept.

Emphasising that the "major innovation in those demands (i.e. of the manifesto) is the imperative to form red bases", David Triesman asserts: "Nor will the red base be an end in itself except in the limited sense of the student role as distinct from any other role. The seizing and holding of the red bases is clearly the last act the students can undertake

---

[1] Patrick Seale and Maureen McConville: *French Revolution 1968*, London, 1968, p. 105.
[2] ibid., p. 109.

as students, for once they have engaged in that course, they are a fair way down the road to abolishing the intellectual-manual worker distinction, as they will have liberated the University from selectivity."[1]

Triesman sums up the tasks of "revolutionary students" in these words:

1. Create red bases.
2. Make it clear to the workers why we are doing so.
3. Hold them for as long as possible in order to reap their full benefit.[2]

David Fernbach writes in similar fashion:

The Red Base is the most important weapon that the student movement can produce for the socialist revolution, and makes the link with the working class at the revolutionary political level.[3]

He adds that the "*most important*" fact is that "the university or college with a red strategic majority can function as a revolutionary political presence or *foco*, concretely expressing the ideas of a socialist revolution to which the working class must be won. Within the educational institution as elsewhere, the struggle has two aspects: the struggle with force (mass mobilisation → occupation → resistance → armed struggle) and the struggle with ideas. The strategy of the Red Base is premised on the fact that in any institution essential to the forces of production forms of dual power can be created here and now."

He concludes with a defiant threat that if the authorities, in the face of such a move by the students, threaten to close the college, "we must show that we are prepared to run it—as a Commune—and that we don't fear our own strength".[4]

Anthony Barnett likewise believes that "in the universities the question of power is being posed. Revolutionary students must have the determination to resolve it—to help all students free themselves from the hegemony of the authorities by establishing red bases which will detach the student body from the institution's controls, set up dual power on the campus, and create the permanent possibility of revolutionary action at the highest level. . . . In bourgeois society red bases could be Latin Quarters with an internal life that is open

[1] *New Left Review*, January–February, 1969, "The Impermanent Stronghold", p. 34.
[2] ibid., p. 35.
[3] *New Left Review*, January–February, 1969, "Strategy and Struggle", p. 40.
[4] ibid., p. 42.

and militant, and a majority ready to switch (to) the offensive over-night."[1]

Arguing that "capitalist power can be thrown back in particular limited contexts"[2] Barnett refers to the establishment of red bases in the colleges as "territory gained" and then goes on to draw an analogy with the struggle of the Vietnamese peasants against "one particular link of the chain of international power". Barnett emphasises:

> Turning the universities into red bases now means: *First and foremost the mass of students liberated from the clutches of the authorities:* from the controls of the administration, from the hegemony of bourgeois ideology, from the safety catch of their Unions, from the mystique of the institution, from the strait-jacket of institutionalisation and from the sugar-coated bullets of participation.[3]

In short, "Red bases for the future overthrow of the ruling class and the immediate liberation of the students."

After such a display of "revolutionary" rhetoric, it is perhaps not surprising to find that Barnett wants to "abolish the union", since he regards the students' unions as "the invisible occupation of the student body by the authorities".[4]

Having been presented with a rather extravagant comparison of the idea of red bases in the colleges with the Commune, dual power, Soviets, the *foco*, and the Vietnamese struggle, one should perhaps not be surprised to find another advocate of red bases in the colleges draw-ing a parallel with the liberated areas established in China prior to the victory of 1949.

"It should not be thought", writes James Wilcox,[5] "that the call to make the creation of Red Bases a strategic goal of our struggle is merely a flight of rhetoric. The time has come to take seriously the images we use, to explore the limits of the analogies we invoke to the boundary of the possible. We must learn to penetrate the disguises in which history

---

[1] *New Left Review*, January–February, 1969, "A Revolutionary Student Movement", p. 43.

[2] Barnett evidently has a confused conception as to what is meant by "capitalist power", not grasping that the basis of the power of the capitalist class is connected with their control of the State machine.

[3] ibid., p. 45.

[4] The attempt by the Tory Government to bring the student unions under the control of the Registrar indicates that the ruling class fears the potential of the student unions, as well as of the trade unions, and wants to tame them. When the unions are under attack by the ruling authorities it is strange to find a call from allegedly revolutionary quarters calling for their abolition.

[5] *New Left Review*, January–February, 1969, "Two Tactics", p. 23.

advances. Red Bases first appeared in China disguised as Soviets—perhaps Soviets will re-emerge in Europe disguised as Red Bases."[1] Later in his article, Wilcox returns to this analogy with China, pointing out that in the course of the liberation struggle there, the revolutionary movement created "a zone of popular power (the Red Bases) with its own popular force (the Red Army)".[2]

Wilcox is not the only proponent of this idea. In a public debate I had in 1969 with Robin Blackburn he, too, elaborated this "theory", arguing that there was an analogy between the role which a "liberated" university could play and that played by the liberated areas in China prior to the victory of 1949.

To draw such a parallel totally ignores the fact that the Chinese liberated areas were defended by their own armed forces, that they had their own independent economy based on centres of production, both agricultural and small-scale manufacturing, that they were inhabited by millions of people, that they had their own form of administration (state power), and that to maintain themselves they had to defend the liberated areas in fierce armed battles over a period of some twenty years against the US-backed armies of Chiang Kai-shek, and eventually to overcome them by large-scale warfare. It was a struggle between two centres of state, political power.

Those who advocate "red bases" in the universities often appear to ignore the realities of real political power in Britain, and talk as if there were no such thing as a powerful capitalist state, with its large army and police force, and as if the ruling class would allow the "liberation" of universities to take place without taking any serious steps to prevent it. This whole theory also ignores a simple fact of economics. Who is to maintain the students and staff of the "liberated" university? Who is to pay for the administration and running costs? Is it seriously believed that the capitalist state would continue to finance such an undertaking? Or is it really maintained that it would be possible to capture a university and run it as an autonomous institution, no longer dependent on state finance—and that the capitalist state would calmly accept this with no other reaction apart from a reproving "tut-tut"? Perhaps the advocates of "red bases in the universities and colleges" have a different perspective in mind and believe (or hope for?) a sharp reaction from the State, a confrontation of forces, a clash with authority, a physical

---

[1] It is difficult to comprehend the meaning of this sentence, and I am not sure whether Wilcox himself knows.
[2] James Wilcox: ibid., p. 30.

battle with the forces of "law and order" which, they think, will help to awaken the "passive", "corrupted" and "integrated" workers as to the realities of class society.

The dangerous consequence of this whole approach is the refusal to accept realistic compromises, sometimes even a refusal to negotiate at all. Coupled with this goes an excessive and unjustified use of violence against persons and buildings, which in the late 1960's reached such an acute and confusing state in Japan. Far from seeking to win immediate advances which would represent an important step forward, such ultra-lefts, in pursuit of "confrontation", try by provocative actions to goad the authorities to use more violent methods against the general body of students in the hope that this will extend the scope of the clash with authority and convince the majority of students that they, too, must rely on violence. The danger of such tactics, of course, is that the student movement as a whole can become a football of rival leftist groups, each one attempting to outbid the other in the extravagance of its slogans and the violence of its actions. This can, and often does, result in disunity, defeats and disillusionment. At the same time it provides an excuse for the right-wing to come to the fore in the defence of "order", and for reformist moderates to present themselves as the only "realistic and reasonable" alternative.

That student militancy should be so pronounced today throughout the capitalist world is a most positive and significant development. But militant feeling and action is not enough to win successes in the struggle against reaction. Clear heads and clear thinking are also needed. It is not the most militant or revolutionary-sounding slogans that achieve the best results, but the demands and forms of action that are best suited to the actual conditions students face at present.

Lenin repeatedly warned against the dangers of ultra-leftism:

By revolutionary phrase-making we mean the repetition of revolutionary slogans irrespective of objective circumstances at a given turn in events, in the given state of affairs obtaining at the time. The slogans are superb, alluring, intoxicating, but there are no grounds for them: such is the nature of the revolutionary phrase.[1]

He ended his article with the following advice:

We must fight against the revolutionary phrase, we have to fight it, we must absolutely fight it, so that at some future time people will

[1] V. I. Lenin: *Pravda*, February 21, 1918, *Collected Works*, Vol. 27, pp. 19–26.

not say of us the bitter truth that "a revolutionary phrase about a revolutionary war ruined the revolution".

Certainly the experience of students in Japan in 1969 should give cause for serious thought. In January, 1969, after many months of campaigning for major reforms in the universities, the Japanese students reached agreement with the authorities for negotiations to take place on January 10 at Tokyo University between a delegation of students and the university authorities. On the very eve of the negotiations Trotskyist students, armed with iron pipes and wooden poles, made an attack on 2,000 students who were using the university buildings in preparation for the next day's negotiations. Shouting "Smash the negotiations meeting" and "Kill the pro-Communist students", the Trotskyists invaded the building.

Despite this provocation, the negotiations meeting was held on January 10 at the Prince Chichibu Rugby Field, Tokyo, in the presence of some 8,000 students, teachers and staff. The student delegates argued in favour of "winning democracy on the campus through the unity of all the people in the university". They put forward a series of ten demands, which included the repeal of the unfair punishment of students (which had led to the struggle at that time), freedom for students to engage in self-governing activities, and the reform of the management and running of the university. After the meeting a further discussion between the student delegation and the authorities resulted in the exchange of a "note of confirmation" regarding the ten-point demands of the students.

In the face of this success for the students, with the possibility of their demands being met and implemented, the Government and the ruling Liberal-Democratic Party announced on January 12 its opposition to settling the dispute on the basis of the "note of confirmation", despite the fact that eight out of ten faculties at the university had called off their previous indefinite strike in order to facilitate agreement.

It was at this point that the Trotskyists and Maoists carried through their major provocation. Armed with stones, wooden staves, iron piping, hand-made bombs and sulphuric acid, they attempted to seize the university building by force, and physically assaulted those students who were opposed to them. Reports indicate that the police made no attempt to prevent the Trotskyist and Maoist students bringing their armoury into the campus, despite the fact that they had previously announced that their aim was to "destroy Tokyo University". These provocative actions culminated in a police action on January 18 to clear the campus. Using this situation, the Government then announced its rejection of the agreed "note of confirmation"; it stationed riot police on the campus and placed the university under *de facto* police control. The struggle for the main demands of the students thus had to be carried forward under more difficult and complex conditions.

There is much to be learned from this experience; in particular to be clear as to the role of the university, the nature of the student struggle, and the absurdity of "theories" regarding the "liberation" of universities or their "destruction".

CAN STUDENTS LEAD THE REVOLUTION?

No one would seriously contend the right of students to conduct militant actions in order to secure satisfaction of their demands. But extremism and ultra-leftism, whether in the nature of the demands, or in the form of action undertaken, only play into the hands of the opponents of democratic change in the universities and colleges. The nature of the struggle understandably arouses strong feelings, but these are not the best counsellors when important political decisions have to be taken. Lenin once referred to revolutionary phrase-making and leftism as "the itch".[1] He pointed out that this distortion "often arises from the best, the noblest and loftiest impulses. . . . But the itch does not cease to be harmful on that account."

This appears to be the conclusion drawn by many students in Britain, West Germany, France, Japan and the United States since 1969. The years 1967–9 witnessed a great explosion of militant student activity in these and other countries, and I have attempted above to provide some explanation for this upsurge. This powerful sweep forward was inevitably accompanied by some extremist trends, expressed both in some of the actions as well as in a number of the concepts advanced. The 1970's have so far witnessed a temporary diminution of the more spectacular actions and more extravagant views (not that this rules out their later emergence once again), the virtual collapse of the more extreme organisations (vide the SDS in West Germany, the RSSF in Britain, and the Trotskyist and Maoist student factions in Japan), and a certain growth of Communist influence, as expressed in the increased votes for UNEF-Renouveau in France, in the election of Communists to leading posts in student unions in Britain, and in the rapid advance of Communists in the West German student bodies.

[1] V. I. Lenin: *Pravda*, February 22, 1918, *Collected Works*, Vol. 27, pp. 36–9.

There is room for much thought and study as to why the years 1967-9 were marked by such effervescent and dramatic actions by the students in a whole series of countries. Such waves of struggle, rippling from country to country, are not unknown in the history of revolutions. The revolutionary year of 1848 in Europe, the aftermath of the 1905 revolution in Asia in the years up to 1911, and the still greater aftermath of October, 1917, throughout the world up to the early 1920's are, perhaps, easier to understand. But undoubtedly among the factors which contributed to this new militancy among students in the late 1960's in addition to the fundamental ones indicated earlier, were the successes of the national liberation movement, the impact of Cuba, the rise of the struggle of Black people in the United States and, probably the most decisive, the war in Vietnam which has so profoundly effected the political situation in all the major capitalist countries.

The present period seems to be one of student consolidation. Some students, at first lured by expectations of "instant revolution" and ready to "storm the heavens", have become disillusioned, dropped out of activity and turned their attention to their future careers. This is always one of the dangerous results of leftism. Fortunately others have learned from the recent experiences and have acquired a more realistic understanding of the nature of the struggle for student progress and of the part students can play, alongside the working class, in the general fight for social emancipation. This has found expression in Britain, for example, in the decision of the National Union of Students to find forms of closer working with the Trades Union Congress.

The experience of the student movement in recent years confirms that, as a collective body, they are unable to act as the leadership of the revolutionary struggle. Individual students will undoubtedly come forward and become part of the vanguard; and as Marxist influence spreads the number emerging in this way will grow. But the role of leadership is a class question. However many talented individuals come forward from the student ranks to take their place in the struggle, they cannot change the objective fact of the role of classes in society. Student militancy and courage are great positive virtues; and so is their readiness to challenge all the shibboleths of capitalist society. But the bourgeois and petty-bourgeois origin of most of them, their upbringing, their future function in society, result in the constant danger of sections of students submitting to confused ideas, of fluctuating between extreme militancy and leftism on the one hand and deep depression or cynicism on the other. It is only in close association with the working-class movement, and especially its advanced, revolutionary sections, its Communists, that students can overcome the built-in dangers that arise from their position in society.

This does not mean that students as a body, or at least, the most progressive sections of them, cannot sometimes act as a catalyst in a given situation and influence the wider struggle of the working class and other sections of the population. This was certainly so in China in the May 4th Movement in 1919: and there have been other such examples. In some countries, too, individual students, along with adult intellectuals, have, in the early stages of the movement in their country, played a vital role in bringing revolutionary and socialist understanding to the people. But these have always been temporary phenomena arising out of particular situations. As the revolutionary movement grows, the working class produces its own intellectuals, its own collective understanding, and, embracing Marxism, the science of revolution, it becomes fully capable of fulfilling its essential function as the leadership of the struggle. Even in those cases where militant student activity has sometimes stimulated and encouraged workers to step up their struggles, once the heavy weight of the working class movement is thrown into battle it quickly becomes clear as to which is the decisive force. As Lenin commented,[1] the proletariat "never yields the palm, and will not do so, in the serious and great revolutionary struggle of the masses".

Students are not dispersed throughout the general population of developed capitalist countries as are the workers, and therefore are not so strategically placed. Numerically, too, they are much smaller. Although they learn quickly, they lack the experience of class struggle, of organisation. Above all, they are not in the factories, at the point of production and exploitation. Yet the means of production and the question of their ownership is a decisive question of the revolution. If the power of the capitalist class is to be broken, then power must essentially pass to another class or coalition of classes—and in modern capitalist society it is the working class which is the basic objective antagonist of the capitalist class.

Only a definite class [stressed Lenin] namely the urban workers and the factory industrial workers in general, is able to lead the whole mass of the toilers and exploited in the struggle for the overthrow of capital, in the struggle to maintain and consolidate the victory,

[1] See above, p. 318.

in the work of creating the new, socialist, social system, in the whole struggle for the complete abolition of classes.[1]

Students have an extremely important role to play, a role which will increase as their numbers grow, as their social composition undergoes more changes, and as their own political understanding advances. Marcuse is justified in drawing attention to their importance in modern capitalist society; but his exaggerated claims on their behalf, and his attempt to place them in opposition to the working class movement itself, could, if his ideas were followed, hinder the building of the necessary alliance between students and workers and, by isolating students from the basis of the revolution, limit their role in the very movement to overthrow capitalism.

FRANCE—MAY–JUNE, 1968

To Marcuse and his followers the events in France in May and June, 1968, must, at first, have come as a great surprise, for here was the "effete" working class in motion, displaying its immense power. But from the complexities of the situation the Marcuseans (and other sections of the "New Left" and old leftists, ironically echoed by the capitalist press) quickly abstracted certain facts, distorted others and attempted to turn the events into a justification for their theories. Here, after all, were apparently a number of the major themes of the "New Left" in action—Fanon's violence, Debray's *foco* translated into the urban "red base", and the student vanguard of Marcuse. And here, too, according to both Marcuse and the capitalist press, was the "reformist" Communist Party, "holding back" the workers and trying to limit their struggle to simple wage demands.

In a speech made to several hundred students and faculty members in the University of California at San Diego on May 23, 1968, Marcuse echoed a number of the major myths which the events in France have given rise to. A few quotations from this speech[2] will indicate Marcuse's line of thought:

> Their (the students) young leader, Daniel Cohn-Bendit, who organised the barricades and was with them all the time till six in the morning,[3] when the street battle was lost, said, Now there is

---

[1] V. I. Lenin: "A Great Beginning", June 28, 1919, *Collected Works*, Vol. 29, p. 240.
[2] Herbert Marcuse: "The Paris Rebellion", *Peace News*, June 28, 1968, pp. 6–7.
[3] i.e. on May 10–11.

only one thing to be done: the General Strike. The following Monday the strike order was followed 100 per cent.

There isn't the slightest doubt that, in this case, the students showed the workers what could be done and that the workers followed the slogan and the example set by the students. The students were literally the avant-garde . . .

The protest movement was at first violently condemned by the Communist-controlled trade unions and by the Communist daily *Humanité*. They were not only suspicious of the students but also they vilified them—they suddenly remembered the class struggle, which the Communist Party has for decades put on ice, and denounced the students simply as bourgeois children . . . the student opposition from the beginning was not only directed against the capitalist society of France beyond the university but also against the Stalinist construction of socialism. . . . The student opposition was very definitely directed against the Communist Party in France. . . . It is a Party which is not yet a Government Party but which would like nothing better than to become a Government Party as quickly as possible. That has indeed been the policy of the Communist Party in France for years now.

. . . a long time before the eruption of these events, there was a systematic attempt to win over workers against trade union prohibition to join the protest movement. The students were sent into the factories, into the plants in Paris and in the Paris suburbs. There they talked with the workers and apparently found sympathy and adherents, mainly among the younger workers. So when the students really went out into the street and started occupying buildings, these workers followed their example and joined their own demands for higher wages and better working conditions with the academic demands of the students. The two came together again in a rather spontaneous and by no means co-ordinated manner, and in this way the student movement actually became a larger social movement, a larger political movement. At this turn of events when already hundreds of thousands of the workers were on strike and had occupied the factories of Paris and the suburbs, the Communist controlled union (CGT) decided to endorse the movement and make it an official strike. This is the policy they have followed for decades. As soon as they see that a movement threatens to get out of hand and no longer remain under the control of the Communist Party, they quickly endorse it and in this way take it over.

I think one thing we can say safely is that the traditional idea of the revolution and the traditional strategy of the revolution are out. They are outdated: they are simply surpassed by the development of our society. . . . This is exactly why I stress the spontaneous nature of this movement and the spontaneous way in which it spread. Now I say spontaneous, and I stick to this concept, but you know there is no spontaneity which doesn't have to be helped on a little in order to be really spontaneous, and that was exactly the case in France . . . compared with traditional organisation of the opposition, this has been a spontaneous movement which, for as long as it could, didn't care about existing organisation, party as well as trade union, and simply went ahead.

To many people the events in France in May, 1968, came as a bolt from the blue. The impression has been created that France was calm and stable until the students of Paris began their militant struggle for their rights. No revolutionary will fail to appreciate the high spirit of the students, their courage and determination; nor can one contest the justice of their demands for university reform. There is wide sympathy and understanding, too, for their desire to participate in the wider movement for shaping a new France, genuinely democratic and moving towards socialism. There is no doubt, either, that police brutality against the students, especially on Friday, May 10th, was a major factor in sparking off the wave of protests that swept over France, culminating in the great strike of nine million workers and the massive factory occupations which tied up the whole country for several weeks.

But this historic nation-wide response, backed by large numbers of scientific and technical workers, by intellectuals, teachers, journalists and other professional people, was produced by something more profound and more fundamental than the immediate events that preceded it, important as these were. Moreover, despite Marcuse, one cannot regard the great upsurge of May–June as an expression of a spontaneous movement, although elements of spontaneity were present, as they are in any major mass upheaval of such a character.

The explosion of May–June, 1968, was largely the expression of the accumulated discontent of the French people after ten years of de Gaulle. Unemployment at 500,000 was at a record level. Wages were largely frozen by the Government and the big employers, while prices and profits had been soaring. There was a big lag in the housing programme. There had been social security cuts—and restrictions on the administrative rights of workers and unions in running the social security system. Small shopkeepers were being squeezed out by the big monopoly distributors, and tens of thousands of small farmers eliminated by large capitalist farming companies. Proposals to reform the outdated university system were being stubbornly refused by the Government and the university authorities. The people, as the Communist Party general secretary, Waldeck Rochet, was to declare on May 21st, 1968, "are fed up with being subjects. They want to be citizens". They were no longer prepared to be pushed around and to see their demands go unheeded.

But accumulated discontent alone would not have produced the movement that shook France so heavily in 1968. For ten years the working people of France had struggled increasingly against these conditions: and the only party which, far from putting the "class struggle on ice" as Marcuse maintained, consistently fought against de Gaulle and his Government right from the very beginning, was the Communist Party. When de Gaulle came to power in 1958 he obtained 80 per cent of the votes in the referendum for his Constitution. The Communist Party was the only Party calling for a "No" vote—and 20 per cent voted "No". On every major issue the French Communist Party strove to rally the French people to struggle for change—against NATO, for extended nationalisation, for higher wages and better conditions, for improved social security. It was the Communist Party which led the fight in France against the US aggression in Vietnam, organising a vast movement of material aid which resulted in the sending from France, a few months before the events of May–June, 1968, of a whole shipload of medicines, machines and other material aid to Vietnam.

It was the Communist Party which worked for the unity of the three main trade union federations—the CGT (General Confederation of Labour), the CFDT (Democratic Trade Union Federation) and the *Force Ouvrière* (FO). It was the Communist Party which had, for ten years, campaigned against the rule of personal power and for an advanced democratic régime. Above all, it was the Communist Party which, from the very beginning of the anti-de Gaulle struggle, fought for unity not only on the trade union front, but on a national political level, striving to unite all left and democratic forces in a common movement against de Gaulle and the big monopolies and to establish a united democratic government which would open the way to socialism.

Marcuse chides the Communists with wanting to "become a Government Party". But what would Marcuse prefer? A government of no parties? Or a government without the Communists? One suspects it is the latter, since Marcuse openly shows his preference for the ultra-left factions of the students who, he avers, were definitely opposed to the Communist Party. With complete contempt for logic, Marcusean critics of the French Communist Party also accused it of failing to turn the events of May–June into a struggle for a change of system, which must surely include a change of government. The French Communist Party, as its consistent voting record shows, enjoys more support among the working class than does any other Party. The presence of the Communist Party in a French Government means the voice of the working class being represented there. Marcuse evidently would prefer that that strong voice be kept outside. For a Communist Party to be prepared to accept the responsibility of being in a government is not, in itself, an aim to be criticised: it depends on what kind of government. The government for which the French Communist Party has been striving is a government based on the united forces of the working class and its allies, expressed in a coalition of all the political forces of the left and the democratic movement. The achievement of such a government would represent an important step forward for the French people and open new prospects for an advance to socialism.

In the ten years leading up to 1968 the French working people increasingly expressed their confidence in the Communist Party, mainly because it had consistently fought for their immediate interests, had raised the banner of unity, and had given a clear perspective for advance. With a membership of over 400,000 and another 50,000 in the Young Communist Movement in 1968, the Communist Party was the strongest single force on the left. No less than 42 per cent of its membership in 1968 had joined since 1959, that is to say in the decade following de Gaulle's assumption of power. Communist electoral strength also grew—from 3,870,000 votes in 1958 to 4,003,000 votes in 1962, and to 5,029,000 in the elections of March, 1967. This vote—equal to $22\frac{1}{2}$ per cent of the total—embraces the key sections of the working class. It is almost equal to the entire Popular Front vote of 1936 which included Socialists, Radical Socialists and others as well as Communists.[1]

This increased support for the Communist Party, especially amongst the workers, leading to whole regions and towns turning decisively towards the Party and electing some 30,000 Communist councillors, helped the Party to win support for its aim of political unity. Thus was

---

[1] That this basic support for the Communist Party is still maintained was shown by the nearly 5 million votes gained by Jacques Duclos, the Communist candidate for the Presidential elections in 1969. This vote, representing 21 per cent of the total, was, it should be remembered, in a straight three-cornered presidential election, without all the advantages to be gained from local electoral agreements in Parliamentary elections, and, in this case with no official backing from other left political forces.

opened up the electoral agreement between the Communists and the Socialists, the Radicals and the Republican Clubs (who together formed the Left Federation), together with the smaller United Socialist Party, in March, 1967. In the 1967 elections the left forces constituting this alliance obtained nearly 47 per cent of the votes—as against just under 43 per cent for the Gaullists. This slight lead for the left reversed the position of the 1965 Presidential election when de Gaulle obtained 55 per cent, and Mitterand, backed by the whole left, including the Communist Party, obtained 45 per cent.

It was these ten years of struggle, led by the Communist Party, which produced a situation in France of such a character that when the Communist Party and the CGT, together with the other trade unions, called for mass demonstrations and a general strike for Monday, May 13th, in solidarity with the students, 800,000 marched in Paris, 60,000 in Lyons, 50,000 in Toulouse, Marseilles and Bordeaux, and 30,000 in Mans, and nine million came out on strike throughout France.

In his treatment of the strike movement and the accompanying actions, Marcuse makes three points which really cannot be sustained. First, that it was in response to Cohn-Bendit's strike call that the nine million responded. Secondly, that the CGT and the Party were at first opposed to the strike and only tailed after events. Thirdly, he implies that the Party favoured limiting the struggle to wage demands, were against a change of system, and were unenthusiastic about the factory occupations.

The fatuous idea that nine million workers, of whom probably at least a third were regular Communist voters, came out on strike because of the appeal of a young, anti-Communist, anarchist student, could only occur to someone completely ignorant of the workings of the labour movement. But let us leave Marcuse's bizarre idea on one side, and deal with what actually happened.[1]

The year 1968, even before May, showed that the workers' discontent was beginning to boil over. Massive industrial actions and demonstrations had already taken place previously in 1967—on February 1, May 17 and December 13. In the famous Renault motor works, a traditional stronghold of the Communist Party and of the CGT, literally scores of stoppages took place between January and May, 1968. Dissatisfaction was also being expressed in other factories. On May 1,

---

[1] As we have noticed previously when analysing Fanon and Debray, bold declamatory assertions often take the place of reality. For this reason the claims of the New Left theoreticians have to be tested by reference to actual facts.

1968, the workers of Paris were given permission by the Government, for the first time in fourteen years, to march in procession through the capital. The demonstration, called by the CGT, drew 100,000 workers.

On May 3, in reply to student protests against a raid by fascists, the Faculty of Letters at Nanterre was closed and police moved into the Latin Quarter. On May 4, post and telegraph workers decided on a series of strikes for economic demands to take place between May 6 and 10. On the same day, seven students were sent to prison. On May 6, on the appeal of the CGT, 100,000 miners stopped work in protest against the lack of safety measures emphasised by the death of six miners on May 3; and technicians in the post and telegraph services came out on strike. The CGT members at the Renault-Billancourt factory, who had already initiated 80 actions since the beginning of March, decided on a further stepping up of their campaign; and civil service employees in the CGT union decided to stop work at the end of the month.

Also, on May 6, the student actions escalated as did police brutality against them. On that same day, the Paris sections of the CGT issued an "energetic condemnation of government provocations and police brutalities against the students", and of the invasion of the Sorbonne by the police; and they "reaffirmed their solidarity with the students and teachers who are struggling for the defence, improvement and democratisation of education". Other CGT sections followed suit, the Bureau of the General Union of Civil Service Federations declaring "its solidarity with the victims of this repression and its demand for the liberation of the arrested students".

On Tuesday, May 7, Georges Séguy, the CGT general secretary, gave a press conference at which he declared:

> The current developments in the university are arousing deep feelings among the workers, who are outraged by the brutal police repression directed against the students. We condemn and denounce the police brutality and their invasion of the University, as well as the closing of two faculties on the eve of the examinations. We demand that the students in prison be released. . . . Solidarity between students, teachers and the working class in their common struggle for social advance, democracy and peace is a well-known concept among all active members of the CGT.

In the course of this same declaration, Georges Séguy also drew attention to the provocative slanders against the working class and the charges that the workers had become bourgeoisified, and warned students against the dangers of leftism which could weaken the struggle of the students' union (UNEF) and bring joy to reactionary circles. Denunciations of the antics of the ultra-lefts, such as that made by Séguy, have been misrepresented by Marcuse as attacks on the students as such. It is quite clear from all the foregoing, however, that from the very start the CGT declared its firm solidarity with the students. The same went for the Communist Party, whose Paris deputies, on May 6, called for solidarity with the students and for a democratic solution to the problems of higher education. At the same time the French Communist Party also warned against the irresponsible position of some groups on the left.

These understandable criticisms of Cohn-Bendit and others (whose anti-communism is admitted by Marcuse) did not prevent the CGT and the Communist Party, however, from continuing to rally support for the students.

But let us continue our chronicle. On May 7 a number of sections of the post and telegraph workers came out on strike, as did Paris taxi drivers, and workers at Renault-Sandouville, at ACH (Le Havre and Harfleur), and at the central office of the Paris region of the Social Security institution. On Wednesday, May 8, the CGT and the CFDT organised a day of demonstrations and strikes by teachers and peasants in nine regions in the West: 30,000 demonstrated in Brest, 20,000 at Quimper, and 10,000 at Rennes. In saluting these demonstrations the Confederal Bureau of the CGT made its energetic protest "against the police brutalities and repression employed against the students engaged in struggle" and reaffirmed its "feelings of solidarity with the students and teachers who are demanding in particular the reopening of their closed faculties, the immediate release of the prisoners and a democratic reform of the system of education".

On Thursday, May 9, in response to an appeal of the National Bureau of the National Union of French Students (UNEF) to all the national trade union centres to publicly affirm their solidarity with the students and to call, for that purpose, a united union demonstration to "defend the right of trade union and political expression and against police repression", the CGT and the CFDT met and quickly reached agreement to organise a joint action. This decision was conveyed the same day to UNEF. Referring to this agreement in the following day's issue of L'Humanité, Madeleine Colin, one of the CGT secretaries, declared that "The CGT will do everything possible to ensure that the agreement reached with UNEF will result in a powerful common mass action of workers and students". Throughout that day (May 9), there were student strikes and demonstrations all over France.

Friday, May 10, was a decisive day. Student strikes and demonstrations continued all day long, and throughout France. A further meeting was held between representatives of the CGT, the CFDT and UNEF and contact made with the autonomous teachers[1] union (FEN). A joint communiqué from the meeting expressed the deep feelings felt by the public over the behaviour of the police against the students and teachers which, it declared, had "provoked the indignation of workers against the government". As a result of this meeting a joint call went out from the CGT, CFDT, FEN, UNEF and SNESup (university teachers' union) for the holding of mass demonstrations in all major towns of France on May 14 and for a massive demonstration in Paris. The FO unions announced their refusal to participate in the demonstrations. On the evening of May 10, after 50,000 students and secondary school pupils had demonstrated in Paris, there were sharp clashes with the police. Students peacefully occupied the Latin Quarter, and put up barricades. Special assault police[2] attacked the students that night, using gas and grenades. Hundreds were wounded.

In the midst of this situation, Georges Séguy (so much maligned by the anti-communist "left") issued a powerful call in the name of the CGT in which he declared:

> The CGT protests vehemently and with indignation against the behaviour of the government; if it really wants to avoid aggravating the situation it must immediately withdraw the police from the Latin Quarter, declare an amnesty for all imprisoned demonstrators and meet the just demands of the students and the university, which in many respects correspond to the demands of the workers. The CGT appeals to the workers to protest . . . and to prepare a powerful mass rebuff in accordance with the decisions of the trade unions of workers, students and teachers.

In the early hours of the morning, the CGT Confederal Bureau issued a statement expressing its "entire solidarity with the students, teachers and university staffs" and calling for the immediate release of the prisoners.

---

[1] Teachers here includes teaching staff in universities.
[2] On a previous, less popularised occasion, in 1962, these special brigades had killed 9 CGT militants at Chavonne

On Saturday, May 11, the CGT proposed an immediate meeting of all trade union centres, together with FEN and UNEF, in order to give a powerful rebuff to the authorities. Early the same morning the Communist Party issued a declaration entitled "Stop the Repression!" This same headline appeared that day in *L'Humanité*, which was issued in 300,000 copies.

Even in advance of the joint meeting, the CGT called on all its organisations and all its members "to make immediate arrangements" to go into action. It appealed to them, acting on the national, regional, and local level, and in the factories, to organise every possible form of protest action.

At the joint meeting there were representatives of the CGT, CFDT, FEN, UNEF and SNESup. (The leaders of FO could not be found.) The CGT proposed a 24 hour general strike on Monday, May 13 (the earliest possible normal working day), accompanied by mass demonstrations throughout France. Since the representatives of FEN, UNEF and SNESup were unable to give immediate assent to the proposals, the CGT and CFDT went ahead and issued a strike call at midday, ending with the words "Long live the unity of workers and students!"

Thus it was not Cohn-Bendit but the CGT which initiated the general strike proposal, and which, together with the CFDT, made the initial public call for the cessation of work.

Shortly afterwards, FEN backed the strike call, and so did the FO. UNEF and SNESup declared that since their members were already on an unlimited strike they could not issue a new call to stop work. The CGT went into immediate action. Millions of leaflets were immediately issued. A special number of the CGT journal, *La Vie Ouvrière*, carrying the headlines "Stop the repression! Long live the unity of workers and students!", was distributed on the Sunday morning (May 12) in millions of copies. In Paris that day a joint appeal was issued by the Paris organisations of the CGT, CFDT, FEN, UNEF and SNESup, in which, along with the demands for amnesty, an end to the repression, and the introduction of democratic educational reform, there was call for full employment and for "the transformation of the economic system by and for the people".

Monday, May 13, was truly an historic occasion. All France seemed to have stopped work. In the Rhone region, 200,000 came out on strike. In the Loire 120,000. In Paris, where the procession stretched for over 4 miles, marching at least thirty abreast, there was indescribable enthusiasm among the 800,000 participants. This day of action confirmed two things: the unity of workers and students and the massive weight of working class participation, demonstrating its decisive character in the struggle of the French people. It also confirmed the leadership and influence of the CGT and the Communist Party.

In the light of the above facts, Marcuse's claim that the general strike was a result of the call of Cohn-Bendit appears too foolish to require further comment.

At the end of the day, the CGT Confederal Bureau, in assessing the significance of that great action, appealed to "workers, and especially the youth, to strengthen their organisations and maintain their unity *in order to bring about economic and social changes which will make possible the real emancipation of the working class*". (Own italics—Author.)

From all the foregoing, it is clear that the CGT and the Communist Party, far from striving to limit the aims of the protest movement, as its detractors have claimed, constantly put before the workers the perspective and need to extend their horizons, and to utilise the immediate struggle for more far-reaching aims.

Now came the next stage of the factory occupations and the strike of nine million workers which was to last several weeks. On May 14, 2,000 metal workers at Sud-Aviation (Bouguenais—Loire-Atlantique) occupied their factory. On May 15 the CGT issued an appeal in four million copies, assessing the events of the past period, calling on the workers to intensify their struggle, and to use all their initiative in the factories and in the localities in order to compel the employers and the government to retreat and meet the workers' demands, and in order to hasten the downfall of the régime. In the course of this appeal it stated:

> Certain petty-bourgeois individuals . . . are slandering the working-class movement and have pretensions of giving it lessons. The working class rejects these stupidities; it reached its age of majority a long time ago; it does not need guardianship; it knows, too, how to avoid provocations aimed at dividing the workers, isolating them and diverting them from their aims. It is with the working class, and around the working class, that all those must act who desire real progress in the direction of profound economic and social change.

The appeal then went on to call for "the replacement of the present power by a popular government".

Thus, once again, while rebuffing the ultra-lefts, the CGT made the clear call for the defeat of the government. This call for a popular government was carried a stage further when the Communist Party, on May 20, issued a call for the creation of thousands of committees of action in favour of "a popular and democratic government". Calling in Parliament next day for an end to the Gaullist government, Waldeck Rochet, the Communist spokesman, declared: "It must get out, and the people be given their say."

On May 16, when factory occupations had already spread to embrace Renault-Cleon, Renault-Flins, Renault-Le Mans, as well as Sud-Aviation Bouguenais, the workers of the huge Renault-Billancourt factory decided to take over the plant. The CGT Metal Workers' Federation announced its immediate "total support". The CGT saluted those who "in response to its (i.e. the CGT) appeal have decided to strike and occupy the factories". On May 17 the Communist Party declared its full support for the factory occupations which were an expression of the will of the workers "to win their pressing demands and, beyond that, to end the Gaullist régime and instal with the least possible delay a democracy opening the road to socialism". In the ensuing days the strikes and factory occupations spread until on May 23 nine million workers were involved.

Those like Marcuse, who argue that the CGT lagged behind the workers because the factory occupations began by initiatives from below, and therefore in a sense spontaneously, do not understand that this is precisely the way important mass movements usually develop. Lenin and the Bolsheviks never took the initiative to set up Soviets in 1905. The workers did it themselves; and this was an expression of what Lenin has always termed the "creative initiative of the masses" which, as he often pointed out, develops forms of organisation and struggle which no revolutionary movement can fully map out, in advance. It was the same with the action by the Upper Clyde shipbuilding workers who decided on their "work-in" not as a result of any preconceived high-level decision of any political party but on their own initiative. Once again, it was the "creative initiative of the masses".

It is of interest here to note the way in which Séguy explained the tactics of the CGT when he addressed a conference of the CGT Youth section, on May 17, 1968:

"Since the Renault workers—and especially those at Boulogne-Billancourt who are a special point of attraction as regards both their considerable influence and the orientation they give to the movement —have decided on a total, unlimited strike and on occupying the factories, we have understood quite clearly that we are entering a phase which is becoming very significant. . . . Renault has set the tone—and, I think, in a good sense. . . . For us, in the Confederal Bureau, it seems that the National Confederal Committee must examine how to carry the movement still further forward. This movement has begun at the base. . . . All the present strikes began by a meeting of the workers, by a discussion on demands and forms of action, often by the election of strike committees under the direct control of the workers. That is to say, a leadership of the movement has arisen, responsible for its actions and decisions directly to the workers themselves. This is the best form we can offer to the workers' struggle. This is always so, and especially in the present circumstances. This is our great strength.

"Of course, some people speculate and say that 'the CGT has been overtaken by the masses', the 'everything is happening down below without the CGT being able to take hold of the leadership'. Such people know nothing about the character of our organisation, or the perspectives and policy which it has mapped out, and above all, seriously underestimate—quite wrongly—the capacity of the CGT members, wherever they may be . . . to demonstrate their fine spirit of responsibility and initiative in such situations. . . . That is why we think it best to let the movement develop along the lines it is already doing, and to place it under the control and watchful eye of the workers themselves.

"As for the CGT itself, we have nothing to fear from submitting ourselves to this control, for there can be no contradiction between the slogans, demands and decisions we put forward and those of the mass of workers.

"This in no sense means that we think that our responsibilities should be restricted to waiting for the workers to approach their trade union officials to call a strike. On the contrary, we believe we must indicate the way forward, that our active members must pay close attention to the way the fighting spirit of the workers develops and that they must act so that, when the conditions are ripe, proposals can be put forward by the CGT members and submitted for the approval of the workers. For the moment, our tactic and our strategy is to extend the strike from below."

In his treatment of the French factory occupations, Marcuse states that the workers acted without caring "about existing organisation, party as well as trade union, and simply went ahead". This, too, shows complete ignorance as to what really happened. The workers were in fact so indifferent to the CGT that 400,000 of them joined in that period: and hundreds of new Communist Party branches were set up.

Marcuse also commented:

They (the workers) occupied the factories and the shops, and they stayed there—but by no means as wild anarchists. For example, only yesterday came a report that they took meticulous care of the machines and saw to it that nothing was destroyed and nothing was damaged. They did not let in any outsiders.

Marcuse seems to be wholly unaware that this initiative was taken mainly by the CGT members occupying the factories, and that the "outsiders" whom they refused to allow in were none other than his preferred ulta-left students, some of whom are reported to have declared to the workers that they would help them to "smash the machines".

It is quite clear that, whatever may have been the influence of the students' struggles—and we have already indicated that their actions and the police brutality against them helped to spark off the events of May–June—Marcuse's claim that "the students were literally the avant-garde . . ." is an over-simplification of what took place. It really shows contempt for the workers and their initiative, quite apart from its misrepresentation of the attitude and actions of the Communist Party and the CGT.

No appreciation of the events in France in 1968 is possible without an understanding of the problem of unity—unity of the working class, and the wider unity of all the existing and potential anti-monopoly forces. Lenin once said it was easy to write the word "UNITY" in letters ten feet high, but that to build it was a long, complex and difficult task.

France is a country with a considerable peasantry or class of small holders (though it is declining), with a large number of small shopkeepers and urban petty-bourgeoisie in general. It has fifteen million workers, but only some four million are in trade unions, and these are divided between three main trade union centres, apart from a number of autonomous unions.

In 1934 the Communist Party and the Socialist Party signed a pact of unity. In January, 1936, this unity of the working class was extended by the agreement reached with the Radical Socialist Party (largely supported by peasants), and with other groups, thus leading to the creation of the People's Front. In 1938, the Socialist leader, Léon Blum, split the unity of the working class; the Radical Socialists deserted, and the People's Front came to an end.

Then followed fascism. Again, in pain and anguish, the lesson of unity had to be learnt. Fascism was defeated—but millions had suffered, and thousands died. The Communist Party itself lost 75,000 of its members, killed by fascism. It had so many martyrs that it became known as the "party of the executed".

The anti-fascist unity established in the Resistance made it possible to set up a broad, united coalition government in 1945, in which the Communists had several Ministries. Important gains were won for the people. Workers secured more factory rights, and a relatively advanced social security system was introduced, in both cases largely due to the proposals by the relevant Communist Ministers. When the cold war began in 1948 the leaders of the Socialist Party split the front once again, both in the trade union and political fields. Ten years of instability followed with constant changes of government, mounting prices, the war in Vietnam, and then the war in Algeria. Then followed ten years of de Gaulle and his personal rule.

Over those four decades it was the French Communist Party which had been the main organiser of unity; it popularised the concept and strove with patience and determination and skill to achieve it in practice. And in the period leading up to 1968 its efforts had made considerable success, as shown particularly by the ability of the united left to win 47 per cent of the votes in the 1967 elections, as against 43 per cent for the Gaullists. The maintenance and further strengthening of this unity held out great hopes at the beginning of 1968 for a radical change of government.

Reaction's only chance was to divide the workers and to separate them from their allies. French big business and de Gaulle knew that democratic unity meant defeat for them. It was only logical that the French rulers should seek their salvation in the people's disunity, and to that end play on every divisive force. In particular, they aimed to turn the people against the Communists, to isolate the Communists and so prevent the working class from having a powerful voice in running the country.

The events of May–June, 1968, which should have been the occasion for strengthening left unity still further became instead the excuse to disrupt the people's movement; and at the heart of that divisive attack were the blows directed against the Communists—from the ultra-left on the one hand, and on the other from de Gaulle and Pompidou who turned the elections of June 23 into an anti-Communist scare.

The British press, in this period, makes wretched reading. Papers such as the *Observer*, the *Guardian*, *The Times*, *New Statesman* and others, which in 1967 had blamed British Communists for the seamen's strike, the dockers' strikes, the Myton building strike, and the Roberts Arundel engineering strike, were lamenting the alleged shortcomings of the French Communists for not being militant enough. While the French Communist Party called for the removal of de Gaulle and his government, the British press referred to a Communist-de Gaulle alliance. *The Times*[1] published an article in which it solemnly declared that the Communists and the CGT had somehow persuaded the simple-minded French workers to occupy the factories "not so much as a method of putting pressure on management" but as "a protection against an invasion by 'irresponsible elements from outside the factories' ". The *New Statesman*,[2] on the other hand, argued that the Communist Party and the CGT "could not halt" the workers taking over the factories. The Party shut the workers up in the factories: the Party could not keep the workers out of the factories. Both myths are based on complete contempt for the workers, on a conception that workers are simpletons who can be manipulated and tricked in this fashion. Only those who have no experience of working-class organisation, or those who have no intention of supporting the movement of the workers towards political power and socialism, would write in this fashion.

One of the central myths produced by the 1968 events in France is that there was a revolutionary situation which was frustrated by the tactics of the Communists. Marcuse, incidentally, said at the time, "it isn't a revolution". But others, who share his hostility to the Communists, assert that it was. *The Economist* (May 25, 1968), for example, claimed to see "A Revolution Set Alight by the Students, Snuffed Out by the Communists". Cohn-Bendit, with one of his typical exaggerations, has stated "The State was completely impotent."[3]

The facts were quite otherwise. A major political and industrial upheaval there certainly was. It was, as the CGT Chairman, Benoit Frachon, has declared, the first major confrontation in the modern period between the working class and the forces of monopoly capitalism. It was, without doubt, one of the most powerful displays of working-class strength and determination witnessed anywhere in the Western world during this century. It was, moreover, a movement which, in its forms and aims, went beyond a normal industrial action. The occupation of the factories was an expression of the workers

[1] May 29, 1968.
[2] May 24, 1968.
[3] Daniel Cohn-Bendit: *Obsolete Communism. The Left-Wing Alternative*, London, 1968, p. 123.

flexing their muscles for their future battles; and the demand for an end to personal rule and for its replacement by a genuinely democratic government, accompanied by the formation of hundreds of popular committees to campaign for such a change, was a clear indication that decisive sections of workers wanted to clear the government out.

But all this does not add up to a revolutionary situation. The majority of wage and salary workers still supported the reformist parties, or even those of the bourgeoisie. Although the industrial workers are strong supporters of the Communist Party, five million votes is still a minority of the total number of wage workers and their families. Secondly, although significant progress towards left unity had been achieved in 1967, the events of May–June, 1968, accompanied as they were not only by ultra-left posturings by the United Socialist Party but by hesitations and manœuvres by leaders of the Left Federation, resulted in a temporary break-up of the political unity so far attained. This was aggravated by the activities of the ultra-left student factions which stoked up hostility towards the Communists, without whom there could be no victory against the régime. Strata of the population beyond the ranks of the workers had been panicked and alienated by the tactics of the ultra-left students whose extravagant behaviour, especially that of continued barricade fighting, burning of private cars, and general vandalism, stampeded the petty-bourgeoisie back into the arms of de Gaulle. This was confirmed by the voting in the June 23 elections, only eleven days after the official ending of the strike; the Gaullists won. The voting figures show that even numbers of workers, including some of the nine million who had been on strike, must have voted for the Gaullist candidates, along with the majority of urban petty-bourgeoisie whose voting against the left was in part a result of the backlash against the stupidities of the ultra-left.

Thus, the relation of class forces in June, 1968, was *not* favourable for a change of social system. Furthermore, Cohn-Bendit notwithstanding, the State was in no way "impotent". Much of the administration had admittedly broken down, but the two key state weapons of repression, the police and the army, were more or less intact. The protests of one section of the Paris police against being used to fight demonstrators in no way meant that the police had been neutralised, let alone won over or in a state of disarray. The army, well-armed and equipped, was ready to act. De Gaulle had visited West Germany during the strike to make arrangements. Tanks were placed ready around Paris Forces were ready to move on to the offices of the

Communist Party and *L'Humanité*. The workers had no arms. All talks of insurrection under such conditions was childish. Perhaps not so childish in one sense but rather sinsister, for some of those who chided the Communists for not trying to "take power" were themselves vehemently anti-communist and would certainly have been against the Communists if they had attempted such an adventure.

Séguy dealt with this whole question in his report to the National Council of the CGT on June 13, 1968:

"In these sharpened conditions of class struggle, some doubtful people, renegades for the most part, have accused us, in insulting terms, of having let slip the opportunity for the working class to take power.

"That is to say with not having attempted to do what de Gaulle accused us of doing, while he nursed the hope of drowning us all in blood after he had made all the necessary military preparations for such an occasion; we have, at all events, good reason to think that that was the case

"To tell you the truth, the question of knowing whether the hour for insurrection had struck or not was never discussed in the Confederal Bureau, nor in the Administrative Committees, composed, as everyone knows, of serious, responsible militants who do not have a reputation for confusing their own desires with the realities of the situation. . . .

"No, the ten million[1] workers on strike were not demanding working-class power, but better living and working conditions, and the great majority of them expressed, by their opposition to the régime of personal power, their attachment to democracy under the slogan: a people's government.

"Such were the objectives and the significance which we gave to the strike movement from the very beginning right up to the end, not because that was our desire but more simply because that was the nature of the movement.

"If, according to an absurd hypothesis, we had abandoned our trade union role and thrown aside that which our critics have described, with contempt, as demands for 'nourishment', in order to set up headquarters for a revolution, or even to take part in sordid political combinations, we would have lost, in one blow, the valuable capital of confidence which the workers have in the CGT.

"We would have alienated, for a long time, the sympathy of other

[1] Subsequent statements have used the figure nine million, as I have done throughout this section.

sections of working people who recognise our seriousness, our authority and our sense of responsibility.

"We would have isolated ourselves, together with the most politically conscious section of the working class, but without the power to avoid being mercilessly crushed.

"Let the 'pseudo-revolutionaries' . . . blame us for having deprived them of the pleasure of helping to bury us!"

Explaining the policy pursued by the Communist Party, Waldeck Rochet stated:[1]

"The unity and strength of the working-class movement, in which our Party and the General Confederation of Labour played the decisive part, compelled the big employers and the government to satisfy important demands of millions of working people, ranging from wage rises to recognition of trade union rights at enterprises. But it was impossible to put an end to monopoly rule and substitute for it an advanced democratic system representing the interests of the working people and other non-monopoly strata.

"*Contrary to the assertions of the proponents of Leftist tendencies, the balance of class forces made it impossible to put on the order of the day the instant establishment of socialist power. On the other hand, it was possible to oust the Gaullist power and set up a régime of advanced democracy, opening the path to socialism. What was lacking for putting this very real possibility into practice was unity of the workers and the democratic forces.* (Author's italics.)

"Our Communist Party spared no effort to achieve firm agreement of the Left Parties and major trade unions on the basis of a common programme of democratic change making possible a genuine alliance of the working class and other anti-monopoly social groups in town and countryside in the struggle for a democratic alternative, opening the path to socialism.

"The socialist leaders obstinately rejected this. In secret, they even agreed to adventurist combinations inspired by anti-communism.

"The situation was exploited by the Gaullist power. Cashing in on irresponsible acts of violence by Leftist groupings, it worked out a plan designed to involve the labour movement, notably the Communist Party in a sanguinary clash with the police and the army. The required forces were put on combat alert.

"Because of the absence of a strong alliance of workers and demo-

---

[1] Speech to the International Conference of Communist and Workers' Parties, Moscow, June, 1969.

cratic forces, the big reactionary bourgeoisie could have put down the working-class struggle for a long time and established a military dictatorship.

"Fully aware of its responsibility to the working class, our Party upset the calculations of its class adversary.

"It succeeded in securing for the working people a sizeable complex of economic and social benefits, retaining and consolidating the conditions for continuing the political battle for democracy and socialism."

It would be idle to suggest that the Communists never put a foot wrong. In fact, in his report to the Central Committee, July 8–9, 1968, Waldeck Rochet mentioned that some mistakes had been made. But in its essentials the strategy and tactics of the Communists during the events of 1968 were correct, and were the only realistic policies to follow. It avoided another Indonesian catastrophe, in which at least half a million Communists and others were massacred in 1965 after an abortive coup against the military leaders; it secured material and democratic gains for the workers; it increased the people's desire to have done with de Gaulle, who was compelled to resign within a year of the general strike; and it provided a basis for resuming the path to left unity by which alone the French working people can advance to end the monopoly régime.

IS THE WORKING CLASS "INTEGRATED"?

None of Marcuse's essays, speeches or books makes clear which period, in his opinion, marked the beginning of the alleged "integration" of the working class in the major capitalist countries. Does it date from imperialism, that is to say, from the beginning of the twentieth century? Is it a post-1945 phenomenon? Or is it meant to describe an entirely new stage, say from the 1960's when these views of Marcuse first began to find consistent and marked expression? Marcuse provides no precise historical setting for his thesis apart from the popular bourgeois term of the "consumer society", which covers approximately the last two decades.

Despite his constantly emphasised arguments on the alleged effete character of the working class in Western Europe and the United States, on its "conservative" and "counter-revolutionary" role, he nowhere analyses the actual struggles of the working class over the past few decades, their scope and character, their demands, their impact and the reaction to them by the monopolies and governments.

It is true, of course, that the capitalist press tends to play down such activities, except when it wishes to stir up anti-working class feeling in order to discredit trade unions and restrict strikes, or when working-class action disturbs the domestic scene so massively that silence is no longer possible; and distortion then takes over.

In the late 1960's, when Marcuse's theories first began to ride high, the press did its best to create a sensation over every student action, to depict these as the only, or the most militant, expression of struggle against the establishment, and to play down or totally ignore much more important mass actions by the working class.

In October, 1968, for example, a few thousand students in Japan, led by a Trotskyist organisation, invaded Parliament and tried to take over the central railway station in Tokyo. Both attempts failed, but they received world-wide coverage and headlines. On the very same day 700,000 Japanese workers demonstrated on the streets, and another 3 million held one-hour strikes and factory meetings against the US war in Vietnam. These latter massive actions were of historical significance for the Japanese labour movement since they were taken by industrial workers on a nation-wide scale on a *political issue*, on a fundamental question of war and peace, and as an expression of international solidarity with the national liberation struggle of the Vietnamese people. But, in noticeable contrast to the press treatment of the relatively small action of the students, the workers' activities received scarcely a mention. This, of course, is no isolated example. When a few thousand Trotskyists and Maoists, in May, 1971, demonstrated in the Père Lachaise cemetery and defiled the tombstones of Maurice Thorez and other former Communist leaders, the press in Britain, without mentioning the barbarous insults to the dead Communists, wrote up the demonstration; but when, in response to a call from the French Communist Party, more than 100,000 demonstrated in reply, the same press ignored it.

That the press should act in this way should not, of course, occasion any surprise; and therefore it is quite understandable that many people, who rely largely on the press or the TV for their knowledge of what takes place in the world, accept this distorted picture. But Marcuse is not just a normal reader of the press, nor a vegetating TV watcher; he is a scholar of world renown, a man who should know the value of historic facts when making judgments of trends in modern society. Moreover, he is no ivory-tower academic, relying on mere documentation or wrapped up in the seclusion of his own thoughts. After all, he

has worked for the US Office of Strategic Studies. He should, therefore, know his way around the world, and it is difficult to believe that
he really knows nothing about the struggles of the workers. But if that
is so, if he is really ignorant of the facts, then he ought to show more
humility before asserting his views about the workers' role in society.
The alternative possibility, that he *is* aware of the immense scope of
working-class activity, immediately poses the question: why then does
he ignore it? The real answer can only be provided by Marcuse himself, but one can hardly be criticised for thinking that his motive must
be political, and that his *a priori* political views prevent him approach-
ing his subject in a scientific manner and basing himself on factual
reality. Political views should not, in themselves, prove a barrier to
scientific examination of modern society, nor to drawing valid conclusions from such an examination. But no valid assessment can be
made if major facts are deliberately brushed aside as of no account
when, indeed, they represent the very heart of the question under
discussion.

To those who appear to think that revolutionary struggles in Europe
only began with the appearance of Cohn-Bendit and Tariq Ali it is as
well to emphasise that since the beginning of this century revolutionary
struggles against capitalism have shaken Europe, that they have continued in a virtually unbroken line for seventy years, that the main
participants in all of them, without exception, have been the workers,
hundreds of thousands of whom have laid down their lives in the cause
of democracy and socialism.

The Russian 1905 revolution; the Easter Rising in Ireland in 1916; the
February and October, 1917, revolutions in Russia; the revolutionary
upheavels in Germany, Austria and Finland in 1918; the Hungarian
revolution and republic in 1919, and the Bavarian and Slovakian
Soviet republics in the same year; the great occupation of the factories
in Italy in 1920; the uprising in Bulgaria in 1923; the Hamburg uprising of 1923; the nation-wide movement in France against the war in
Morocco, 1924; the British general strike of 1926; the rising in Vienna
in 1927; the bloody May Day battle in Berlin in 1929; the revolution
against the Spanish monarchy in 1931; the mass resistance, in many
forms, to the rise of Nazism in Germany, 1932–3; the workers' armed
struggle in Vienna in 1934; the miners' rising in Oviedo, Spain, in
1934; the anti-fascist street battles in France, 1934, leading to the
united front; the battle of Cable Street, London, against the Mosley
fascists, 1936; the Spanish war, 1936–9, and the participation of the

International Brigades; the anti-fascist resistance in Europe, 1939–45;[1] the armed struggle of the Greek people, 1944, and the second Greek resistance war, 1946–9; the assumption of power by the working people in Eastern Europe, 1945 to 1948. As already mentioned, each of these titanic struggles, revolutionary actions in fact, were class actions of a most advanced character—and in each of them, without exception, the main participation as well as the leadership, was provided over-whelmingly by the working class, led in most cases by the Communist Party.

If the last twenty years in Western Europe have witnessed less dramatic developments—no major armed clashes nor actual uprisings —this does not at all signify that the working class has been passive or has reconciled itself to the capitalist system. The forms of struggle may have changed but their scope and significance have not, and without doubt a major facet of the West European scene in the past twenty years has been the increased organisation of the working class, a growth in trade union membership, and a steady expansion of industrial struggles, including strikes, and mass demonstrations, and a growing challenge to the capitalist system.

Between 1919 and 1939 a total of 74,500,000 workers participated in strikes in the industrially advanced capitalist countries. (For the whole capitalist world the figure was 80,800,000.) In the seventeen years following the war, i.e. 1946–63, no less than 224,800,000 workers in the advanced capitalist countries took part in strikes, that is to say, a more than three-fold increase. (For the whole capitalist world the corre-sponding figure was 259,500,000.) The Western industrial countries accounted for 20 million strikers in 1965 and 28 million in 1966. Since then there have been the great strike actions in Italy, especially in the period 1967–9; the events in France in May–June, 1968; and big strike actions in Spain, Great Britain, West Germany, Holland and Sweden. For the ten years, 1960–70, nearly 425 million workers took part in strikes in the whole capitalist world.

An outstanding feature of the post-war strike actions in Western Europe (and Japan, for that matter) is that they are in no sense limited to economic strikes, confined to struggles against a particular factory owner for higher wages or improved conditions. Increasingly they are fought over a wide range of issues—against redundancies and closures,

---

[1] A number of books in the French resistance have established clearly the role of the working class in the anti-fascist struggles, especially André Tollet's *The Working Class in the Resistance*.

for trade union recognition, for a shorter working week, for longer holidays with pay, for better pensions and social security, for the defence of trade unions. It is significant that the number of general strikes, or strike actions of nation-wide importance, has also increased. Between 1960 and 1965 there were over 160 general or major national strike actions in the capitalist world.

All this is abundant proof that the workers are not at all "integrated" into the system, but that they daily give battle to it; and the fact that, in the course of these great strike struggles, demands are raised for fundamental changes in the working of the system, for nationalisation of key industries, for limiting the power of the big monopolies, for an increased say by the workers in the running of industry, testifies, too, to the growing political understanding of the workers which is, in part, indicated by the growth of Communist Party membership, votes, and influence in a number of countries, notably Italy, France, Japan, Spain and Finland.

The extent and significance of the Italian workers' strike struggles, their relationship to the Parliamentary struggle, and the importance of both these forms of struggle for the advance to socialism are well brought out by Enrico Berlinguer, the Deputy General Secretary of the Italian Communist Party:

The large-scale social and political battles of 1968 were politically mirrored in the country's shift to the Left at last year's elections, which brought our Party 8,600,000 votes, or 27 per cent of the electorate. The Socialist Party of Proletarian Unity—a unitarian Left party—in its turn received about 1,500,000 votes. The forces of the Left, working class opposition, which in Italy are fighting for advanced democracy and socialism, thus won 10 million votes, i.e. they obtained the support of nearly one-third of the electorate. The importance of this result of the elections is that it derives from the dedicated struggle of the workers and large sections of the people. . . . After the elections the working people did not display wait-and-see tendencies, in other words, they did not harbour the illusion that tl . strengthening of the Left forces in the parliament, important as that was, could by itself lead to a change in the government's policies. On the contrary, they showed the understanding that the success at the elections created more favourable conditions for the struggle of the working classes and for the political battles of our Party and other Left forces. Indeed, after the elections the struggle of the working people acquired a broad scale and a high level of militancy. In 1968 the number of strike hours exceeded 68 million, the highest in recent years. Yet in the first two months of 1969 more than 44 million strike hours were registered. . . .

The actions of the working class, vanguard of the entire front of the popular masses, is not confined to demands for higher wages. They embrace the entire range of problems concerning the social, human and civic position of the working people in and outside factories and offices. A struggle is being waged for broader bargaining rights of the working people, for new trade union and political rights, for a substantial reduction of working time, for various forms of control over the rhythm of labour, for an improvement of sanitary conditions and for the right to hold meetings at factories and in workshops.

Essentially, it is a struggle to change the class balance of strength. In all this are manifested broader tendencies towards activating the masses, towards their participation in political life, towards the promotion of democracy. . . . The struggle of the working people increasingly brings to the fore problems connected with structural changes in the economy and the state system and more and more concretely shows that the working class and other working people must assume the administration of the state and national life. Increasingly large numbers of working people are coming to realise that in Italy major problems of economic, social and cultural progress and democracy can only be resolved by remaking the very foundations of society, in other words, through socialist revolution.[1]

This analysis by Berlinguer is largely confirmed by the events in Italy since the above speech. Both 1969 and 1970 were major strike years for Italy, 300 million working hours being lost through strikes in 1969 and 150 million in 1970. Even the smaller latter figure was twice the 1970 figure for Britain, which was itself the highest recorded since the 1926 General Strike. Commenting on the significance of these developments in Italy, Daniel Singer[2] has emphasised that this strike movement did not confine itself to wage demands (although the wage increases won were, in fact, an all-time high), but "set itself new objectives" showing that Italy had reached a "new era of class struggle". Singer's summation— ". . . enough has happened in the last three years to sow seeds of future conflicts: this is why the ghost of revolutionary change is haunting the boardrooms of Turin and Milan"—is not far off the mark. It is certainly closer to reality than Marcuse's sweepingly derogatory estimate of the working class in Western Europe.

[1] Speech at the International Meeting of Communist and Workers' Parties, Moscow 1969. See published report, Prague, 1969, pp. 375–8.
[2] Daniel Singer: "Italy after the 'Miracle' ", *New Statesman*, September 17, 1971.

These experiences in Italy clearly refute Marcuse's contention that Communist Parties, such as that in Italy, have become a "non-radical" legal opposition relying on "the parliamentary game" and "moving towards Social Democracy". They also refute his assertion that "class struggles are attentuated", that "former conflicts within society are modified", and that "there is a definite tendency for political opposition—working class opposition—to grow weaker".[1]

Faced with overwhelming evidence of working-class struggle, some New Left commentators have tried to dismiss strike actions as of no significance, even as a danger to revolutionary development.

> Strikes, even general strikes, tend to induce passivity in the working class: after all, in itself, a general strike is simply workers doing nothing on a large scale. . . . Usually they last not more than nine days and they can even be a salutary tonic for an ailing capitalist class leading to demoralised workers and higher profits.[2]

If that were so, one would have to explain why the British ruling class took such vindictive measures against the British workers for the 1926 general strike, and why the right-wing trade union and labour leaders (who presumably desire to see "passivity" in their ranks) declared: "Never again!" One would also have to explain why, if strikes, and especially general strikes, are so useless and induce such passivity amongst the workers, did both the Wilson Government and the Heath Government, following months of press and TV propaganda against strikes, introduce Bills to tame the trade unions and restrict strikes?

Marcuse and the New Left may not rate the industrial struggles of the workers very highly, but the big monopolies, and the ruling political circles, both conservative and right-wing labour (and the pattern in Britain is repeated throughout the Western world), have no such illusions. They appreciate only too well that their main enemy is the working class, even if the workers are not yet fully conscious of their historic destiny; and that is why every effort is made to bend the workers, blunt their class understanding, and, above all, try to cripple their organisations and their capacity to struggle. If the economic trickery, the so-called "consumer society", and the allegedly all-powerful propaganda media (to which Marcuse makes such obeisance) were being successful in "integrating" the workers, the rulers would

---

[1] See above, pp. 285-7.
[2] James Wilcox: "Two Tactics", *New Left Review*, January–February, 1969, pp. 24-5.

not have to deploy such strength to hold them in check. Far from the workers becoming integrated, every year sees the capitalists faced with bigger challenges, requiring, on their part, an ever new riposte and counter-blow to keep back or divert the workers' movement.

Strikes by themselves will never bring about a change of political system; but no Marxist has ever suggested that they would. In any case strikes, in actual life, do not really exist "by themselves"; in actuality, they influence and in turn are influenced by other factors. Strikers are one of the forms of class struggle in which the workers are schooled and in which those who have a more advanced political understanding can raise the level of political consciousness of those participating.

> Strikes [as Lenin stressed] teach the workers to unite; they show them that they can struggle against the capitalists only when they are united; strikes teach the workers to think of the struggle of the whole working class against the whole class of factory owners and against the . . . government. This is the reason that socialists call strikes "a school of war", a school in which the workers learn to make war on their enemies for the liberation of the whole people, of all who labour, from the yoke of government officials and from the yoke of capital.[1]

Of course, such a comprehension does not take place spontaneously amongst the workers solely by their taking part in strike action. In the midst of their actions there needs to be an advanced section, a political vanguard, which assists the workers to draw political class conclusions from their experience. But just as certainly, the majority of the workers will never learn these essential political lessons solely through the medium of propaganda, from speeches, or from leaflets and pamphlets; they must have their own experience, too, and such experience must include experience of class struggle of which strikes constitute an important part.

Even in the United States, where admittedly the working class, including those sections organised in the trade union movement, is still very much under the influence of capitalist ideas and led by men who uphold the system and, in many cases, stand well to the right of the political spectrum, it would be wrong to ignore the growth of other trends which are challenging the positions of the reformist leadership. On the decisive question of the war in Vietnam, the trade union were initially slow to react. But increasingly over the past five years they have begun to express their firm opposition to the US aggression and to demand the withdrawal of US troops.[1] Not only has the five million strong Alliance for Labor Action (Automobile Workers, Teamsters and Chemical Workers) come out against the war; so have important ALF–CIO unions such as the Amalgamated Clothing Workers of America, Amalgamated Meatcutters and the American Newspaper Guild, apart from hundreds of individual leaders and local organisations of many other unions. Protests have not been confined to paper, but many thousands of workers and trade unionists have participated in recent years in the big demonstrations, notably in the Moritorium Day of October 15, 1969, and in the massive march on Washington on November 15, 1969. Many more union leaders have spoken out against the war since then, as indicated in part by the declaration published in the *Washington Post* on February 25, 1970, signed by 123 trade unionists including the leaders of 22 unions. Declaring "We cannot and will not have both guns and butter", this statement was signed by more trade unionists and included more trade unions than any previous manifesto against the war.

One of the spin-offs from this development has been the building of many forms of student-labour unity, both in relation to anti-war activities as well as in connection with workers' strike struggles and student battles for democratic rights.[2]

In view of Marcuse's arguments and those of his followers regarding the role of the working class, it is of interest to note the findings of US sociologists and political scientists. An article in *Dissent* by Harlan Hahan (May–June, 1970), entitled "Dove Sentiment Among Blue-Collar Workers", points out that national studies as well as analyses of local referenda held on the subject of the Vietnam war show that "the . . . vote against the war in nearly every referendum was concentrated in working class rather than upper-class segments of the communities". The studies in question had been carried out since 1964, and reveal that the greatest degree of support for the complete withdrawal of all US troops from Vietnam came from people who had never finished their secondary education and who had annual incomes below $5,000. The findings showed that it was the "blue-collar workers" in particular who were becoming increasingly opposed to the war. This may come as a surprise to many people who have been led to believe, by the mass

---

[1] For full details of this important development, see *American Labor and the Indo-China War* by Phillip S. Foner, New York, 1971.

[2] See Philip S. Foner· op cit pp. 98 115 for further details.

media, that the protest movement in the US against the war in Vietnam has been mainly an affair of students, middle class and professional people. This, again, is an example of how modern myths are created, and Marcuse's theories have undoubtedly lent credence to such myths.

Is there, then, nothing valid in Marcuse's warning as to the extent to which tne working class in the advanced capitalist countries, and especially in the United States, can, by a combination of economic benefits and ideological pressure, be won to identify its hopes and standards with the existing capitalist system? It would be entirely wrong to discount this problem. It is, of course, not new, although in today's conditions it operates under a number of new conditions. Reformism, that tendency in the working-class movement that limits itself to obtaining better conditions from the capitalist system but fails to challenge the system itself and to work for its defeat, has undoubtedly been the major problem facing the workers of the advanced capitalist countries during the past hundred years. Basically it is a much greater, more fundamental and persistent problem in these countries than are the various manifestations of leftism with which this book mainly deals.

Marcuse is right to draw our attention to the enormous propaganda power which the modern mass media place at the disposal of the capitalists. He is correct to emphasise the extent to which the big monopolies, through economic concessions and by ideological conditioning, persuade large sections of the proletariat that its fate and its standards are tied up with the maintenance of the capitalist system. But to see this is to see only one aspect of the problem—and to see it in a distorted fashion, too.

The deepening crisis of world capitalism, faced with the advance of the socialist countries, the challenge of national liberation, and the opposition of its own workers, is a reality which Marcuse does not recognise. He appears to have unbounded faith in the capitalist system which he claims to oppose. He appears to think that the system's ability to buy off and mislead a section, even for a time the majority of the workers, is unlimited. His brave words, in fact, despite all their bravado and apparent militancy, are a sorry and pessimistic belief in the omnipotence of capitalism and the inability of the working class.

Taking up the cudgels against Lenin, Marcuse argues that the labour aristocracy is no longer a minority of the working class but "its vast majority". Marcuse is confusing here two quite different things. Certainly the aristocracy of labour, and especially in the United States, is a powerful factor in the labour movement, finding its expression particularly in the upper corrupt circles of the American trade union movement. But to see all those temporarily misled by these leaders as identical with them leads only to an inability to grasp the main tactical task of revolutionaries in such a situation, namely to win over the mass of workers still influenced by reformism, to break the ideological hold of the labour right-wing, of the labour aristocracy, and to turn the mass of the workers on to the revolutionary road. If the majority of workers in the United States still have a vision restricted to the fight for higher wages and other concessions, then it is the duty of revolutionaries not to damn them and turn their backs on them, but to raise their sights and give them socialist understanding.

Lenin said it was always necessary to have faith in the workers, even when they apparently no longer had faith in themselves. It has always been a standpoint of Marxism, one that has stood the test of time, that the working class in the capitalist countries has within it two main trends—one that accepts the system, and the other which works for its overthrow; in brief, the reformist trend and the revolutionary trend.

After 1917 the revolutionary trend in the working-class movements of the capitalist countries came to be embodied largely in the Communist Parties. Other sections of the revolutionary movement stayed outside the communist ranks, and some who today are also challenging the capitalist system are not in the Communist Parties. But this does not alter the fact that these Communist Parties became, and still are, the major expression of the revolutionary trend in the working-class movement in the capitalist countries, its most consistent, far-sighted, scientific, organised and dedicated section. That is why it is these parties which, in the main, led the major working-class and revolutionary struggles in the capitalist world over the past fifty years. And the fact that, in the more recent period in France, Italy, Spain, Japan, and in Britain, too, the hold of reformist ideas has become weakened, and that the labour movements have been won to a more left-wing position, is itself living proof that the working class is not one reactionary mass but a battlefield of two trends, reformist and revolutionary, a battlefield in which revolution, the wave of the future, is showing itself capable of winning big advances today and even greater advances tomorrow.

But Marcuse cannot accept this; even more, despite what he must know is the reality of this century, he cannot admit it. For, by doing so, he would destroy his entire anti-working-class and anti-communist thesis. Yet one who, to protect his thesis, will even shut his eyes to reality, cannot claim to be a scientist.

CHANGED COMPOSITION OF THE WORKING CLASS

Some theorists have argued that the emergence of a growing army of white-collar, managerial, technical and scientific personnel, as a major component in the economy is (*a*) either pushing aside the industrial working class as the main revolutionary force amongst the workers: or (*b*) gradually absorbing the majority of the working class, producing a process of bourgeoisification which is turning the proletariat into a conservative "middle class". Marcuse's approach tends to contain elements of both these conflicting views.

The undoubted changes in the composition of the working class in the developed capitalist countries do not, however, warrant either of these conclusions. These changes, which can be traced over some decades, are mainly a consequence of the changing division of labour in the production processes arising from technical transformations.

In the first case, throughout the twentieth century, and particularly marked in the most developed countries, there has been a decline in the number of workers engaged in agriculture, a process which took a further stride forwards after the second world war when large-scale capitalist farming, the use of chemicals, the increased employment of farm machinery, and the introduction of factory farming, became widespread. The percentage of the population engaged in agriculture dropped in the United States from 26·5 to 5·6 between 1920 and 1965, in Great Britain from 7·3 to 4·1 (1921–59), in France from 42·6 to 20·4 (1921–62), in Italy from 59·8 to 30·8 (1901–60), and in Japan from 50·9 to 33·4 (1920–60; it has dropped considerably since).

Secondly, there has been a change in the number of workers engaged in light industry (mainly textiles) and coal, compared with the number engaged in heavy industry, producing the means of production. In Great Britain the percentage of manufacturing workers employed in light industry dropped from 51 in 1911 to 25 in 1964, while those engaged in heavy industry rose from 49 to 75 per cent. New industries account largely for this transformation—electronics, production of polymers, rocket building, space engineering—as well as the militarisation of production. Coal has made way for oil and natural gas, as well as for electricity. Synthetics are replacing traditional textiles, leather, wood and even metal; while cars and planes replace railways. Manufacturing processes have developed greatly in food production, and chemicals have expanded in all directions.

The extent of the changes is revealed in the following tables:

Changes in the Number of Industrial and Office Workers in Various Industries

United States	1962 (Index—100 in 1947)
Electrical Engineering	147·6
Transport Engineering	129·0
Power and Gas	121·8
Chemical industry	130·9
Coal	31·9
Railway equipment	53·0
Textile industry	67·8
Railways	51·8
Great Britain	1961 (Index—100 in 1948)
General engineering, shipbuilding and electrical engineering	123·1
Iron and steel	118·6
Chemical industry	119·9
Coal	83·2
Textile industry	90·3
Garment and footwear	94·0
Tanning	80·0

The figures for Great Britain are not yet so marked as those for the United States, but the trend is obvious. Similar figures can be provided for the other developed capitalist countries.

The changes in the composition of the working class that concern us most in relation to Marcuse, however, are those relating to skill, technique and science, the question of the relative weight of white-collar and blue-collar workers, and what effect the changing pattern has on the role of the working class in the struggle to end capitalism and introduce socialism.

The development of mass production based on the conveyor system already, in the first four decades of this century, resulted in a great simplification of the worker's function. The process of production was broken down into the most elementary operations, and the skilled worker made way for the semi-skilled with only a narrow speciality, which consisted in performing a limited number of the simplest operations. The number of semi-skilled workers grew quickly, and by 1940 half of all workers in the United States belonged to this category. At the same time the introduction of specialised equipment and large-scale serial production required a number of categories with higher qualifications, such as fitters, maintenance-men, inspectors, tool-makers and foremen. This latter category was, however, smaller than the former. This period therefore saw a relative reduction in the number of skilled workers.

The development of automation, of electronics and cybernetics, has brought about further dramatic changes in the composition of the working class, creating new occupations and modifying its skill structure. Many traditional trades, based on manual labour, are disappearing; some old trades are becoming modified; and new specialities are coming into being. The long-established trades which used to include a large part of the skilled workers are gradually being eliminated. In building, the mass production of standard parts reduces the number of carpenters and bricklayers. In engineering there is less demand for boiler-makers. Fewer spinners and weavers are needed in textiles. The 1965 edition of a handbook of the US Department of Labour which provided information about different occupations, listing 22,000 types of employment, revealed that 8,000 types of occupation had been dropped since the previous edition in 1949, and a further 6,432 had had to be added.

Automation has meant a big increase in the number of skills required. This is seen most markedly in the United States where automation is most advanced. Between 1950 and 1960, the number of electricians and specialists in radio-electronics increased nearly eightfold. Automation has also meant a big increase in the number of men required for servicing and repair; at Renault's, in France, for example, there is one repair man for every two machine operators in the automated departments, compared with one to every eight in the non-automated departments. In the US oil-processing industry, which has an exceptionally high degree of automation, the relationship between repair men and machine operators is one to one.

Another change arising from technical advance is the necessity for the worker to be prepared to change his occupation more than once, instead of, as previously, spending all his life perfecting his one particular skill. One result of this is the need for the worker to have a broader general education and wider specialised training. The skills of a new type rely less on manual dexterity and physical labour and more on general education, technical ability and knowledge and the capacity to make decisions. The semi-skilled operatives, employed on repetitive monotonous operations, are the first to be displaced, since these are exactly the type of operation which can be most easily automated. On the other hand, highly skilled workers, with a grounding in electronics, hydraulics, pneumatics, etc., who are called upon to service and repair automatic units, are increasingly demanded by the new processes.

In this way [write Lyubimova and Gauzner][1] integrated automation objectively brings up the question of the elimination of the antithesis of physical and mental work and calls for workers' qualifications to be raised to the level of those of technical specialists.

Under capitalism, however, this is not a simple straight line process. In the first case, the capitalist state is not so eager to provide the necessary funds to give the working class an essential broad education combined with skilled vocational training. Secondly, the introduction of automation, even in the United States which is the most advanced in this respect, is still in no sense complete. Alongside the introduction of automation the conveyor system continues. Employers usually find it more profitable to introduce automation only partially, continuing to employ a certain number of machine-hands to perform repetitive operations. Partial automation frequently results in the replacement of skilled labour by unskilled labour.

The unevenness with which automation is being introduced in the United States, and its complex impact on the structure and skill of the working class, is shown by an investigation carried out in 1960 in the United States metal-working industry. At 25 per cent of the factories where automation had been introduced, the skill of machine operators had gone up, whereas at 27 per cent it had actually declined. A similar investigation in France revealed that 80 per cent of the enterprises employed men of lower skill to operate automatic machines. One factor here, which cannot be ignored, is the tendency for the monopoly companies to classify new occupations as unskilled or semi-skilled in order to keep down wage rates.

Despite all these factors, statistics tend to reveal that there is a gradual increase in the percentage of skilled workers and a decline in

[1] V. Lyubimova and N. Gauzner: *Workingclass on the Wane?* (Moscow, undated), p. 40.

that of the unskilled. Of significance is the fact that in the United States the average period of studies for all workers went up from 9 years in 1948 to 10·7 years in 1964; even for unskilled, it increased in that period from 8 years to 9·3 years, clearly indicating the increased needs of developed capitalism to have at its disposal a more educated working class.

In the capitalist countries there has been one additional consequence of the scientific and technological revolution, and that is unemployment. Alongside the "normal" unemployment created by capitalism's inner contradictions and its deliberate policy of creating a reserve army to weaken the struggle of the working class, there is taking place a considerable speed-up in rationalisation and the replacement of men by machines. Production is being concentrated in a limited number of factories, plants are being closed down and workers dismissed, with no immediate alternative job to go to and with no facilities for training for other employment. Unemployment is not only affecting the traditional industries, nor just the unskilled or the new school leaver, but skilled workers and technicians are also finding themselves out of a job. Even so, this has not stopped the overall growth of the working class in the industrialised capitalist countries.

In all the advanced capitalist countries there has been a considerable numerical growth in the army of the working class during the twentieth century. Alongside this numerical increase, there has been an advance in education and skill. This quantitative and qualitative growth of the working class creates new conditions for the proletariat, the principal productive force in society, to acquire a scientific world outlook and play a still greater role in society and in political life. This will not come about spontaneously; but neither is there any iron social law that will automatically transform a more skilled and educated working class, enjoying all the social benefits which accompany such accomplishments, into the army of passive, conservative, brainwashed, gadget-seeking morons which Marcuse apparently believes modern monopoly capitalism has produced.

WHITE-COLLAR WORKERS

But what of the salaried managerial, engineering[1] and technical personnel and office workers, all those who are covered by the all-

---

[1] The team "engineer" in this section is employed to describe someone with a degree in engineering or a high technical qualification, and not in the general sense in English of a skilled metal worker.

embracing term "white collar"?[1] Can one so easily place them in an entirely different category to the "blue-collar" workers?

It is first necessary to examine the changes taking place amongst those sections which are characterised as white collar. The first significant thing is their relative and absolute numerical growth compared with other sections of the labour force.

Engineering and Technical Personnel and Office Workers[2]
as percentage of Total Manpower in Industry

Year	US	Britain	Germany	France
1901–10	12·0	8·6	7·6	10·4
1921–30	17·9	13·7	11·9	12·8
1931–40	17·7	15·0	14·0	14·6
1941–50	21·6	20·0	—	—
1962–64	26·0	23·0	23·0*	23·6

* Data from Federal Germany.

As regards the increase in the number of white-collar workers employed in industry, engineering and technical personnel and scientific workers have, in the past decade, accounted for the greater part of this growth. This is, of course, a natural consequence of the scientific and technological revolution; it is also a result of the increased militarisation of the major capitalist countries. The massive outlays on research have led to a considerable growth in scientific and technical personnel. The giant monopolies possess their own big research centres. In the United States, two thirds of scientific and technical personnel are engaged in research for the Pentagon. At the universities richly endowed research centres work both for the military and for private industry.

The growth in the number of office workers is similarly connected with changes in production and distribution methods, which have increased the need to receive, process and classify the information which modern large-scale production requires. There is more accounting, registering, recording—paper work of all kinds, for Government

[1] The term "white-collar worker" is not really a scientific term. As used by bourgeois statisticians and sociologists it tends to lump together quite disparate categories, from the lowly paid clerical worker to the top manager linked with the executives and with the capitalist class. If I use the term in this section it is mainly for purposes of brevity; but it should be noted that my use of the phrase, white-collar *worker*, is intended to cover wage and salaried personnel who have become part of the working class, excluding the small executive section whose destinies are linked with the employing class.

[2] See Lyubimova and Gauzner: op. cit., p. 54.

departments, for the military,[1] for the police and security organs, for credit systems, for social insurance, taxation, etc. The big companies employ a growing army of salesmen, public relation experts, and market research personnel. Much of the growth of white-collar labour is connected with the parasitic nature of monopoly capitalism and with the enlargement of the repressive apparatus of the state along with that of the bureaucratic administration in other spheres. All this leads to a big increase in the number of white-collar workers and the relative decline in the proportion of workers directly engaged in production. In the manufacturing industry in the US, for example, the proportion of the latter dropped from 72·7 per cent in 1952 to 66·5 per cent in 1961, while the proportion of engineers, technicians, office employees and sales personnel rose from 20 to 25 per cent. During this period, which saw a growth of 3·4 per cent in the manpower employed by the US manufacturing industry, the number of engineers, technicians and specialists rose by 75·2 per cent, of sales staff by 25·8 per cent and office employees by 9·8 per cent.

In the newer industries the proportion of engineering and technical personnel is particularly marked, reaching 26 per cent in the West German electrical engineering industry, and 32 per cent in its chemical industry. In the US the figures for the chemical and atomic industries are respectively 50 and 60 per cent.

Between 1947 and 1965 the number of white-collar workers in the US increased by 9·6 million, while the number of blue-collar workers declined by 4 million. By 1965 white-collar workers accounted for 44·5 per cent of the total, and service workers 12·9 per cent; blue-collar workers accounted for 36·7 per cent, and agricultural workers 5·9 per cent.

In other major capitalist countries the same stage has not yet been reached but a parallel trend is taking place.

Can it be argued that the simple fact of the growth in the number of white-collar workers compared with the decline in the proportion of blue-collar workers means that the working class is becoming "bourgeoisified", being transformed into a new "middle class"? Those who argue in this way are confusing changes within the ranks of the working class with basic shifts in the class structure.

As Lyubimova and Gauzner comment:

[1] At the time of the disclosure of the Pentagon papers on Vietnam in the summer of 1971, it was revealed not only that these papers themselves comprised 7,000 pages of narrative and documents, totalling some 2½ million words; but that the Pentagon possesses literally *millions* of classified documents.

The factor determining to which class a person, or a group of people, belongs is not the existence of calluses on a man's hands, or the absence of them, but the relationship of the individual, or group, to the means of production.[1]

In the last century the majority of engineers, technicians and even white-collar workers engaged as clerks and administrative workers enjoyed privileges, salaries and certain tokens of status which divorced them from the production workers and drew them nearer to the capitalists with whom they tended to identify themselves. In the twentieth century this position of the white-collar sections began to break down; and in conditions of modern state monopoly capitalism and the scientific and technological revolution this process has become accentuated. Many who were, in former periods, private self-employed professionals, are now just salaried employees of the big enterprises, subject to capitalist exploitation whatever may be their salaries. The majority of engineers, technicians, draughtsmen and clerical and administrative workers have become an important new section of the working class.

This is borne out by figures demonstrating the decline in the number of specialised workers enjoying the status of self-employed. In the US, for example, the proportion of hired labour among engineers and technicians rose from 62·1 per cent in 1870 to 88·1 per cent in 1960. In Britain, the percentage of engineers, technicians and specialists who were salary earners rose from 83·5 per cent in 1921 to 91 per cent in 1951.

In other words, an increasing proportion of engineering and technical personnel, as well as clerical employees, have to sell their labour power to the big monopolies in the same way as do other sections of the working class. They suffer exploitation at the hands of the capitalists in the same way as other sections of workers. Their actual work nowadays is much closer to the actual work processes than hitherto.

In the most developed capitalist countries engineering and technical personnel are no longer a relatively small, exclusive stratum. The big firms now employ thousands of such specialists who no longer feel themselves a privileged group close to the owners and directors. These specialists, moreover, are far more occupied these days with the supervision and functioning of machines, and less with the control of people.

The introduction of automation has had a profound effect on the

[1] V. Lyubimova and N. Gauzner: op. cit., p. 63.

character of work of both engineer and worker, increasing the mental and nervous strain on both.

> If in the conventional plant the worker and the run-of-the-mill engineer fulfil different functions—the worker expending physical energy, while the engineer expends mental energy, in the automated plant the two are straining their nerves all the time. By obliterating the difference in the conditions and operations, capitalist automation presupposes intensified exploitation not only of skilled and unskilled workers but also of engineers and technicians.[1]

Office work, too, is undergoing radical change. Mechanisation is making giant strides there, and offices are coming to resemble factory departments, with batteries of typists or other operators in a single open office, linked by a single continuous flow of work in place of numerous individual clerical operations. The office worker who does a bit of typing, some shorthand, odd accounting, looks after the stamps, sorts the mail, files letters and documents, and makes tea still exists; but is no longer the typical office employee of the big firms where business machines, calculators, computors, photostat equipment, and electrical duplicating by processes which come close to printing, are taking over. Figures provided by the IBM Corporation in the US show that over 7 per cent of all office work in the United States is now being done by automatic equipment, and that in the near future about a third of all office work will be automated.

By their role in production processes and the character of their work, all white-collar sections are coming closer to the blue-collar workers and thus becoming part of the growing army of wage workers.

A number of theoreticians, including some who claim to be Marxists, tend to use the term "proletariat" to signify only manual workers, or even the lowest stratum in society. On the basis of this misrepresentation of the views of Marx and Engels they then deduce that the decline of manual work and the extension of all kinds of non-manual work, "white-collar work", including especially that of technicians, engineers and scientific workers, signifies the decline of the proletariat and the growth of the "middle class" or of a "labour aristocracy".

But did Marx and Engels regard only manual labourers as proletarians? Did they exclude clerical and commercial labour from this category? Did they exclude so-called "mental" labour?

[1] A. M. Rumyantsev, Editor: *Structure of the Working Class*, New Delhi, 1963, p. 97.

Nothing that Marx or Engels ever wrote can justify such a conclusion. As already noted in Chapter 1, Lenin's definition of a social class demonstrates that what is decisive is one's relationship to the means of production. In other words, what distinguishes the proletariat from the capitalist class and petty bourgeoisie is that the former is deprived of the means of production and thus compelled to hire itself to the capitalists to whom it sells the only commodity it has, namely labour power. Engels noted this point in the preface to the English edition of the *Communist Manifesto*, where he wrote that the proletariat is "the class of modern wage-labourers who, having no means of production of their own, are reduced to selling their labour power in order to live".

Marx in no sense limited his concept of the term proletariat to those directly handling the object of production. He included as belonging to the working class all those whose labour creates surplus value or assists this surplus to come into the hands of the capitalists. The capitalist is not concerned whether the worker produces the surplus value directly, in the form of commodities, or in an indirect way, using his labour to create the conditions for a redistribution from other sectors of the economy.

The different roles which workers play in the modern production process, Marx points out, in no way excludes them from playing their part in creating surplus value.

> With the spread of the specifically capitalist mode of production in which a considerable number of workers jointly produce one and the same commodity, the direct relations between the labour of some or other workers and the object of the production inevitably become very different. For example, general workers in a factory are not directly related to the processing of raw materials. Workers acting as overseers over those workers who do the processing stand still farther away. The attitude of the engineer is again a different one, and in the main he works only by his brains, etc. But *the combination of all these workers*, possessing labour-power of varying value . . . produce a result which . . . finds expression in *commodity*, in a *material product*. These workers in the aggregate, as a single production body, constitute a living machine for the manufacture of these *products*. . . . A feature of the capitalist mode of production is that it sunders the different kinds of labour one from the other, and consequently, also divides mental and manual labour . . . and allocates the two types of labour to different people. . . . But this separation does not alter the fact . . . that the relation of each of these people to capital is invariably the relation of a hired worker, the relation of a

productive worker in this specific sense. In the aggregate, these people . . . *directly* exchange their labour for money as capital, and consequently not only reproduce their wages but, in addition, directly create surplus value for the capitalist.[1]

In this passage Marx develops the same point that he made in *Capital*, where he brought forward his concept of "the collective labourer":

> In order to labour productively, it is no longer necessary for you to do manual work yourself; enough, if you are an organ of the collective labourer, and perform one of its subordinate functions.[2]

Returning later to this thesis concerning the collective labourer, Marx notes that "all these workers taken together" (he is referring here to a whole range of workers, varying from labourers to those supervising other workers directly engaged in production and to engineers working "chiefly with their brains") act as a single collective labourer.[3] According to Marx, the differences in forms of labour amongst different people, especially the gulf between mental and manual labour, does not prevent the material product being the product of the collective labour of all these workers.

Referring specifically to the commercial employee, Marx expressed the view that a "commercial employee is a wage worker like any other". Mercantile wage workers, he wrote, "produce direct profits for their employer without creating any direct surplus value (of which profit is but a transmuted form). . . . Just as the labourer's unpaid labour directly creates surplus value for productive capital, so the unpaid labour of the commercial wage worker secures a share of this surplus value for merchant capital."[4]

It is true that, unlike industrial workers, commercial workers, i.e. shop assistants and office workers, take no direct part in production, yet their labour is essential for the working of capitalism which could not function without circulation. "The unpaid labour of these clerks," noted Marx, "while it does not create surplus value, enables him (i.e. the capitalist—Author) to appropriate surplus value, which, in effect, amounts to the same thing with respect to his capital. It is, therefore, a source of profit for him."[5]

[1] Karl Marx: *Theories of Surplus Value*, Selections, London, 1951, pp. 195–6.
[2] Karl Marx: *Capital*, Vol. 1, pp. 508–9.
[3] Karl Marx: *Theories of Surplus Value*, Selections, London, 1951, pp. 195–6.
[4] Karl Marx: *Capital*, Vol. III, Moscow, 1959, pp. 287–8.   [5] ibid., p. 294.

Marx, of course, emphasised that the decisive core of the working class was the *industrial* proletariat, that is to say that section of the working class connected with factory production. But, as we have already noticed, more and more sections of white-collar labour are becoming linked more closely and more directly with factory production.

Moreover, more branches of material production are taking on an industrial character. As a consequence of the scientific and techno-logical revolution, the developing social division of labour tends to transform such services as heating and lighting, public catering, various repair services, laundries, cleaning, etc., into independent branches of large-scale capitalist production. An increasing number of functions in the sphere of distribution, such as storage, weighing and packaging, have become a continuation of production. All wage workers employed in these branches of the economy are part of the army of the industrial proletariat.

From all of the foregoing, one can conclude that the industrial proletariat, and not just the proletariat in general, far from diminishing is actually growing numerically and in proportion to the total labour force.

In the size of their earnings, too, the position of white-collar workers is approximating that of the blue-collar workers. In the past several decades the gap between the salaries of office employees and production workers has first closed and then started to move in the opposite direction.[1] At the beginning of the present century office workers received several times the pay of industrial workers. In the US, for example, average annual earnings of an office employee in manufacturing were 232 per cent of those received by a manufacturing worker. By 1926 the percentage was down to 177 per cent. After the second world war the shift continued even more rapidly, so that today the average earnings of male office employees in the United States are below those of a skilled industrial worker, being 97 per cent in 1947 and 91 per cent in 1963. British Ministry of Labour figures show that whereas the average weekly earnings of male employees (excluding executives and technical personnel) were 1s. 10d. higher than those of workers in manufacturing in 1959, by 1960 they were 4s. 11d. *less*, and by 1963 they were 9s. 1d. less.

Understandably enough, the pay of engineers and scientific workers

[1] An advertisement for the Association of Scientific, Technical and Managerial Staffs carries the significant slogan: "Why did I choose a pen instead of a pick."

is higher than that of industrial workers—but here, too, the gap is narrowing.

The pay of technicians, draughtsmen and laboratory assistants, who make up more than half of all engineering and technical personnel, is beginning to approximate that of skilled workers. Already by 1959 the average earnings of US engineers, technicians and other male specialists was only 24 per cent more than that of skilled workers. In Federal Germany by 1961, the figures were approximately the same.

Thus, far from the mass of workers becoming part of a new "middle class", the process that is taking place is one of an increasing tendency for new sections to be added to the working class, for the working class to grow numerically and in proportion to other sections of the population, and for the new sections to find that their conditions of work, their functions in production and their earnings make them part of the working class.

As a consequence, and to protect their interests in the face of increased exploitation, these new sections enter upon struggle, organise into trade unions, and commence to link their organised activities and even their political destinies with those of the already established trade union and labour movement. This has been a marked feature in recent years in Britain, as shown by the surging membership figures of the Association of Scientific, Technical and Managerial Staffs, and those of the Draughtsmen, of the National Union of Teachers, of Local Government Officers[1] and others, as well as by the decisions of unions such as those of the teachers, bank employees and local government officers to join the Trades Union Congress. In the United States, the membership of the International Union of Office Employees rose from 26,200 in 1949 to 55,000 in 1962, and that of the American Federation of State, Country and Municipal Employees went up from 75,000 in 1949 to 200,000 in 1962.

Whatever may be the views of some theoreticians and even, in some cases, of the leaders of these bodies, the organisational link-up of their union with the traditional industrial trade union movement is an indirect recognition of the realities of class struggle and of their own place within it.

Over seventy years ago Lenin noted:

> In all spheres of people's labour, capitalism increases the number of office and professional workers with particular rapidity and makes

[1] ASTMS: 87,000 in 1967 to 220,000 in 1970 (includes mergers); DATA: 73,000 in 1967 to 105,000 in 1970; NALGO: 367,000 in 1967 to 440,000 in 1970.

a growing demand for intellectuals. The latter occupy a special position among the other classes, attaching themselves partly to the bourgeoisie by their connections, their outlook, etc., and partly to the wage-workers as capitalism increasingly deprives the intellectual of his independent position, converts him into a hired worker and threatens to lower his living standard.[1]

Since Lenin wrote, the factors bringing all sections of white-collar workers closer to the rest of the working class have become predominant. Certainly the composition of the modern working class has changed and become more complex. As we have noted, the agricultural labour force is declining, there is a run down in the older established industries, expecially mining, textiles and the railways, a growth in manufacturing, especially in its newest sectors, and an increase in white-collar work, especially in its technical, engineering and scientific branches.

None of this, however, signifies any decline in size of the working class itself; on the contrary, it marks its further growth by its extension into further fields of economic and social activity which require wage labour. This process is drawing different sections of the working class closer together, consolidating their organisation, strengthening their unity and promoting their struggle. The basis of the working class is becoming broader and this, far from weakening, strengthens the capacity of the workers to build a powerful movement against monopoly-capitalism.

It would, of course, be foolish to present an over-simplified picture. In rejecting Marcuse's negative and pessimistic assessment of the modern working class we have no intention of following in the wake of that school of over-optimistic Marxists who are reluctant to recognise problems, are afraid to admit setbacks and who tend to present the struggle for socialism as one straightforward, uncomplicated and triumphant march to victory.

Proletarian status is not identical with proletarian consciousness. The position of white-collar workers, often their social origin and family connections, too, tend to submerge them in a wave of individualism and petty-bourgeois ideas. Life itself constantly breaks down the individualism, and that is why there has been such a remarkable growth in the membership of white-collar unions in the major capitalist countries in recent years; but even here, the process is far from complete. Furthermore, while it is a great step forward for unions of non-manual

[1] V. I. Lenin: *Collected Works*, Vol. 4, p. 202.

workers to link their destinies with those of the long-established industrial workers, as has happened with the British trade union movement, one should recognise that this vital accession of strength is also a means by which non-working-class ideas can be brought into the trade union movement, blunting its class edge and even sowing a measure of confusion and division. There is no automatic certainty that these dangers will assume disastrous proportions; but neither can there be any easy assumption that a proletarian and socialist outlook will be rapidly and spontaneously acquired by these new sections of the working class. It is the conscious effort of those who already have a political awareness and a class understanding that can ensure that the decisive majority of the expanding army of workers is won for socialism.

THE MAJOR CONTRADICTION

Many of those following in the wake of Marcuse—as well as those who pre-dated him[1]—have undoubtedly drawn attention to important new phenomena in modern capitalist society. No Marxist can afford to ignore the significant changes taking place in the structure and composition of the working class to which a number of these studies have drawn attention; although many of the conclusions are open to debate.

Marcuse, as we have noticed, is not too specific on some of the consequences of these changes. While in general he believes that the majority of the working class in the developed capitalist countries is becoming a labour aristocracy, thus rendering it in the main a conservative and even counter-revolutionary force, he nevertheless considers that the "technical intelligentsia", that is to say, "highly qualified employees, engineers, specialists, scientists"—all those, in fact, whose higher income levels and social status would tend to place them in the ranks of his rejected labour aristocracy—may be expected to play an important part in the ranks of the opposition. The contradictions in his position seem to have eluded him.

Apparently, the receipt of higher salaries and the possession of such

---

[1] Many of Marcuse's propositions, which found expression mainly in the latter half of the last decade, are not entirely his original ideas. Elements of his theories concerning the role of the working class in modern capitalist society have found expression earlier in the writings of C. Wright Mills, Ralf Dahrendorf, Theodor Geiger, T. H. Marshall, Reinhard Bendix and others. Numerous later neo-Marcuseans have also produced voluminous studies, short monographs, theses galore, to "prove" the decline, corruption, bourgeoisification or even disappearance of the working class.

material benefits as a decent house, a car, television set, washing machine and so forth, which these categories of technicians undoubtedly enjoy, do not in Marcuse's eyes have the same corrupting effect on such individuals as they do on the generally lower paid industrial workers who are struggling for a better life. Marcuse, who also enjoys these benefits of a higher standard of living and who, presumably in his own opinion, has not been corrupted by this so-called "consumer society", evidently believes that for him and for those who have a similar social position and income, there is a different social law than that which he applies to the majority of the working class.

A recent sociological study carried out in Luton,[1] and which tends to reject a number of Marcuse's assumptions regarding the working class, rightly comments:

> For our own part, we would simply observe that it is not to us self-evident why one should regard our respondents' concern for decent, comfortable houses, for labour-saving devices, and even for such leisure goods as television sets and cars, as manifesting the force of "false" needs; of needs, that is, which are "superimposed upon the individual by particular social interests in his repression".[2] It would be equally possible to consider the amenities and possessions for which the couples in our sample were striving as representing something like the minimum material basis on which they and their children might be able to develop a more individual style of life, with a wider range of choices, than has hitherto been possible for the mass of the manual labour force. And in particular, given the harsh dilemma that our respondents frequently faced between more inherently rewarding work and greater economic resources with which to carry through their family projects—a dilemma largely avoided by those in more advantageous class positions—we would not be inclined to speak *de haut en bas* of "stunted mass-produced, humanity", "made-to-measure consumers" or "sublimated slaves".

This is well said. We are not of course, questioning the sincerity of Marcuse and his supporters who argue in this way. What seems to be far more basic is Marcuse's refusal to face up to the fundamental contradiction in capitalist society. He appears to be obsessed with what

---

[1] John H. Goldthorpe, David Lockwood, Frank Bechofer and Jennifer Platt: *The Affluent Worker in the Class Structure*, Cambridge, 1969, p. 183.
[2] This phrase is a quotation from H. Marcuse's *One Dimensional Man.*

he terms "the consumer society" and repeatedly, in the way he develops his line of argument, presents the problem as if it arises from a conflict between the capacity of modern society to produce an abundance of material goods and its incapacity to provide a higher *quality* of life. This is certainly an important problem, although for many millions, including an estimated 40 million in the United States alone, the satisfying of the minimum material requirements is an essential prerequisite for any fuller and more meaningful life.

By his emphasis on "the consumer society" Marcuse diverts attention from the major contradiction in capitalist society. The point is not how many workers own a car, a fridge, a TV, or even a house or other item of *personal* property. The crucial thing is that *the means of production* are owned by the capitalists.

Nowhere is there any evidence that Marcuse understands or accepts the Marxist theory of surplus value. He provides no indication as to the role and method of exploitation in capitalist society, nor even if he is cognisant of it. Because he seems unaware of the source of capitalist profit, namely the expropriation by private capital of the surplus value created by the worker through the expenditure of his labour power, he fails to establish that private ownership of the means of production, distribution and exchange is the fundamental source of the injustices and inequalities of our society, and that to end this system, which he claims to reject, it is necessary that the expropriators be expropriated, that the means of production, distribution and exchange be taken out of the hands of their private owners and turned into public property. Since those who own the means of production dominate the capitalist state and control the mass media, an immense struggle, the action of millions of people is required if that power is to be broken; and the decisive social force, the force that grows larger, more cohesive and better organised all the time, is the working class, which constitutes the overwhelming majority of the population in all the advanced capitalist societies.

The very nature of modern capitalist production, the creation of giant monopolies, the carrying through of mergers between these giants and the creation of super-giants which spread their branches and subsidiaries throughout the capitalist world, the growth of international firms, the accumulation of huge sums of capital, the impact of the scientific and technological revolution now embracing capitalist industry—all this brings capitalism nearer to the threshold of its demise. Already, in 1916, Lenin, in the concluding pages of his study

Imperialism, the Highest Stage of Capitalism, pointed to the process taking place:

> When a big enterprise becomes a gigantic one and, working on the basis of exactly computed mass data, systematically organises the supply of primary raw materials to the extent of two-thirds or three-fourths of all that is necessary for tens of millions of people; when these raw materials are transported to the most suitable places of production, sometimes hundreds or thousands of miles from each other, in a systematic and organised manner; when one centre controls all the successive stages of working up the raw materials right up to the manufacture of numerous varieties of finished articles; when these products are distributed according to a single plan among tens of hundreds of millions of consumers (the marketing of oil in America and Germany by the American Oil Trust), then it becomes evident that we have socialisation of production going on right before our eyes, and not mere "interlocking"; that private business relations, and private property relations, constitute a shell which is no longer suitable to its contents, a shell which must inevitably begin to decay if its removal is postponed by artificial means; a shell which may continue in a state of decay for a comparatively long period (particularly if the cure of the opportunist abscess is protracted), but which will inevitably be removed.

The processes now under way in the most developed capitalist countries are creating the basis for revolutionary change. For too long, owing to the presence of the "opportunist abscess", the shell of private capitalist relations has been allowed to continue its decay. Capitalism will not disappear by itself. There will be no automatic collapse. Whatever its difficulties and crises, the system will continue unless the working people themselves take purposeful action to end it; and at the centre of that action must be the many millions strong army of the working class. Despite its detractors, of whom Marcuse is an outstanding exponent, and despite, too, the lack of understanding which the majority of workers themselves may have regarding their historic mission, there can be no fundamental change in the present system unless it is based on the ever expanding legions of the workers. It is the task of revolutionaries to awaken and kindle that understanding, both among the workers and also among their potential and actual allies, including the students, intellectuals, and middle strata alongside the most oppressed sections of society.

By his theories concerning the working class Marcuse undermines the trust and confidence of non-working-class strata in the revolutionary role of the workers, and weakens, too, the confidence of the working class itself. Objectively, therefore, whatever may be his motives, Marcuse does a disservice to the anti-capitalist cause for which he claims to be a spokesman.

Chapter Five

Conclusion

5

Conclusion

Fanon, Debray and Marcuse have come to somewhat similar conclusions on many basic questions of revolutionary theory, especially on the role of classes in the modern world and in their estimates of the Communist Parties.

All three lament to some extent the town—urbanisation, technological advance and material benefits for the working people. For Fanon and Debray the town is a source of corruption and decay. According to Marcuse material advance, the "consumer society" turns the worker into a conservative supporter of the capitalist system. Fanon, too, derides technological progress. In opposition to the "corrupted" working class, Fanon hails the peasantry of Africa; Debray calls on Latin American revolutionaries to go up into the "mountain" and win the unsullied peasants; while Marcuse looks to the exploited millions in the Third World whom he sees as unaffected by the rotting fruits of the metropolis. Both Fanon and Marcuse find the only potential revolutionary mass force in the towns to be that of the outcasts of society, the *lumpenproletariat*, the poorest of the poor, the unemployed and unemployable, and, in the United States (and presumably now also in other Western countries), among the Black minorities. Debray and Marcuse place special emphasis on the allegedly leading role of students and intellectuals; and while Fanon does not express such views directly, implicit in his analysis and his hopes that militants from the African towns will go to the countryside to organise is the concept that it will be intellectuals from the towns that will play this role of leadership.[1] This intellectual élitism or paternal

[1] At a first glance Fanon's writings might convey a different impression, especially since so much of his effort is devoted to attacking the shortcomings of African careerist intellectuals. For this reason some commentators, such as Prof. E. Shils, have described Fanon as "only an eloquent Sorel"—anti-intellectualism being a particular facet of Georges Sorel's views. (See, for example, James Joll: "Anarchism, a Living Tradition", *Anarchism Today—Government and Opposition*, Vol. 5, No. 4, 1970, pp. 550–1.) But if one takes Fanon's thought as a whole it is clear that he expects that from amongst the main body of intellectuals, most of whom he depicts as hypocrites, there will emerge a number who will provide the leadership of the revolution. After all, for whom was Fanon writing? Certainly not for his despised workers—nor for his mainly illiterate peasants and *lumpens*.

guidance by non-working-class intellectuals, has nothing in common with the concept of a vanguard party, based primarily on the working class.

The theme of violence is a major element in the views both of Fanon and Debray. At different phases of revolutionary struggle the question of violence can arise; no revolutionary shrinks from such a necessity, especially if he understands that the working people have to be ready at all times to exert their force, by whatever means are necessary, in order to overcome the violence or potential violence of the ruling class.

But Fanon and Debray approach this question in a different fashion. For them violence is not just a means to an end but a necessary experience in itself; violence is liberation; it is the cleansing fire which tests and purifies revolutionaries. It is, according to Fanon, by practising violence that the long-subjected colonial peasant overcomes his fear of the enemy and acquires a readiness to take part in revolutionary change. Debray propounds his belief that by the physical act of taking up arms and fighting man transforms himself into a dedicated revolutionary.

Marcuse is not so outspoken a champion of violence; in fact in an interview in November, 1970,[1] while defending the big student protest actions then sweeping the Unites States, he claimed that "much of the supposed work of extremists can be laid at the door of agents infiltrated into their ranks. 'But in any case I consider this kind of violence self-defeating. It is welcomed by those who long for still stronger measures.'" This notwithstanding, Marcuse had nothing but praise for the prolonged violent barricade fighting that went on in Paris in 1968 long after there was any political advantage to be gained by such tactics.

A certain worship of spontaneity, too, is to be found in both Marcuse and Debray. Debray downgrades the role of ideology, while Marcuse, who acclaims what he regards as "the spontaneous nature" of the events in France in May–June, 1968, approves, too, the "opposition to all ideology", which he claims to find among young people today. Fanon, by contrast, laments Africa's lack of an ideology.

All three scorn existing institutions, and certainly see little or no point in revolutionaries working within the framework of such bodies, even to expose them and utilise them as a political platform. Above all, they share a common hostility towards the organisations of the labour movement, especially the trade unions; in the case of

[1] Interview in the *Observer*, November 22, 1970.

Debray and Marcuse this is particularly directed against most Communist Parties.

Other commentators have drawn attention to the close parallels between many of the ideas of Fanon, Debray and Marcuse and the traditional ideas of the anarchists—hatred of the town and of the material benefits of modern capitalist society, the idealisation of the peasantry (*vide* Proudhon and Bakunin) and of the *lumpenproletariat* ("that rabble which, being very nearly unpolluted by all bourgeois civilisation . . . alone is powerful enough today to inaugurate the Social Revolution, and bring it to triumph"—Bakunin),[1] and the worship of violence and spontaneity. Even Debray's *foco* theory has its counterpart in the attempt of the anarchist, Errico Malatesta, in 1876 to "set the big motor into action" in Italy by first setting the "small motor" going in the form of a peasant assumption of power in a small area.

In common with anarchists, Fanon, Debray and Marcuse give the impression that they fear the organised, disciplined ranks of the proletariat; they resent above all, that such organised discipline should wield political power. Anarchism and élitism are more attractive to petty-bourgeois intellectuals than the patient, organised, disciplined work of preparing and winning *millions* for revolutionary change.

Anarchism, as Lenin once remarked, is the price the working-class movement has to pay for the sins of opportunism. But there are some specific reasons for the recent renewal of anarchist trends in the major capitalist countries, trends which express themselves not in any strengthened organisational form, but rather in the field of a number of general ideas of which Fanon, Debray and Marcuse are in a sense, spokesmen.

The continued grip of reformism and right-wing social democracy in the labour movements of most imperialist countries, especially in the face of the high hopes of so many after 1945, and the growing disgust, particularly of many young people, with the existing capitalist system and with the shameful compromising antics of the reformist leaders have resulted in quite desperate moods in some circles, moods which find their political expression in forms of anarchism. Writing on another occasion, Lenin noted: "Certain people who were inattentive to the conditions for preparing and developing the mass struggle, were driven to despair and anarchism by the lengthy delays in the decisive struggle against capitalism in Europe."[2] Understandably

---

[1] Michael Bakunin: *Marxism, Freedom and the State*, London, 1960, p. 48.
[2] V. I. Lenin: *Collected Works*, Vol. 18, p. 584.

enough, to many people, especially the young, the delays today seem interminably long. As far as material conditions go, the major capitalist countries are over-ripe for revolution, and it is therefore not surprising that there should be mounting impatience in the ranks of those who want to finish with the existing system. Unfortunately, however—and here is the kernel of the problem—the majority of workers, let alone the majority of people, in the advanced capitalist countries, have not yet been won for this idea of basic change. And without this majority there can be no revolution.

Lenin was quite adamant on this question. In Russia itself, throughout the summer of 1917, he and the Bolsheviks worked consistently to win a *majority* in the main Soviets. Only then did they call for the uprising. After 1917, within the Communist International, he fought strenuously for this same necessity to win the majority. Writing specifically on the defeats of the armed uprisings in Germany in March, 1921, Lenin warned: ". . . however heroic it was, *in future* such a challenge, provoked by the government, which, since 1919, has already killed by provocations 20,000 workers *should not* be accepted until the Communists have the majority behind them all over the country, and not just in one small district."[1] In the preparations for the Third Congress of the Communist International in 1921, the importance of winning the *majority* of the workers was again a key point of contention. Criticising a draft thesis by Karl Radek, Lenin opposed the latter's proposal to remove the reference to winning the majority of the working class and to replace it with the thesis that it was essential to win the socially decisive section of the working class. Calling Radek's proposal "the height of absurdity", Lenin wrote: "To win power you need, *under certain conditions* (even when the *majority* of the working class have already been won over *to the principles of communism*), *a blow* dealt at the decisive place by the majority of the socially decisive sections of the working class."[2] Insisting that winning the majority of the workers was "the basis of everything", Lenin declared: "The tactics of the Communist International should be based on a steady and systematic drive to win the *majority of the working class*, first and foremost *within the old trade unions*. Then we shall win for certain, whatever the course of events."[3] In his speech to the Congress itself, which opened in Moscow on June 22, 1921, Lenin spoke against the proposal of the German, Austrian and Italian delegations to delete

[1] V. I. Lenin: *Collected Works*, Vol. 42, p. 323.   [2] ibid., p. 320.
[3] ibid., pp. 320–1.

the word "majority" in reference to the necessity of winning the majority of workers to the principles of communism. Commenting on these amendments, Lenin said:

> An absolute majority is not always essential; but what is essential to win and retain power is not only the majority of the working class—I use the term "working class" in its West European sense, i.e., in the sense of the industrial proletariat—but also the majority of the working and exploited rural population.[1]

Such views may appear anathema to those who are anxious to "trigger off" a revolution—but the concept of the small, heroic, active group which, by example, or its own acts, would get things going, is no new problem to the revolutionary movement. Anarchism, Blanquism, the Narodniks, the "Left" Communists—Marxists have always had to contend with such trends. Lenin once remarked to Clara Zetkin: "We need tireless Party agitation and propaganda and then Party action. *But this Party action must be free of the mad idea that it can replace action by the masses.*"[2] (Author's italics.)

Anarchist ideas today are not the result of mere impatience with opportunism, however. There is no doubt that an additional source of current anarchist modes of thought is the impact of the world wide revolution in the Third World, and especially the Chinese revolution. Distorted views concerning the course of events in China, and attempts to generalise from the rather special circumstances of China, have led some people in the West to conclude that the peasantry is the most revolutionary class, that the struggle must start in the countryside, that armed struggle is the only way. One-sided assessments of the Cuban revolution, as we have seen, have similarly led to over-simplified conclusions which some people have attempted to apply mechanically in quite different circumstances. Over-generalised con-clusions from the experience of the African revolution, too, have added their quota of ideas to the new anarchism.

A contributory factor has been the divisions in the international communist movement, including the differences between several socialist states and a number of unresolved problems of socialist democracy. The revelations that followed the Twentieth Congress of the Soviet Communist Party in 1956 profoundly shocked progressive people, especially the younger generation; and the further departures

---

[1] V. I. Lenin: *Collected Works*, Vol. 32, p. 476.
[2] *On Lenin. Reminiscences of Foreign Contemporaries*, Moscow, 1966, p. 37.

from socialist democracy that took place later, including the events in Czechoslovakia and Poland, have caused some sections of the progressive movement in the West to have reservations about the Communist Parties. Under these conditions the slogans of anarchism, as well as those of the "New Left", the several brands of Trotskyism, and the various groups which claim to be "Maoist", have had a certain attraction.

Anarchism is a form of rejection of the *status quo*. But it is also an expression of the viewpoint of the petty bourgeoisie. David Stafford[1] has pointed out that analyses of the readership of the anarchist press and other observations tend one to conclude that "in Britain—as elsewhere—the social basis of the movement has shifted significantly since the heydey of the classical anarchists, and that anarchist ideas find their greatest support in highly developed societies amongst the middle class". Noting anarchist preference for the peasantry as against the working class, Horowitz[2] has commented: "And even though anarchism may not have worshipped at the shrine of petty-bourgeois life as such, . . . it certainly did respond to petty-bourgeois values—individualism, enterprise, dissociation and antipolitics."

Such petty-bourgeois values are also reflected in the anarchist disdain for modern science and technology, and in its hopes for a return to small-scale individualist production.

> The anarchist never confronted the problems of a vast technology, and ignored them by trying to find his way back to a system of production that was satisfying to the individual producer rather than feasible for a growing mass society. . . . The anarchist literature contains a strong element of nostalgia, a harking back to a situation where workshops were small, where relationships were manageable, where people experienced affective responses with each other. Technology and the material benefits of science were never seriously entertained by the anarchists except in a ministerial contempt for that which destroys the natural man.[3]

The anarchist, in his search for "the natural man", untainted by civilisation, by modern capitalism in particular, believes that such a man is to be found among the peasants and *lumpenproletarians*, neither of whom have been physically embraced by modern production. Such "outsiders", in the eyes of the anarchist, are destined to fulfil the role of

---

[1] David Stafford: "Anarchists in Britain Today", *Anarchism Today*, op. cit., pp. 492–3.
[2] Irving L. Horowitz: ed., *The Anarchists*, New York, 1964, p. 34.
[3] ibid., pp. 590–1.

rebels against society. In the eyes of Fanon and Marcuse, too (not so clearly in the case of Debray), these "outsiders" are the only natural revolutionaries.

The present-day defects of capitalism, to many of which Marcuse draws such necessary attention, seem to the anarchist to confirm him in his views:

> Mass society and mass culture become a permanent feature of the State apparatus. So that anarchy, because of its nihilistic elements, becomes a cry against manipulation. The anarchist is a man who won't be manipulated.[1]

This appears to be Marcuse's cry, too; and echoes of it are to be found in Fanon and Debray, as well.

But does it all really stand up as a contribution to revolutionary theory? Can the ideas of Fanon, Debray and Marcuse be accepted as genuine additions to Marxism, as new weapons in the struggle for socialism?

It seems very central to me that all three reject the organised working-class movement, and that Debray and Marcuse specifically reject the Communist Parties, alleging in both cases that the Parties have become virtually reformist. If the strictures of Fanon, Debray and Marcuse concerning the working class arose out of a sincere and genuine concern to overcome weaknesses, to assist the workers to cast aside their illusions and to throw in their lot with the revolution, that would be perfectly understandable. Marxists have never hesitated to criticise faults in the ranks of the workers. Marx and Lenin, for example, battled constantly against opportunism, pointing out repeatedly the great harm caused to the movement by the ideas of reformism. But Fanon, Debray and Marcuse make no appeal to the working-class movement. They are not concerned with winning the workers for the revolution. On the contrary, they reject the proletariat—and appeal to the students, the intellectuals, the peasants and the *lumpenproletariat* to do the same. In the eyes of Fanon, Debray[2] and Marcuse the workers are not misguided people who have to be helped; on the contrary, they are depicted virtually as the enemy standing on the other side of the barricades. Even a cursory reading of all three reveals a singular lack of direct contact with and knowledge of the working-class movement; and this is not at all surprising since they have all decided,

[1] ibid., p. 594.
[2] In his latest work Debray has modified his views a little on this question, but he has never repudiated his earlier hostility to the Latin American working class.

without any real scientific study, that the working class is no longer a major revolutionary force.

It is the logic of their anti-working-class position—more pronounced in Marcuse, less in Debray—that they should display an intense hostility to the Communist Parties. In Fanon this is not directly expressed, but since he is concerned mainly with Africa where only a handful of such Parties exist, this is perhaps understandable. But the anti-communism of Marcuse and Debray (and of a number of post-Fanonists) has to be understood as arising from their faulty analysis of the role of classes in the socialist revolution. If they reject the working class, then logically they must reject the most disciplined, highly organised, and militant detachment of that class; and whatever may be the faults and weaknesses of Communist Parties, they are all based on the working class to which they endeavour to bring socialist understanding, confidence and the spirit of struggle and unity.

After all the arguments have been examined, and all the secondary questions put on one side, the socialist revolution boils down to one essential question—the change of class power, the taking of political power away from the capitalists and the assumption of political power by the working class and its allies in order to replace private ownership of the means of production by public ownership. Those who turn their backs on the working class have, in reality, and whatever may be their hopes, turned their backs on the socialist revolution. And those who adopt the anti-communist mantle, even if it bears "Left" colours of the reddest hue, are only weakening the revolutionary movement. No socialist revolution has ever been carried through without the working class or under the banner of anti-communism.

Fanon, Debray and Marcuse may appear more radical, more militant, even more revolutionary, to those untutored in class struggle and not schooled in the revolutionary mass movement—but an anti-communist standpoint from the "left" is no more progressive than the anti-communism of the traditional "right". We are not here concerned so much with motives. Fanon, Debray and Marcuse may have expounded the most sincerely-held views. They may have the deepest desire to end the capitalist system. But this is not the point. What we are concerned with is the objective results of their theories. After all, there is no sincerometer with which to gauge people's honesty of purpose. The only judgment a Marxist can make of such theories is that of objective results.

The anti-working-class and anti-communist views brought forward by Fanon, Debray and Marcuse are a form of élitism which envisages the intellectuals and students leading the illiterate peasants and poor townfolk, and creating a new utopian society in their own petty-bourgeois image, without working-class power and without Communists. This is a luxury in the field of ideas which the capitalists can tolerate. Hence the irony of the position that the writings and views of these three "revolutionary" thinkers are given space and publicity in the mass media, their books are issued by bourgeois publishers, their theories debated on TV, and in the national press. Marcuse claims that all "radical opposition" in the capitalist countries is "absorbed", becomes a victim of "repressive tolerance". One cannot help noting the different treatment meted out to these three writers compared with the virtual blackout which greets the views and writings of Communists. Is it really the Communists who are "integrated", or is it not the thinkers of the "New Left"? By joining in this ruling class hostility to the working class and the Communists are not Marcuse *et al.* acting as partial administrators of the repression, and not as its victim?

The main slogans and tenets of Fanon, Debray and Marcuse have caused considerable confusion in student and intellectual circles, but fortunately not so much in the ranks of the working class for whom they were never intended, and whose feet are too firmly planted in the stern realities of their daily class struggle. Perhaps it sometimes appears to impatient revolutionaries that the feet of the workers are too firmly planted; and it may be true that, at times, there seems to be a certain inertia, a kind of passivity, a reluctance to "storm the heavens".

But it is the responsibility of revolutionaries to maintain confidence in the working class even at times when it has apparently lost confidence in itself. All the major tests of the twentieth century, all the revolutionary clashes over the past seventy years have made abundantly clear that at the testing time the working class will be there, massively and decisively. When the really serious questions of class struggle, of revolutionary struggle, arise it is the workers who, as a class, display indomitable courage, self-discipline, dedication, organisational ability and creative initiative. So it has always been. And so it will be in the coming battles of tomorrow.

Index

DATE DUE

FEB 13 2006		
FEB 15 2012		